// piste // parks

our top 50 recommendations

pat sharples // vanessa webb

foulsham
LONDON • NEW YORK • TORONTO • SYDNEY

foulsham
Capital Point, 33 Bath Road, Slough, Berkshire, SL1 4UF, England

Foulsham books can be found in all good bookshops and direct from www.foulsham.com

ISBN: 978-0-572-03631-7

Train information provided by Daniel Elkan
Cover photographs top right and bottom left © Melody Sky; top left © Arosa Tourism

A CIP record for this book is available from the British Library.

Skiing and snowboarding, especially off-piste, are potentially dangerous activities that should only be attempted by professionals and experts, having taken all safety considerations into account and following professional advice where advisable. Neither the editors of W. Foulsham & Co. Ltd nor the authors nor the publisher take responsibility for any possible consequences from any activity by any person reading or following the information in this book.

While every effort has been made to ensure the accuracy of all the information and the source of all the images contained within this book, neither the author nor the publisher can be liable for any errors. In particular, since laws change from time to time, it is vital that each individual checks relevant legal details for him or herself.

Printed in Great Britain by Thomson Litho, East Kilbride

Contents

Acknowledgements

We would like to thank all the people who helped us, allowing us to travel to each of the Top 50 Resorts. We could not have done this without them. Thank you to tourist offices and their press and marketing departments, and to friends and family who have helped us out, providing information and accommodation. In particular we would like to thank the following:

Andorra: Arinsal: Pete and Adrian. Pas de la Casa and Soldeu: Silvia Encinas and Sira Puig, Tyler Charlton.

Austria: Bad Gastein: Markus Papai. Ischgl: Dominik Walser. Kitzbühel: Sascha Reitsma and Tamara Prömer. Lech: Claudia Lengenfelder. Mayrhofen: Kathren Egger and Jon Weaver. Saalbach-Hinterglemm: Jason Hough. St Anton: Wilma Himmelfreundpointner.

France: Les Arcs: Helen. Avoriaz: Cosima Zinck. Chamonix: Glen and Caroline. Courchevel: Laurence Bourgeois and all the regulars at the Signal. Les Deux Alpes: Elodie Lavesvre, Héléna Hospital, Pete and Lynn and Matt Sharples. La Grave: Robin and Marlene, Niels and Didier, and Jean-Charles. Meribel: Françoise Daviet, Adam Johnson, The Taverne hotel/bar. Morzine: Sturan Erskine, Johnny Mclaren, Bruno Robinet. La Plagne: Giles and Claire, Marcus, Paul and Monica Sharples. Ste Foy: Anne Royer, Adrian Myers. Serre Chevalier: Ben Hawker aka Bungle. Tignes: Simi Johnson, Euan at Les Mélèzes, James Vernon. Val d'Isère: Chris Howarth, Jane Jacquemod. Val Thorens: Stefanie.

Italy: Alagna and Gressoney: Lara, Hotel Villa Tedaldi. Cervinia: Elsa and Andy North. Selva in Val Gardena: Jolanda Senoner.

Sweden: Jon Olsson, Jens H. Bond. Åre: Bengt Ullström.

Switzerland: Heidi Reisz at Swiss Tourism. Arosa: Beatrice Gerber and our film crew Rachel and Simon. Champéry: Sonja Collet, Kina Ojdahl, John Mitchell, Paul and Rhonda. Crans Montana: Stefanie Ambuehl. Davos: Clair Southwell, Daniel Waechter, Chris Southwell, Carin Gisep-Caligari, Othmar Thomann. Engelberg: Maria Ferretti and Slavemonkey. Klosters: Clair Southwell, Daniel Waechter, Hotel Alpina, Lukas Durr, Al Thony and Chris Southwell. Mürren: Rahel Mazenauer and Ursula Mühlemann. Saas-Fee: Robbie and Therese, Adrian Schnyder. St Moritz: Alexandra Blaha. Verbier: Warren Smith, Melody Sky, Nick Southwell, Pierre-Yves. Jamie and Kerry. Zermatt: Karin Schmid.

Photographers: Adrian Myers, Ross Woodhall, Melody Sky. Magazines: Zack Ragg and Daniel Crawford at Dark Summer, Jamie Cameron at Falline.

A big shout out to all of Pat's sponsors who have supported him in his career as a professional skier and now are considered close friends. Thank you. Oakley Marketing Manager, Stewart Morgan. Oakley team manager, Jeremy Festa. Salomon Marketing, Sonia Prior, Richard Seymour, Mike Stoker and Eric Davis. Natives.co.uk, Iain Martin, Snow and Rock, Kevin Young and Gregor Brealey, Ignite, Neil Thompson, Tracker and BCA, Mark Staddle, Giro, Gregor Urquhart.

A special thanks to all at Foulsham Publishing who believed in us and gave us the chance to write our book. Also, we would like to thank our families and friends for their support. A special thanks to David and Carol Webb, Vanessa's parents, who have let us take over their home, and provide unconditional help and support and to Paul and Monica Sharples, Pat's parents, for our European base, and for refuelling us when we needed a break.

We are so sorry if we have missed people out, but you know who you are and we won't forget your support. Many thanks, Vanessa and Pat.

Introduction

While sitting on a ski bus in April 2004 we had the idea of writing a travel guide on the best locations to ski and snowboard. The first edition was published in 2005 and, since then, we have worked hard to improve on the first year, travelling and researching the information, with plenty of help from locals, tourist offices and friends. We skied with some of the world's best skiers and snowboarders and checked out some of the biggest events in the world.

When you choose a ski resort, the decision is a very personal one – what suits one person will not suit another. If you are there with a group of friends, you won't want a family-oriented resort. If you are a beginner, a resort with plenty of black runs is not for you. So we have tried to provide you with the information you need to make your choices so that your skiing holiday – whether it's the first or you are already a ski addict like we are – is just great.

About the authors

Pat Sharples: Pat is a big name on the British freestyle scene. He is head coach of the British Freeski camps and a former England Freestyle team captain. Pat has earned many titles, such as England Champion and European Mogul Challenge champion. His sponsors include Oakley, Salomon, Snow and Rock, BCA, Giro, Ignite hats and Natives.

Pat is currently the team manager for Salomon and Oakley's skiers and spends his time looking for and coaching new talent. He has also started his own training camps in the UK and France (www.patsharples freestylecamps.co.uk), providing high-performance coaching for all abilities and ages.

The information in this book about the mountains – including parks, and off-piste and backcountry – was compiled by Pat, with the help of many of his contacts and friends in the industry.

Vanessa Webb: Vanessa has always had a passion for skiing, travelling and writing. She has skied all her life and has spent winters in Canada, France and New Zealand and is also a qualified ski instructor and coach. Vanessa has a first class degree in Psychology and Philosophy, and has recently been the manager for a number of events in the mountains, including the ever popular Snowbombing in Mayrhofen, Austria.

Vanessa is responsible for writing about the resorts themselves, including the hotels, restaurants, activities and nightlife, and for the editing of Pat's dubious spelling.

How to use this book

Use this book exactly how you like, but if you want to find the best resort for you, we recommend that you start by checking out the list of 'Top 5s' (page 7). Decide which features of a resort you value the most (nightlife, lift pass price, off-piste/backcountry, parks…) and see which resorts we recommend in these categories; you might find that some overlap. Make a shortlist of three or four that you think would suit you, then refer to them in the main text of the book and decide which one you think is more your cup of tea. We've rated them – in our opinion – out of 5 for snow reliability, the parks and off-piste, après ski, nightlife, eating out and resort charm, and whether they are suitable for expert, intermediate or novice skiers. If you think you might like similar resorts to us, you could also check out how we rank all 50 resorts. The latest snow reports and piste maps for each resort are usually available on the tourist office website, the address of which is given under Useful facts and phone numbers.

Our top 50 resorts

Please be clear that these ratings are based purely on our opinion and have been included for interest and as a talking point. Some people may hate our favourite resorts, some may fall in love with those we are not so keen on. A favourite resort is a very personal thing and should be chosen on the qualities you think are the most important. It is also important to note that we would not have included a resort that we do not rate highly, so even those at the bottom of our personal list have some great plus points and might shoot to the top of your list.

1 St Anton, Austria, page 59
2 Chamonix, France, page 82
3 Verbier, Switzerland, page 210
4 Saas-Fee, Switzerland, page 199
5 La Grave, France, page 99
6 Zermatt, Switzerland, page 215
7 Mayrhofen, Austria, page 51
8 Courchevel, France, page 87
9 Tignes, France, page 123
10 Val d'Isère, France, page 128
11 Champéry, Switzerland, page 170
12 Morzine, France, page 107
13 St Moritz, Switzerland, page 205
14 Lech, Austria, page 47
15 Ste Foy, France, page 116
16 Engelberg, Switzerland, page 181
17 Klosters, Switzerland, page 188
18 Bad Gastein, Austria, page 31
19 Ischgl, Austria, page 39
20 Les Deux Alpes, France, page 93
21 Serre Chevalier, France, page 119
22 Avoriaz, France, page 78
23 Mürren, Switzerland, page 195
24 Åre, Sweden, page 160
25 Soldeu, Andorra, page 26
26 Les Arcs, France, page 74
27 Gressoney, Italy, page 150
28 Crans Montana, Switzerland, page 173
29 La Plagne, France, page 111
30 Meribel, France, page 103
31 Saalbach-Hinterglemm, Austria, page 55
32 Arosa, Switzerland, page 170
33 Laax Murschetg, Switzerland, page 192
34 Kitzbühel, Austria, page 43
35 Zell am See, Austria, page 67
36 Selva in Val Gardena, Italy, page 158
37 Courmayeur, Italy, page 147
38 Val Thorens, France, page 133
39 Alpe d'Huez, France, page 70
40 Arinsal, Andorra, page 18
41 Hintertux, Austria, page 36
42 Alagna, Italy, page 137
43 Cervinia, Italy, page 140
44 Sölden, Austria, page 63
45 Hemsedal, Norway, page 157
46 Davos, Switzerland, page 177
47 Riksgränsen, Sweden, page 163
48 Pas de la Casa, Andorra, page 22
49 Flims, Switzerland, page 184
50 Cortina d'Ampezzo, Italy, page 144

Travelling by train

We are grateful to Daniel Elkan for providing the information on train travel. Routes tend to remain fairly constant, but since fares change, it is best to get up-to-date information online when you book. Most journeys offer the best value sharing a 6-berth standard-class couchette. Once confirmed, most companies do not permit change or refund. All trains and times are daily, except journeys that use the Bergland Express, which leaves on a Friday night.

On all routes, children under 4 travel free of charge unless they require their own accommodation. The exception is the Bergland Express where a reduction only applies in a sharing couchette cabin. On the fares to Swiss resorts, children under 16 do not pay the rail fare in Switzerland if travelling with their parents. Special fares may be available for groups of 6 or more (10 or more for Eurostar and in France).

Our top 5s

Top 5 resorts for après ski
1 St Anton, Austria, page 59
2 Verbier, Switzerland, page 210
3 Mayrhofen, Austria, page 51
4 Ischgl, Austria, page 39
5 Saalbach-Hinterglemm, Austria, page 55

Top 5 resorts for resort charm
1 Saas-Fee, Switzerland, page 199
2 Klosters, Switzerland, page 188
3 St Moritz, Switzerland, page 205
4 Val D'Isere, France, page 128
5 Mayrhofen, Austria, page 51

Top 5 resorts for extreme skiing/powder
1 La Grave, France, page 199
2 Chamonix, France, page 82
3 St Anton, Austria, page 59
4 Verbier, Switzerland, page 210
5 Ste Foy, France, page 116

Top 5 resorts for the family
1 Courchevel, France, page 87
2 Soldeu, Andorra, page 26
3 Mayrhofen, Austria, page 51
4 Lech, Austria, page 47
5 Klosters, Switzerland, page 188

Top 5 resorts to go to with a group of mates
1 Morzine, France, page 107
2 Meribel, France, page 103
3 St Anton, Austria, page 59
4 Val D'Isere, France, page 128
5 Les Deux Alpes, France, page 93

Top 5 resorts for parks
1 Mayrhofen, Austria, page 51
2 Les Deux Alpes, France, page 93
3 Laax Murschetg, Switzerland, page 192
4 Meribel, France, page 103
5 Morzine/Avoriaz, France, pages 107 and 78

Top 5 resorts favoured by the rich and famous
1 St Moritz, Switzerland, page 205
2 Courchevel, France, page 87
3 Klosters, Switzerland, page 188
4 Lech, Austria, page 47
5 Kitzbühel, Austria, page 43

Top 5 resorts for a romantic weekend
1 Saas-Fee, Switzerland, page 210
2 Val D'Isere, France, page 128
3 Klosters, Switzerland, page 188
4 St Moritz, Switzerland, page 205
5 Chamonix, France, page 82

Top 5 resorts for guaranteed snow
1 Saas-Fee, Switzerland, page 210
2 Zermatt, Switzerland, page 215
3 Hintertux, Austria, page 36
4 Les Deux Alpes, France, page 93
5 Tignes, France, page 123

Top 5 resorts for value for money
1 Soldeu, Andorra, page 26
2 Arinsal, Andorra, page 18
3 Mayrhofen, Austria, page 51
4 Pas de la Casa, Andorra, page 22
5 Morzine, France, page 107

Ski and snowboard banter for dummies

Backcountry
Some people use the terms off-piste and backcountry interchangeably, but backcountry really refers to riders heading out into the really remote and untouched areas of the mountain.

Backcountry kicker
You will sometimes see skiers and boarders building their own jumps in the backcountry. This enables you to hand pick your location, size and landing, and many people will session these kickers for hours.

Big air
Snowboarding and skiing competition in which riders are judged on the height of the jump, the difficulty of the manoeuvre and the accuracy of the landing.

Big Bertha
A big jump.

Big booter
A massive jump that really stands out from the rest.

Boardercross
A snowboarding course that includes various obstacles, such as jumps.

Box
Budding freestylers will practise sliding on boxes in the park before progressing to rails.

Cornice
A big chunk of snow (caused by wind and such like) that is dangerously balanced on the side of the mountain. Look out for cornices in the backcountry; whilst it may seem enjoyable to jump off them, they are very unstable and have a tendency to break and cause an avalanche that could sweep you away in the process.

Couloir
A gully in the mountain. Couloirs range from little more than a narrow run that many people could have a bash at, to steep and tight shoots only to be attempted by experts.

Drop-off
This involves riding off a cliff on your board or skis.

FIS standards
The Fédération Internationale de Ski (FIS) organises many world-class events, so if something is to FIS standards it means it's pretty damn good.

Freeride
Freeriding has been attributed to many different kinds of riding. We use the word to refer to backcountry, bigmountain and off-piste riding.

Freestyle
Freestyle can mean anything from skiers in the moguls to skiers and snowboarders hitting the jumps in the park. Sometimes freestyle is related too closely to the park; many freestyle riders enjoy jibbing off natural hits all over the mountain.

Freshies
You can get freshies if you are the first person up the mountain immediately after a fresh snowfall, as they refer to the first tracks in fresh powder.

Fun boxes
A long thin box on which skiers perform various manoeuvres.

Gap jump
This is when a rider has to clear a gap from the take-off to the landing.

Half pipe
Take a big pipe, cut it in half and put snow in it – voilà! Variations are a quarter pipe (take a big pipe, cut it in half, and cut that half in half so that you just have one wall to hit) and a super pipe (take a really really big pipe, cut it in half and put snow in it). These pipes have massive walls and are used in all the world-class competitions.

Hip
See spine.

Hit
A jump.

Hook
To hook is to throw yourself off something, eg a cliff. If somebody refers to you as a hooker it's not necessarily a compliment, as hookers will throw themselves off anything, but without any element of control or style.

Jibbing
This is when riders play around on the pistes or in the park. In the park you might jib on rails or fun boxes, whilst on the piste you might be doing nose or tail presses or playing on natural hits wherever you spot them.

Kickers
Jumps used for launching aerial manoervres.

Line
As well as being a top brand of ski, the term 'line' also refers to the route you take down the mountain. In bigmountain competitions, judges rate the line a competitor chooses, as well as his or her technique, style, etc.

Magic carpet
The moving walkway that is used in some children's/beginners' areas instead of a lift.

Motorway runs
Wide, easy trails.

Mogul field or bumps
A slope covered in natural or manmade bumps.

New School
This is a term that has emerged fairly recently in the skiing world, referring to the new movement in freestyle skiing. Skiing has gone through a huge change in the past decade, and the gap between skiing and boarding has closed in. There is no longer the rift between skiers and boarders that there used to be, and there is no real difference in the image or desires of freestyle skiers and boarders. As always, it will take probably another decade or so for the new style of skiing to be recognised by everyone – some resorts are still seriously Old School, only allowing snowboarders into their parks and other guidebooks have separate sections for skiers and boarders, or deal exclusively with one or the other.We are the first to acknowledge that the new generation of rider, whether skier or boarder, is after the same thing.

Off-piste
This is the natural terrain, outside the marked areas of the piste.

Park
Area used by snowboarders to perform stunts.

Piste
A ski run.

Pisteurs/ski patrol/ski monitors
These are the lifeguards of the mountain. They will come and help you if you've injured yourself on the slopes and they know everything there is to know about the mountain and weather conditions. These are the people to consult before you venture off-piste, as they will inform you how safe it is and which areas should be avoided.

Powder
Good, light, deep snow.

Rails
These are just like hand rails that you see in the street and you'll mainly find them in parks. Skiers and snowboarders use them to slide down, or up, and they come in many different shapes and sizes, such as a rainbow rail, kinked rails (flatdown, up-flat-up, Y-down, etc), C-rail, S-rail or rollercoaster rail. If you want to start learning rails, most parks provide a fun box on which to learn and practise.

Rainbow box
A box gently rising up to the peak, followed by a gentle slope down.

Ratrac piste basher
A machine that packs snow tightly on the trails.

Ride/Rider
This refers to both skiers and boarders. We don't differentiate between them; we all ride the same mountain.

Run
A ski slope; green is easiest (although not all countries have green runs), followed by blue, red then black.

Seasonaires
Skiiers who return every season.

Sessioning
This means hitting a jump or rail once, walking back up and repeating this process for as long as you fancy.

Shapers
These are the people who maintain and look after the park. Some resorts leave their parks to fade away once they have been built, whilst others employ a number of shapers, who take huge pride in their work and are a great asset to the resort.

Skiing switch
This means skiing backwards.

Slopestyle
A course of jumps, rail slides or obstacles.

Spine
A jump shaped like a spine, where you can land on either side of the landing. Also called a hip.

Step up
A type of jump where you land at a higher point than where you took off.

Table top
A jump with a platform that you must clear to reach the landing. Table tops are less intimidating than gap jumps, and small ones are suitable for learning on.

Tracked out
An area of snow that has been ridden so much it is no longer worth riding.

Wall ride
A steep wall, found in the park, for boarders and skiers to ride up and jib around on.

Safety

Avalanche safety

For anyone who is venturing off-piste, it is vitally important to be equipped, not only with all the relevant safety gear (see pages 14–15), but also with the required knowledge.

Skiing and snowboarding are not without risk. Around 100 people die every year in the Alps as a result of avalanches, so you need to be physically and mentally prepared.

Ultimately there are three key areas of knowledge in which skiers and boarders should be proficient before they step off the pisted areas. These are:

1 **Avalanche avoidance:** This is by far the best method of avalanche safety!
2 **Avalanche survival:** What to do if the worst occurs.
3 **Search and rescue:** How to rescue an avalanche victim effectively.

Avalanche avoidance

While it is vitally important to carry avalanche survival equipment such as transceivers, probes and shovels, it still remains that 55–65 per cent of buried victims die even when they are equipped with all the gear. Therefore, the most successful way to deal with avalanches is to avoid them, and the key to this is skiers'/boarders' knowledge and experience, and their ability to engage in effective risk analysis. Here are a few pointers to get you started.

Plan your route

Your route should be well considered and carefully planned, taking into account:

- **Slope aspect and gradient.** Carry an inclinometer and compass for gauging slope aspect and steepness. Remember that the majority of avalanches occur on north-west to east aspects on slopes greater than 30 degrees. Slopes between 30 and 60 degrees have a potential to slide, and the gradient most likely to slide is 38 degrees.
- **Recent weather conditions.** Include new snowfall. Rain on fresh snow leads to a high risk of avalanches.
- **Evolution of the snowpack.**
- **Predominant wind direction and speed.**
- **Humidity.**

Gain experience

The better your knowledge and experience, the better able you will be to cope with problem situations. Find ways to expand your knowledge:

- **Attend courses.**
- **Read up on the subject.**
- **Check www.backcountryaccess.com**
- **Go out with experienced people and listen to their advice.**
- **Study the avalanche bulletin.** Do this in great detail, especially if there is a mention of local risk factors.

Don't fall into common traps

A run is not safe just because:

- You've done it before; familiarity is dangerous and can mean that you do not assign the risk-analysis procedure that you would to an unknown slope.
- You can see other people doing it.
- You've already started so you will finish; always be prepared to admit the danger and head back, even if it means a long hike.
- You've got an avalanche transceiver and all the other equipment. A transceiver is a search-and-rescue device; it should not affect the risk-analysis procedure.

Avalanche survival

In the case of an avalanche there are three main factors that will affect whether a victim survives and there are a few things you can do to enhance your chances of survival.

Depth of burial

Approximately 90 per cent of victims caught in avalanches are alive when the avalanche has stopped moving but most are buried beneath the surface and cannot free themselves. Their chances of survival decrease rapidly with time, and statistics show that

55–65 per cent of buried avalanche victims are recovered dead.

Help yourself

If you can, try to swim in the slide. This may avoid you being entirely buried.

The ABS Airbag (a fantastic but expensive piece of equipment) has been designed to protect the victim from complete burial; airbags are triggered by the victim, making their bodies less dense than moving snow.

Air supply

Suffocation accounts for 50 per cent of all avalanche fatalities and is not easily avoided if your rescuers cannot reach you quickly.

Help yourself

Try to clear your airways to breathe. It may be possible to clear an air pocket around your mouth as the slide slows down.

The Avalung is a unique piece of equipment that can be used to buy the victim valuable time. Working on the principle that avalanche debris is mostly air, it extracts air from the surrounding area and deposits exhaled air into the snow behind the victim.

Rescue time

It has been found that victims recovered during the first 15 minutes of avalanche burial have a 93 per cent chance of survival.

The only fatalities tend to be those who sustained injuries as a result of the fall during the avalanche itself. Between 15 minutes and 45 minutes recovery time is a crucial half hour known as the asphyxiation phase.

After 45 minutes, the chances of survival decrease to less than 30 per cent. After 45 minutes, even if you have managed to find an air pocket, the risk of death from hypothermia is high.

Help yourself

Visual clues can give rescuers an indication of your location, and speed up the rescue process. If you can push a ski pole or arm out to the surface, statistics show you have a much greater chance of being rescued.

The Avalanche Ball is another useful piece of equipment that will give a visual clue to the victim's location. Pull a cord on the waist belt and the ball inflates and floats to the surface of the slide, whilst remaining attached to the victim via a cord. This will greatly increase the victim's chances of a swift rescue.

An effective rescue team is by far the best way to decrease rescue time. If all parties have avalanche transceivers it is vital that the rescuers start the search immediately and have prior training. The rescuer can alert the rescue services quickly if they have a phone (be aware that using a phone may interfere with the transceiver signals) but they should not go for help; they should start their rescue immediately the avalanche ceases.

Search and rescue

Using transceivers

We have talked about the importance of carrying and knowing about transceivers. However, there are a few details that are very important and not immediately obvious. For example, think about the impossibility of trying to find more than one buried body using transceivers; the signals given out by a number of transceivers will cause confusion and may render them useless. The best way to avoid this is to ensure that only one person is skiing/boarding at a time. Others should wait in safe areas, not in the way of a potential avalanche. This also provides a greater number of rescuers should the worst occur.

Help yourself

- Ensure that one person at a time is skiing or boarding.
- Ensure that transceivers are functioning and turned on.
- Practise using them in the local park or back garden so you use them as a reflex action in an emergency.
- Do not carry your transceiver in your rucksack. Wear it as close to the body as possible to avoid it being torn from you.
- Assign a leader whose job it is to ensure that every member of the group has a functioning transceiver.
- Turn your transceiver off at the end of the day and remove the batteries if it is to be stored for a long period of time. Use new batteries at the start of each season.
- Effective probing and digging is also essential for a successful search and rescue.

Park rules and etiquette

1 No snaking. Make sure you know when it is your turn to take your run up to the jump or rail; never cut people off by jumping in front of them and stealing their turn.

2 Never stand on top of the jumps unless you are marking the fact that there has been an accident, in which case you should make this obvious to those waiting at the top of the jump – make a cross sign with your arms or poles.

3 Never stand or sit on the landing of a jump – for obvious reasons – the jumper can't see you, could land on you and this could lead to death.

4 If you crash on a landing, try to get out of the way of the landing area as quickly as possible, and alert those around you to indicate your crash to those at the top.

5 Never start your run-in until you know the person before you has landed safely and made their way out.

6 Always stick to jumps within your ability. Don't try something that you don't feel comfortable with.

7 Wear a helmet, and back and hip protector. Landings can be hard-packed and it's easy to mess up on rails. Many people have died when a helmet could have saved them, although resorts obviously try not to advertise this fact. Helmets are not unfashionable, you can get some wicked-looking ones (see page 8), and they could save you from a crushed skull.

8 Don't walk out across run-ins or landings unless you can see exactly where everyone else is and what they're doing, and they can see you.

9 Never ride down the park in a group; always go one at a time.

10 Store the resort's mountain rescue/emergency number in your phone so that you're prepared if you witness an accident. The international emergency number from a mobile phone is 112.

11 Don't intimidate people who have just started using the park – you were there once.

In your backpack should be:

- Compass
- Emergency food and water
- First aid kit
- Inclinometer
- Map
- Pocket-knife
- Probe
- Shovel
- Torch

Equipment guide

Boards and skis

If you're in the market for a board or skis, the following companies bring out a new range every year with improved performance and updated graphics. Make your choice according to your ability and the style of riding or skiing that you enjoy. The companies design some of their equipment specifically for the park, piste or powder and some to enable you to enjoy all areas of the mountain. Lighter and shorter boards and skis are made for women. For boards, see Salomon (www.salomon.com) and Burton (www.burton.com). For skis, go to Armada (www.armadaskis.com), Völkl (www.volkl.com) and Salomon (www.salomon.com) or www.k2skis.com

Body armour

There is no doubt that skiing and snowboarding are dangerous. Whether you are sticking to the pisted runs, hitting the parks or venturing into the backcountry, we strongly advise the use of safety equipment. There are numerous examples of people who have seriously injured themselves, sometimes fatally, who could have protected themselves simply by wearing the basic safety equipment of a helmet and a back and short protector.

Helmets

In America, there are a number of resorts in which it is illegal not to wear a helmet and this attitude is spreading to Europe. You should consider a helmet as important as your skis/board, if not more so, as it could be a lifesaver. There is no excuse for not wearing one – and they make you look hardcore.

We don't go anywhere without our Giro helmets. In particular we recommend the following:

The Revolver: Perfect for the park and the pipe, this helmet has just enough brim on the durable, hard shell to hint at your style. It features an interior subliner and an interior goggle channel, which allows space for your strap. What's more, the Stack Vent technology keeps your goggles fog free. The Audio version of this helmet features 40mm speakers so that you can enjoy crystal clear treble and thumping bass while you're on the move.

The G10: Lightweight and with a low-profile shape, the G10 is hugely popular. The fit is great and the three ventilation settings make it suitable whatever the weather throws at you.

Giro ski and snowboard helmets can be bought at www.sailandski.co.uk, www.ellis-brigham.com or www.snowandrock.com

Back protectors

If you fill your days in the park hitting huge kickers and sketchy rail slides or going off cliff drops in the backcountry then you need a back protector. Your spine is pretty vulnerable when you crash and needs protecting; if you value the use of your limbs invest in one. Contrary to popular opinion they are perfectly comfortable and don't restrict body movement. We like the Forcefield Pro L2 Back Protector, it's comfortable and flexible, but also provides optimum performance and protection. For more information visit www.forcefieldbodyarmour.co.uk

Short protectors

Not everyone feels the need to wear a short protector but it can be very handy in a crash over rocks or on a rail in the park. The Dainese Impact Short Plus features soft composite protection for the hipbone, sides and gluteus with rigid composite femur protectors. Buy Dainese products at Snow and Rock. Forcefield also offer board shorts.

Safety equipment for backcountry riding

Venturing into the backcountry is risky, no matter how good your knowledge of the terrain. Each year there are more reports of avalanches taking people's lives because an increasing number of skiers and boarders are exploring off-piste without the required experience or equipment. There are a few essential pointers. For starters, never go alone. No one will be there to witness your amazing Rodeo 720 off the 24m cliff and if you get caught in an avalanche – you're stuffed. Ensure that at least 1 person in the group has extensive experience and substantial knowledge of the local terrain. If your group does not have these qualities, hire a guide.

Additionally, it is vital to invest in the right equipment – it could save your life or someone else's.

Avalanche transceivers

This is arguably the most important piece of equipment to have when exploring off-piste. It is used to locate someone who has been enveloped in an avalanche and also allows a fellow transceiver carrier to find you. It should be worn under your jacket at all times. Remember, it is completely useless unless you know how to use it. Details on vitally important courses can be found at www.backcountryaccess.com/education or www.natives.co.uk

Tracker2: This is one of the simplest and most reliable avalanche transceivers on the market (www.backcountryaccess.com). Tracker's unique architecture and crossed 'X' antenna provide something no other digital beacon can offer: real-time display. Faster processing and display speeds provide instantaneous feedback on the victim's location. Unlike delayed displays, there is minimal offset between your lowest distance reading and the victim's actual location. Tracker 2 is even faster and easier than its predecessor, the Tracker DTS, and it is the industry's fastest, most precise pinpointing, with triple receive antenna. Other features include simplified mechanical search/transmit switches, a multiple burial indicator, and 40m+ search strip width. It measures 13.2cm x 8.6cm x 2.5cm and weighs approximately 181g.

Probe pole

The probe is used to stick into the snow to find someone who has been buried.

Profile 240 probe: This is the mainstream top-selling probe at Backcountry Access (www.backcountryaccess.com). It has depth markings in 1cm increments, 6-section 7075 aluminium tubing, an extended length of 240cm and a collapsed length of 40cm.

Carbon 340 probe: This top of the line probe from Backcountry Access also has silk-screened depth markings in 1cm increments with clear protective coating and 7-section carbon fibre tubing. It has an extended length of 340cm and a collapsed length of 47cm.

The depth markings on these probes encourage proper excavation. If you know exactly how deep the victim is, you should dig your hole accordingly. Probing and shovelling is the most time-consuming part of any avalanche rescue so it's important to be equipped with the right knowledge (see www.backcountryaccess.com).

Avalanche shovels

Shovels are now ultra light so you can't use weight as an excuse for not carrying one. They are designed for digging people out of an avalanche, but also come in handy for building big backcountry kickers. Backcountry Access only makes high-quality aluminium shovels because plastic doesn't work in avalanche debris. The oval shaft and 6061 aluminium make their shovels the strongest and lightest.

Tour Shovel System: At just 454g, this is a seriously light shovel/probe combination. It has a super-strong oval shaft with T-grip and can be fixed-length (63cm) or extendable (88cm).

Chugach Pro EXT: The biggest, baddest digging machine in the range, this has an extendable oval shaft with D-grip and an oversized blade for moving lots of snow, which also makes it popular for building and shaping kickers. The Chugach Pro has an extended length of 104.5cm and a collapsed length of 28.6cm

ABS backpacks

This is one of the most invaluable avalanche safety devices. It is designed to keep you above the surface during an avalanche by making the body less dense than moving snow.

Burial is a huge factor in avalanche fatalities (see pages 12–13) and an ABS backpack can massively increase your chances of survival. The airbags are stowed in the backpack until the trigger on the shoulder strap is pulled, which activates the nitrogen-air cartridge, releasing 2 75-litre air bags within 2 seconds. The ABS has to be released by the user and practising this is vital. Find out more information on www.abssystem.com

For the gadget mad

Hydration

Backcountry Access (www.backcountryaccess.com) pioneered the concept of freezeproof winter hydration, having realised that you don't want to let dehydration caused by a frozen tube to your water source ruin your day. Its Stash system harnesses body heat to warm the water in the bite valve and hose, which are typically the most vulnerable to freezing. Specialised mesh lining on the underside of the shoulder strap transfers heat directly to the Stash sleeve.

Stash Rider: This has a simple, dedicated snowboard attachment system. There is also a reservoir, stormproof zip and internal shovel and probe pockets. Its low profile also makes it chairlift-friendly.

Stash BC: Made for full-day backcountry expeditions, this pack has a 3-litre reservoir, stormproof zippers, an external shovel pocket, diagonal and A-frame ski mount and a removable plastic/foam framesheet.

Helmet cameras

Helmet cameras are the ultimate toy for use on the piste, in the park and in the backcountry. You can view an extensive range at www.actioncameras.co.uk

For the beginner: Wireless helmet cameras are perfect for those new to on-piste filming as they are self-contained units that record on to SD cards, eliminating the need for a camcorder. The tiny cameras clip or Velcro to your helmet.

For the all-round entertainment package: Archos' helmet camera (around £100) is made especially for the Archos 5 or 7. This is the option if you want a fantastic media machine for music and movies. The camera has a 420 TV line resolution and comes with a 6mm Sony CCD lens. The helmetcam, which is powered off the Archos unit, can record several hours of footage directly on to the hard drive of the Archos. The camera has some fantastic features: it can capture in any environment without an extra light source, even in near darkness; the MPEG-4 SP files are compatible with both PCs and Macs; data can be transferred via USB 2.0 directly to a computer and, it has slow motion capability (½, ¼, ⅛ speeds).

The disadvantage is obviously the cost, as you have to buy the Archos (£250–350), in addition to the camera above.

For the pro: There are a variety of top-quality helmet cameras providing DVD-quality footage. All that you will need is a compatible camcorder with AV-In.

Music on the mountain

Oakley Thump Pro: The Thump Pro is compatible with most music programmes including iTunes® (unless music is bought from the iTunes music store), Windows Media Player® and WinAmp®. Thump Pro offers memory storage up to 1GB (240 songs). Listen to music virtually anywhere with speaker booms that adjust easily for a customised fit, and just swing them out of the way when you need to hear your environment. The Thump Pro will play up to 6 hours of playback time on a single charge.

O ROKR™: From Oakley and Motorola, the O ROKR™ provides stereo music and wireless connectivity, using the next generation of Bluetooth® eyewear, letting you stay connected to calls and music while you're riding. O ROKR™ can wirelessly stream music from a compatible Bluetooth®-enabled phone or a portable music player with an add-on Bluetooth adapter (you can use O ROKR™ with your iPod by adding the optional NAVIPLAY© adapter). When you want to pause the music, adjust the volume or change songs, just use the buttons on O

ROKR™. You can switch instantly between stereo music and wireless communication – when you need to take a call, answer it from O ROKR™ while your compatible mobile phone rests up to 10m away. You get up to 5 hours of talk time and more than 100 hours of standby time in a hands-free link that is part of something you're already wearing. Impressive…

More gadgets

Suunto wristop computers: Depending on the model that you choose (with costs of £100–500), you will be able to take advantage of a range of features, such as an altimeter, barometer, compass, chronographic functions, logbook and on certain models, GPS (SUUNTO X10).

The altimeter gives you an insight into your vertical speed, online cumulative descent and number of runs and altitude profile. The barometer will show you the sea level pressure, absolute pressure, weather trend graph, temperature and has a 48-hour memory and weather alarm. The compass provides information on bearing and bearing tracking and the ski chronograph shows the degree of the slope, maximum speed, average speed and vertical drop for individual runs. The logbook keeps a record of the total and cumulative vertical ascents and descents, as well as the number of runs. Most models also store data for later analysis – you can view, compare, and analyse your riding performance through a specially designed PC interface and compare it with others over the internet.

Portable boot dryer: The Therm-ic dryer dries all kinds of boots or gloves overnight and warms them up again for cosy feet and hands in the morning. It also gets rid of bad odours. It dries ski boots in 60–90 minutes and the compact collapsible design makes it easy to pack away. You can buy the dryer from Snow and Rock (about £40).

Nixon watches: The snowboarders' choice, and an instant eyecatcher, these watches are superb presents. The range is massive: check out www.nixonnow.com and make your choice.

Surfster Ice: The Surfster Ice (around £60) is an inflatable toboggan, with neolite knuckle guards, webbing handles and left and right leash tags. Its Dual Density core makes for a comfortable and exhilarating ride. Traditional toboggans can be very cumbersome; the joy of the Surfster Ice is that it packs down to little more than a roll mat, and yet inflates in a couple of minutes (it comes with a pump).

Radica SSX Snowboarder: Play SSX for real, in the comfort of your own lounge (around £40). Grab a few mates and a few beers and hit the pipe.

Andorra

The Brits' choice: perfect for beginners, an awesome party scene and it won't break the bank

Arinsal

A fun and friendly resort, if you've been once, you'll certainly want to come again.

On the slopes	Rating
Snow reliability	❄❄❄½
Parks	❄❄❄❄
Off-piste	❄❄½
Off the slopes	
Après ski	❄❄❄½
Nightlife	❄❄❄½
Eating out	❄❄
Resort charm	❄❄❄

The resort

The Vallnord ski area comprises the connected areas of Arinsal, Pal and La Massana, and the separate area of Ordino-Arcalis, a great ski area to visit but with no associated village. Arinsal is the most popular base as it is home to most of the amenities in the Vallnord. It is full of Brits, which has its good and bad points. Families will be happy, as will beginners, intermediates and park enthusiasts. The après ski bars will not disappoint and are far better value for money than many other European resorts.

The slopes in Arinsal, Pal and La Massana are great for beginners and low intermediates, but competent riders may get bored after a couple of days. A trip to Ordino-Arcalis is definitely worth the effort, as there are some great freeriding areas. You can get to Arcalis on a local bus or take a trip organised by the tourist office. It takes about 30 minutes by road. The great freestyle parks in Vallnord provide another option for experts.

The investment in Vallnord continues, with much being spent on high-speed lifts, snow cannons and even the refurbishment of restaurants. Accessing Vallnord has been made far easier by the new 1.2km Pont-Pla tunnel between La Massana and the centre of Andorra. This also encourages trips to the capital, Andorra La Vella, a great place for shopping.

The mountains

Height: 1550–2620m

Ability	Rating
Expert	❄❄
Intermediate	❄❄❄
Beginner	❄❄❄❄

Getting about

There are 89km of pistes in Vallnord (63km in Arinsal and Pal and 26km in Ordino-Arcalis), most of them geared towards beginners and intermediates. A gondola ride from the centre of Arinsal or a chair from the end of town will begin your ascent up to Pic Negre (2569m), from which you can take some easy runs back towards Arinsal or take a gondola over to Pal's slopes, which are generally less crowded and have more to keep the keener riders happy.

Ordino-Arcalis is a 30-minute bus trip away but it's well worth it. Snow reliability is fairly good here, with the base 400m higher than Arinsal. Experts will find more challenging runs, from a steep, often mogully, black run from the ridge to the base of Arcalis to plenty of off-piste – particularly in the Cercle de la Coma. Heliskiing is also an option. Go midweek for almost empty runs.

The park

There are now three parks in the Vallnord area. A small beginners' park in Pal in the La Tossa zone includes three rails and a small jump to get you started. The Arcalis snowpark, at 2100m at the end of the Portella del mig slope, also has a couple of jumps and a few rails. The main park is in Arinsal. This boasts a fantastic super pipe with 4/5m high walls that is groomed nightly, a huge selection of rails, kickers of all sizes, a spine and a 500m boardercross. Check out www.vallnordfreestyle.com

Off-piste and backcountry

Arinsal seems to get its fair share of snow each year, which means you can always find a bit of fresh powder. There are a few good tree lines around and a couple of faces but nothing over-challenging. On the plus side, Arinsal attracts mostly beginners so the off-piste that there is won't get tracked out and you can find fresh powder weeks after it has dumped. The La Cappa area is one of the best and there's a massive cornice that's great for getting huge air. Here is also the steepest marked run in Andorra.

Lift passes

See www.vallnord.com for the latest prices.

Instruction

Arinsal Ski School
00376 73 70 29

Pal Ski School
00376 87 80 50

See www.vallnord.com for the latest prices.

Other activities

Shopping: The main activity in Andorra is shopping on all the duty-free delights: alcohol, clothes, electronic gadgets – everything is as cheap as chips. Take care, though, as you are only allowed to take back certain quantities and values of products.

Ski bikes, paragliding, heli-skiing, mushing, speed riding: See www.vallnord.com.

Thermal water centre: Andorra la Vella is the best place for this, and it's only about 10–15 minutes' drive from Arinsal. The Caldea Andorra (00376 80 09 99, www.caldea.ad) is Europe's biggest mountain thermal water centre. It is an impressive place offering 6000m^2 of indoor and outdoor lagoons, Jacuzzis, Turkish baths, pools and waterfalls, with a variety of cultural influences – from Roman to Japanese. On top of this there is a fitness room and a variety of beauty treatments available.

> 'A variety of cultural influences – from Roman to Japanese'

Events

The **Big Snow Festival** (www.thebigsnowfestival.com) in March features some of the world's best DJs and live acts. There are also skiing and snowboardng competitions.

Accommodation

If you're planning a holiday in Arinsal there are a number of cheap options to consider. Just take care that you're not too far away from the action – there's no need to be, as you can get some great deals right in the centre of town and next to the gondola.

Aparthotel Poblado (00376 83 72 37, www.aparthotel-poblado.com) is in a handy location and is great value.

The **Micolau** (00376 73 77 07, www.hotel-micolau.com) is a cosy and charming converted farmhouse with simple, snug rooms. There is a separate lounge for guests and the relaxed restaurant has an inviting log fire.

'A charming converted farmhouse with simple, snug rooms'

Hotel **Husa Xalet Verdú** (00376 73 71 40, www.husalamontana.com) is friendly, clean, comfortable and well located.

For ritzy accommodation, head to the 4-star **Princesa Parc** (00376 73 65 00, www.hotelprincesaparc.com), which has swish spa facilities as well as 10-pin bowling and a games area. Finally, the **Sant Moritz apartments** (00376 73 78 78, www.santmoritz.com) are fully equipped, perfect for families or groups of friends, with 17 apartments with 1 or 2 bedrooms, ranging from 50 to 85m^2 (most have a terrace or balcony, some have a Jacuzzi).

Eating out

On the mountain

The restaurants on the mountain are mainly self-service and usually crowded, offering the standard assortment of snack food. **Panoramix** (00376 83 58 03), a British bar-restaurant, has a good reputation for its extensive sun terrace and Pal's main building has a decent array of options, including a large cafeteria and a proper restaurant, **La Borda** (contact through Pal Ski Station, 00376 73 70 00), serving Andorran cuisine. Vallnord's mountains have a range of international cuisine on offer. In the Setúria sector you can have barbecue ribs in **Coll de la Botella** (contact through Pal Ski Station, 00376 73 70 00). **Igloo** serves Chinese and **Mexicobelix** nachos and burritos (both in the Arinsal sector).

In town

Our favourite restaurant in Arinsal is **Cisco's**, which does fab Tex-Mex food in a converted cattleshed, with a relaxed and rustic feel. The fajitas are especially tasty, as is the mango chicken. The staff are a riot, and the bar downstairs is really popular with the locals and those in the know. All in all, this is a great place for a night out. **El Moli** (www.moliarinsal.com, 00376 83 52 81) is a cute pizzeria in the centre of town, with great food and even better cocktails. They also do takeaway. **Surf** (00376 83 80 69) is a great place to munch on a plate of steak and chips. **Micolau** (00376 73 77 07) is open all day and serves some great snacks, such as all-day breakfasts, bacon and sausage sandwiches, and good tasty salads. At night the warming fire is very inviting and cosy. **Borda d'Erts** (00376 83 67 82) is a few minutes' drive down the road, and is great for a more upmarket night out.

'At night the warming fire is very inviting and cosy'

Bars and clubs

The bars in Arinsal are plentiful and it's pretty difficult not to have a good night here (although that could be something to do with the size of the measures). All of the bars are open from après ski (unless they serve food at lunchtime) and stay open until 3am on weekdays and 4am on Friday and Saturday. **Cisco's** is a favourite with the locals and is a snowboarder hangout. It has a great atmosphere, wicked staff, table football, free internet and the awesome Tex-Mex restaurant upstairs.

El Derbi is a fun Irish pub that is especially heaving on karaoke night. **El Cau** is a bar for the real locals. They have giant TV screens for sports, too, and free toasties are sometimes offered with a drink between 3 and 6pm! **Quo Vadis** (00376 83 76 00, www.quovadis-arinsal.com) is famous as the longest running bar in Arinsal, has a small restaurant and is very popular with tourists. The **Solana** hotel is owned by local instructors and has a big open log fire to relax by. **Red X** is a theme bar that often has fancy dress and live music, and at the end of the day they show video analysis from the day's skiing/boarding.

> 'The longest running bar in Arinsal is very popular with tourists'

Getting there

By car

Arinsal is not an easy drive from the UK, but if you are planning a road trip you should take the A 71 motorway from Paris (860km) as far as Clermond Ferrand, then the A 9 motorway through Narbonne and the A 61 to Toulouse. Next, head towards Foix on the N 20 and to Andorra via the Envalira Tunnel (for which there is a toll), towards La Massana. From the La Massana cable car roundabout, Arinsal is signposted.

By plane

Toulouse (190km) Transfer to Arinsal available from the novatel airport transfer service (www.andorrabybus.com).

Barcelona (200km) Transfer to Arinsal available from the novatel airport transfer service (see above).

By train

Take the Eurostar from London St Pancras to Paris (Gare du Nord). Cross by métro to the Gare d'Austerlitz. Then travel from Paris to l'Hospitalet près l'Andorra overnight by sleeper train. Then get a bus to Andorra la Vella (90 minutes), and then another bus (25 minutes) to the resort. Contact Rail Europe (0870 830 4862, www.raileurope.co.uk) or European Rail (020 7387 0444, www.europeanrail.com). Bus tickets (Andorra Bus) are purchased on the bus.

Useful facts and phone numbers

Tourist office

T: 00376 73 70 20
F: 00376 83 62 42
W: www.vallnord.com

Emergency services

- Police: 110
- Ambulance/Fire: 118
- Emergency health care: 116
- Mountain rescue: 112
- Hospital: 00376 87 10 00

Taxis

- Associacion de Taxistas de Andorra (00376 86 30 00)

Pas de la Casa

Take Blackpool, add some snow and you've got Pas de la Casa

On the slopes	Rating
Snow reliability	❄❄❄
Parks	❄❄
Off-piste	❄❄
Off the slopes	
Après ski	❄❄❄
Nightlife	❄❄❄❄½
Eating out	❄½
Resort charm	❄

The resort

If you don't like drinking and shopping to excess, stop reading now. Pas de la Casa is the biggest and most well known of the six resorts in Granvalira (the others being Grau Roig, Soldeu, El Tarter, Canillo and Encamp). It is big and pretty ugly, but it's very friendly and it's very cheap, so the shopping is tremendous and loads of people come here to buy electrical gadgets, designer clothes, alcohol and perfume. The nightlife could be a plus or a minus point depending on how you look at it. It's a 'lads on a stag night' kind of place and when night falls the urge comes over you to wave your hands around, shout 'Wehey' and drink until you drop. The dropping bit might not be completely your fault as Andorran drinks are as cheap as British pub prices and you get around a triple measure into the bargain. So it does tend to get a tad rowdy. We prefer to stay in Soldeu (see page 26) – you get all the benefits of cheap drinks and there's still a great night-time scene, but you're in much nicer surroundings and you can always pop over for an afternoon's shopping in Pas de la Casa or Andorra la Vella.

If you are thinking of coming to Pas de la Casa, it is worth checking out the Soldeu chapter, too, as the resort is only 20 minutes away by car and the mountain areas are directly accessible.

The mountains

Height: 1710–2640m

Ability	Rating
Expert	❄❄
Intermediate	❄❄❄❄
Beginner	❄❄❄❄

Lift passes

Check the latest prices at www.skiandorra.ad The 5 non-consecutive days pass gives you 10% discount on one of a number of adventure activities, including a ride in a snow mobile.

Getting about

The Grandvalira mountain contains 6 sectors that correspond to the 6 towns; Pas de la Casa, Grau Roig, Soldeu, El Tarter, Canillo and Encamp. From Pas de la Casa head up the Solana chairlift. Complete beginners should use the green slopes by the Les Abelletes car park. From Grau Roig there are a number of options to take you up the hill, all directly accessible from the car park. There is 193km of runs in Grandvalira, all of which come under the same lift pass and most of which are geared towards the beginner/intermediate skier or boarder, with lots of long 'motorway' runs. Grau Roig is home to the best slopes – the masses tend to stay on the beginners' slopes in Pas de la Casa and Soldeu so you can enjoy the sunny slopes in peace.

The park

If you've just got to grips with your skiing or boarding and want to start practising some tricks, the fun park in Pas de la Casa is a perfect place to learn. There are a couple of small jumps and the odd rail. If you're pretty good and looking for a sick park, make your way over to the superb Snow Park in El Tarter (covered in detail in the Soldeu chapter, see page 26). There is also a nice new rail park in Grau Roig with several lines and a good range of rails. If you fancy a shot on a skier/ boardercross course, there's one near the bottom of the resort. Check out www.grandvalira.com

'The fun park in Pas de la Casa is a perfect place to learn'

Off-piste and backcountry

Pas de la Casa doesn't have much off-piste of its own but within the Grandvalira region there are some good areas to be found. Some of the best riding can be found at the top of the mountain by Grau Roig, where there are a few long powder fields to be had. There is also some decent freeriding over towards Soldeu (see Soldeu chapter, page 26).

Instruction

The Andorran ski and snowboard school has seven different centres with instructors that speak loads of languages. Check out www.grandvalira.com.

Pas de la Casa

00376 87 19 20

Grau Roig

00376 87 29 20/00376 87 29 27

Other activities

Adventure activities (based in the Cubil in Grau Roig): The Grau Roig Adventure Activities Centre is the place to go to organise any activity you may want to try your hand at. They organise individual activities as well as catering for large groups of 100 or more. Here are a few of the popular choices (contact the tourist office for more details). Other activities offered by the Adventure Activities Centre include cross-country skiing, snowshoeing, igloo building, orienteering and avalanche rescue courses.

Helicopter flights: 10 or 20-minute helicopter flights can be organised, taking off from Grau Roig or Soldeu.

Husky sled trip: Take a romantic husky sled trip, driven by a guide over 1.5km or 3km.

Mushing: There is a mushing circuit at Grau Roig where you can learn to ride a sled pulled by a team of huskies.

Paintball: This takes place in the battlefield in Grau Roig. All equipment is provided.

Paragliding: Take off from Tossa d'Espiolets (in El Tarter) and land at the bottom of El Tarter. The flights last for 20 minutes and you are accompanied by an instructor.

Shopping: Shopping is the main activity of choice here (unless you're too busy drinking). Remember to check the permitted quantities of alcohol, perfume, cigarettes, etc, but take as much as you are allowed or you'll regret it. Shop around before you buy as prices do differ from shop to shop.

Snowmobiling: This takes place along guided routes. Trips can last 15 minutes, 30 minutes, 1 hour, or you can take a 2-hour excursion to Port d'Envalira which has fantastic terrain for snowmobiling.

Snow track: The Audi snow track is located at the Pla d'Espiolets in Soldeu and you can rent 4WD cars and learn to drive on the snow. Contact the tourist office for more information.

Sports and socio-cultural complex: Pas de la Casa sports and socio-cultural complex (00376 85 68 30) contains a multi use court with floating floor and spectator seating, squash courts, table tennis, saunas and an indoor pool.

Events

The **Snowgames** take place in March each year and run over consecutive weekends. The main events are a snowrunning competition (a snowshoe race) and the San Miguel Snowbike, a bike-cross for mountain bikers on snow. There is also a cross-country endurance test, 'Snowtop'. The best comps (freestyle festival and freestyle series) happen in Soldeu and El Tarter (see Soldeu, page 26).

Accommodation

Hotel Himàlaia Pas (00376 73 55 15, www.hotansa.com) is close to the slopes and offers pretty good accommodation and facilities, including a pool, spa area, gym, games room, internet access and disco. There are 98 rooms, equipped with satellite and mini bar. **Hotel Màgic** (00376 75 69 00) is owned by the same company and is also 4-star (Andorran rating systems, however, appear to be slightly more lenient than those elsewhere in Europe). It has a similar level of comfort and price, internet access, and although there is no pool, there is a sauna, Turkish bath, gym and sunbeds.

Apartments are popular because they are often good value, and you can cook for yourself, which (personally speaking) looks more hygienic and enjoyable than eating at some of the dodgy buffets that are around. Being honest, those who don't fall into the '18–30, on a mission for carnage, the cheaper the better' category shouldn't really stay in Pas de la Casa anyway (the neighbouring Soldeu would be far better) and those who do fall into this category probably won't give a monkeys about the type of accommodation they're in as they won't see much of it.

Eating out

On the mountain

You'll find very few places that you want to linger in Pas de la Casa and Grau Roig – apart, that is, from the restaurant at **Llac dels Pessons** (00376 75 90 15), by far the best on the mountain. Reach it from the Comi del Pessons path running from the Llac del Cubil chair. It's situated on the edge of a frozen lake and is cosy and inviting. It's a table-service restaurant with superb food, specialising in grilled meats on their indoor wood fire. **Xirixuca Costa Rodona** is a good burger stop.

In town

Most of the restaurants in Pas de la Casa serve sketchy food in a dingy atmosphere with shocking service. Then they have the cheek to add a mandatory 10 per cent service charge to your bill. If you find comfort in the familiar you could always head to **Burger King** (Pas de la Casa), **McDonald's** (Pas de la Casa) or **Pizza Hut** (Grau Roig).

However, all is not lost; there are a couple of places that every Pas de la Casa victim should head to. We love the **Perla Negra** (00376 85 68 38), a fun place to take a group of mates, where you can play some darts and then tuck into some tasty ribs and meat skewers. **El Raco** (00376 85 51 99) is a Moroccan-style restaurant and smells of incense. **Vertigo** has a gorgeous, candlelit restaurant, with smart food and the sweet choice of 'big plates' or 'little plates' depending on your appetite.

A real find is a tucked away restaurant called **L'Husk**y (00376 85 52 48). It has a big open fire and old wooden skis and woodwork on the walls, creating the cosy ski lodge feel rarely found in Pas de la Casa. The T-bone steak is very tasty, although at 10oz, it might not satisfy the most hardened steak-eater.

'A real find is a tucked away restaurant called L'Husky'

Bars and clubs

If you didn't feel like you were in Blackpool before, you will when you hit the bars. They are cheesy, rowdy and most of the best clubs are down seedy backstreets (don't worry: Andorra has one of the lowest crime rates in Europe). It's great fun though.

Milwaukee is the place to start the evening with a few pints – between 5 and 7pm there is a good atmosphere and an enticing happy hour. After this it gets absolutely rammed. The **Underground** is a great bar: the Dutch/English owners really make the atmosphere and the music is tailored to British tastes. It's one of the few bars in Pas de la Casa where you can actually have a conversation over the music. **KYU** is a great bar/club and **Bilbord** (00376 85 62 36) is the place to drink when everywhere else has closed, but keep hold of your beer – put it down on the bar and it may well be danced upon. The music is generally commercial hits and the crowd Dutch and British.

'Bilbord is the place to drink when everywhere else has closed'

Getting there

By car

From Paris, take the A6 to Nantes, the A10 to Toulouse, the A62 to Carcassone, the A61 to Foix (direction Hospitalet – RN 20).

By plane

There are no airports in Andorra although there are plans for one at Seu d'Urgell. Until then, the closest are Toulouse, Barcelona and Girona.

Toulouse (200km) Novatel Minibus Services (00376 80 37 89, www.andorrabybus.com) runs a transfer service from the airport.

Barcelona (200km) Novatel Minibus Services (see above) and Direct Bus (00376 80 51 51, www.autocarsnadal.com) run transfer services from the airport.

Girona (219km) Novatel Minibus Services (see above) runs a transfer service from the airport.

By train

Take the Eurostar from London St Pancras to Paris (Gare du Nord). Cross by métro to the Gare d'Austerlitz. Then travel from Paris to l'Hospitalet près l'Andorra overnight by sleeper train. Then get the connecting bus (40 minutes) to the resort. Contact Rail Europe (0870 830 4862, www.raileurope.co.uk) or European Rail (020 7387 0444, www.europeanrail.com). Bus tickets (Andorra Bus) are purchased on the bus.

Useful facts and phone numbers

Tourist office

T: 00376 85 52 92 (Pas de la Casa)
00376 80 10 60 (Grandvalira)
W: www.grandvalira.com
www.skiandorra.ad

Emergency services

- Fire brigade/ambulance: 118
- Police: 110
- Police station: 00376 87 20 00
- Emergency medical service: 116
- Medical centre: 00376 85 52 25
- Hospital: 00376 87 10 00

Taxis

You won't find any taxi ranks out of Andorra la Vella, but you can call any of the numbers below to order one:

- Associació de Taxis d'Andorra: 00376 86 30 00
- 00376 86 10 05
- Més Taxis: 00376 82 80 00

Soldeu

One of Andorra's finest resorts. Great slopes for beginners and intermediates and a perfect park for the freestylers.

On the slopes	Rating
Snow reliability	❄❄❄
Parks	❄❄❄❄
Off-piste	❄❄❄
Off the slopes	
Après ski	❄❄❄
Nightlife	❄❄❄½
Eating out	❄❄½
Resort charm	❄❄½

The resort

Soldeu has undergone massive changes in recent years with smart new hotels and lifts popping up. Fortunately it hasn't lost its fun, friendly atmosphere and is still our favourite base in Andorra. Budget skiers and party people abound, but a new clientele has emerged since the opening of the 5-star Hermitage Hotel and spa and its counterparts.

The resort is set along the busy main road from Pas de la Casa through to Andorra la Vella and the buildings are far prettier than that of its neighbour, Pas de la Casa. There are some great pubs (which are packed every Saturday with British footie fans), and good restaurants and hotels. Another great thing about the six resorts in Grandvalira (Pas de la Casa, Grau Roig, Soldeu, El Tarter, Canillo and Encamp) is that they are so close together that you can be in any one of them in half an hour. The mountains are also linked, making it one of the largest ski areas in Europe, although the terrain is fairly flat and easy compared to other similar-sized European resorts. Soldeu is a great base for anyone visiting the superb snow park in El Tarter, a reason to come to Andorra in itself. If you are thinking of coming to Soldeu, it is worth checking out the Pas de la Casa chapter too (see page 22) as the resort is only 20 minutes away by car and the mountain areas are directly accessible.

The mountains

Height: 1710–2560m

Ability	Rating
Expert	❄❄½
Intermediate	❄❄❄❄
Beginner	❄❄❄❄❄

Lift passes

Check the latest prices at www.skiandorra.ad. The 5 non-consecutive days pass gives you 10% discount off 1 of a number of adventure activities, including a ride in a snow mobile.

Getting about

The Grandvalira mountain contains 6 sectors that correspond to the 6 towns: Pas de la Casa, Grau Roig, Soldeu, El Tarter, Canillo and Encamp. From Soldeu, the cable car takes you up to Espiolets, where you can start your journey through Grandvalira. Alternatively you can head up the mountain from nearby El Tarter, which has a chairlift and a gondola that take you up to the experts' snow park and general meeting place. Canillo and Encamp are slightly more inconvenient places from which to begin your journey up the mountain, being at the far end of Grandvalira, and you also have to take the gondola back down at the end of the day. From Encamp, the long Funicamp might take a while, but it does set you down bang in the heart of Grandvalira.

Grandvalira is geared to the beginner/intermediate skier or boarder with 'motorway' style runs and long paths. It also caters very well for kids, and has a great Disney run (at the top of the El Tarter gondola) past pictures of Mickey, Donald, Cinderella and Buzz Lightyear. There are a few things to interest the more advanced/expert rider as well, not least the superb park in the El Tarter sector. El Tarter also holds the Guinness world record for having the longest bumps run in the world at 1300m.

The park

There are three parks in Grandvalira, a beginners' park in Pas de la Casa, a slopestyle in Grau Roig with a decent rail park, and the amazing park in El Tarter. The latter (accessed from el Pla de Riba Escorxada) consists of three big kickers with a smaller side kicker by the side of each one. They range from 22m to 5m gaps, and are always perfectly shaped. There's a 120m half pipe, a selection of rails and a massive wall ride. The quarter pipe and gigantic hip are also wicked after they've been shaped.

> 'The quarter pipe and gigantic hip are also wicked after they've been shaped.'

Off-piste and backcountry

The off-piste in Grandvalira is all really accessible and requires a minimum of hiking. It isn't over challenging but there's more than you would think and you can find fresh powder in the trees, even when it hasn't snowed for a few weeks. The big tree run back to the bottom of Soldeu is a must after a snowfall and has been nicknamed 'the land of the giants' because the trees are so huge. The hike off to the right of Riba Escorxada is amazing in the right conditions and is a favourite among the locals.

For some low-risk off-piste and an interesting experience (weather conditions permitting), there is a ratrack pistebasher that will drag you with ropes to the Pic d'Encampadana (El Tarter sector), from where there are four possible routes down. It's free, so why not give it a go?

Instruction

The Andorran ski and snowboard school has seven different centres with instructors who speak loads of languages.

Soldeu

00376 75 31 91

El Tarter

00376 89 06 41/00376 89 06 44

Canillo

00376 89 06 91

Protec Coliflor Freestyle Camps

Camps run regularly and all the coaches are pro-riders, ex-competitors or qualified instructors specialising in teaching freestyle. A 1-day camp involves 3 hours' coaching, video analysis and safety equipment. The most intensive training is during Protest Riding Week (usually late January/early February) and includes theory lessons, photos, trampolining, an equipment raffle and parties. 00376 89 05 41 or e-mail freestyle@grandvalira.com

Other activities

In Andorra the main activities are shopping for all the duty free delights (alcohol, clothes, electronics – everything is cheap as chips, take care though as you are only allowed to take back certain quantities and values of products) and drinking. However, for the more discerning holiday maker there are a fair few things to try your hand at.

Adventure Activities: The Adventure Activities Centre in the Cubil, Grau Roig (covered in more detail in the Pas de la Casa chapter, see page 22) has a huge number of activities available. These include igloo building, orienteering and avalanche rescue courses, mushing, husky sled trips, snowshoeing, parapent flights, helicopter flights, snowmobile riding, paintballing and cross-country skiing.

Bowling: A 2-lane bowling alley can be found in the Hotel Nòrdic in El Tarter (00376 73 95 00). It closes at 1am.

Ice skating, go-karting and curling: In Canillo, the Palau de Gel D'Andorra (00376 80 08 40) contains an ice rink that is equipped for ice skating, ice go-karting or curling. There is also a large pool, tennis and squash courts, and lots more things to do.

Snow track: At the Pla d'Espiolets in Soldeu, Audi has designed a snow track where you can learn to drive 4WD cars on the snow. Contact the tourist office for more information.

Sports: Encamp's Sports and Socio-Cultural Complex offers facilities including badminton, basketball, volleyball, a climbing wall, tennis courts, martial arts room, squash courts, boules area, gym, solarium, saunas and indoor pool.

Spa: Sport Wellness Spa (00376 87 05 10, www.sportwellness.ad) at Hotel Hermitage is a superb complex offering 4500m^2 of facilities over 5 floors. There are pools, Jacuzzis, Turkish baths, hammam, beauty treatments and a hairdresser. Make sure you take flip-flops – they won't let you in the spa without them and they are expensive to buy there.

Thermal water centre: Caldea Andorra (00376 80 09 99, www.caldea.ad) is Europe's biggest mountain thermal water centre, located in Andorra la Vella. It is a massive and impressive place offering 6000m^2 of indoor and outdoor lagoons, Jacuzzis, Turkish baths, pools and waterfalls, with a variety of cultural influences – from Roman to Japanese. On top of this there is a fitness room and a variety of beauty treatments available.

Events

The park in El Tarter hosts the Freestyle series, which is composed of 3 freestyle events and is entered by a mix of pros and amateurs. The **Vans Snowboard Academy Awards** is an invitational event at which teams of snowboarders and cameramen are given 24 hours to prepare the best video. The next day the films are shown and judged in Nemo's pub in El Tarter.

The **Burton Senoritas** is a slopestyle event for female riders in El Tarter in February. In March the **Grandvalira Total Fight Masters of Freestyle** event takes place. Check out http://blog.grandvalira.com/freestyle for more events.

Accommodation

The **Sport Hotel Hermitage** (00376 87 06 70, www.sporthotels.ad) is a 5-star hotel. You can expect all the luxuries and comforts of a 5-star, including heated bathroom floors, hydromassage baths, room service massages and staff to take your skis to the lockers when you arrive. Most impressive is the 5-floor, 4500m^2 wellness centre (see Other activities).

The **Sport Hotel Village** (with 4 well-deserved stars, 00376 87 05 00, www.sporthotels.ad) has an immense reception area with a gorgeous bar, acres of lounge areas, all in a wooden, modern-chalet-style décor. There are 148 gorgeous rooms (25 with Jacuzzi) and the hotel has a sauna and gym. As if all this isn't enough, the hotel is in the centre of town and built over the lift system, so has direct access to the slopes. Slightly less deserving of 4 stars, but still very nice are **Piolets** and **Himálaia**. Piolets, also in the centre of town, is a pleasant hotel, very spacious, with a massive balcony that's in the sun all day. The pool and spa area is the best feature of the hotel with sun loungers, a huge gym, sauna, solarium, Turkish bath and massage. The 4-star Himálaia hotel (00376 87 85 15, www.hotansa.ad) is spacious and comfy with underground parking, sauna, Jacuzzi, Turkish bath and fitness area.

In Canillo, **Els Meners** (00376 75 14 54) has 15 clean airy apartments with a Spanish feel. **Casale Chalet** in El Tarter is another great value option.

For the cheapest deals, tour operators (Thomson, Crystal, etc) and the internet can have some real bargains. Just make sure your accommodation isn't too far from town.

Apartments are also worth considering; you will pay less if you self-cater and there are loads of good apartments around.

Eating out

On the mountain

Both Soldeu and El Tarter have a collection of restaurants at the top of the bubble cars from the villages that are good meeting points, especially if you have skiers and boarders of different abilities.

At the Soldeu area, Espiolets, you have the self-service restaurant (00376 89 05 81) if you don't have much time, and the Gall de Bosc building, which contains a cafeteria on the ground floor, **Fun Food** (00376 89 06 04), selling sandwiches, burgers and salads and on the upper level a gourmet restaurant, **Gall de Bosc** (00376 89 06 07). At El Tarter, at the top of the gondola, is **Restaurant Riba** (00376 89 06 36), a self-service restaurant, and a terrace overlooking the snowpark where you can grab a burger or sandwich.

The comfortable **Pi de Migdia** (00376 89 06 35) is situated next to the arrival of the El Tarter gondola. The restaurant opens for lunches and on Friday and Saturday evenings. Reservation is essential.

At **Collada d'Enradart**, at the top of the Funicamp gondola from Encamp, is a panoramic restaurant with great views. There is a gourmet restaurant upstairs, a self-service restaurant on the lower floor and a burger/sandwich counter outside.

We recommend heading over to a restaurant called **Llac des Pessons** (00376 75 90 15) in the Grau Roig area; a table-service restaurant that is by far the best in the area, with cosy wooden tables, a great view over the frozen lake of the Circ del Colells mountains and superb food – choose from sandwiches or their meat specialities, grilled on the indoor wood fire.

In town

In Soldeu, there are a fair few decent eateries. For a full English breakfast head to **Slim Jims** (00376 85 25 67), an English-run café where you can also check your e-mails. If you're not up the mountain at lunchtime, **Hotel Bruxelles** (www.hotelbruxelles.ad), right in the centre of town, has a big terrace in the sun overlooking the mountain. It serves massive sandwiches, paninis, burgers and salads.

'It serves massive sandwiches, paninis, burgers and salads'

Fat Albert's (00376 85 17 65) has a restaurant in a converted barn, serving a mix of meat, fish and pasta. For some traditional cuisine, try **Borda del Rector** (00376 85 26 06, www.bordarector.com), a lovely wooden and stone, chalet-style restaurant. It has an open fire and a gorgeous bar/lounge area. It's a little out of Soldeu, closer to El Tarter, but they'll pick you up from Soldeu if you're eating. The **Red Dragon** has a cosy and inviting atmosphere. It serves Chinese, Thai and Vietnamese dishes (as well as steaks and other dishes, if you prefer).

Bars and clubs

Going out in Andorra is an experience. Once you've got used to the dirt-cheap booze (actually similar to British pub prices, but compared to typical European ski resorts it's cheap), poured freely (a triple shot is the norm) until there is little room for mixer, you can join in with the other delighted Brits in causing havoc.

The **Aspen Bar** (00376 85 19 74) has a cool atmosphere, very much like a British pub. There are loads of TV screens for the Saturday footie matches (on Saturdays the bars are far more packed than the slopes), tons of comfy seating, and pool tables and video games to keep you entertained. On a Thursday, don't be surprised to walk in and find two guys/girls boxing in big kangaroo suits, and Saturday night traditionally entails a School Disco theme. From 2pm they serve good Tex Mex food. **Fat Albert's** is a really popular place, with great après ski, an excellent restaurant downstairs and a locally renowned live band.

The **T-bar** is known by the locals for its après-ski snacks and, more interestingly, for the opportunity to hang upside down from the roof for a shots challenge. **Pussycat** opens from 9pm until late and is the place to be later on in Soldeu (although you can go early to make full use of the special drinks deals). They have live music, DJs and theme nights and pole-dancing competitions. What's even better is that it's free entry.

'Pussycat opens from 9pm until late and is the place to be later on in Soldeu'

Getting there

By car

From Paris, take the A6 to Nantes, the A10 to Toulouse, the A62 to Carcassone, the A61 to Foix (direction Hospitalet – RN 20).

By plane

There are no airports in Andorra. The 2 closest are Toulouse and Barcelona.

Toulouse (200km) Novatel Minibus Services (00376 80 37 89, www.andorrabybus.com) runs a transfer service from the airport.

Barcelona (200km) Novatel Minibus Services (see above) runs a transfer service from the airport.

By train

Take the Eurostar from London St Pancras to Paris (Gare du Nord). Cross by métro to the Gare d'Austerlitz. Then travel from Paris to l'Hospitalet près l'Andorra overnight by sleeper train. Then get the connecting bus (65 minutes) to the resort. Contact Rail Europe (0870 830 4862, www.raileurope.co.uk) or European Rail (020 7387 0444, www.europeanrail.com). Bus tickets (Andorra Bus) are purchased on the bus.

Useful facts and phone numbers

Tourist office

T: 00376 89 05 60 (Soldeu)
00376 80 10 60 (Grandvalira)
W: www.grandvalira.com
www.skiandorra.ad

Emergency services

- Fire brigade: 118
- Police: 110
- Police station: 00376 87 20 00
- Emergency medical service: 116
- Medical centre: 00376 85 52 25
- Hospital: 00376 87 10 00

Taxis

You won't find any taxi ranks out of Andorra la Vella, but you can call any of the numbers below to order one:

- 00376 86 30 00
- 00376 86 10 05
- 00376 82 80 00

Austria

Charming traditional towns with crazy après ski parties – Austria makes it work perfectly.

Bad Gastein

The spa facilities and spectacular scenery make the Gastein valley an exceptional place to visit

On the slopes	Rating
Snow reliability	❄❄❄½
Parks	❄❄
Off-piste	❄❄
Off the slopes	
Après ski	❄❄
Nightlife	❄❄❄
Eating out	❄
Resort charm	❄❄❄❄❄

The resort

The Gastein valley is famous for its spas and wellness facilities – the 17 thermal springs produce 5 million litres of radon-enriched water each day, which are used for their restorative qualities. Many of the hotels have superb facilities, and there are some huge health centres in the resort, too.

There are a number of towns along the valley floor. Bad Gastein is the most well-known, but it's not necessarily the best place to stay – it depends completely on what you are looking for. Dorfgastein is the first stop. It's a lovely quiet village, with the disadvantage that the slopes are not connected to the valley's main network. Bad Hofgastein's slopes are connected to Bad Gastein's and it has the major pull of the Alpen Therme Gastein (see Other activities) – Europe's most modern alpine health and leisure world. Bad Hofgastein is a genuine village, with a pleasant and relaxed atmosphere, whereas Bad Gastein's buildings are regal and majestic. Although some of the interiors of the buildings in Bad Gastein could do with updating, it is impossible not to be impressed by the setting – the whole resort is built on the sides of a steep gorge, with a massive waterfall roaring through the centre of town. The furthest resort is Sportgastein, which you wouldn't want to stay in, but it's a great place to visit for powder runs if the snow is bad elsewhere. Good restaurants and nightlife are somewhat lacking in the valley, so it is a better destination for relaxing spa and skiing weeks than for crazy nights of partying.

A car is a good idea to ferry yourself around or you could always look into renting an electric quad bike (contact the tourist office for details).

The mountains

Height: 1080–2230m

Ability	Rating
Expert	❄❄❄
Intermediate	❄❄❄❄
Beginner	❄❄❄

Getting about

There are four mountains to choose from in Gastein, providing 200km of slopes, although they are not all connected by lift. The Schlossalm (2050m), above Bad Hofgastein, has a number of easier slopes for the beginner/low intermediate rider. This mountain is connected to the main area in Bad Gastein, the Stubnerkogel (2246m), from which you can ride back down to town. At the end of the valley is the small area of Graukogel (2492m), a blessing for its tree runs and lack of queues. Graukogel also has the most difficult run, B6. You could also take the short (15–20 minute) drive to Sportgastein's mountain, Kreuzkogel (2686m), sacred for its snow reliability when all other areas fail. Sportgastein is definitely worth a look, and not only when the snow is bad, as it has some great runs on and off-piste, even though it is only served by a 2-stage gondola and 1 drag lift!

The park

The freestyle scene appears not to have captured the hearts of the locals in Gastein, so although they actually have a half-decent park, they aren't fussed about advertising it. You can find the park in Grossarl, above Dorfgastein. It has a half pipe, 2 quarter pipes, a small selection of jumps (ranging from 3 to 10m long), and a couple of fun boxes.

Off-piste and backcountry

Sportgastein is the highest area, and therefore has the best snow and some of the best powder runs in the Gastein valley. There are some good spots of off-piste that are accessible via ski routes 1 and 2 and they're unlikely to be tracked out, although you should really employ the services of a local guide to make the best of the ski area (contact the ski schools/tourist office to find an available guide). From the top of Sportgastein, at Kreuzkogel (2686m), there's a great run down the valley that is a marked route (Ski route Nord), but is not prepared or patrolled (you do need avalanche equipment and a good skill level for this run). You will come out at Heilstollen, on the road from Sportgastein back to Bad Gastein and from here you can catch the bus back into town (8am–6pm). On Stubnerkogel you can find some good powder off the B18 (though this is prone to avalanching) and the tree lines at Graukogel around the B3 and B6 runs are worth a look in bad weather.

Lift passes

Check the latest prices at www.badgastein.at

Instruction

Ski School Schlossalm, Bad Hofgastein

T: 0043 (0)6432 3298
W: www.schischule-schlossalm.at

Ski and Snowboard School

T: 0043 (0)6434 2260 (Bad Gastein)
0043 (0)6432 6339 (Bad Hofgastein)
W: www.schneesportgastein.com

Other activities

Ice skating: Bad Hofgastein has an artificial ice skating rink and curling lanes.
Nine-pin bowling: In Pub Gastein, Hotel Bellvue, Bad Gastein.

Snowbiking, frozen waterfall climbing, and tobogganing: All these are offered by Schneesport Schule Gastein (see Instruction), if you can squeeze them in around your spa treatments (see below).

Spas: As well as venturing to the wellness area that you are almost guaranteed to have in your hotel, visiting one of the massive spas in resort is an absolute must. Far more than just something to do on a bad weather day, these places rock.

In Bad Hofgastein is the **Alpen Therme Gastein** (0043 (0)06432 82930, info@alpentherme.com, www.alpentherme.com), Europe's most modern alpine health and leisure world covering an area of more than 32 000m^2. It contains 6 adventure and vitality worlds: leisure world, adventure world (with lazy flow river, 'black hole' slide with flashy lights and a speed slide which really is pretty speedy), sauna world, ladies wellness and beauty world, fitness world and taste world (a restaurant and sky bar with a 360-degree panoramic view of the mountains). There's also a 360-degree cinema screen in adventure world that you swim into. So that you don't have to faff around with money, you have a band around your wrist that records everything you buy. Clever. If you want to be extra clever, bring your own towel and dressing gown from the hotel because it's extra to hire them. Don't be shy if you're a bloke – there are loads of men there.

'So that you don't have to faff around with money, you have a band around your wrist that records everything you buy'

In Bad Gastein is a similar construction, the **Felsentherme Gastein** (0043 (0)6434 2223, www.felsentherme.com). The Felsentherme indoor area includes a pool surrounded by rocks for relaxation, a 600m^2 adventure area with 2 layered pools, massage beds, geysers and a wild water channel, a 70m water slide and a rock grotto. There is also a fitness area and a new panorama wellness area with 7 different saunas, solariums, a juice bar, a nudist area and 2 mountain-top pools. Outdoors is a 34°C relaxation pool, a 24°C sport pool and a children's fairytale pool with interactive fairytale figures.

The **Healing Gallery** ((0043 (0)6434 37530, office@gasteiner-heilstollen.com, www.gasteiner-heilstollen.com) is an intensive, natural and rare spa remedy, 2.5km deep inside the Radhausberg mountain. The healing air inside the mountain was discovered by miners searching for gold, but the unique climate they revealed is far more valuable. The healing effects are due to the radon content of the air, a temperature of 37–41.5°, speleotherapy conditions (pure, dust-free, allergy-free and bacteria-free air) and a high humidity (70–100 per cent). The vast majority (80–90 per cent) of visitors have reported alleviation of medical complaints, as well as relaxed muscles and joints. The healing gallery is thought to be the most effective natural treatment of rheumatic illness and may also relieve joint infection, muscular injury, respiratory disease and allergic illness.

Tandem paragliding: In Bad Hofgastein (0043 (0)664 4232322, www.tandem-flying.com).

Tobogganing: Go up the Schlossalm lift (Bad Hofgastein) and enjoy 3.3km of floodlit fun.

Events

The International Ski Federation's **Snowboard World Cup** competition is held in Bad Gastein. The event features a floodlit parallel slalom competition followed by the snowboard cross, and there is also live music and food for spectators.

Accommodation

Bad Gastein

In Bad Gastein you should look at location pretty carefully, especially if you're not a fan of walking with skis or board, as some hotels involve a fairly long, steep ascent. The hotel **Cordial Sanotel** (0043 (0)6434 25010, www.cordial.at) is close to the lifts of the fairly small area of Graukogel but not to the others. It is a beautiful hotel though, with a fantastic wellness facility (Jacuzzi, indoor pool, sauna, steam bath, solarium and treatments), and it is right on the famous Gastein cascades waterfall. Make sure you're in the main building or you'll have a walk to the pool and other facilities. The **Hotel Salzbergerhof** (0043 (0)6434 20370, www.salzburgerhof.com), is in a fairly good location for the lifts. As well as containing a couple of the best bars in town (see Bars and clubs), and a good wellness area, all rooms now have plasma TV (family rooms have a DVD player) and mini bars.

The **Grüner Baum** (0043 (0)6434 25160, www.hoteldorf.com) is in the middle of nowhere and is a beautiful and romantic retreat from the world. It's not really a place for the hardcore riders as it takes about 20 minutes to get to the slopes. It is, however, the place to go for the most comprehensive list of beauty and slimming treatments, with packages such as a Shiseido beauty week or a slim and fit purification week. No matter what ailment you go in there with, you're bound to come out feeling as fit as a fiddle.

> 'Grüner Baum is a beautiful and romantic retreat from the world'

Bad Hofgastein

Bad Hofgastein is a great place to be based. It's more of an active town than the touristy Bad Gastein, with shops, bars and atmosphere. The **Klammer's Kärnten** (0043 (0)6432 67110, www.hotel-kaernten.com) is our favourite hotel. It is friendly but luxurious, calm and classic. The wooden bar is cosy and welcoming, with new papers each day and free cakes in the afternoon. The rooms are beautiful and spacious, some even with baths in the centre of the room. Yet it is the wellness area where the hotel really excels. The indoor and outdoor pools, and range of saunas, therapeutic treatments, solarium and plunge pool are set in an idyllic, serene and perfectly designed sanctuary.

Some hotels in Bad Hofgastein have partnered up with the Alpen Therme to give free access to their guests. They even have underground tunnels to access it so you can wander through in your dressing gown. These include the **Hotel Norica** (0043 (0)6432 8391, www.hotel-norica.at), **Österreichischer Hof** (0043 (0)6432 62160, www.oehof.at), **Kurparkhotel** (0043 (0)6432 6301, www.kurpark hotel.at) and **Panorama Apartmenthotel** (0043 (0)6432 67590, www.panoramagastein.com).

Eating out

On the mountain

The best places to eat on the mountain are **Jungerstube** (0043 (0)6433 7370) on the Bad Hofgastein side of Stubnerkogel (at the bottom of the Fleischleiten run and Jungeralm lift), **Treff** on **Graukogel**, at the mid-station of the chairlift up the mountain and Knappenstub'n on Sportgastein, a self-service restaurant at the first station of the gondola, with a great terrace and great views.

In town

This is 1 resort where we would probably opt for half-board accommodation as there isn't a great variety of restaurants to check out. **Hotel Mozart** (0043 (0)6434 26860, www.hotelmozart.at) and **Hotel Elisabethpark** (0043 (0)6434 25510, elisabethpark.at) do good food and the **Weinfassl** has an old, traditional atmosphere and a good view. **Grüner Baum** (see Accommodation) has one of the most acclaimed restaurants in the valley. For a change, there's the **Sancho Mexican** (0043 (0)6434 21762) – the only restaurant in town with a relaxed atmosphere that serves Mexican and British dishes. You will find it next to the waterfall in the centre of town. There's a kebab shop if you get desperate.

> 'Some hotels in Bad Hofgastein have partnered up with the Alpen Therme to give free access to their guests'

Bars and clubs

The Salzbergerhof has all the best bars, with the spirited **Silver Bullet Bar** (www.silverbulletbar.com, 0043 (0)6434 225360) offering great live music at après ski and the **Gatz Music Club** (www.gatz-club.com, 0043 (0)6434 225340). Of the other bars in town, the best are **Häggblom's Bar** and the bar at **Eden**. The casino is also definitely worth a look. In Bad Hofgastein, the **Piccolo** ice bar has a great atmosphere and we loved the pool bar downstairs with three pool tables where you pay a trifling amount for an hour's play. The sky bar also gets pretty busy. The best club is the **Almstadl** in the Hotel Norica.

Getting there

By car

From Innsbruck take the motorway via Wörgl, followed by road number 312 via St Johann/Tirol to Lofer. Take the road number 311 via Zell am See to Lend and then road number 167 into the Gastein valley.

By plane

Salzburg (90km) Transfer takes around 1 hour (book online at www.gastein.com).

Munich (290km) Transfer takes around 2 hours.

Innsbruck (200km) Transfer takes around 2 hours.

By train

Take the Eurostar from London St Pancras to Brussels; then the Bergland Express overnight skitrain, changing at Wörgl, to arrive in Bad Gastein station, in resort. Contact European Rail (020 7387 0444, www.europeanrail.com).

Useful facts and phone numbers

Tourist office

T: 0043 (0)6432 3393 560
F: 0043 (0)6432 3393 537
W: www.badgastein.at

Emergency services

- Police: 133
- Ambulance: 144
- Fire:122
- Mountain rescue: 140
- Doctors' emergency call out: 141
- Kardinal Schwarzenberg Hospital: 0043 (0)6415 7101/0

Doctors

- Emergency service for drugs and medicine: 0043 (0)6432 85000
- Dr Foisner: 0043 (0)6432 8293
- Pharmacy Bad Gastein: 0043 (0)6434 22180
- Pharmacy Bad Hofgastein: 0043 (0)6432 62040

Taxis

- Taxi Rainer: 0043 (0)6432 3000
- Taxi Rudigier: 0043 (0)6432 6622
- Taxi Schneeberger 0043 (0)6434 6633

Hintertux

Reliable snow all year round attracts large numbers of people to this lovely little resort

On the slopes	Rating
Snow reliability	❄❄❄❄❄
Parks	❄❄❄❄½
Off-piste	❄❄
Off the slopes	
Après ski	❄❄❄
Nightlife	❄❄
Eating out	❄
Resort charm	❄❄❄

The resort

The major pulling point of Hintertux is its height (1500–3250m), which makes it one of the most snowsure resorts in Austria. Snow is guaranteed all year round and the extent of the glacier is far less confining than that of many of the glaciers in the European resorts.

Hintertux is at the end of the Tux valley and is accessible by car or bus from Mayrhofen and from the other towns in the Tux valley: Lanersbach and Vorderlanersbach.

Hintertux itself is an attractively compact hamlet with some lovely hotels and guest houses and a few amusing bars and clubs. Though small, it has a definite charm, as all of the buildings maintain a traditional, yet new and glossy feel. The lifts are a few minutes down the road from the village centre, where there are more hotels and 1 bar with a great après ski vibe.

Hintertux is most suited to those who consider guaranteed snow to be the primary requirement of a holiday, with the provision of bars and off-slope activities as only secondary.

The mountains

Height: 1500–3250m

Ability	Rating
Expert	❄❄❄
Intermediate	❄❄❄
Beginner	❄❄

Getting about

There are 225km of ski runs, collectively named the 'Ski and Glacier World Zillertal 3000'. Of these, 86km are on the glacier and to get to the rest you take a 15-minute bus journey to Lanersbach. In summer, there are 18km of pistes open, and up to 10 lifts, with the longest descent being 2km. Spring also offers good value skiing/boarding, with around 60–70km open until May. Hintertux has won a prize for sport facilities for the disabled. You can ascend from the underground parking to 3250m without using steps.

The park

The Hintertux park (www.hintertuxergletscher.at) is on the large glacier next to the Olperer drag lift, and is one of the highest in the world, so you are almost guaranteed to find good snow. It does mean that it can get windy and cold, but if you keep hiking up instead of catching the lift, you'll keep your muscles warm. They have some of the top pros up on the glacier, shaping the hits, hence their immaculate condition. They also have a perfectly shaped pipe that is used for World Cup Half Pipe events (snowboard), a choice of jumps for different standards and a mixture of rails. One of the best features of this great park is that it is rideable practically all year round.

Off-piste and backcountry

Hintertux's snowsure glacier mountain makes it one of the best places to go when other resorts are lacking in powder; you can sometimes start exploring the backcountry from as early as October. Make sure you take real care exploring this glacial area – the weather can change completely within minutes and you could easily find yourself lost in winds and mist. It's not a good place to be in bad weather as it's too high up for trees to grow, so you're stuck in vast areas of open terrain. There are also crevasses to watch out for.

When the weather's right, the off-piste around the marked black runs is steep and a good place to get in some powder turns. Don't underestimate the dangers of the glacier – take a guide.

Lift passes

Check the latest prices at www.tux.at

Instruction

Luggis Ski and Snowbard School, Tux

0043 (0)5287 86808
www.luggis-schischule.at

Ski and Snowboard School Hintertux

0043 (0)5287 87755 or 87363
www.skischule-hintertux.at

Ski School Tux 3000

0043 (0)5287 87747 or 86112
www.tux-3000.at

Other activities

Ice skating and curling: The 1000m^2 natural ice rink in Lanersbach is open from December until the end of February. For reservations call 0043 (0)5287 87385.

Shooting range: Air rifle shooting takes place every Monday from 7pm at the shooting range in the Tux primary school in Lanersbach. Contact Tux riflemen's guild: 0043 (0)5287 87337.

Sleigh rides: Book 1 day in advance at Café Brentnerstall (0043 (0)5287 87782 or 0043 (0)5287 87604).

Sports Centre Tux: This centre in Vorder-lanersbach offers bowling 3pm–midnight. (0043 (0)5287 87297, info@testerhof.at).

Tandem paragliding: Take off from the Hintertux Glacier, the Sommerbergalm or the Eggalm in the double-seater glider (with qualified pilot). Contact Natursport Tirol (0043 (0)5287 87287 or 0043 (0)676 307 0000) or Tandem Funflights (0043 (0)676 328 1996 or 0043 (0)5287 86109).

Tobogganing: There are 3 natural toboggan runs on Bichlalm (3km run), Grieralm (5km run) and Höllensteinhütte (4km run). All runs can be accessed by taxi.

Events

Hintertux hosts its version of **Oktoberfest** on the first weekend in September. In mid-October there is a **powder weekend** to celebrate the first powder of the winter. The **Snowboard World Cup Halfpipe** event also takes place in Hintertux's superb park.

Accommodation

Hotels and pensions in Austria are a cut above the rest – all you need to worry about is how far it is to the slopes and the bars. **Hotel Kössler** (0043 (0)5287 87490, www.koessler.at) is a friendly, pretty and in the centre of Hintertux. The **Bad Hotel Kirchler** (0043 (0)5287 8570, www.badhotel-kirchler.at) is slightly more upmarket, with suites and apartments as well as standard and superior rooms. Bad means spa – the hotel has a swimming pool fed by the highest thermal springs in Europe, 2 saunas and a Turkish steambath.

If you are looking for the utmost in quality, choose one of the hotels next to the slopes (and therefore a 20-minute walk to the village). Of these, the smartest is probably the **Neuhintertux** (0043 (0)5287 8580, www.neu-hintertux.com) with stunning pools and large wellness facilities. **Hotel Vierjahreszeiten** (0043 (0)5287 8525, www.vierjahreszeiten.at) and **Der Rindererhof** (0043 (0)5287 8558, www.rindererhof.at) are also top quality 4-star hotels by the lifts.

Staying in Lanersbach is also an option, as it is now linked to the Mayrhofen and Finkenberg slopes and is only a 15-minute drive from the glacier at Hintertux. We'd prefer to either stay in Mayrhofen or Hintertux though.

Eating out

On the mountain

Gletscherhütte (0043 (0)6644 3504099) at 3012m is a lovely hut at the peak of the Gletscher. It is open all year and the views are fantastic. **Spannagelhaus** (0043 (0)5287 87707) is a popular après ski joint, and is a good place for a bite to eat. It is also open all year. **Tuxer Joch Haus** (0043 (0)5287 87216) at the top of the Tuxerjoch chair lift (ski run 17) is good, but is only open December to April. Each of the latter 2 offers the possibility of staying over – call the restaurant for more details.

In town

There aren't too many independent restaurants, most are hotel-based. **Didi's** is a really nice pizzeria and **Tuxersübl** has great food in a cosy atmosphere. Tasty burgers can also be picked up from the Hohenhaus pub by the lifts.

Bars and clubs

Après ski starts with a couple of beers at the **Spannagelhaus** and continues at the crazy **Hohenhaus Tenne** (0043 (0)5287 8501), just opposite the lifts back in town. Après ski is massive here, in a really atmospheric, big chalet-style bar. This is how an après ski bar should be, with loads of drinking until around 9pm, when it closes up for the night. Between après and dancing, there aren't too many bars to choose from, mostly hotel bars. Later on, back in Hintertux 'centre' (if you can call it that), there are a couple of amusing places to continue. **Tux 1** (0043 (0)5287 8501) is bizarre, but cool. The atmosphere is mixed up; it has a typical, Austrian-style chalet interior, yet mingled into the décor is an '80s-style DJ box, a dance floor, disco ball, plasma TVs, a dancing pole, pool, darts and table footie. The clientele is equally bizarre, but it's great fun all the same. Look out for karaoke Wednesdays and '70s and '80s nights. At the **Batzen keller** (0043 (0)5287 8570), there are once again the '80s style features – smoke machine and neon – but it's quite fun after a few pints.

Getting there

By car

From the A12 take the exit for the Ziller valley. Take the Federal Highway B169 to Mayrhofen and then the Tux road to Hintertux.

By plane

Innsbruck (90km)
Salzburg (160km)
Munich (230km)

By train

Take the Eurostar from London St Pancras to Brussels; then the Bergland Express overnight skitrain, changing at Jenbach, to Mayrhofen, and then a local bus (41 minutes) to the resort. Contact European Rail (020 7387 0444, www.europeanrail.com). Bus tickets are purchased on the bus.

Useful facts and phone numbers

Tourist office

T: 0043 (0)5287 8506
F: 0043 (0)5287 8508
W: www.tux.at
www.hintertux.com

Emergency services

- Police: 133
- Ambulance: 144
- Rescue helicopter: 0043 (0)800 207 070
- Mountain rescue: 140
- Fire: 122
- Schwaz District Hospital: 0043 (0)5242 600
- Innsbruck Hospital: 0043 (0)512 5040

Doctors

- Dr Katharina Weber-Gredler and Dr Simon Gredler: 0043 (0)5285 62550
- Dr Pavel Kriz (dentist): 0043 (0)5285 63341
- Dr Peter Peer: 0043 (0)5287 86180

Taxis

- Siegfried's Taxi: 0043 (0)5287 1718, www.taxi-tux.at
- Taxi Siebzehnwölf: 0043 (0)5287 1712
- The Tuxer nightbus carries on until 2am from Vorderlanersbach to Hintertux

Ischgl

Glamorous and chic, with great terrain and superb après ski.

On the slopes	Rating
Snow reliability	❄❄❄❄
Parks	❄❄❄❄
Off-piste	❄❄½
Off the slopes	
Après ski	❄❄❄❄½
Nightlife	❄❄❄❄
Eating out	❄❄❄❄
Resort charm	❄❄❄❄

The resort

If you like comfort and style, and return year after year to big-name resorts such as Val d'Isère, Zermatt, Verbier or St Anton, you should give Ischgl some serious consideration. The hotels are glamorous and plush, the après ski is as crazy as it gets, and the terrain is superb. You can also ride over to the duty-free Samnaun, pack your bags with cheap booze for the evening and clink your way back to Ischgl.

> 'the hotels are glamorous ... and the terrain is superb'

The resort is compact and focused around a pedestrianised street. The most convenient place to stay is close to the Silvrettabahn lift in the centre of town. There is a moving walkway from town to the other 2 lifts, the Pardatschgratbahn and Fimbabahn, where you will find more great après ski bars. The icing on Ischgl's cake is the superb free music events on the mountain in April. The 'Top of the Mountain' Easter Concert and end of season concerts have pulled in the biggest names in the business (see Events).

The mountains

Height: 2000–2782m

Ability	Rating
Expert	❄❄❄
Intermediate	❄❄❄❄
Beginnner	❄

Getting about

Ischgl has over 230km of snowsure terrain to explore, as well as a superb park and some great backcountry areas.

Ischgl is good for most intermediates and for experts, but beginners should perhaps look elsewhere, partly because of the lack of decent slopes to learn on and also because many instructors speak less English than you would expect.

The 3 lifts from the resort will all take you to Idalp, the main meeting point for ski schools. This does get busy so it's best to stay clear if you can – head over to the more secluded runs from Palinkopf to Gampenalp or take a trip to duty-free Samnaun.

To ski over to Samnaun from Idalp, take the Höllkarbahn chair then one of the chairs up to Palinkopf. The only routes from here are red, though intermediate skiers should not have too many difficulties. You will pass customs on your way back to Austria so, while there is free-flowing cross-border movement, you should still carry your passport and only buy the amount of alcohol that customs regulations allow.

The park

Ischgl claims to have one of the biggest and best parks in Europe, 'Boarders' Paradise'. It was one of the first resorts in Europe to start pushing the freestyle ski and snowboard scene, and it held the first official World Championships for snowboarders.

The park has a long list of features: tons of different sized kickers (from beginner to professional), one quarter pipe, World Championship half pipe named 'the tube', rails for all levels of rider, a big fun box, a boarder/skier-cross course, a giant slalom (boarders only), wave rides (from advanced to pro), and a kindercross (boarder/skier-cross for children with waves and jumps).

> 'Ischgl claims to have one of the biggest and best parks in Europe ... Boarders' Paradise'

Off-piste and backcountry

Ischgl mainly attracts intermediate skiers who stick to the pisted areas, so there are plenty of fresh untracked areas around. Like a lot of other resorts, Ischgl has marked areas for freeriding. The Palinkopf (2864m) is a favourite and not too challenging, and the Greispitz (2872m) also has a freeride trail.

For the more advanced there is the extreme trail on the Hollenkar face; this is one of the most challenging parts of the mountain and should be undertaken only by those in the know. Even though these runs are marked on the map, there is still the danger of avalanches so check out the avalanche danger rating and take the advice of pisteurs if you're not sure. Towards the bottom of the resort are some good tracks through the trees; a great place to head in flat light.

Lift passes

Check the latest prices at www.ischgl.com

Instruction

Ischgl Ski School

0043 (0)5444 5257 or 5404
www.schischule.ischgl.at

Other activities

Beauty treatments: Alpenhotel Ischglerhof (0043 (0)5444 5330), Hotel Trofana Royal (0043 (0)5444 600), Hotel Madlein (0043 (0)5444 5226) and Hotel Seiblishof (0043 (0)5444 5425) offer beauty treatments to the public.

Horse-drawn sleigh rides: Take a 2-hour ride to Mathon, where there is a short stop. Book on 0043 (0)5444 5365 or via www.ischgl.com.

Ice skating and curling: The ice rink is open daily from 2pm, late night closing 3 times a week (0043 (0)5444 52660).

Recreation centre: On the outskirts of Ischgl (in the direction of Mathon), the centre has 4 indoor and 4 outdoor tennis courts. Call 0043 (0)5444 5265 for court reservations. Private lessons are also available on request.

Silvertta centre: This centre (0043 (0)5444 606950) has an indoor pool, sauna, steam room, sunbed, massage, reflexology, internet café, bowling alley and restaurant.

Squash: At the Hotel Solaria (0043 (0)5444 5205). The courts are open 9am–9pm.

> 'Year after year Ischgl attracts the biggest names in the music business'

Tobogganing: Every Monday and Thursday, from 7pm, take the Silvrettabahn to take a ride down the huge, 7km-long, floodlit toboggan run from Idalp to Ischgl. Toboggans can be rented from Silvretta Sports.

Events

Year after year Ischgl attracts the biggest names in the music business for their season opening and closing events, and for the legendary **Top of the Mountain Easter concert**. Michael Jackson, Tina Turner, Pussycat Dolls, Beyonce, Kylie, Katy Perry and Alicia Keys have been headline acts in the past. These concerts are totally free – all you need is a lift pass, so check out this year's line up with the tourist office and book your ticket.

Accommodation

There are loads of plush hotels in Ischgl, most with a traditional luxurious feel, the most extravagant of which is the **Trofana Royal** (0043 (0)5444 600, www.trofana.at). There are nearly 20 styles of room, each with their own hefty price tag. The minimalist **Madlein** (0043 (0)5444 5226, www.madlein.com), however, is significantly different, with vast open spaces filled only with marble, spotlights and the occasional square pouf or artily positioned candle. Stylish and glamorous it is, cosy and inviting it isn't. The pool and fire room are very cool, but the jury's still out on the Zen garden.

> 'There are loads of plush hotels in Ischgl, most with a traditional luxurious feel'

Other good hotels are the **Yscla** (0043 (0)5444 5275, www.yscla.at), in a very central position on the main street, and the **Elisabeth** (0043 (0)5444 5411, www.ischglelisabeth.com), another glamorous choice, right opposite the Pardatschgratbahn lift, with a great après ski bar.

The expensive hotels aren't the only option, there are loads of guesthouses and apartments. Contact the reservations department of the tourist office (see Useful facts and phone numbers). They will help you find something to suit your budget; just make sure it's not out of town, or on the wrong side of the bypass.

Bars and clubs

Ischgl is top of the tree for proper, sweat-inducing, sing-along, après ski mania. Each side of the town has its own après scene going on. At the base area of the Pardatschgratbahn and Fimbabahn lifts, our favourite bars are the **Ice bar** and **Schatzi bar** of the Elisabeth hotel, **Niki's Stadl** and the **Nevada Alm**. If you ski down to the other side of town head straight to the buzzing **Fire and Ice** bar or the infamous **Trofana Alm**. When the night sets in you need to head either to the **Tenne** club at the Trofana or go Ibiza style and hit the crazy **Pacha** nightclub in Hotel Madlein. If you tire of dancing and would prefer to watch some lovely ladies strut their stuff, the Hotel Madlein also has a **Coyote Ugly** table dancing club.

> 'Ischgl is top of the tree for proper, sweat-inducing, sing-along, après ski mania'

Eating out

On the mountain

Towards Fimbatal, the **Paznauner Taja** (0043 (0)5444 5176) and **Bodenalpe** (0043 (0)5444 5285) are atmospheric chalet-style restaurants with busy bars. The Paznauner often has live music. The **Alpenhaus** restaurant on Idalp, at 2300m, has great views and a huge terrace. On the Swiss side, the **Alp Trida Sattel** has great views and good food as does the table-service restaurant **Schmuggler Alm** in Samnaun.

In town

Ischgl's restaurants cater to most demands, from après ski munchies to gourmet cuisine. Trofana Royal's gourmet restaurant, **Paznauner Stube** (0043 (0)5444 600), will suit the more refined palate. For a good steak or pasta, try the **Allegra** (0043 (0)5444

527564) attached to the Hotel Yscla in the centre of town with a Frankie and Benny's-style atmosphere and menu, and a happy pasta hour. For pizzas, the **Salz & Pfeffer** (0043 (0)5444 5919) takes some beating, with fantastic wood-fired pizzas and an open feel, reminiscent of Pizza Express. For something a little cosier, try the **Grill Alm** (0043 (0)5444 5293), which serves up tasty traditional treats, or the gorgeous **Trofana Alm** pizzeria (0043 (0)5444 602), which you will find tucked behind the Trofana Royal.

Getting there

By car

Take the Inntal motorway towards Arlberg and exit at Pians towards Paznaun. From here it is signed to Ischgl and should take 20 minutes.

Parking is free during the day, so you can pop in for a day on the mountain, but if you stay overnight you will have to pay.

By plane

Innsbruck (100km) Around 1 hour by road.
Friedrichshafen (170km) Around 1.5 hours by road.
Munich (300km) Around 2.5 hours by road.
Salzburg (300km) Around 3 hours by road.

By train

Take the Eurostar from London St Pancras to Brussels; then the Bergland Express overnight skitrain, changing in Innsbruck, to Landeck, and then a local bus (60 minutes) to the resort. Contact European Rail (020 7387 0444, www.europeanrail.com). Bus tickets are purchased on the bus.

Useful facts and phone numbers

Tourist office

T: 0043 (0)50990 100
F: 0043 (0)50990 199
W: www.ischgl.com

Direct reservations

T: 0043 (0)5444 526618

Emergency services

- Police: 0043 (0)59 133 71 42
- Fire brigade: 122
- Rescue squad/Red Cross: 144
- Mountain rescue: 0043 (0)5243/140 (emergency number)
- Hospital St Vinzenz: 0043 (0)5442 60 00

Doctors

- Dr Walser: 52 00 (in office hours and emergency)
- Dr Treidl in Galtür: 0043 (0)5443 82 76

Taxis

- Alpentaxi Ischgl: 0043 (0)5444 5757, www.alpentaxi.at
- Ischgler Taxi: 0043 (0)5444 5999, www.taxi-ischgl.com
- Taxi Express: 0043 (0)5444 20120 or 5824, www.20120.com

Kitzbühel

One of Austria's most beautiful and traditional resorts.

On the slopes	Rating
Snow reliability	❄❄
Parks	❄❄
Off-piste	❄❄❄
Off the slopes	
Après ski	❄❄❄❄
Nightlife	❄❄❄❄
Eating out	❄❄❄
Resort charm	❄❄❄❄❄

The resort

Kitzbühel's distinguishing feature is its fairytale pedestrianised centre with colourful buildings, sparkly lights and exclusive cocktail bars and shops. Reflected in this cosmopolitan atmosphere are the clientele, most of whom are elegant and sophisticated. Aside from all this, however, is a great après ski scene, in which the less sophisticated Brits can revel. It's a shame that Kitzbühel's charm and character does not extend far out of the square though – you quickly reach far less attractive suburbs and congested roads.

Kitzbühel's slopes are great for cruising, although altitude is a problem and you may have to go searching for good snow on higher peaks. The resort also has a seriously Old School attitude, hiding the snowboarders away on a separate mountain wherever possible. For the typical Kitzbühel skiers, the focus is definitely more on the pit stops than the powder.

The mountains

Height: 760–2000m

Ability	Rating
Expert	❄❄❄
Intermediate	❄❄❄❄❄
Beginner	❄❄❄

Getting about

Kitzbühel's slopes are extensive, but largely disjointed. The 3S lift has alleviated this problem to an extent by connecting the Hahnenkamm/Pengelstein area to the terrain of Jochberg and Pass Thurn, but the others are still out on a limb. From Pengelstein, you can begin the Ski Safari right over to Pass Thurn, a great place to head if conditions are bad, as it offers the highest terrain in Kitzbühel. On this route you will cover around 35km of runs. The Hahnenkamm mountain is also home to the Streif piste: the Hahnenkamm downhill run. The run's not as difficult as it may sound – confident red run riders will be fine.

The Kitzbüheler Horn is home to the park (see below) and Bichalm has been left ungroomed to encourage freeriders to make the effort to get to this inconvenient area.

The park

The park, on the Kitzbüheler Horn, consists of a boardercross and half pipe, and a few jumps and rails that are changed regularly according to the snow conditions. The maintenance of the park is decent, if sporadic.

Off-piste and backcountry

Some of the best off-piste is really accessible, so first-time freeriders can easily find some good spots to practise on and even the more experienced backcountry rider won't need to do massive hikes to locate good areas. There aren't too many people looking for it either, so you should find untracked spots.

Look out for the fairly steep Ehrenbachgraben bowl, or try the 'freeriding mountain' Bichalm. To hire a guide, give Alpinschule Kitzbühel a call on 0043 (0)5356 73323.

Lift passes

Check the latest prices at www.bergbahn-kitzbuehel.at/en

Instruction

Rote Teufel (Red Devil) Kitzbühel

The one and only school in Kitzbühel.
0043 (0)5356 62500
www.rote-teufel.at

Other activities

Boutique shopping: Shopping and sipping wine in cafés is the usual activity of those who choose not to hit the slopes.

Curling: Available at a couple of places: the Alpenhotel (0043 (0)5356 642540, www.alpenhotel-kitzbuehel.at) has ice stick shooting; there is curling at the Lebenberg (0043 (0)5356 62444).

Fitness centre: Contact the centre (0043 (0)5356 63412, www.fitnessforfun.at) for more details.

Horse-drawn sleigh rides: Call Eberl Hubert (0043 (0)5356 66380) or Henntalhof (0043 (0)5356 64624).

Hot air ballooning: For this popular option, call Ballooning Tyrol (0043 (0)5352 65666, www.balloningtyrol.com).

Ice skating: You can skate at the Sportpark centre (0043 (0)5356 20222) or the Alpenhotel (see Curling).

Paragliding: Two schools offer paragliding in Kitzbühel: Alpin Experts (0043 (0)664 3423309, www.alpin-experts.at) and Element 3 (0043 (0)5356 72301 www.element3.at).

Sports: The leisure and sports centre has facilities for climbing, tennis, curling, ice hockey/skating, bowling and there is a restaurant. Call 0043 (0)5356 20222 and check out www.sportpark.kitz.net.

Tobogganing: There is a natural 5km tobogganing run at Gaisberg, above the nearby town of Kirchberg. It is free during the day (with valid lift pass) but you have to pay at night. On Thursdays and Fridays there is also nightskiing at Gaisberg. The lifts are open 6.30–9pm but the runs stay lit until 11pm so you can stop for a drink or two on your way down. There is another, 2.5km, toboggan run at Bichalm. You can rent toboggans at the lodge and it is open in the evening but is not lit.

Water sports and spa: The Aquarena (0043 (0)5356 6951215, www.bergbahn-kitzbuehel.at), situated close to the Hahnenkamm lift, is pretty impressive, with a big pool, adventure slides, sauna, hammam, massage and other treatments.

Wellness facilities: You can find these in many of the smart hotels. For example, at the Sport Hotel Reisch you can visit the Aveda wellness facility (0043 (0)5356 633660, www.sporthotelreisch.at) and the A-ROSA Spa Hotel has amazing facilities (0043 (0)5356 65660 992, www.a-rosa.de).

Events

The **Kitzbühel Hahnenkamm Downhill** is now the most famous downhill event in the world. It's held every year in January and thousands of people flock to the resort to watch the best downhill skiers from around the globe battling it out on 1 of the toughest alpine courses.

Accommodation

There's a great range of accommodation, with lots of places to find 5-star luxury and equally as abundant guest houses and pensions where you can find cheaper beds. Of the luxury options, we love the **Zur Tenne** (0043 (0)5356 644440, www.hotelzurtenne.com), a stunning 4-star hotel, right in the heart of the beautiful town centre. The **Schwarzer Adler** (0043 (0)5356 6911, www.adlerkitz.

at) has superb wellness facilities and a gorgeous, traditional atmosphere. If you like the sound of a secluded alpine castle, try the imposing **Hotel Schloss Lebenberg** (0043 (0)5356 6901, www.austria-trend.at/leb). The location is inconvenient for the slopes and town, but there are shuttle buses to take you around.

The 5-star **Grand Spa Resort A-ROSA** (0043 (0)5356 65660 992, www.a-rosa.de) is a modern-day castle. Its pulling point is the opulent spa, whose 3000m^2 incorporate indoor and outdoor connected pools, 7 different saunas, 16 treatment rooms and dedicated yoga rooms. Opposite the Streif ski run, A-ROSA isn't in the most convenient location for town but there is a good shuttle service. You can pay for a spa day without accommodation.

'A modern-day castle with an opulent and extensive spa'

If you are looking for B&Bs, you can get very good value places on the outskirts of town, such as pension **Thurner** (0043 (0)5356 62275), or something slightly more expensive to be closer to the main lifts, such as pension **Rosengarten** (0043 (0)5356 625280).

Eating out

On the mountain

The mountain restaurants in Kitzbühel have a fantastic reputation. The bars that are dotted around on the snow make good pit-stops too. **Berggasthof Hagstein** (0043 (0)5356 65216) makes a great glühwein stop on the way down from Kitzbüheler Horn. Our 2 favourite restaurants in the Hahnenkamm sector are the beautiful and rustic **Melkalm** (0043 (0)5356 62119, www.melkalm.at), with fantastic food and the friendliest service, and the **Sonnenbuhel** (0043 (0)5356 62776), that has a great terrace with deckchairs. Over towards Kirchberg, the **Schi Alm** (0043 (0)5357 3282, www.schi-alm.at) has a great little bar out on the snow.

In town

For good, traditional Tyrolean dishes, as well as the odd tasty Asian dish, the **Schwedenkapelle** (0043 (0)5356 65870) is the place to go. To get into the swing of things, pop along to the dinner dancing on Saturdays. The **Neuwirt** (0043 (0)5356 691158, www.restaurant-neuwirt.at) at the Hotel Schwarzer Adler provides award-winning food (2 red rosettes, 1 Michelin star), with just as astonishing a price tag. For Austrian cuisine in less formal surroundings, the **Chizzo** (0043 (0)5356 62475, www.chizzo.info) is good value and has a lovely terrace and bar outside. You will find it just outside the gated town centre entrance. Our favourite was the Mexican restaurant **La Fonda** (0043 (0)5356 73673), where you can enjoy some fajitas and a margarita in a cosy and well-designed restaurant/bar. The **Shanghai Chinese** (0043 (0)5356 62178) has great Chinese food and an extensive menu, and looks like your typical Chinese restaurant inside. If you're missing Italian food, head to the bustling **Barrique** (0043 (0)5356 62658) in the centre of town. If you get post-après munchies, **McDonald's** is across the street from the Londoner.

Bars and clubs

The ice bars at the bottom of the slopes (**Hahnenkamm Pavilion Bar** – 0043 (0)402 6950 – for example) are good places to start the après. Most tourists head straight to the **Londoner** (0043 (0)5356 71427, www.thelondoner.at), which has a great atmosphere but gets really jam packed and is more expensive than other bars. Brit-run **Brass Monkeys** is another good loud après ski venue. The American-themed **Highways** music bar (www.highways.at) and the cute **s'Lichtl** (0043 (0)5356 63924) with its ceiling of fairy lights are also well-liked. **Jimmy's** wine bar (0043 (0)5356 64409), in the centre of the square, is great for a more civilised glass of wine and a plate of bruschetta.

‘The Bergsinn is modern and futuristic’

The **Bergsinn** (0043 (0)5356 66818, www.bergsinn.at), just at the edge of the pedestrianised area, is modern and futuristic, with a great cocktail list. Late-night dancing can be had at **Take 5** (0043 (0)5356 71300), a smarter and more expensive club. The **Casino** (0043 (0)5356 62300, www.kitzbuehel.casinos.at) has French and American roulette, blackjack, poker and slot machines.

Getting there

By car

From Munich take the E53, A9, A99 and A8, all in the direction of Salzburg. Then take the A93 to Kufstain Süd, highway 178 towards St Johann and the 161 to Kitzbühel.

From Salzburg take the highway to Walserberg, the 21 towards Bad Reichenhall, the B178 towards St Johann and the 161 to Kitzbühel.

By plane

Salzburg (80km) A recent initiative provides cheap, convenient transfers to resort. The Kitzbüheler Alpen shuttle must be booked 48 hours in advance at www.eurotours.at/airportshuttle. This is only available on Saturdays but Andi's Taxi (see opposite) also offers a good service.

Innsbruck (95km)

Munich (135km)

By train

Take the Eurostar from London St Pancras to Brussels; then the Bergland Express overnight skitrain to arrive at Kitzbühel station, in the resort. Contact European Rail (020 7387 0444, www.europeanrail.com).

Useful facts and phone numbers

Tourist office

T: 0043 (0)5356 777

F: 0043 (0)5356 77777

W: www.kitzbuehel.com

Emergency services

- Police: 133 or 0043 (0)5356 62626
- Mountain rescue squad: 140 or 0043 (0)5356 62265
- Mountain patrol: 0043 (0)5356 74544
- Rescue squad – Red Cross: 144 or 0043 (0)5356 691000
- Hospital Tilak: 0043 (0)05356 6010

Taxis

- Andi's Taxi: 0043 (0)5356 66222, www.andis-taxi.com
- Silver Star: 0043 (0)5356 63500
- Taxi Aufschnaiter: 0043 (0)5356 6969, www.kitz-tour.at

Airport transfer

- Four Season Airport transfer: 0043 (0)512 584 157, www.airport-transfer.com
- Transferbus.net: 0043 (0)820 600802, www.transferbus.net

Lech

A chic, yet relaxed resort, with something for everyone.

On the slopes	Rating
Snow reliability	❄❄❄❄
Parks	❄❄½
Off-piste	❄❄❄❄
Off the slopes	
Après ski	❄❄❄
Nightlife	❄❄
Eating out	❄❄❄❄❄
Resort charm	❄❄❄❄

The resort

Lech is a stunning resort. Every building has the traditional chalet look and a stream trickles through the town, adding to the relaxed ambience. The resort's planning and construction laws cleverly maintain not only the traditional look of the hotels and chalets, but also space in-between buildings, providing an open feel and the convenience of being able to ski back to many hotels. The Rüfikopf cable car can be accessed from the main street and the Schlegelkopf chairlifts are just a short walk from here.

Oberlech is a small, traffic-free gathering of hotels just above Lech, only accessible by cable car. The cable car does stay open until 1am so you could sample some of the nightlife in Lech and then rush back up to your hotel, but we prefer it for a lunch stop rather than as a base for the holiday. Families might enjoy the seclusion though, and there is the ski-in ski-out option from any of the hotels there.

Lech attracts the rich, famous and royal – residents of Lech are proud that Princess Diana was a regular visitor, whose signed painting hangs proudly from the wall of the Hotel Arlberg. You could quite easily be wandering past Princess Caroline of Monaco, Boris Becker, Vladimir Putin or members of the Dutch or Jordanian royal families. Despite the abundant prosperity, the resort is by no means pretentious or elitist – it's friendly and welcoming.

The mountains

Height: 1450–2450m

Ability	Rating
Expert	❄❄❄❄
Intermediate	❄❄❄❄❄
Beginner	❄❄❄❄

Getting about

The main slopes of Lech and Oberlech are accessed by the Schlegelkopf chairlifts. These slopes are great for low intermediates and cruisers as they are primarily wide and flat (boarders may find the flats a tad annoying). As in many resorts now, there are a number of off-piste routes marked on the piste map. In some resorts this is a little infuriating as it can hinder your chances of fresh tracks, but in Lech there are few people to compete with.

From the Rüfikopf cable car on the main street in Lech, you can make your way over to Zürs, although this is a one-way trip; you'll have to catch the bus back. These reds and blues are geared to intermediates, but you'll also find some decent challenges.

The park

Short but sweet! The park is well-shaped and groomed. There are 6 kickers, ranging from 3m to 12m in length and 2 rails, including a superb rainbow rail. It would be a great place to learn freestyle, and get your tricks dialled, but could be a little dull for the experts – apart from the rainbow.

Off-piste and backcountry

Lech has off-piste for all levels of backcountry rider. For the less experienced freerider, there are a fair few marked ski and board routes on the map, which are not pisted or patrolled. For backcountry trips, hire a guide. There is quite a bit of hiking and climbing to be done to access some of the big powder bowls, but this all adds to the adventure. On bad weather days, with high winds and flat light, the Krieferhorn area has some good off-piste spots that wind up at the bottom of Lech. Environmentalists have banned off-piste through the woods and being caught could cost you your lift pass.

Lift passes

Check the latest prices at www.skiarlberg.at

Instruction

Alpin Center Lech

0043 (0)5583 39880
www.alpincenter-lech.at

Lech Ski School (Ski and Snowboard)

It can also arrange guiding and heliskiing.
0043 (0)5583 2355
www.skischule-lech.at

Other activities

Beauty treatments: The following hotels offer treatments and are open to the public: Burg-Vital-Hotel (0043 (0)5583 3140, www.burgvitalhotel.at), Romantik Hotel Krone (0043 (0)5583 2551, www.romantikhotelkrone-lech.at), and Gasthof Rote Wand (0043 (0)5583 34350).

Helicopter rides: For information about helicopter rides call the ski school on 0043 (0)5583 2355.

Horse-drawn sleigh rides: Reserve your horse-drawn sleigh rides from Haus Angelika (0043 (0)664 3443 730, or 0043 (0)5583 4140), Pension Zugerhorn (0043 (0)664 6520510 or 0043 (0)5583 2749) and Duftner/Bischnau (0043 (0)664 2842645).

Ice skating: Skating is really popular in Lech at the indoor ice skating rink at the Hotel Monzabon (0043 (0)5583 21040). You can also have a go at curling.

Paragliding: Ring Flight Connection Arlberg on 0043 (0)664 141 5166 for more information.

Squash: There are courts at Hotel Enzian (0043 (0)5583 22420).

Tennis: The Tennis centre Lech (0043 (0)5583 21610) offers tennis, table tennis, football, table football and a climbing wall.

Therapeutic massages and remedies: Call the Physiosport Muxel (0043 (0)664 1229 923).

Tobogganing: Tobogganing on the 1.2km long slope from Oberlech to Lech is open 9am–10pm. Bobsleds are available for rent from the Bergbahn Oberlech (mountain railway).

Wild animal feeding: Watch deer feeding from a seat in the Engerle forest on Zugerstraße. Guided tours can be booked by calling 0043 (0)5583 2161 222.

Accommodation

For 5-star luxury, choose the central **Hotel Arlberg** (0043 (0)5583 21340, www.arlberghotel.at) with indoor and outdoor pools, a fantastic outdoor whirlpool, sauna, beauty treatments and a gourmet restaurant. The **Hotel Post** (0043 (0)5583 22060, www.postlech.com), a Relais & Châteaux hotel, is also a favourite of royalty from many countries. In fact, it is so luxurious any non-royals may find it a bit uncomfortable. The cosy lounge bar is the place for whisky and cigars and the numerous elaborate suites are exceptional. Jackets and ties are essential for meals in the dining room. The more affordable 4-star **Tannbergerhof** (0043 (0)5583 2202, www.tannbergerhof.com) is right in the centre of town and has a decent spa area. Bear in mind that it is also the most popular après ski venue – great unless you plan to lie in bed peacefully with a good book.

Hotel Gotthard (0043 (0)5583 3560, www.gotthard.at) is yet another highly recommended 4-star hotel with a superb new indoor pool, great wellness facilities and excellent food (champagne may even appear at breakfast). The prices are a welcome surprise given the top quality service.

However, you don't need to stay in the gorgeous 4 and 5-star hotels to get quality service and lovely rooms. The charming **Hotel-Pension Felsenhof** (0043 (0)5583 2524, www.felsenhof.at) has great rooms and the staff are first class. Alternatively, **Pension Angerhof** (0043 (0)5583 2418) is an attractive and central B&B and the cute **Pension Odo** (0043 (0)5583 2358) is in a great, ski-in ski-out location, has only 17 beds and has reasonable half-board accommodation.

'You don't need to stay in 4 and 5-star hotels to get quality service'

Eating out

On the mountain

The **Rud-Alpe** (0043 (0)5583 41825, www.rud-alpe.at), on the slopes just above town, is just how you would hope a chalet-style restaurant would look. It's big but still manages to be cosy with a nice fire. Typical Austrian food is on offer and it is very good value. You can also have an evening meal up here. The **Panorama** restaurant (0043 (0)5583 2336 501) at the Rüfikopf top station also serves traditional Austrian food, and the views from the terrace are pretty good.

The sunny terraces in car-free Oberlech are one of the best places for lunch. The **Goldener Berg** (0043 (0)5583 22050, www.goldenerberg.at) has a huge menu, although it is a little pricey, and is popular for its fondues at night. **Hotel Montana** (0043 (0)5583 24600, www.montanaoberlech.at) is also a great gourmet lunch stop in Oberlech and the **Trittalm** (0043 (0)5583 2831) in Zürs has a good atmosphere. **S'Murmele** (0043 (0)5582 288) is a well-kept secret, where those in the know pop in at lunchtime.

In town

Lech/Zürs has the largest number of gourmet restaurants in Austria. Those wanting to sample such exclusive treats should try the restaurants at the **Arlberg Hotel** (0043 (0)5583 21340, www.arlberghotel.at), the **Berghof** (0043 (0)5583 2635, www.derberghof.at), the **Burg** (0043 (0)5583 2291, www.burghotel.at) or the **Rote Wand** in Zug (0043 (0)5583 34350). For more information, collect a booklet from the tourist office and look for restaurants with pictures of chefs' hats next to them.

By far the most atmospheric and charming restaurant is **Hus Nr. 8** (0043 (0)5583 33220, www.hus8.at), a restored old farmhouse. The restaurant is split into sections of the old house (the owner himself was born in 1 of the rooms). The food is fantastic, from its traditional Austrian specialities to fondues, raclettes, salads and soups.The best thing about this restaurant is that it's not at all expensive. For a romantic night, the **Älpele** (0043 (0)5583 3388) in Zugertal is beautiful and the evening is completed by the restaurant's seclusion – you cannot reach the restaurant by car, you must walk or take the snowcat. In Zürs, the **Flexenhäusl** (0043 (0)5583 4143) is another special place to dine, largely because it's so small, with only 20 covers. Reservation is a must.

'This restored farmhouse is by far the most atmospheric and charming restaurant'

The **Schneggarei** bar (0043 (0)5583 39888, www.schneggarei.com), a little hut near the chairlifts, looks like nothing from the outside, but it's beautifully decorated inside and the wood-fired pizzas and ribs are great and reasonable. The **Italiener** restaurant (0043 (0)5583 3734) is a lovely little pizzeria, serving food from 6pm until midnight. The futuristic **FUX** restaurant and bar (0043 (0)5583 2992, www.fux-mi.net) caters for those who tire of local delicacies. Choose between an American steakhouse and the Euro-Asian option with woks, sushi and other oriental dishes. The lounge bar is great for curling up in front of the fire with a whisky and a cigar.

Bars and clubs

When après ski kicks off you have 2 choices: either join the mainly local crowd at the outdoor **S'Pfefferkorndl** (0043 (0)5583 2525-424) ice bar in the centre of town, where you can get some good snacks if you're peckish (burgers, oysters, the works); or head to the tourist favourite, the **Tannbergerhof** (0043 (0)5583 2202, www.tannbergerhof.com). This is the most popular après venue, with fab happy hours, a great atmosphere and a heaving crowd until early morning. The **FUX** (0043 (0)5583 2992, www.fux-mi.net) has a bar/club and is a good place for a whisky in front of the fire, and the **Post** hotel (0043 (0)5583 22060, www.postlech.com) has a cosy, upmarket bar with a comprehensive cigar menu. For seriously late-night partying you'll need to catch a taxi into Zürs, where you will find 2 great clubs, the **Zürserl** (0043 (0)5583 2662, www.edelweiss.net) in the Hotel Edelweiss, and the **Vernissage** (0043 (0)5583 2271) bar/club in the Robinson Club.

Between 7.30pm and 4am Night Taxi James (0043 (0)5583 2501) will take you to various stops in Lech.

Getting there

By car

The route finder on the tourist office website will help you find your way. There are tolls on Austrian motorways. You can pay at border crossings, petrol stations, post offices, tobacconist's, through your road recovery service or at Lech Zürs tourist office.

By plane

Innsbruck (120km)

Friedrichshafen (130km) For bus transfers check out www.airport-bus.at.

Zürich (200km) Reserve your transfer at Lech travel agency (0043 (0)5583 3155, reservation@lech-zuers.at) or Arlberg Express (0043 (0)5583 2000, www.arlbergexpress.com).

By train

Take the Eurostar from London St Pancras to Brussels; then the Bergland Express overnight skitrain, changing in Innsbruck, to Langen, and then a local bus (25 minutes) to the resort. Contact European Rail (020 7387 0444, www.europeanrail.com). Bus tickets are purchased on the bus.

Useful facts and phone numbers

Tourist office

T: 0043 (0)5583 21610
F: 0043 (0)5583 3155
W: www.lech-zuers.at

Emergency services

- Police: 0043 (0)5583 2203 or 0043 (0)591 338 1051
- In case of emergency call 144
- Fire: 0043 (0)5583 3445
- Mountain rescue: 0043 (0)5583 3446

Doctors

- Dr Elmar Beiser: 0043 (0)5583 2032
- Dr Reinhard Muxel: 0043 (0)5583 3300
- Dr Harald Rhomberg: 0043 (0)5583 2234/2294
- Dr Christoph Murr: 0043 (0)5583 4242 (also emergency services ambulance): 0043 (0)664 411 8787

Taxis

- Taxizentrale Lech: 0043 (0)5583 25010, www.taxi-lech.at
- Taxi Zürs: 0043 (0)5583 3110

Mayrhofen

Legendary park, lively nightlife and good-looking town... practically perfect.

On the slopes	Rating
Snow reliability	***
Parks	*****½
Off-piste	***
Off the slopes	
Après ski	*****½
Nightlife	****
Eating out	***
Resort charm	****

The resort

Mayrhofen feels like a ski resort should feel; with a charming main street, traditional architecture, bars brimming with people from 4pm onwards, great nightlife and a snowpark to rival the best in Europe.

Mayrhofen has so much going for it that we can forgive it for having no runs back to town, and for the resulting queues for lifts. And if you need another reason to visit, prices are far more reasonable than at most of the top resorts.

Advanced riders may tire of the few challenging runs, but intermediates, beginners and children are well catered for and the ski schools are superb. Snow reliability is a general concern with Austria, but with the Hintertux glacier just down the road there is at least a backup plan.

The mountains

Height: 630–2500m

Ability	Rating
Expert	**
Intermediate	****
Beginner	***

Getting about

The main riding area can be reached from the Penken gondola in the middle of town. If you can be bothered, you can skip the queues by catching a bus to Finkenberg or Hippach. Most of the riding here is geared towards the intermediate rider. The more daring should try Austria's steepest piste, the Harakiri piste, with a 78 per cent gradient. If you're undecided, you can pick up a leaflet that gives you a choice of 5 routes: the Ahorn circuit for beginners, Penken and Zillertal 3000 for intermediates, the 'fun and action' circuit for racing, the Harakiri run and the snowpark and the challenging Höhenemeterfresser (or altitude tour) where you will cover 13000m in altitude in 1 day and receive a certificate for your efforts. The Ahorn area is a bus ride away and the place to go for peace and quiet; best suited to families and kids.

The Ahorn cable car can carry up to 160 people to the Ahorn plateau in just over 6 minutes. This lift is only 200m from the Penken cable car base, making the Ahorn area easily accessible. The snowsure Hintertux glacier is a short drive away for more off-piste options (see Hintertux chapter, page 36).

The park

The VANS Penken Park (www.vans-penken-park.com) has to be one of the best in Europe in terms of kickers and rails. It has 5 separate lines plus a half pipe. There are kickers up to 20m long and also a kids' park with 11 obstacles and its own lift. The park is very well maintained – it is constantly shaped and the landings are groomed each morning so that they're not too solid.

Off-piste and backcountry

Mayrhofen is not known for its steep and deep, more for its lively nightlife and freestyle scene. There are, however, a few areas that are worth checking out. After a big snow fall, head to the Zell am Ziller area, which is a superb place to get freshies, and look underneath the Larchwald trees in flat light. For getting some easy powder turns in, make your way up in the Horbergjoch area, the highest point of the mountain. Word has it, you can always find some virgin snow!

'Known for its lively nightlife and freestyle scene'

Lift passes

Check the latest prices at www.mayrhofnerbergbahnen.com

Instruction

Die Roten Profis Skischule and Snowboardschule Mayrhofen

0043 (0)5285 63900
www.skischule-mayrhofen.at

Mount Everest Ski School

The founder of this ski school, Peter Habeler, was the first to ascend Everest without artificial oxygen, in 1978. Off-piste tours are on offer as well as instruction for all levels.
0043 (0)5285 62829
www.habeler.com

Skischule Mayrhofen 3000

A great ski and board school offering lessons and guiding.
0043 (0)5285 64015
www.skischule.mayrhofen3000.at

Skischule Mayerhofen Total

SMT is a superb ski school.
0043 (0)5285 63939
www.mayrhofen-total.com

Snowboardschule Mayrhofen Total

A great snowboard school offering a range of disciplines. Video analysis is also available.
0043 (0)5285 63939
www.snowboard-mayrhofen.at

Other activities

Adventure pool: The Erlebnisbad adventure pool (0043 (0)5285 6760, www.erlebnisbad-mayrhofen.at) has a water chute, saunas, crazy river, cascade, bubble pool, mountain lake and restaurant.

Adventure sports: Action Club Zillertal (0043 (0)664 44 13074, www.actionclub-zillertal.com) offers loads of activities such as tobogganing evenings, skidoo driving, paragliding, freeriding tours and snow shoes.

Aqua centre: The Aqua Centre – Fun and Spa at Hotel Strass (0043 (0)5285 6705) has sauna, solarium, massage, table tennis and squash. There are 3 indoor and 9 outdoor tennis courts and 3 more squash courts at other venues. Contact the tourist office for more information.

Curling: There is an artificial ice rink with lanes for curling.

Nine-pin bowling: This can be found in La Fontana (0043 (0)5285 62578); open 4pm–1am on weekdays and 11am–1am at the weekend.

Paragliding: There are a couple of companies offering tandem paragliding flights. Stocky Air (0043 (0)664 313 9800/0043 (0)664 872 5913, www.fly-zillertal.com) has a good range of options. They fly daily at 9am and can provide you with photos and film on request. Zillertaler Flugschule (0043 (0)5285 64906/0664 3588 435, www.zillertaler-flugschule.com) offers flights too.

Tobogganning: A natural toboggan run starts from Gasthof Wiesenhof, with a total length of 2.5km.

Events

In January a **snow and avalanche awareness camp** is held to introduce you to freeriding (www.saac.at). In February there is a great street festival on the main street with live music, street performers and shows from 6pm. In March, the Ästhetiker Tour **'Wängl**

Tängl' Snowboard Jam takes place. Those not invited can attend qualifiers in an attempt to compete against the top pro boarders from America, Australasia and all over Europe. As well as the snowboard contest, there is a skate contest and street art. **Snowbombing** takes place right at the end of the season and lasts for a week. This mad event brings some world-class DJs and live acts to the resort such as DJ Yoda, De La Soul, Fatboy Slim, The Enemy and Editors. For the 2011 line-up see www.snowbombing.com If you are already in resort you can buy a wristband for the events or you can book the full package through Snowbombing – accommodation, transfers, event wristband, etc. There is no official ski/snowboard competition to accompany this event, although there is sometimes a jam session and a few DJs on the mountain.

Accommodation

Location is particularly important in Mayrhofen as the lifts and nightlife are all focused at one end of the main street. The 4-star **Hotel Strass** (0043 (0)5285 6705, www.hotelstrass.com) has the best location in town, right next to the Penkenbahn lift, and it has great spa facilities with pool, sauna and solarium. It is also home to the Ice Bar, the Speak Easy Bar, the Sports Bar and Grill and the Arena nightclub (see Bars and clubs). Ask for a room on 1 of the top floors to avoid the thumping music.

> 'It has great spa facilities with pool and sauna'

Alternatively, ask for a room in the **Aparthotel Strass**, a few doors down the road. These rooms are cheaper, you can use all the facilities in the main hotel, the accommodation is just as nice and you are still central yet away from the noise. Contrary to the name, these rooms do not have any self-catering facilities. Another favourite is the **Sporthotel Manni** (0043 (0)5285 633010, www.mannis.at), well known for its rooftop pool. It also has a fantastic position on the main street, just a minute or so's walk from the Penkenbahn lift. The central **Hotel Waldheim** (0043 (0)5285 62211, www.hotelwaldheim.at) is a cosy and welcoming 4-star hotel. The charmingly traditional **Kramerwirt** hotel (0043 (0)5285 6700, www.kramerwirt.at) has lovely restaurants, and staff clad in lederhosen. The only 5-star is the beautiful **Hotel Elisabeth** (0043 (0)5285 6767, www.elisabethhotel.com), a little bit further out of town. The rooms have mini bars and balconies, and you can pay extra for a whirlpool, Jacuzzi and steambath. There are some very reasonable and pleasant pensions (B&Bs) in Mayrhofen and apartments for those who prefer to self cater. You can book these through the tourist office at www.mayrhofen.at

Eating out

On the mountain

The **Schneekar hütte** (0043 (0)5285 64940), at the top of the Schneekar chairlift on Horberg, is cosy and traditional with good food (fresh prawn and salmon steaks) and a great terrace. The **Grillhofalm**, by the snowpark, has good pizzas and Josefs Biohütte, down from Tappenalm lift, serves organic food.

In town

Restaurants in Mayrhofen cater to most tastes. For ribs, burgers, salads, pasta, wings, and a pint or 2, in Hard Rock Café-style surroundings, **Mo's bar** (0043 (0)5285 63435) is definitely the way forward. The **Café Tirol** in the centre of town has cheap internet and good food. The food in the **Sports Bar and Grill** in the Hotel Strass is also very tasty. For pizza, the best are **Mamma Mia's** at the Hotel Elisabeth (0043 (0)5285 6767) and the **pizzeria** at the Sporthotel Manni (0043 (0)5285 633010). For a change, head to **Singapore Chinese** (0043 (0)5285 63912), near the tourist office. For the best traditional cuisine in superb surroundings head to the **Wirtshaus zum Griena** (0043 (0)5285 62778), a 400-year-old farmhouse that has been converted into an enchanting restaurant. Not the place to go if you have a dairy allergy – most dishes come in a pan, covered in cheese.

Bars and clubs

The best bars for après ski are pretty obvious as you step off the lift; right opposite you is the **Happy End Bar** (0043 (0)5285 62333), and to your left is the **Ice Bar** (0043 (0)5285 6705), which is very lively, busy and bare; so you can be as rowdy as you like. The Ice Bar is part of the Strass Hotel (see Accommodation), as is the **Speak Easy Bar**, which is also popular. In the centre of town, **Mo's** is great for a pint and a bite to eat (see Eating out), and **Apropos** for a game of pool (open 8.30pm–4am). Towards the older part of town and the tourist office, you will find the ever popular **Scotland Yard Pub** (www.scotlandyard.at – you'll recognise it by the painted British flags and Old School English phone box). This pub has a great atmosphere and is always busy. Club-wise, you can choose between the house/techno/metal music at the **Arena**, or the more commercially biased **Schlussel Alm** (0043 (0)5285 62232), just a minute's walk from the main lift station (away from town).

When the pubs shut, make your way down to the Cuban atmosphere of the late-night drinking hole, the **Cohibar**.

Getting there

By car

Take the A12 to Wiesing, then B169 on for another 30km.

By plane

Innsbruck (75km)
Salzburg (175km)
Munich (190km)

By train

Take the Eurostar from London St Pancras to Brussels; then the Bergland Express overnight skitrain, changing at Jenbach, to arrive at Mayrhofen station in the resort. Contact European Rail (020 7387 0444, www.europeanrail.com).

Useful facts and phone numbers

Tourist office

T: 0043 (0)5285 6760-0
F: 0043 (0)5285 6760-33
W: www.mayrhofen.at

Emergency services

- Police: 133
- Ambulance: 144
- Mountain rescue service: 140

Doctors

- Dr Alois Dengg: 0043 (0)5285 62992-0
- Dr Simon and Katharina Gredler: 0043 (0)5285 62550
- Dr Jörg Ritzl: 0043 (0)5282 3758
- Dr Wilfried Schneidinger: 0043 (0)5285 63124
- Dr Armin Zumtobel: 0043 (0)5285 62054
- Schwaz Hospital: 0043 (0)5242 600
- Innsbruck Hospital: 0043 (0)512 504
- Physiotherapist Stöckl Hermann: 0043 (0)5285 624366

Taxis

- Apfolter's Taxi: 0043 (0)664 2500250
- Taxi Sandhofer: 0043 (0)5282 3604
- Reini's Taxi: 0043 (0)650 463 75 75
- Taxi Kröll: 0043 (0)5285 62260

Saalbach-Hinterglemm

Accessible and extensive terrain, a charming town and crazy après ski.

On the slopes	Rating
Snow reliability	❄❄
Parks	❄❄½
Off-piste	❄❄❄❄
Off the slopes	
Après ski	❄❄❄❄❄
Nightlife	❄❄❄❄
Eating out	❄❄❄❄
Resort charm	❄❄❄❄

The resort

Saalbach-Hinterglemm attracts a huge variety of clients: swanky bankers roll in from Munich for the weekend to visit 1 of Saalbach's swish hotels, families enjoy the charming village and quaint mountain huts, ardent skiers choose the ski-in ski-out benefits of Hinterglemm and the big drinkers flock to dance on the tables all night.

Saalbach is a charming, typically Austrian town, and pulls in the mid to high end of the market. Prices aren't cheap, but you certainly get what you pay for – the quality of accommodation is superb. Hinterglemm is slightly less glam, with fewer top end hotels, but it still has charm, and has fantastic access to the Ski Circus (see below).

The mountains are great – loads of terrain, perfect for the intermediate, but also with plenty of off-piste to keep freeriders happy. Freestylers shouldn't get too excited about the two parks – there are OK for beginners, but not for the serious jibbers.

The mountains

Height: 1003–2100m

Ability	Rating
Expert	❄❄❄
Intermediate	❄❄❄❄
Beginner	❄❄❄

Getting about

There are 200km of pistes covering the Saalbach-Hinterglemm Leogang mountains, and they are immaculately groomed and pleasingly accessible. The mountains are great for all levels of skier, but intermediates will be particularly happy with the Ski Circus. This is the name for Saalbach's circuit of pistes, which covers both sides of the Glemm valley. Start wherever you like and make your way back to the beginning. Don't drag your hungover bones out of bed at midday and expect to coast round – you have to get your skates on to make it in a day.

Snow reliability is far from perfect due to altitude and the large number of south-facing slopes, but the snowmaking facilities are good.

The park

There are two snowparks: one at the base of Hinterglemm and the other in Leogang. The Hinterglemm park has improved over the years and now has 3 separate kicker lines each featuring 3 or 4 large booters. The park at Leogang has a huge array of rails and a separate kicker. Beginners are no longer well catered for in these parks, but there are some small jumps and boxes next to the Hinterhagalm t-bar in Saalbach.

Off-piste and backcountry

The off-piste is superb. It is off-piste rather than backcountry – you can hop on and off pistes to your heart's content and spot your lines on the lift up. The off-piste itineraries through the trees towards Leogang are great in bad weather and check out the powder bowls around the Zwölferkogl, Seekar and Schattberg areas after a snowfall.

Lift passes

Check the latest prices at www.saalbach.com

Instruction

Hinterglemm

Hinterglemmer Ski & Snowboardschule
0043 (0)6541 634640 or 0043 (0)6542 7511
www.skischule.com

Ski & Snowboardschule Activ
0043 (0)676 5171325
www.skischule-activ.at

Saalbach

Snowboardschule Saalbach
This snowboard school has a huge range of courses on offer. Aside from the usual, the school offers freestyle lessons for different levels of rider and freeride days. Backcountry courses are on offer, with a theory unit and 2 days on the mountain.
0043 (0)6541 20047
www.board.at

Snow Academy
0043 (0)664 5059 933
www.snowacademy.com

Skischule Fürstauer
0043 (0)6541 8444
www.skischule-saalbach.at

Other activities

Bowling alley: Bobby's Bowling Alley, (0043 (0)6541 63 89, www.bobbys-pub.at). There are 4 bowling alleys, as well as darts, quiz machines, pool and table football.

Floodlit toboggan runs: The Simalalm run is 4.5km long and the price covers transport up to the run, toboggan rental and welcome drink. The Spielberghaus run is 3km long and the price covers transportation and rental. The Maisalm run is 1.5km long. The Reiterkogel is fairly new – you can take the Reiterkogel cable car in the centre of Hinterglemm (open Monday–Saturday 6.30–9pm). Rent a toboggan from the bottom.

Ice skating: Located after the Zwölferkogelbahn lift towards the end of the valley on the left (0043 (0)6541 7403).

Paragliding: Air star (0043 (0)6582 70708, www.airstar.at) offers a variety of flights.

Sleigh rides: Trips are 1 hour long.

Swimming pool: This large (25 x 12.5m) indoor pool is in Hinterglemm and has a sauna (0043 (0)6541 7131).

Tennis: After the Zwölferkogelbahn lift towards the end of the valley on the left. The courts are open 9.30am–10pm (0043 (0)6541 7403).

> 'Try a 30°C Jacuzzi in the snow or a salt water steam bath'

Accommodation

Hinterglemm

Hotel Theresia Gartenhotel (0043 (0)6541 74140, www.hotel-theresia.co.at) is superb. The water features are one of the hotel's best facilites, including a 30°C indoor pool, a 30°C Jacuzzi in the snow, and a 70m^2 adventure pool (outdoor). There's also an aroma grotto, salt water steam bath, and five different types of sauna. The staff are welcoming and the rooms are excellent; they even provide free soft drinks in your room. The **Aparthotel Theresia** costs less and you still have use of all the water facilities.

Hotel Glemmtalerhof (0043 (0)6541 7135, www.glemmtalerhof.at) has great facilities, including an indoor swimming pool and sauna. Saalbach's pensions are fantastic value, although check the location carefully. **Pension Blasius** (0043 (0)6541 6423, www.eberharter.at) is run by a very friendly family, is centrally located and has a small sauna and solarium.

Saalbach

The luxurious **Alpenhotel** (0043 (0)6541 6666-0, www.alpenhotel.at) has 2 bars, 3 restautants and 1 nightlub, the exclusive Arena. It also has fantastic wellness facilities that include an indoor swimming pool, whirlpool, sauna and exercise room. The **Kendler** (0043 (0)6541 6225, www.kendler.at) is another expensive luxury hotel that has an excellent location next to the Bernkogel chair. The **Haider** (0043 (0)6541 6228, www.hotel-haider.at) is quaint and traditional and is also well located near the main lifts. It has a sauna and hot whirlpool.

Eating out

On the mountain

The **Pfefferalm** (www.pfefferalm.at) is a fantastic mountain hut. It's as rustic as they come – the only light comes from candles and warm open fires, and bear skins cover the walls. The **Wieser Alm** is the place to go in the sun for views over the whole valley and the Westernstadl Altachhof (0043 (0)6541 87150) has a great western theme. Not just the place for carnage, the **Hinterhagalm** (0043 (0)6541 7212) is also a beautiful place to dine. It serves traditional Austrian dishes and was also a backdrop for *The Sound of Music.*

In town

Most of the hotels are half board and have good restaurants. For a night out, the **Heurigenstube** (0043 (0)6541 6345-58) in Hinterglemm is a casual restaurant, famous for its ribs. **Wallner Pizzeria** (0043 (0)6541 6234) on the main street in Saalbach is good value. For meat, head to **Peter's Restaurant** (0043 (0)6541 6232, www.hotel-peter.at). The Alpenhotel's (0043 (0)6541 6666-0) 3 restaurants serve a variety of cuisines – **La Trattoria** is an Italian and Spanish restaurant, **Pipamex** serves Mexican and **Vitrine Asian** wok specialities. The restaurant in the Hotel Kendler, the **Herzl Stube** (0043 (0)6541 6225), is highly rated for its cuisine and rustic atmosphere.

Bars and clubs

Some people come to Saalbach-Hinterglemm purely for the après ski scene. If you are staying in Hinterglemm you should start at the **Goaßtall** (www.goass.at). It has an outside area with patio heaters. Inside it just gets strange, with robotic goats dressed in lederhosen and real goats behind glass. There is a good restaurant, too, if you get peckish. In town, the Hotel Dorfschmiede (0043 (0)6541 7408) has a great après ski bar – the **Harley Davidson and Bikers Pub**, which has a good atmosphere and loads of motorcycle memorabilia – the bar stools are motorcycle seats, that kind of thing. The **Hexanhäusl bar**, with its weird witchcraft theme, is absolutely bizarre (check out www.hex.at). The **Tanzhimmel** restaurant and bar (0043 (0)6541 649795, www.apresworld.at) is also huge for après; and later on, under it is the **London Bar** – an underground warren with pub, disco, lap dancing rooms (the lap dancing is thankfully behind closed doors so you can ignore it if you want to).

'A good atmosphere and loads of motorcycle memorabilia'

In Saalbach, you will start your evening at the **Hinterhagalm** (www.hinterhag.at), above the Turm T-bar on the beginners' slope, a crazy place for après, with live music and dancing on tables. Down at the bottom of the Taum T-bar, the next stop should be **Bauer's Schi-Alm** (www.bauers-schialm.at) – another mad après spot. **Bobby's Pub** (www.bobbys-pub.at, 0043 (0)6541 6389) serves good-value pints and you can have a game of pool, darts or table football, play on quiz machines or even try out the bowling alleys (see Other activities). Later on you can head to the **Arena** (0043 (0)6541 6666), an upscale nightclub. Live bands are often playing. Things kick off here around 11pm. The disco in Berger's **Sporthotel** (0043 (0)6541 6577) is less exclusive and tends to be populated by the younger crowd.

Getting there

By car

The tourist office website has links to a route planner.

If you are travelling from the north by road, you will escape the toll charges if you use the Munich–Salzburg motorway (take the Siegsdorf exit before Salzburg–Inzell–Schneizlreuth–Lofer– towards Zell am See).

By plane

Salzburg (90km).
Innsbruck (173km).
Munich (190km).

By train

Take the Eurostar from London St Pancras to Brussels; then the Bergland Express overnight skitrain to Zell am See station, and then a local bus (32 minutes) to the resort. Contact European Rail (020 7387 0444, www.europeanrail.com). Bus tickets are purchased on the bus.

Useful facts and phone numbers

Tourist office

T: 0043 (0)6541 6800-68
F: 0043 (0)6541 6800-69
W: www.saalbach.com

Emergency services

- Ambulance: 144
- Police: 133
- Fire brigade: 122

Doctors

- Dr Scheuch: 0043 (0)6541 6287
- Dr Spatzenegger: 0043 (0)6541 7878
- Dr Schernthaner: 0043 (0)6583 8447
- Dr Hartmann: 0043 (0)6583 8237

Taxis

Saalbach

- Taxi 6620: 0043 (0)6541 6620, www.taxi6620.at
- Taxi Hörl: 0043 (0)6541 6573, www.hoerl.at

Hinterglemm

- Taxi Schmidhofer: 0043 (0)6541 7163
- Taxi 6969: 0043 (0)6541 6969

St Anton

Our top resort – you'll get hooked on the 24-hour addictive atmosphere.

On the slopes	Rating
Snow reliability	❄❄❄❄
Parks	❄❄
Off-piste	❄❄❄❄❄
Off the slopes	
Après ski	❄❄❄❄❄
Nightlife	❄❄❄❄
Eating out	❄❄❄❄
Resort charm	❄❄❄❄

The resort

St Anton is without a doubt one of the best resorts in Europe. For competent riders with an appetite for challenging mountains and non-stop nightlife there is no better place to be. Note the term 'competent' – beginners and timid intermediates may well struggle with the formidable terrain. Despite its infamous party scene, the resort retains its charm, with the long, pedestrianised main street full of attractive, traditional buildings. This street is the focus of the action; the best bars and clubs and most of the restaurants are located here, and the main lifts are only a minute's walk away.

The mountains

Height: 1304–2811m

Ability	Rating
Expert	❄❄❄❄❄
Intermediate	❄❄❄❄
Beginner	❄

Getting about

St Anton provides 276km of pistes and 174km of backcountry runs to get your teeth into. What's more, the snowfall (and superb snowmaking facilities) is sufficient to maintain the slopes up to mid/end April. The slopes don't really suit the beginner, but all others will be ecstatic with the terrain, especially the backcountry enthusiasts, who have a wide range of options from the top of the Valluga alone. The ski routes are handy to guide those who wish to venture off-piste without a guide, but don't expect fresh tracks: these routes are well known. Have good insurance, too, as the resort takes no responsibility for accidents on these routes.

The most demanding on-piste runs are the Schindlerkar, the Kandahar run on the Galzig and the Gampberg run on the Rendl.

The lift company has invested heavily in the lift system in St Anton, and the Galzigbahn in particular is an incredible piece of architecture that whips you up to the top of the mountain in no time and is a great step towards banishing those nasty queues. The Muggengrat 6-seater chairlift even has heated seats! Most people will head up the Galzigbahn each morning or take the 4-person chair up to Gampen. The Galzig and Gampen sections are connected and form the focal point of the ski area. From Galzig you can head up to the daunting peak of the Valluga or cruise down to the charming village of St Christoph – a popular lunchtime pit-stop.

The park

The snowpark on the Rendl has jumps, boxes, obstacles, rails, tabletops and kickers of various sizes. There is also a well-maintained half pipe, and a funpark for beginners. If you're here to push your limits though, head into the backcountry and build something.

You see a lot of the world's best pros filming here and making the most of natural hits; Jon Olsson, Tanner Hall and Simon Dumont have been spotted filming segments in St Anton's backcountry.

Off-piste and backcountry

St Anton is up there as one of the best freeriding locations in the world. We were totally blown away with what there was on offer. Like so many other resorts, especially in Austria, there are marked off-piste routes. The best, and most extreme, is the Pfannenköpfe, by the Valfagehr chair. It is fairly challenging, and there are some good cliff drops and gullies, a perfect place to get the heart racing. Don't think that just because it's marked on the map you don't need all the proper avalanche safety gear; it's not protected from avalanches.

To step it up a level, head to the summit of the legendary Valluga and the massive powder bowl below. This eventually leads out on to another marked ski route where you have 2 choices: you can either traverse left and head down the Mattun route, or keep on down the steeper face, the Schindlerkar. On a powder day this is a great place to play in the steep, deep terrain, but if it hasn't snowed for a while you will probably find black run mogul fields, which are great only if you like moguls.

Indiana Jones types should explore over the other side of the Valluga (strictly with a guide; they won't let you up the last part of the lift with skis or board without one). It's hairy in places, but a very exciting area to check out. This leads you all the way into Zürs. A mountain guide is invaluable in St Anton to take you to hidden couloirs, bowls and cliffs.

Lift passes

Check latest prices at www.ski-st-anton.com

Instruction

Piste to Powder Mountain Guided Adventures

This British-run school, owned by Graham Austick, provides a first-class off-piste guiding service.
0043 (0)664 1746 282
www.pistetopowder.com

Ski and Snowboard School St Anton

0043 (0)5446 3563
www.skistanton.com

Ski School Arlberg

0043 (0)5446 3411
www.skischool-arlberg.com

Other activities

Conference and sports facilities: The arlberg-well.com (0043 (0)5446 4001, www.arlberg-well.com) has an impressive combination of conference, sporting event and wellness facilities. It contains 3 swimming pools: an indoor pool, a children's pool and an outdoor pool, and tons of sauna facilities (Finnish sauna, kelo sauna, samarium, steam bath, 2 solariums and massage showers), as well as a fitness studio and an ice skating rink. Except for the ice skating rink, which closes at 6pm, the facilities are open until 10pm.

Horse-drawn sleigh rides: These can take you into the Verwall valley. For reservations call Martin Tschol on 0043 (0)5446 2380. Sleighs leave from Hotel Mooserkreuz.

Paragliding: Tandem flights and courses can be booked through Flight Connection Arlberg (0043 (0)5524 8439, www.fca.at).

Squash, tennis, bowling, climbing wall: These are all available at the arl.rock sports centre (www.arlrock.at, 0043 (0)5446 26259)

Tobogganing: The 4km floodlit toboggan run from Gampenplateau down to the valley takes 10–15 minutes and covers a 500m drop in altitude. Call the Arlberger Bergbahnen (0043 (0)5446 23520) for more information.

Events

Right at the beginning of December (usually the first weekend) is the official opening of the resort when there are people partying all over the place all weekend. The **Intersport spring festival** in April includes a freeride competiton. In April the **Weisse Rausch** (White Rush) is a Chinese downhill event in which all competitors (on boards, skis, telemark, anything) throw themselves from the top of the Vallugagrat (2650m) as fast as possible (1300m drop in altitude). The White Rush is also the first stage of the Arlberg Eagle triathalon, with a half marathon in July and a mountain bike marathon in August.

Accommodation

St Anton really does have all types of accommodation available, from low-cost B&Bs to luxurious hotels. Unless it's high season, you are usually safe just turning up in St Anton as they have a great electronic system outside the tourist office that finds all available rooms for your required dates, and lets you know the price, location, etc. The tourist office packages are also worth checking out; the Powder Snow Weeks in January allow you to take advantage of the low-season prices and more-than-likely fantastic snow conditions.

If you are looking for a comfy room in a great location, for the best value in town, we have the place for you. It is **Haus Flatscher** (0043 (0)5446 3603, www.haus-flatscher.com), run by Emma Flatscher, who will do anything to make your holiday enjoyable. The rooms are excellent quality (with TV and phone). A good 3-star is the simple but cosy **Ehrenreich** (0043 (0)5446 2353, www.arlberg.com/hotel.ehrenreich), only a minute's walk from town and lifts.

Those in search of luxury should look at either the Hotel Alte Post or the Schwarzer Adler (both are 4-star – there are 2 5-star hotels but they are not particularly convenient for town or lifts). The **Hotel Alte Post** (0043 (0)5446 2553-0, www.hotel-alte-post.at) is absolutely stunning both outside and in, and has blended modern and traditional looks perfectly. The pool, spa and beauty facilities are incredible. Take your pick of rooms from a double (28m^2), a junior suite (39–56m^2), the Alte Post suite (98m^2) or the Alte Post Deluxe (190m^2) that sleeps 5–10 people! The **Schwarzer Adler** (0043 (0)5446 2244-0, www.schwarzeradler.com) is an old, traditional hotel, with very similar facilities to the Alte Post.

Eating out

On the mountain

The **Rodelalm** (0043 (0)5446 3745/0676 886486100) at Gampen is one of the cosiest restaurants on the mountain. This original Tyrolean hut has an open fireplace, a good terrace and superb local specialities. It is also open at night when the toboggan run is open. The **Hospiz Alm** in St Christoph (0043 (0)5446 3625) is a notorious lunchtime spot. Equally famous for its spectacular wine cellar and slide to the toilet, the Hospiz Alm should not be missed. The **Free-Flow Rendl** restaurant on Rendl (0043 (0)5446 2352–550) serves international cuisine, including tasty wok dishes, and the ice bar outside has live music on Tuesdays and Thursdays. The Galzig run home provides lots of opportunities to stop for a meal or, more usually, a shot or 2. The **Sennhütte** (0043 (0)5446 2048) is popular for its huge sun terrace, and sometimes has live music. The **Krazy Kanguruh** (0043 (0)5446 2633, www.krazykanguruh.com) serves a great burger, and a stop here on the home run is destined to mark the beginnings of a messy après ski session. At the **Mooserwirt** (0043 (0)5446 3588, www.mooserwirt.at) the fun persists, and if you get the munchies, the food's good here, too. In December the TV cameras hit the Mooserwirt to film the RTL *Après Ski Hits* programme.

In town

Some of the best restaurants are also the best bars. The offbeat **Hazienda** (www.hazienda.at, 0043 (0)5446 2968) has top notch steaks, fish, salads and pasta, which should always be preceded by cocktails in front of the open fire. Food is served until 11pm and then the place turns into a night-time hotspot. **Bobo's** (0043 (0)5446 2714, www.bobos.at) similarly turns from a busy Mexican restaurant into an even more hectic bar later on. Staff and punters are all on a mission, which creates a great atmosphere, as long as you don't mind the occasional jarring of the shoulder. Spanish tapas dishes are served in the **Bodega Bar** (0043 (0)5446 42788), open until 1am. **Pomodoro** (0043 (0)5446 3333) and **Scotty's** (0043 (0)5446 2400) are both great pizzerias. For traditional food, **Fuhrmannstube** (0043 (0)5446 2921) is simple but cosy, and great value for money. Traditional dishes are also superb at the rustic chalet **Alt St Anton** (0043 (0)5446 2432) in Nasserein.

For something a little different, the contemporary **ben.venuto** (0043 (0)5446

30203, www.benvenuto.at), at the arlberg-well.com building is worth a visit to sample its fabulous food and stylish, minimalist décor. Though gourmet food (an eclectic mix from Italy and the Orient), it is not ridiculously expensive.

Bars and clubs

The **Krazy Kanguruh** (0043 (0)5446 2633, www.krazykanguruh.com) and the **Mooserwirt** (0043 (0)5446 3588, www.mooserwirt.at) are the best places to celebrate a marvellous day on the mountain and kick start the evening activities, both on the slopes just above the town. The staff at Krazy's 3 bars (Krazy bar, Down Under bar and Ice bar) are ready to quench that thirst but the really crazy parties are going on across the piste at the Mooserwirt.

Back in town you could stop for a drink at the **Anton bar** (0043 (0)5446 2408, www.hotelanton.com) right at the bottom of the slopes – a modern bar with good snacks and meals until 9.30pm. From there it's a short walk to the ever popular **Funky Chicken** (0043 (0)664 4043 360), a crowded après spot, that serves dinner (tasty roast chicken or curry), followed by the dangerous margarita happy hour (11pm–midnight). The nearby **Platzl** bar is rustic, cosy and well lit with a large open fire and live music 10pm–2am. At the centre of the main street is the **Piccadilly** (www.piccadilly-bar.com), more of a British-style pub, once again with live music from 4pm. **Hazienda** is a great night spot, with perfect cocktails (see Eating out) and the tireless **Bobo's** is constantly buzzing with activity (see Eating out). **Post Keller** and **Kandahar** (www.kandaharbar.com) are the clubs to head to, and they often don't chuck you out until gone 6am.

Getting there

By car

Plan your route at www.stantonamarlberg.com

By plane

Innsbruck (100km)
Friedrichshafen (140km) Book your transfer (bus or taxi) on www.airport-bus.at
Zürich (200km) Book your transfer at www.arlbergexpress.com
Munich (250km)
At weekends there are regular bus services from the airports to St Anton.

By train

Take the Eurostar from London St Pancras to Brussels; then the Bergland Express overnight skitrain, changing at Innsbruck, to arrive at St Anton am Arlberg station, in resort. Contact European Rail (020 7387 0444, www.europeanrail.com).

Useful facts and phone numbers

Tourist office

T: 0043 (0)5446 22690
F: 0043 (0)5446 2532
W: www.stantonamarlberg.com

Emergency services

- Police: 0043 (0)5446 2237/236 213
- Mountain rescue: 140 or 0043 (0)5446 2970
- Ambulance: 144
- Fire: 122
- Report ski accidents by calling 2352 (or 2889 in Rendl)
- Hospital (Zams): 0043 (0)5442 600
- Avalanche warning: 0043 (0)512 1588

Doctors

- Day Clinic Arlberg: 0043 (0)5446 42666
- Dr Sprenger: 0043 (0)5446 3200
- Dr Knierzinger: 0043 (0)5446 2828
- Dr Helene Hall: 0043 (0)5446 30392

Taxis

- Taxi Arlberg-Car/Taxi Greisser: 0043 (0)5446 3730
- Taxi Harry: 0043 (0)5446 2315 or 2368
- Taxi Isepponi: 0043 (0)5446 2275 or 2179
- Taxi Lami: 0043 (0)5446 2806

Sölden

Austria's most reliable snow, and raucous, Ibiza-style nightlife.

On the slopes	Rating
Snow reliability	❄❄❄❄❄
Park	❄❄❄
Off-piste	❄❄❄
Off the slopes	
Après ski	❄❄❄❄
Nightlife	❄❄❄❄
Eating out	❄
Resort charm	❄❄

The resort

Sölden is a sprawling town, encompassing around a mile of shops and bars. The buildings are kept traditional and are mostly pretty attractive, although the busy road is a drawback. The après ski is as crazy as it gets and is the reason why some people flock to the place in droves, and others flee as fast as they can.

Though far prettier, the general atmosphere of Sölden's 'party mile' isn't far off that of Blackpool's 'golden mile', so make sure it's your cup of tea before you book your ticket.

The riding is superb for both intermediates and experts, with good on and off-piste terrain, and an excellent park.

Sölden's original events draw crowds, who might gather to watch a re-enactment of Hannibal crossing the Alps (snow cats act as elephants and horsemen fly around on skidoos) or try to build the craziest waterslide vehicle in a bid to win €1000. Sölden isn't a typical picture of Austrian charm but it doesn't try to be – it's all about the fun here.

The mountains

Height: 1350–3250m

Ability	Rating
Expert	❄❄❄
Intermediate	❄❄❄❄
Beginner	❄❄

Getting about

Sölden's mountains have far more redeeming qualities than the town itself. Sölden can happily claim to have the largest glacier terrain in Austria, and connects 3 3000m peaks by lift: Gaislachkogl (3058m), Tiefenbachkogl (3309m) and Schwarze Schneid (3370m). It's worth taking a few hours to tour the 'Big 3 Rally', covering all the peaks and over 50km. Thanks to the altitude, there is good snow right until the end of the season, which is usually early May. However, the lifts on the glacier are no longer open for summer skiing in July and August although they occasionally open in September, depending on conditions.

The 150km of pistes are mostly intermediate and can be reached by 2 cable cars at either end of town. The experts will also be happy with the off-piste potential and great park. For those who enjoy a spot of mogul munching, Sölden has kept areas ungroomed and you can often find some great bumps here. Beginners will be less happy, with their learning area not being particularly convenient.

The park

The 6ha Base Boarders Park can be accessed by taking the Giggijochbahn cable car and then the Heinbachkar chair. The park has a good 70m half pipe, 3 lines of kickers for all standards of rider, and a choice of rails that the shapers change throughout the season. These vary between a gondola rail, snake rail, wallride,2 kinked rails, double-kinked rail, straight rail, 2 boxes, Y down rail, flat down rail and rainbow rail. There's also a boardercross here, although it's not always in the best of conditions.

Off-piste and backcountry

Sölden has some great freeriding areas and there are loads of huge big open faces, but unfortunately a lot of areas are avalanche prone as they get the sun for most of the day. When the conditions are right, start at the top of the Gaislachkogl (3058m) and make your way down the Wasserkar valley, a great spot with a few good cliffs to hook off. It's best to do this one before lunch as it does get tracked out really quickly.

Underneath the Giggijoch bubble lift is another hot spot for some powder turns. There are some nice open runs for first-time freeriders. This leads out into some decent tree runs, but be careful you don't get lost as you could end up with a long walk back to town. It's also worth checking out the unpisted ski routes marked on the map; there's a good track from the top of Rettenbach (2684m) that takes you through the Rettenbachtal Valley and eventually leads back on to the piste. The Freeride centre is opposite SPAR in the town centre – it's worth popping in to check out conditions and avalanche reports. You can also book a guide here (see Freeride Center below).

Lift passes

Check the latest prices at www.soelden.com

Instruction

Freeride Center

Certified mountain guides and experienced freeriders can show you round the mountain.
0043 (0)650 415 3505
www.freeride-center.at

Ski and Snowboard School Aktiv

0043 (0)5253 6313
www.skiaktiv.at

Ski and Snowboard School Sölden-Hochsölden

0043 (0)5254 2364
www.skischule-soelden.com

Ski and Snowboard School Vacancia

0043 (0)5254 3100
www.vacancia.at

Ski and Snowboard School Yellow Power

Organises off-piste guiding.
0043 (0)5254 2255 22
www.yellowpower.at

Other activities

Aqua dome: On a bad day it might be worth taking a 15-minute drive down to the massive aqua dome in Längenfeld (0043 (0)5253 6400, www.aqua-dome.at).

Helicopter rides: Book a flight around the Big 3 (0043 (0)5550 38800, www.wucher.at).

'Romantic nights in your double sleeping bag with a bottle of champagne'

Ice skating: The skating rink, behind the sports centre, is open Sunday–Thursday 2–9pm and Friday 2–5 pm.

Igloo village: Austria's first igloo village sits at 2700m, at the heart of the Rettenbach glacier. There are 8 igloos, each sleeping 2 or 4 people. Igloo activities range from an igloo-building workshop to romantic nights when you settle into your double sleeping bags with a bottle of champagne. Call the tourist office for more information.

Night skiing: This is usually Wednesdays – check with the tourist office – 5.30–8.30pm (last ride up). Passes can be bought at the ticket counters of the Gaislachkogl valley station.

Sledding: A 5km floodlit sledding run is open from the Gaislachalm to the Gaislachkoglbahn station..

Sports centre: The Freizeit Arena sports centre (0043 (0)5254 2514, www.freizeit-soelden.com) offers a water slide, pool, samarium, sauna, steam and herb baths, fitness room, tennis, bowling, badminton and shooting.

Events

The **Back On Snow** parties kick off the season in October. In March/April, Sölden hosts **Gay Snowhappening**. Hundreds of gay men from across Europe in the first and only pan-European gay ski and party week. Another new feature is gay-only ski lessons. Karaoke night and moonlit bowling is popular, as is the non-stop partying. In mid–late April, the re-enactment of **Hannibal crossing the Alps** is pretty impressive, involving 500 actors, planes, paragliders, helicopters, bikers and fireworks. The **Winter Finale** (end April/beginning May) is a massive party weekend, with ski tests and jam sessions on the mountain, live music and DJs throughout the day and night and the **glacier waterslide event** – win €500 for the biggest jump and €1000 for the craziest 'water vehicle'.

'Hannibal crossing the Alps is pretty impressive'

Accommodation

The big and beautiful 5-star **Central Hotel** (0043 (0)5254 22600, www.central-soelden.at) has amazing spa facilities and beauty treatments. **Hotel Regina** (0043 (0)5254 2301, www.hotel-regina.com) is attractive and traditional and has a great pool, and beauty treatments such as wraps and special baths. The 4-star ambience may be slightly spoilt as you sip champagne on your balcony, by your full-frontal view of the naked plastic mermaid on top of the Rodelhütte table-dancing club.

There are tons of good value B&Bs and pensions in and around Sölden. Your best bet is to contact the tourist office, or search online (www.soelden.com) for your specific requirements and dates of travel. If you want to be near the action, double check that the location isn't too far from the main street, as some of the B&Bs are a fair way from town.

Eating out

On the mountain

At the mid station of Gaislachkogl, the **Almstubn** (0043 (0)5254 2214) has 2 big self-service restaurants, a massive sunny terrace and an ice bar. It's also open on Wednesdays during night skiing. At the top station of the Gaislachkogl, on the second floor, is **Tre Milla** (0043 (0)5254 508 888), the Alps' highest pizzeria at 2058m. The views of peaks are superb from here. The quaint **Huhnersteign** (0043 (0)5254 2872), on the Rettenbach glacier ski route, is one of the best huts on the mountain for a good lunch in the sun.

Gampe Alm (0043 (0)5254 2144) and **Gampe Thaya** (0043 (0)664 240 0246) on ski trail 11, between Hochsölden and Gaislachkogl, are both good rustic mountain huts with cosy atmospheres and table service. **Eugens Obstlerhütte** (0043 (0)5254 2186), on the run from Hochsölden to Sölden, is a great place to stop for a beer at the end of the day.

In town

The restaurants in town aren't the best selection we've ever seen, but as you'll probably be too drunk to remember them it shouldn't cause you too much heartache.

The best pizzeria in town is the **Nudeltopf** (0043 (0)5254 2010, www.nudeltopf.at), and **Armin's Törggle** (0043 (0)5254 3535) has good-value local fare. Mexican food can be found at the **Hacienda** restaurant (0043 (0)5254 3526), above the tourist office. The restaurant in **Hotel Dominic** (0043 (0)5254 2646, www.dominic.at) is one of the smarter places to dine. There's nothing we'd get too excited about.

Bars and clubs

As you ride down the mountain at the end of the day you cannot miss the après ski hangouts, with folks clomping around on tables, happily swinging their beers. If you come down the slopes into Ausserwald, stop at **Philipp's** (0043 (0)5254 2351, www.philipp-soelden.at) for a few beverages.

Back in town, the atmosphere continues in many bars along Sölden's sprawling streets. **Fire and Ice** (www.apresskisoelden.at), **Bierhimml** and the glass-housed **Bla Bla** at the Dominic hotel are 3 of the best bars to start at. **Hinterher** (0043 (0)5254 2771), **Ötzi Keller** (0043 (0)5254 2240) and **Lawine**, under hotel Tyrolerhof, are all good bar/clubs to move on to and are open late. To see some naked ladies strutting their stuff, head to the classy-looking **Rodelhütte** (0043 (0)5254 3133).

Getting there

By car

Sölden's website (www.soelden.com) has a very user-friendly route planner to help you find your way there by car.

By plane

Innsbruck (85km) Transfer time is just 1 hour. *Munich, Zürich, Salzberg* and *Bozen* (all 210–280km) Transfer time is 2.5–3.5 hours. Transfers with Four Seasons travel (www.airport-transfer.com).

By train

Take the Eurostar from London St Pancras to Brussels; then the Bergland Express overnight skitrain, changing in Innsbruck, to Otzal, and then a local bus (60 minutes) to the resort. Contact European Rail (020 7387 0444, www.europeanrail.com). Bus tickets are purchased on the bus.

Useful facts and phone numbers

Tourist office

T: 0043 (0)5254 5100
F: 0043 (0)5254 510 201
W: www.soelden.com

Emergency services

- Police: 0043 (0)5254 2206
- Ambulance (Rotes Kreuz): 0043 (0)5254 2360
- In the case of an accident on the mountain: 0043 (0)5254 508 825

Doctors

- Dr Gerhard Leys: 0043 (0)5254 2040
- Dr Edgar Wutscher: 0043 (0)5254 2207
- Dr Wolfgang Drapela: 0043 (0)5254 30399

Taxis

- Taxi Quaxi: 0043 (0)5254 3737, www.taxiquaxibusreisen.com
- Taxi Lenz: 0043 (0)5254 2133, www.taxi-lenz.at

Zell am See

A small, attractive resort, geared towards the intermediate rider.

On the slopes	Rating
Snow reliability	❄❄❄
Park	❄❄
Off-piste	❄❄
Off the slopes	
Après ski	❄❄❄❄
Nightlife	❄❄❄
Eating out	❄❄❄
Resort charm	❄❄❄

The resort

Zell am See is a small resort by the side of a lake, full of character and Austrian charm. Despite its size, there are a decent number of good shops, bars and clubs. The mountains are just as beautiful as the town, and perfect for cruising and taking in the views. The terrain is great for beginners and intermediates but it's not extensive, and the experienced rider will cover the mountain quickly. The snowsure Kaprun glacier ensures that Zell is also popular in the summer for glacier skiing in the morning and watersports in the afternoon.

The mountains

Height: 755–3030m

Ability	Rating
Expert	❄
Intermediate	❄❄❄❄
Beginner	❄❄❄

'Zell is also popular in the summer'

Getting about

There are 130km of piste in Zell am See and the longest is 4km. To ski the Schmittenhöhe, avoid the main cable car from town as the queues can be pretty hideous. It's best to catch the newly extended Areit gondola from neighboring Schüttdorf direct to the Breiteck peak. If the snow suffers in Zell am See you can always head to the glacier at Kaprun, beneath the peak of the Kitzsteinhorn, which is less than 10km away.

Zell am See will appeal to beginners and intermediates, but is less suited to experts. There are a couple of runs that are used for the World Cup and other downhill races, which are open to the public when events aren't on but that's about it. It is also not the place to find the steep and deep. There are a few areas just off the pistes and in the trees, but nothing major. Try the Magnetköpl and Langwiedbahn routes. The slopes also receive a lot of sun, so the snow can suffer.

The park

From the Sonnenkarbahn chair (2600m) you can drop into the easy or central park. These two parks combine 9 rails and 15 kickers and between them have 2 easy lines with small kickers, easy rollers, a funbox and a straight rail, two medium lines with 5–10m tables, kinked boxes and a 6m rainbow box. The one pro-line has a black 8m step-down kicker, two 15m table tops and a trickier 8m kinked box. There is also a smaller 200m park at 3000m – the Gletscher Park with an easy and medium line. Check out http://snowpark.kitzsteinhorn.at.

Lift passes

Check the latest prices at www.europasportregion.info

Instruction

Offpiste Adventures
0043 (0)6542 20214
www.offpiste.at

Sport Alpin Zell am See
0043 (0)664 4531417
www.sport-alpin.at

Ski and Snowboardschule Zell am See
0043 (0)6542 56020
www.ski-zellamsee.at

Other activities

Bowling alley: This is located at Schlosstrasse (0043 (0)6547 8222).

Drive on ice: This can be done in cars or on quads in Kaprun (067684 652235, www.winterpark.at), open Sunday to Friday, 2–8pm. There is also a bouncy castle and snow tubing for kids.

Horse ride in the snow: Call Porsche Reitanlagen on 06542 57362 or Reitanlage Badhaus on 0664 551902.

Paragliding: Contact Flugplatz Zell am See (06742 56041).

Snow kiting: Practise your tricks at up to 75km/hr on Lake Zell. You can also ice skate and curl on the lake.

Sports Centre: The Kaprun Optimum has a fitness room and indoor and outdoor swimming pool (06547 7666). There is also an indoor swimming pool at Freizeitzentrum in Zell am See (06542 7850).

Tobogganing: There is a floodlit toboggan run from Gasthof Köhlergraben in Zell am See.

Accommodation

Hotel Berner (0043 (0)6542 799, www.bernerhotel.com) is beautiful and a great place to relax after a hard day on the slopes. It's run by 2 brothers who take great pleasure in making sure that you get well looked after. The restaurant and food are fantastic and you can take advantage of the outdoor pools and games room. The best thing about the hotel is that you can ski or board right from the door.

To bling it up, stay in the only 5-star in town, the **Hotel Salzburgerhof** (0043 (0)6542 765, www.salzburgerhof.at). The hotel includes a wellness centre, sauna, beautiful indoor and outdoor swimming pools, solarium, massage facilities and amazing food in its award-winning restaurant.

For slightly cheaper accommodation, check out the excellent **Gasthof Steinerwirt** (0043 (0)6542 72502, www.steinerwirt.com), a 2-star hotel that's not far from the slopes or the main shops and bars.

Eating out

On the mountain

There are some lovely mountain huts in Zell am See. The **Ebenbergalm** (0043 (0)664 351 2307), on Schmittenhöhe, is a cosy hut with a small terrace, just above the main town. The **Pinzgauer Hütte** (0043 (0)6542 7861) serves a good variety of food, including local specialities, and has great views. The **Schmitten Pfiff** (0043 (0)6542 789 221) has amazing panoramic views. The **Schmittenhöhe** at the Berghotel (0043 (0)6542 72489, www.berghotel-schmitten.at) has parties on the terrace and is a good choice of hotel if you want to be the first person on the slopes.

In town

For a tasty steak head to the **Tauernstüberl** (0043 (0)6542 57174) or the **Steinerwirt**. **Pizzeria Giuseppe** (0043 (0)6542 72373) or **Zum Cäsar** (06542 47257, www.caesar.at) serve great pizzas and the **Crazy** restaurant at Crazy Daisy's (www.crazy-daisy.at) has a Mexican restaurant attached to the bar and it's good value food too. For award-winning gourmet food, head to the **Schloss Prielau** (0043 (0)6542 72609) or the **Zur Einkehr** bistro (0043 (0)6542 72363).

Bars and clubs

The most popular place in Zell am See is **Crazy Daisy's** – there is a band playing every night and it's always jam packed. If you want to hang around with the locals head to the Bierstadl. If you're feeling a bit more chilled, head to the **Hirschenkeller** where you can listen to blues, rock and reggae music. The **Pinzgauer Diele** is a great venue for après ski and it is also one of the best spots for dancing until the early hours. The **Viva Club** gets quite crazy late at night and has live music and DJs.

> 'One of the best spots for dancing until the early hours'

Getting there

By car

From the north of Austria head towards Munich and continue on the motorway towards Salzburg. At Siegsdorf follow the street south to Lofer, Saalfelden and Zell am See. Drivers coming from the east should take the motorway Vienna – Salzburg – Bischofshofen. There get off and follow the signs through St Johann, Schwarzach, Bruck to Zell am See. Coming from the west gives you the choice between the motorway Stuttgart – Munich – Salzburg or Bregenz – Innsbruck – Wörgl.

By plane

Salzburg (100km) There is a regular bus from Salzburg to Zell am See. Check out http://engl.salzburg-airport.com/bus.html or book a transfer through www.vorderegger.at or www.holiday-shuttle.at
Munich (250km)

By train

Take the Eurostar from London St Pancras to Brussels; then the Bergland Express overnight skitrain to arrive at Zell am See station, in resort. Contact European Rail (020 7387 0444, www.europeanrail.com).

Useful facts and phone numbers

Tourist office

T: 0043 (0)6542 770
W: www.europasportregion.info

Emergency services

- In all emergencies call 112/122
- Hospital: 0043 (0)6542 777

Doctors

- Dr Helmuth Barth: 0043 (0)6542 56766, office@meddoc.at
- Dr Wolfgang Göttlicher: 0043 (0)6542 72136
- Dr Johann Hanl: 0043 (0)6542 47360

Taxis

- Taxi Rainer: 0043 (0)6541 6261, zellamsee@taxi-saalbach.at
- Taxi for You: 0043 (0)664 33 44 888, info@taxizell.at www.taxizell.at

France

The home of many of the big commercial resorts, with a few hidden gems.

Alpe d'Huez

A great resort for all levels of rider.

On the slopes	Rating
Snow reliability	❄❄❄❄
Parks	❄❄❄
Off-piste	❄❄❄½
Off the slopes	
Après ski	❄❄❄
Nightlife	❄❄❄
Eating out	❄❄❄
Resort charm	❄❄

The resort

Alpe d'Huez is a fantastic all-round resort. The mountain is extensive, and suits all standards of rider. The resort has great snow conditions and off-piste, and it also gets a lot of sun, which can take its toll on the piste, but is great when there is a big snowfall and bluebird skies the next day.

We like the town, and find the locals really friendly, but this opinion is not universal; many people think that the resort is fairly ugly and has retained little of its traditional French charm. Alpe d'Huez is less well known than the big resorts, but it's starting to give them a run for their money, and the following of Brits who return year after year is steadily rising. As snow reliability is increasingly important, the snowsure, high-altitude slopes add to the value of Alpe d'Huez. It also helps that Alpe d'Huez is only an hour from Grenoble airport. Your ski pass also covers a day in Les Deux Alpes – take the bus or travel in style in a helicopter (contact Delta Evasion, 0033 (0)6 08 32 49 59, www.deltaevasion.com).

The mountains

Height: 1100–3330m

Ability	Rating
Expert	❄❄❄❄
Intermediate	❄❄❄❄
Beginner	❄❄❄❄

Getting about

Pic Blanc is the highest peak in the Grandes Rousses Massif at 3330m and offers breathtaking views of the national Ecrins Park and its peaks. The altitude almost guarantees good snow, although the sun can do some damage later in the season. There are 245km of pistes, offering a wealth of slopes for all levels of rider. Make sure that you explore the far corners of the ski area, such as the runs to Oz and Vaujany, as you will find some lovely peaceful slopes and great pit stops for lunch. The 16km Sarenne black run is the longest in Europe, but it isn't as difficult as your average black. Le Tunnel and Combe Charbonniere are also great places to push yourself.

The park

Alpe d'Huez has 2 snowparks. The beginners', kids' and freestylers' park has boxes, rails, whoops and a slide bar area. The experts' park is near the Lac Blanc lift and offers 4 big air jumps, slide bars, a wave rail, a C-box, a hip, a street rail, 2 totems, a half pipe and a boardercross.

Off-piste and backcountry

Alpe d'Huez has some of the best areas for backcountry riding in the Alps. Most of the terrain is above the tree line, which can cause a problem if there is a big storm or serious cloud cover. The 3300m Pic Blanc is the starting point for a number of itineraries including the Grand Sablat, which runs through the east face of the Massif des Grandes Rousses. Other routes from the Pic Blanc are the Combe du Loup and a long descent via Couloir de Fare.

> 'Most of the terrain is above the tree line'

Other places to explore are the back bowls of Auris and the bowls on Dome des Petites Rousses where you will find couloir l'impossible, couloir 263, col de l'Herpie, the chimneys and many more. With a helicopter you can drop into the Pyramids by rope, which is challenging but superb. You definitely need a guide to explore these areas safely.

There are some tree runs under the Villarais chair and above Vaujany. As well as a guide, for many routes you will also need to organise transport to get back to the resort.

Check with the Bureau des Guides for booking and more information.

Lift passes

Check the latest prices at www.alpedhuez.com

Instruction

British Masterclass

The Masterclass are top ski and snowboard instructors, with a great reputation.
0033 (0)4 76 80 93 83
www.masterclass-ski.co.uk

Bureau des Guides

As well as guides, they also offer a number of other activities, including off-piste skiing in groups, heliskiing, ski touring and ice climbing.
0033 (0)4 76 80 42 55
www.guidesalpedhuez.com

ESF

The ESF has a big range of ski and snowboard instructors, most of whom are English speaking.
0033 (0)4 76 80 31 69
www.esf-alpedhuez.com

ESI

0033 (0)4 76 80 42 77
www.ecoledeskiinternationale.com

Other activities

Ice driving: The Eclose ice track is a highly specialised training ground for professional racing drivers. Here, you can have a lesson on how to drive on ice and snow, or learn more advanced skills. Call 0033 (0)476 806 997.

> 'The ice track is a highly specialised training ground'

Ice skating: The public open air rink on the Avenue des Jeux (0033 (0)476 112 116) is open daily 10am–11pm except when it is hosting events. It also has a curling rink.

Indoor heated swimming pool: Entry is free with a VISALP lift pass, open daily 10am–8pm. There is also a sauna and Jacuzzi. Don't wear swimming shorts – only trunks are allowed.

Night skiing: The signal slalom stadium is a 950km piste, floodlit for 2 nights a week.

Night skiing is free for those who have a VISALP pass for 2 days or more.

Paragliding: Alpe d'Huez Parapente (0033 (0)6 89 09 49 39), Element'air (0033 (0)6 73 37 03 39 or 0033 (0)046 113 172) and Delta Evasion (0033 (0)6 08 32 49 59, www.deltaevasion.com) offer paragliding. You can also hang-glide and microlight.

Sports and convention centre: There is a wide range of activities from martial arts and orienteering to squash and tennis (0033 (0)4 76 11 21 41). Many activities are free with the VISALP pass.

Tobogganing: The night-time toboggan run on the Butte de l'Eclose slope (Tuesday and Thursday, 5.30–7.30pm) is free for those with the VISALP pass.

Yoga: Contact 0033 (0)6 25 54 79 73 for details.

Accommodation

The 4-star **Hotel Au Chamois d'Or** (0033 (0)4 76 80 31 32, www.chamoisdor-alpedhuez.com) is in a fantastic location for access to the pistes and lifts, and it is equally well suited for the shops, restaurants and bars. It has good facilities, with swimming pool, Jacuzzi and fitness room.

'Good restaurants, fitness centre and swimming pool'

The other 4-star hotel in town is the **Royal Ours Blanc** (0033 (0)4 76 80 35 50, www.hotelroyaloursblanc.com), a huge hotel, not in the prettiest building, but with good restaurants, fitness centre and swimming pool. **Hotel Les Grandes Rousses** (0033 (0)4 76 80 33 11, www.hotel-grandes-rousses-alpe-huez.federal-hotel.com) is a beautiful and charming, 3-star, chalet-style hotel, in the centre of Alpe d'Huez, 50m from the lifts with a nice little pool.

Eating out

On the mountain

For some tasty gourmet food, head to the bottom of the Marmottes gondola, where you will find **La Cabane du Poutat** (0033 (0)4 76 80 42 88). The **Auberge de l'Alpette** (0033 (0)4 76 80 70 00) has the best omelettes and salads and the **Chalet du Lac Besson** (0033 (0)4 76 80 65 37) is a superb restaurant for rustic French charm, with a big open fire and a sun terrace. Make sure you book in advance. **Le Signal** (0033 (0)4 76 80 39 54) has some of the best views around.

In town

Alpe d'Huez has a good selection of restaurants – from high-quality, gourmet cuisine, to snack bars with great value burgers and slices of pizza. **Le Génépi** (0033 (0)4 76 80 36 22) has superb traditional Savoyard food to be enjoyed in the cosy, rustic atmosphere. **P'tit Creux** (0033 (0)4 76 80 62 80) is a great place for top of the range food, but it's not cheap. **Smithy's Tavern** (0033 (0)4 76 11 32 29, www.smithystavern.com) is one of our favourite places to stop for a bite. The Tex Mex can be a welcome break from the traditional raclettes and fondues and there is always a good, busy atmosphere. **Les Epiciers** at L'Ours Blanc (0033 (0)4 76 80 41 14) is another real favourite.

Bars and clubs

Smithy's (see In town) is one of our favourite bars in town, run by 2 brothers, who also have a Smithy's branch in Les Deux Alpes. Loads of action is guaranteed in here. Our other favourite bars are the **Pacific** bar and the **Underground** (0033 (0)4 76 80 31 39, www.holidayalps.com/the-underground-bar). Live music is often on at the **Sporting bar,** and **O'Sharkey's** (0033 (0)4 76 11 36 39) and **The Crowded House** are popular. To finish the night off in true fashion, you can dance the night away in the **Igloo**.

Getting there

By car

There are 682 covered parking spaces. Call the Town Hall (0033 (0)4 76 11 21 21) for more information.

By plane

Grenoble (99km)
Lyon (150km)
Chambéry (140km)
Geneva (220km)

By train

Take the Eurostar from London St Pancras to Paris; then by TGV to Grenoble; and then a bus (90 minutes) to the resort. Contact Rail Europe (0870 830 4862, www.raileurope.co.uk) or European Rail (020 7387 0444, www.europeanrail.com). Bus tickets must be purchased in advance from VFD coaches (0033 (0)4 76 60 46 37, www.vfd.fr).

Useful facts and phone numbers

Tourist office

T: 0033 (0)4 76 11 44 44
F: 0033 (0)4 76 80 69 54
W: www.alpedhuez.com

Emergency services

- Ambulance: 0033 (0)4 76 80 28 00
- Fire: 18 or 0033 (0)0 00 00 00 18
- Police station (Alpe d'Huez): 0033 (0)4 76 80 32 44
- Police station (Bourg d'Oisans): 0033 (0)4 76 80 00 17
- Mountain rescue: 0033 (0)4 76 80 65 49
- Piste safety: 0033 (0)4 76 80 37 38

Doctors

- Dr Darmon and Dr Achkar: 0033 (0)4 76 80 37 30
- Dr Robert: 0033 (0)4 76 80 69 29
- Dr Burghgraeve and Dr Decoster: 0033 (0)4 76 80 35 84

Taxis

- Agence de taxi S Chalvin: 0033 (0)4 76 80 38 38
- F Duclot: 0033 (0)4 76 80 20 81

Les Arcs

An extensive, versatile mountain and some great places to stay, if you do your research.

On the slopes	Rating
Snow reliability	❄❄❄❄
Parks	❄❄❄
Off-piste	❄❄❄❄
Off the slopes	
Après ski	❄❄❄
Nightlife	❄❄❄
Eating out	❄❄❄
Resort charm	❄❄❄❄ for 1950
	❄❄ for 1800

The resort

Les Arcs has 4 resorts at different levels: Arc 1600, Arc 1800 (which itself is split into Charvet, Villards and Charmettoger), the beautiful new Arc 1950 and Arc 2000. We don't particularly like Arc 1600 or Arc 2000. Arc 2000 has good access to the slopes but that's about it. However, we like the rest of Les Arcs, so we're going to ignore them and refer to only Arc 1800 and Arc 1950.

Arc 1800 (Charvet, Villards and Charmettoger) isn't beautiful, but it's not ugly either and there's lots going on. Charvet and Villards are centred round slightly claustrophobic open-air shopping centres and Charmettoger is prettier in the trees but it's a 10–15 minute walk to the bars in Villards.

The brand-new Arc 1950 is stunning. It's in the last stages of being built by the Canadian company Intrawest, and it has a certain Canadian feel to it. The apartments are spacious and modern and the buildings are colourful. With its friendly, village atmosphere, 1950 is becoming a focal point of Les Arcs and is a perfect base for families. The success of 1950 seems to be catching on – another satellite resort, Edenarc 1800, consisting of 330 apartments, is being built on a new site above the village of Les Arcs 1800, with a gondola to link it to the slopes.

The mountains

Height: 1200–3326m

Ability	Rating
Expert	❄❄❄❄
Intermediate	❄❄❄❄
Beginner	❄❄❄❄

Getting about

In Les Arcs there are 200km of pistes (105 pistes in total) and within the whole Paradiski area (combining Les Arcs and La Plagne) there is a massive 425km. The terrain is fabulously varied, with slopes for all levels, good backcountry areas, and woodland runs for bad-weather days. Most of the runs are ideal for cruising intermediates. The Aiguille Rouge is the highest point in the ski area at 3226m and from here there are some great steep runs down to Le Planay or Le Pré. Some of the best runs are down to Villaroger and the reds to Vallandry. Les Arcs is 1 of the few resorts to have its own speed skiing area: the Flying Kilometre. See how fast you can go; the world record at the moment is 256kph.

The park

The Les Arcs park, named Apocalypse (www.lesarcs.com), has always been popular amongst the ski and board bums who live in the resort or travel up from Bourg St Maurice. Three shapers are keeping it in tiptop condition, and Apocalypse Parc now consists of 1 hip, 4 rails, 10 table tops and 1 pipe. Set out in green, red and black runs, this park has a great, friendly atmosphere and it's good for all standards. There's also a flood-lit half pipe in Arc 2000.

Off-piste and backcountry

Les Arcs is a tremendous place for freeriding as so much terrain is available now that it is linked with La Plagne. If the conditions are good and the lifts are open, it's worth heading up the Aiguille Rouge cable car. Underneath there are loads of steeps and couloirs and it's here that they hold the famous North Face Freeride competition, which attracts the best big mountain freeriders in the world. The cable car is often closed due to high winds, but on a perfect powder day, you will love it. It's an area for the experts as it is quite challenging. If the weather's not so great, it doesn't matter as there are loads of tree lines above 1600m. Also the Trans Arc cable car gives you easy access to some wicked riding down to Nancroix that always seems to be in good condition. For more off-piste exploits in the Paradiski area, check out La Plagne (see page 111). To make the most of this amazing mountain, it's worth hiring a guide to show you all the secret backcountry hide-out spots.

Lift passes

Check the latest prices at www.lesarcs.com/ www.arc1950.com

Instruction

Arc Aventures (1800)

Arguably the best school in Les Arcs.
0033 (0)4 79 07 60 02
www.arc-aventures.com

ESF Arc 1800

There are 90 qualified instructors here.
0033 (0)4 79 07 40 31
www.esflesarcs.com

Privilege (1800)

0033 (0)4 79 07 23 38
contact@ecoledeskiprivilege.com

Spirit 1950

Heliskiing and freeriding, group and private lessons for skiing and snowboarding.
0033 (0)4 79 04 25 72
www.spirit1950.com

Other activities

Bowling: (Arc 1800) Call the Aiguille des Glaciers (0033 (0)4 79 06 97 76).

Helicopter trips: Call Heli Mountains (0033 (0)6 11 74 38 83, www.helimountains.com) for details of trips over Mont Blanc or the Paradiski area.

Hot air balloon rides, overnight igloo stays, dog sled trips: You can do any of these with Nordic Adventures (0033 (0)6 09 49 32 07).

Ice drive: Drive on ice with Ecole de Pilotage (0033 (0)6 08 06 67 22 or 0033 (0)6 07 06 34 42).

Massage: Be soothed and re-energised in your own accommodation (0033 (0)6 12 65 34 52).

Night skiing: Take to the slopes at night on Tuesdays and Thursdays on the Chantel chair in 1800 (free).

Paragliding: Arc Aventures (0033 (0)4 79 07 60 02) offers paragliding.

Skidoo: With Arc Aventures (see above) you can take out a skidoo after the lifts have shut, either as a passenger or driver, led by a guide. You have to ride round a selected track and follow speed limits and safety guidelines so you won't be able to go crazy.

Events

The **Columbia Speedflying Pro** takes place in Les Arcs usually in January, a hugely acclaimed event that attracts the world's professionals. The **Robert Blanc Derby** is a fun race from Grand Col to Pré St Espirit.

Accommodation

Most accommodation is in the form of apartments, although there are 1 or 2 hotels. You can book apartments directly with the tourist office (0033 (0)4 79 07 68 00), but you can also expect to pay a booking handling fee, tourist tax, damage deposit and for bed linen.

1800

The best of the hotels is the smart **Grand Hotel Paradiso** (0033 (0)4 79 07 65 00, www.grand-hotel-lesarcs.com), about a 10-minute walk from Villards, which has more bars and restaurants than Charmettoger.

The **Latitudes Hotel du Golf** (0033

(0)892 35 04 02) in Charvet has a great location. Inside are 2 restaurants: the Petit Zinc restaurant is massive and impersonal, but the Restaurant du Golf is good. The hotel also contains the Bar Le Swing jazz bar and the Mont Blanc Bar, which is pretty cool.

1950

Book your apartment with either **Pierre and Vacances** (www.pierreetvacances.com), whose comfortable apartments sleep 2–10 people, or with the 4-star **Radisson SAS Resort Arc** 1950 (0033 (0)4 79 23 10 00, www.arc1950.radissonsas.com). They have apartments with 1–4 rooms. All of the apartments for Pierre and Vacances and Radisson SAS have access to a health spa with a swimming pool, sauna and Turkish bath, fitness training and solarium as well as an open-air heated swimming pool and Jacuzzi and the apart-hotel has underground parking and WiFi internet connection. The tour operators Erna Low and Neilson do packages to 1950.

Eating out

On the mountain

The mountain restaurants in Les Arcs aren't amazing on the whole. One that is outstanding is **Chalets de l'Arc** (0033 (0)4 79 04 15 40, www.restaurant-savoie.com), above Arc 2000. It is really cosy with a wood and stone décor and fantastic service and it's also open in the evenings. For good views, try **The Solliet** (0033 (0)6 65 65 61 44, www.solliet.com), above Le Pré, or the restaurant at the **Col de la Chal**. The **Chalet de Luigi** (0033 (0)6 08 57 23 36), in 1950 town, has a large, south-facing terrace alongside Marmottes piste. This smart restaurant offers a welcome break from Savoyard food and burgers, with homemade pastas and proscuitto its speciality. Inside, the high ceilings and wooden beams complete the luxurious European/American chalet feel.

In town

Charvet (1800)

In Charvet (1800), the **Mountain Café** (0033 (0)4 79 07 00 89) is a popular Tex Mex restaurant with long wooden tables. **L'Hedoniste** (0033 (0)4 79 01 40 02) wine bar and eatery is a tiny restaurant (14 covers) and really cute. They serve soups, oysters and a number of different boards of food such as the gourmet board (including duck and homemade foie gras), a Savoyard board or a butcher's board. A number of wines and sparkling wines are served by the glass. **Chez Les Filles** (0033 (0)4 79 04 14 55) has fantastic views and is really friendly. They serve pancakes, local specialities and salads at lunchtime and traditional Savoyard fare in the evenings. The Italian-run **Casa Mia** (0033 (0)4 79 07 05 75) is a charming restaurant. At lunchtimes it serves the usual pizzas, etc and at night the gastronomic Italian and Savoyard specialities are brought out. **Chez Boubou** (0033 (0)4 79 07 40 86) serves English breakfast and good-value burgers and chips.

Villards (1800)

There are loads of places serving Brit-friendly foods, including the **Jungle Café** (0033 (0)4 79 07 19 62) and **Red Hot Saloon** (0033 (0)4 79 07 74 52, www.redhotsaloon.com).

1950

In 1950 the lovely, spacious and smart **Chalet de Luigi** (0033 (0)6 08 57 23 36) serves fresh, homemade pasta and other delights at lunchtimes and in the evenings. **Café Hemmingway** (0033 (0)4 79 07 34 36) is a nice café serving fish, meat dishes and local specialities. The Asian restaurant **EAST** (0033 (0)4 79 00 19 57) is a great additon to 1950 and **Los Chicanos** (0033 (0)4 79 00 22 58) brings a trendy and colourful Spanish/South American feel. Try **Il Valentino** (0033 (0)4 79 07 56 48) for pizza.

Bars and clubs

Charvet (1800)

In Charvet (1800), **Chez Boubou** (0033 (0)4 79 07 40 86) and the **Gabotte** (0033 (0)4 79 07 41 86) are popular with the locals for a cheeky après beer.

Villards (1800)

The largest selection of bars is to be found in Villards (1800). **Ambiente** (0033 (0)4 79 07 49 51, www.ambientecafe.fr) is a cool après bar. The **Jungle Café** (0033 (0)4 79 07 19 62) serves steaks, pastas, omelettes and not-cheap burgers. Their cocktails are great, but also pricey. The tables can be folded up to allow dancing. In the massive

Red Hot Saloon (0033 (0)4 79 07 74 52, www.redhotsaloon.com) there's a lot to keep punters entertained: live music, theme nights, pool, and sports on big TVs. They serve salads and sarnies 12–4pm and a full menu 4–10pm. Happy hour is 5–6pm. When you stumble out of the Saloon, head to the **Apokalypse** nightclub (0033 (0)4 79 07 43 77, www.theapokalypse.com).

1950

In 1950 **Les Belles Pintes** (0033 (0)4 79 04 25 55) is an 'Irish pub' (as perceived by Canadians, not the Irish) open 11am–1am. Happy hour is 5.30–6.30pm and they also have pool and darts. They serve hot dogs and sandwiches, burgers and chips, croque monsieurs and bruschetta 12–2.30pm. **Le Chalet de Luigi**, as well as having a top restaurant, has a bar and a nightclub, **Le Club 1950** (0033 (0)4 79 00 05 17). The bar is open every day from early morning until 4am.

Getting there

By car

You will need to park in the underground car park in 1950 if you drive there. Contact 0033 (0)4 79 04 12 37, www.resaplace.com.

By plane

Lyon (200km) Transfers can be booked through Satobus (0033 (0)4 37 255 255, www.satobus.com.

Geneva (145km) Transfers can be booked through www.alpski-bus.com or www.altibus.com (0041 (0)22 798 20 00).

Heliport transfers can also be booked on 0033 (0)6 11 74 38 83.

Chambéry (120km) Transfers can be booked through Trans'neige (0033 (0)4 79 68 32 90).

By train

Take the Eurostar from London St Pancras to Paris; then an overnight train to Bourg St Maurice, and then a funicular train (7 minutes) to the resort. Contact Rail Europe (0870 830 4862, www.raileurope.co.uk) or European Rail (020 7387 0444, www.europeanrail.com). Funicular tickets are purchased at the station.

Useful facts and phone numbers

Tourist office

T: 0033 (0)4 79 07 30 20 (1950)/0033 (0)4 79 07 61 11 (1800)
W: www.lesarcs.com/www.arc1950.com

Direct reservations 1800

T: 0033 (0)4 79 07 68 00
F: 0033 (0)4 79 07 68 99
W: www.lesarcs.com

Direct reservations 1950

T: 0033 (0)4 79 23 10 00
W: www.radissonblu.com

Emergency services

- Slopes rescue: 0033 (0)4 79 07 85 66
- Fire: 18

Doctors

- Cabinet Médical Arc 1600: 0033 (0)4 79 07 78 57
- Cabinet Médical Arc 1950: 0033 (0)4 79 00 44 43
- Cabinet Médical Arc 2000: 0033 (0)4 79 07 30 01
- Centre Médical du Charvet: 0033 (0)4 79 07 46 41
- Centre Médical des Villards: 0033 (0)4 79 07 49 99
- Hospital in Bourg St Maurice: 0033 (0)4 79 41 79 79

Taxis and airport transfers

- Taxi Boirat: 0033 (0)6 13 61 63 10/0033 (0)6 03 22 72 68
- Borne taxis à Bourg St Maurice: 0033 (0)4 79 07 03 94
- Airport transfers: 0033 (0)4 79 07 04 49

Avoriaz

The most convenient resort in the Alps – spectacular and charming.

On the slopes	Rating
Snow reliability	❄❄❄
Parks	❄❄❄❄
Off-piste	❄❄❄
Off the slopes	
Après ski	❄❄❄
Nightlife	❄❄❄
Eating out	❄❄
Resort charm	❄❄❄½

The resort

Avoriaz is unique. The design and architecture of the town is very '60s, but it was nevertheless well thought out and there is something spectacular and charming about its crazily angled structure, enhanced by its impressive setting on the edge of a cliff. One of the really exceptional features is that practically all the accommodation is ski-in ski-out. As the village is car-free and very wide, everyone whacks on their equipment outside their apartment and cruises down to the lift – a much preferable way to start the day than cumbersome bus journeys and long walks. The mountains are unquestionably superb, with Avoriaz being bang in the centre of the massive Portes du Soleil circuit that unites the slopes of France and Switzerland. In 1993 Avoriaz was the first resort in France to build a terrain park and half pipe and the resort still pulls in the best freestyle snowboarders and skiers in the world to its international competitions.

If you are looking for luxurious accommodation think again – there is only 1 hotel that could be described as such, Les Dromonts (see Accommodation); most of the apartments are pretty cramped.

The mountains

Height: 975–2466m

Ability	Rating
Expert	❄❄❄
Intermediate	❄❄❄❄
Beginner	❄❄❄

Getting about

This resort is great for mixed ability groups, but Avoriaz particularly appeals to intermediates who can cruise around the 650km of pistes in the Portes du Soleil cicuit choosing a new area to explore each day (might be an idea to ditch the unhelpful piste map and look to the on-piste signage). For a challenging black run, Plan Brazy is a good bet, and you will end up (weather permitting) in Les Prodains or head to the notoriously mogully Swiss Wall.

Transportation within Avoriaz

Within Avoriaz you can get about in sledges or shuttles. You have 3 options when it comes to transporting you, your mates/family and your luggage to your accommodation:

Using the baggage sledges should be fine if you are staying in the Falaise area (chalets de la Falaise, Chapka, Douchka, Elinka, Kouria, Malinka, Néve, Saskia, Tilia) as it's really close to the car park/dropping-off point.

Between 8am and 7pm you can hire a sledge to transport you. Between 7pm and 8am you will need a shuttle.

If you are travelling on a Saturday as most people are you don't need to worry about organising or calling up for transportation, as there are assistants all over the place and they'll call a sledge for you. At any other time you will need to call 0033 (0)4 50 74 01 55.

The park

Avoriaz definitely knows how to build and look after its 3 parks. They have some big sponsors putting money behind them so they can now afford to have 6 full-time shapers working hard to keep it sweet! In Arare, the upper park has some decent sized kickers, rails, a corner jump and a half pipe, and sometimes you will find a step-up, quarter pipe or a spine. In La Chapelle on the field of Super-Morzine, there are 6 kickers of all different dimensions, 5 rails, a skier and boardercross and a super pipe where they hold the O'Neill freestyle pro event. The Avoriaz parks are among some of the most respected in Europe, so if parks are your thing, you should give Avoriaz a try. Check out the website www.snowparkavoriaz.com The Stash is in the forest of Lindarets accessed from the Prolays chair, and includes various obstacles for jibbing. Great fun for all levels of freestyler.

You also have access to 1 of the best parks in Europe at Les Crozats, on the Swiss side (see Champéry chapter, page 170). There is also a new snowpark for kids aged 5–12, called 'Trashers'.

Off-piste and backcountry

Avoriaz has a fair bit to offer in terms of off-piste, never mind the whole of the Portes du Soleil (see Morzine and Champéry chapters, pages 107 and 170). The top of the Combe du Machon chairlift is a great place to start. From here, you can explore either the terrain off the back of the Coupe de Monde run (with a guide/local) or the more accessible powder on the Crozats side. From the Fornet lift you can traverse to a cornice and bowl that winds up at the Valée de la Manche (Mine d'Or lake). You can then commence the 45-minute hike down the road to Morzine, or you could arrange for someone to pick you up. The foolhardy riders can take the Cubore lift and attempt the sketchy hike to a big, fun, and untracked bowl.

Lift passes

Check the latest prices at www.paradiski.com

Instruction

Alpine Ski and Snowboard School

T: 0033 (0)4 50 38 34 91
W: www.avoriazalpineskischool.com

ESF

The ESF teach skiing, boarding and free ride.
0033 (0)4 50 74 05 65
www.esf-avoriaz.com

International Ski and Snowboard School

As well as ski and snowboard lessons, the school offers tandem paragliding.
0033 (0)4 50 74 02 18
www.ecoledeglisse.com

Mint Snowboard School

Mint has been set up by two enthusiastic British snowboarders. They offer lessons to all levels of rider.
0033 (0)6 80 77 66 09
www.mintsnowboarding.com

Snowboard Camps

More Mountain runs separate men's and girls' camps.
www.moremountain.com/camps

Other activities

Biotop Winter Forest Park: This adventure park in the Lindarets Forest is designed with equipment made entirely out of wood, e.g. tree trunk slides, staircases, etc.

Bowling, pool, table footie, video games: These activities can all be found in Le Studio 9 in the Place des Dromonts (0033 (0)4 50 74 06 77).

Diving under ice: Try the amazing experience of diving under the ice. Contact the Cameleon Organisation on 0033 (0)4 50 74 00 59 for more details.

Hang-gliding, paragliding and parasailing: These are arranged by the International Ski School (0033 (0)4 50 74 02 18).

Hot air balloons: Contact the Cameleon Organisation on 0033 (0)4 50 74 00 59 for more details.

Ice skating: Contact 0033 (0)4 50 74 08 52.

Jacuzzis, sauna, therapies and sports hall: Check out the Altiform fitness centre (0033 (0)4 50 74 18 48).

Mountain biking on the snow: This involves riding down the hill to Prodains. Contact the Rustine school of mountain biking on 0033 (0)6 14 52 41 82.

Night sledging: This takes place every day from 6pm (except Sunday) on the Crôt slope (0033 (0)6 07 75 92 48).

Sledge rides: To ride in a sled pulled by dogs call 0033 (0)4 50 73 15 17.

Events

Avoriaz starts its winter season with a 2-day **fête de la glisse**, with demos, games, competitions, live music and entertainment. In January, **La Grand Odyssee** sees over 300 dogs racing through the Portes du Soleil. In March the **Jazz Up Festival** comes to town. Snowboard comps are also regularly held on the super pipe in Avoriaz.

> 'Snowboard comps are regularly held on the super pipe'

Accommodation

Most of the accommodation is in the form of self-catering apartments. It doesn't really matter where your apartment is – they are all pretty similar and you can usually ski to the door. **Pierre et Vacances** is one of the largest rental companies (0870 026 7145 (UK)/0033 (0)1 58 21 55 84, www.pv-holidays.com/avoriaz), but don't expect a spacious apartment, they are usually on the cosy side, although they have been making an effort to renovate as many apartments as possible. The service you will receive is also minimal – expect to make your own beds, etc.

There are just 3 hotels in Avoriaz. One is down in Les Prodains so not ideal if you want to sample the Avoriaz nightlife. In Avoriaz centre you have **Hotel de la Falaise** (0033 (0)4 50 74 26 95), owned by the Pierre et Vacances group. This has absolutely no atmosphere or character so you would be better getting an apartment. The final hotel, **Hotel des Dromonts** (0033 (0)4 94 97 91 91, www.christophe-leroy.com/dromont.htm), is an incredible contrast to the others. From the outside it is a deceptively dull building, camouflaging itself perfectly in the less-than-stunning surroundings. However, once inside those dreary doors the innovative architecture is captivating. All rooms have something to gawp at, with crazy lines and unexpected angles fashioning fantastic spaces. The Thalgo spa area is great.

You can leave your luggage at the luggage room at the ice rink office on your arrival or departure day if you have to move out of your room or apartment and don't want to lug it round everywhere. You pay per item of luggage and can pay extra for a shower. It is open 8.30am–6pm.

Eating out

On the mountain

The Yeti on the slopes near Avoriaz is the place to stop for a crêpe, with deckchairs, a terrace and great après ski. There are a bunch of restaurants under the half pipe, at the top of the cable car from Les Prodains. **La Tanière** (0033 (0)4 50 74 13 10) and **Les Trappeurs** brasserie (0033 (0)4 50 74 17 33) are also worth a visit. There are more restaurants at Lindarets – our favourites are **Pomme de Pin** and **Crémaillère** (0033 (0)4 50 74 11 68). On the Super Morzine side of town, **Les Cretes de Zorre** (0033 (0)4 50 79 24 73) is by far the best.

In town

If you are in desperate need of a hangover cure before you take to the slopes, the **Tavaillon** (0033 (0)4 50 74 14 18) bar serves English breakfasts. The **Cabane** (0033 (0)4 50 74 20 60) is a popular and informal bar/restaurant that is great for food and beers. **La Falaise** (0033 (0)4 50 74 10 48) is the best pizzeria, with really friendly and helpful staff who are more than willing to cater for large groups. **Intrets** (0033 (0)4 50 74 15 45) is also good for pizza and pasta. **Fontaines Blanches** (0033 (0)4 50 74 12 73) has a lovely alpine feel and serves all the usual French fare. **Duchess Anne** (0033 (0)4 50 74 12 50) has a nice terrace for lunch and serves pizzas, local specialities and steak haché. **Le Chalet**

D'Avoriaz (0033 (0)4 50 74 01 30) is a really cute alpine restaurant up by the slopes, near the car park with great pierrades. For gourmet fodder, the uniquely designed **Hotel des Dromonts** (see Accommodation) has a fantastic restaurant. You can even attend one of Mr Leroy's 3-hour cookery courses.

Bars and clubs

For après ski on the slopes the **Yeti** is good (see Eating out). In town, **Shooters** (0033 (0)4 50 74 07 22) is the place to go, populated with Brits, Deutsch and Danish, bopping away to the live music 4.30–6pm and the disco beats until 2am. There are theme nights every week and on Saturdays the bar is usually dominated by seasonaires. **Globe Trotters Café** (0033 (0)4 50 74 06 21) is also popular with Brits. For dancing, there is a late-night club called **Le Yak**. All the best bars and clubs are around the same area so it's pretty easy to check them all out without getting too chilly.

If you fancy a change from the usual bars and clubs there is a cool and atmospheric bowling bar (0033 (0)4 50 74 06 77) in the Place des Dromonts with 2 lanes, pool, darts, air hockey and arcade games.

Getting there

By car

When you arrive in Haute-Savoie, follow the signposts to Chamonix by the A40. Take the Cluses Exit n° 18, head towards Taninges by the D90, then follow les Gets, Morzine and finally Avoriaz. Avoriaz is only an hour or so away from Geneva. If you drive, you will be required to leave your car at the car park at the entrance of Avoriaz. There is an indoor and an outdoor car park. Reserve your spot on www.avoriazparkings.com

By plane

Geneva (80km) Transfer by taxi (see numbers left), bus (0033 (0)4 50 38 42 08) or or a more 'bling' entrance into resort, a helicopter will pick you up from Geneva and drop you in Avoriaz (0033 (0)4 50 92 78 21).

By train

Take the Eurostar from London St Pancras to Paris; then an overnight train to Cluses, and then a bus (85 minutes) to the resort. Contact Rail Europe (0870 830 4862, www.raileurope.co.uk) or European Rail (020 7387 0444, www.europeanrail.com). Bus tickets must be purchased at least 7 days in advance from Altibus (0033 (0)4 79 68 32 96, www.altibus.com).

Useful facts and phone numbers

Tourist office

T: 0033 (0)4 50 74 02 11
F: 0033 (0)4 50 74 24 29
W: www.avoriaz.com

Emergency services

- In an emergency call 18 or 112 from a mobile phone.
- Police: 17
- Medical centre: 0033 (0)4 50 74 05 42 (for emergencies, general medical care, physiotherapy, etc)

Taxis (for transfers)

- Hubert Buttet: 0033 (0)4 50 79 64 54
- Momo Cheraiet: 0033 (0)4 50 79 03 40/ 0033 (0)6 07 94 58 35
- Richard Gourvil: 0033 (0)4 50 75 97 12
- Laurys France Taxi: 0033 (0)4 50 74 69 77, www.laurys.com
- Sarl Evason: 0033 (0)4 50 26 29 29

Chamonix

A base for the serious extreme community, this town has everything; bring a car if you can.

On the slopes	Rating
Snow reliability	❄❄❄❄
Off-piste	❄❄❄❄❄
Off the slopes	
Après ski	❄❄❄½
Nightlife	❄❄❄❄
Eating out	❄❄❄❄
Resort charm	❄❄❄❄

The resort

The first thing that hits you about Chamonix is the scenery; you can't possibly drive into the place without being impressed. Being at the foot of Mont Blanc, Chamonix was destined to be a popular resort from the start, nearly a century ago. Amazingly, it seems to have developed and matured into the perfect town, rather than being destroyed by ugly buildings and tourists like so many resorts. It has plenty of olde worlde charm, streets that you could wander round for days, a diversity of nationalities and more facilities than anyone could need. On top of the beautiful town, the mountains are the best, without a shadow of a doubt, and the nightlife is incredible. The commute between the town and the mountains isn't ideal but it's this fact that lets Chamonix maintain the feel of a real town, as opposed to a purpose-built resort, so we'll forgive this slight inconvenience.

The mountains

Height: 1035–3840m

Ability	Rating
Expert	❄❄❄❄❄
Intermediate	❄❄
Beginner	❄❄❄

Getting about

On 1 side of the valley are Flégère and Brévent, both perfect for panoramic views in the sun. Brévent can be accessed close to Cham centre and Flégère a little further down in Les Praz, although the 2 are linked. The Aiguille du Midi and Les Grands Montets, home of the steep and deep, are on the opposite side of the valley and Le Tour, at the far end, has some great tree runs. In total there are 155km of runs with the longest downhill run coming in at 7km.

Learning to ski/board in Chamonix

You might not think Chamonix would be a great place to learn how to ski and snowboard and in some respects you would be right as it is geared towards the more extreme market. However, once you have been wiped out a few times by speedy riders hurtling through the beginners' slope to get to the bottom of the mountain you might appreciate the fact that Chamonix has 4 beginners' slopes (1 attached to each of the mountains except Flégère) with no other runs going through them. Progression is difficult though, and for intermediates it's not all that great; Chamonix really comes into its own for the experts and pros. There are 4 beginners' areas: La Vormaine in Le Tour, Les Chosalets at Argentière, 500m from the Lognan–Grands Montets cable car, Le Savoy at the foot of the Brevent and Les Planards, 2 minutes from the centre of town.

Off-piste and backcountry

The infamous ski movie *The Blizzard of Aahhhs* – starring Glen Plake and Scot Schmit – changed the lives of every professional big-mountain skier out there and it was mainly filmed in Chamonix on the Grands Montets. There is so much off-piste and backcountry terrain in Chamonix that we can hardly do it justice. The Grands Montets is a good place to start. The drop is around 2000m and you don't even need to hike. Just drop over the back at the top of the gondola and you're off. One of the routes from here is actually marked on the piste map but it's completely ungroomed and gets bumped up at the bottom (you have the option of trees rather than bumps at the other side if you prefer). From the Brevent lift you can hike for about 10 minutes to the face (marked as a black on the map). You start on a couloir that's pretty steep and has the tendency to avalanche but they do bomb it. A great run.

From the Aiguille du Midi, the infamous Vallée Blanche is a 22km descent. The run isn't too difficult, but you could probably do with a guide, especially if you want to go down some steeps. Off the back of the Tête de Balme are some steep and dangerous couloirs if you fancy a challenge. The only disadvantage about the powder in Chamonix is that it's there for a matter of minutes – you'll have to camp out by the lifts in a snowstorm if you want some fresh tracks.

Lift passes

Chamonix Le Pass provides unlimited access to Brevent–Flégère, Domaine de Balme, Les Grands Montets (not including the cable car from Lognan to Grands Montets, which costs extra) and Les Planards, Le Savoy, Les Chosalets and La Vormaine.

Mont Blanc Unlimited is the above plus Aiguille du Midi and Helbronner cable car, Montenvers train, Lognan–Grands Motets cable car, Les Houches and 1 day at Courmayeur.

You can pay the supplement to upgrade to an unlimited pass at any time.

Check the latest prices at www.chamonix.com

Further information

The Vamos edition of *Chamonix* is a good off-piste guide book written by 2 mountain guides based in Cham. It's written in good English and sold in Snow and Rock.

Avalanche risk

The avalanche risks in Chamonix are less than you might think. There is a huge potential for avalanche but a fairly small chance of being caught in 1. Because all and sundry want to hit the off-piste when they head to Chamonix, the local officials are very paranoid and keep everything shut unless it's safe.

Instruction

The tourist office will provide you with a list of guides and schools to choose from but these are the 2 that we were recommended by local experts.

Chamonix Experience

A good reputation but pretty expensive.
0033 (0)4 50 54 09 36
www.chamex.com

Evolution 2

EV2 is well thought of by the locals and can provide you with any kind of instruction or guide.
0033 (0)4 50 55 3 57
www.evolution2.com/cham

Touring

Chamonix is the place to tour; the Haute Route is the classic 6-day hut-to-hut journey from Chamonix to Zermatt with some interesting variations. Other week-long itineraries include 5 days touring and a 2-day ascent of Mont Blanc (training required).

> 'Chamonix is the place to tour'

Local day tours allow you to keep Chamonix as your base. There are many tours – Col de Passon from Les Grands Montets, Col du Belvedere from Flégère, Col de Toule from the Aiguille du Midi are three classics.

For tour guides contact EV2 or Chamonix Experience (see above). Chamonix Experience also offer good taster courses covering all the skills you will need to complete a multi-day tour.

Other activities

Bowling: Open 5pm–2am (earlier in bad weather), the bowling alley is situated on the Avenue de Courmayeur in Chamonix Sud (0033 (0)4 50 53 74 37).

Casino: Situated on the Place de Saussure, the casino (0033 (0)4 50 53 07 65) has slots open from noon and French and English roulette, black-jack, and poker from 9pm. The restaurant is open from 7.30pm until midnight.

Cinema: Bang in the centre of town, the cinema (0033 (0)4 50 55 89 98) has 3 screens with several shows per day. Films are shown in French and English (with French subtitles).

Paint ball: Contact 0033 (0)6 07 36 01 51, www.paintballcham.com.

Panoramic flights: These are pretty popular around Chamonix. Chamonix Mont Blanc Hélicoptères (0033 (0)4 50 54 13 82, www.helico.fr) organise trips on the Aiguille Verte and over the Massive. SAF Chamonix Hélicoptères (0033 (0)4 79 38 48 29) organise 30-minute flights for 5 people.

Paragliding: This can be done on Aiguille du Midi, Brevent, and Les Grands Montets. Contact Alpine Flying Centre (0033 (0)6 10 63 45 58, www.flyers-lodge.com), Centre Ecole Parapente Mt Blanc (0033 (0)4 50 34 77 37, www.cepmontblanc.com) or Summits (0033 (0)4 50 53 50 14, www.summits.fr).

Richard Bozon Sports Centre: Situated at 214 Av. de la Plage, this centre contains a swimming pool, sauna and hammam (0033 (0)4 50 53 23 70), tennis and squash (0033 (0)4 50 53 28 40), skating rink (0033 (0)4 50 53 12 36 – night sessions on Wednesday), weights and fitness room (0033 (0)4 50 53 23 70) and climbing hall (0033 (0)4 50 53 23 70).

'Shopping in Chamonix is an absolute pleasure'

Shopping: With 400 shops to choose from, shopping in Chamonix is an absolute pleasure.

WiFi for free: The tourist office has wireless connections and if you have the right equipment you can use it for free during your stay.

Events

The **Boss des Bosses** is a mogul competition without many rules; anything goes. It began 16 years ago when all the Chamonix ski bums challenged the Val d'Isère ski bums to a mogul challenge. Since then a number of the major ski resorts have become involved and enter their own teams. A resort's team must consist of 5 male skiers, 2 female skiers, 2 snowboarders and 1 telemarker. It's a great day (around mid-March) and a legendary competition.

'It's a great day and a legendary competition'

Accommodation

High Mountain Holidays (www.highmountain.co.uk) has a number of catered and self-catered accommodations in locations across Chamonix, from dead in the centre, to quieter areas near the ski lifts.

The **Park Hotel Suisse** (0033 (0)4 50 53 07 58, www.chamonix-park-hotel.com) is a good 3-star hotel opposite the tourist office. The modern 3-star **Oustalet** (0033 (0)4 50 55 54 99, www.hotel-oustalet.com) is near the Aiguille du Midi. **Hotel La Savoyarde** (0033 (0)4 50 53 00 77, www.lasavoyarde.com), technically a 3-star, is great value but it is a little run down and could do with a revamp. You can't get a more central location than the 4-star **Grand Hotel des Alpes** (0033 (0)4 50 55 37 80, www.grandhoteldesalpes.com) that is right smack in the centre, next to the Chanel shop. It's an excellent hotel, with swimming pool, sauna and Jacuzzi, although the parking's a tad difficult.

Mountain Retreats (0033 686 54 72 40 (FR)/ 01635 253 946 (UK), www.mountainretreats.co.uk) also has 3 great chalets.

Eating out

On the mountain

There are 14 restaurants on the mountain, and pretty much the lot have incredible views over the Mont Blanc mountain range. In the Brevent/Flégère region, **La Flégère** (0033 (0)4 50 55 82 23) and **Le Panoramic** (0033 (0)4 50 53 44 11) have amazing terraces and views over the Mont Blanc range, and not-so-bad food. **La Bergerie** (0033 (0)4 50 53 05 42) has a beautiful atmosphere with both table and self-service options and **Altitude 2000** (0033 (0)4 50 53 15 58), at the top of the gondola in Planpraz, has great food, service and terrace. On Les Grands Montets, the **Plan Joran** (0033 (0)4 50 54 05 77) offers quick snacks, a pizzeria, a picnic area, a terrace and a smart restaurant. The **Lognan** (0033 (0)4 50 54 10 21) is pretty smart and has a good 'pasta corner' and the **Refuge de Lognan** (0033 (0)6 88 56 03 54) is rustic and off the beaten track. The food is fantastic. At the summit of the Aiguille du Midi is **Le 3842**, a café with salads, sandwiches, pies and remarkable views. Over on Le Tour, the **Charamillon** (0033 (0)4 50 54 09 05) is a good self-service eatery.

In town

Le Munchie (0033 (0)4 50 53 45 41) on the Rue des Moulins has some of the best food in Cham. It's mid range, fresh and tasty. **La Maison Carrier** (0033 (0)4 50 53 00 03, www.hameaualbert.fr), just out of town, is pretty smart (wear a shirt) but relaxed at the same time. The chef has a Michelin-starred reputation and for the food and service you get it's not too expensive. **Chez Valereo** (0033 (0)4 50 55 93 40) is a great Italian with tasty pizzas and a renowned wine list. It's a popular place with the locals. The **Bistrot des Sports** (0033 (0)4 50 53 00 46, www.bistrotdessports.com) is a very French restaurant/bar right in the centre of town on the main street. Savoyard food is the speciality and the bar is legendary, and frequented by hardcore locals as well as passing tourists. The **Calèche** (0033 (0)4 50 55 94 68, www.restaurant-caleche.com) in the town centre (just past the cinema) is atmospheric and also serves a large selection of good traditional Savoyard food. It's a little touristy and mid price range. For Tex Mex, the **Cantina** (0033 (0)4 50 53 83 80, www.cantina.fr) is great. It can be found down a little back alley just off the main street and does good food at a good price. **Belouga** serves the best takeaway burgers in town.

Bars and clubs

Since Chamonix has loads of permanent residents (about 10000) and 180 licences, there are loads of good bars, pubs and clubs to pick from.

L'M is a hotel and restaurant in the centre of town that has a great Austrian-style après ski bar outside with big outdoor heaters and a large outdoor screen for footie and other sports.

> 'A great Austrian-style outdoor après ski bar with big heaters'

Just opposite the station are a few cool bars. **Chambre Neuf** (0033 (0)4 50 53 00 31) is a classic après ski bar, popular with the locals and the Scandinavians. **La Terrasse** (0033 (0)4 50 53 09 95) in the centre of town sometimes has live music. **Clubhouse** (0033 (0)4 50 9 96 56, www.clubhouse.fr) is more London than Chamonix and it does great cocktails. It's the sister bar of Milk and Honey in London and New York.

MBC (0033 (0)4 50 53 61 59, www.mbchx.com) is about 5 minutes' walk from the centre of town, has a good reputation for homemade beer and a year-round clientele, both English and French. **South Bar** (0033 (0)4 50 53 98 56, www.southbar.se), right at the end of town is a hip and full-on après ski bar. **Bar'd Up** (0033 (0)4 50 55 80 92) attracts a more British and Aussie crowd and is on the rue des Moulins, just off the main street in the centre of town,

Getting there

By car

Chamonix is really easy to access by road. From Paris take the A6 towards Lyon then the A40 towards Lyon/Geneva then the N205.

By plane

Geneva (88km) is only an hour's transfer away. There is a daily coach transfer 3 times daily. Contact the tourist office/www.chamonix.com for timetables or call 0033 (0)4 50 53 01 15.

Lyon (220km) Bus connections are via Satobus (0033 (0)4 37 255 255).

For taxi transfers contact the airport transfer services:

ATS: 0033 (0)4 50 53 63 97 (in France), 0709 209 7392 (in the UK), www.a-t-s.net

Chamonix Transfer Service: 0033 (0)6 62 05 57 38, www.chamonix-transfer.com

By train

Take the Eurostar from London St Pancras to Paris, then an overnight train, changing at St-Gervais-Les-Bains to arrive in Chamonix. Contact Rail Europe (0870 830 4862, www.raileurope.co.uk) or European Rail (020 7387 0444, www.europeanrail.com).

Useful facts and phone numbers

Tourist office

T: 0033 (0)4 50 53 00 24
F: 0033 (0)4 50 53 58 90
W: www.chamonix.com

Direct reservations

T: 0033 (0)4 50 53 23 33

Emergency services

- In a medical emergency dial 15, for the fire brigade call 18, or 112 for either from a mobile
- Mountain rescue: 0033 (0)4 50 53 16 89
- Ambulance: 0033 (0)4 50 53 46 20
- Hospital: 0033 (0)4 50 53 84 00
- Weather information: 0033 (0)8 92 68 02 74

Doctors

In Chamonix

- Drs Dartigue-Peyrou, Dehlinger and Plumerault, 350 avenue de la Plage: 0033 (0)4 50 53 15 27
- Dr Roncin, 10 avenue du Mont-Blanc: 0033 (0)4 50 55 85 74
- Drs Cadot and Richard, 275 rue des Allobroges: 0033 (0)4 50 55 80 55
- Doctor on call (nights, Sundays and bank holidays): 15

Taxis

- ABAC Taxi Gopée: 0033 (0)6 07 02 22 13, www.abactaxichamonix.com
- Cham Taxi: 0033 (0)6 07 26 36 62
- Taxi Monard: 0033 (0)4 50 55 86 28
- Taxi Rousseau: 0033 (0)6 07 67 88 85, www.taxi-chamonix.fr

Courchevel

Endless pistes and a resort with kudos.

On the slopes	
Snow reliability	❄❄❄❄
Parks	❄❄
Off-piste	❄❄❄❄❄
Off the slopes	
Après ski	❄❄❄
Nightlife	❄❄❄❄
Eating out	❄❄❄❄
Resort charm	❄❄❄

The resort

Les Trois Vallées is worlds apart from most resorts in terms of the miles of pistes and powder to explore. Any level of skier and boarder will be pushed to the next level here. Within Courchevel, there are a number of areas to choose as a base, although the frequent free buses make travel between villages pretty easy.

Courchevel 1850 is the highest and most cosmopolitan of the Courchevel resorts. It has a reputation for attracting the rich and famous and many a celebrity has been spotted on the slopes. This brings with it inflated prices, Michelin-starred restaurants, exclusive and well-hidden cocktail bars and plush chalets.

1650 has a more relaxed and friendly community feel with fewer glitzy hotels and restaurants, although the cosmopolitan vibe of 1850 is gradually filtering down. The slopes of 1650 may be off to the far side of Les Trois Vallées, making it a slightly longer journey over to Meribel or Val Thorens, but the runs are also some of the best, with quiet sweeping blues and access to some of the best powder.

Less expensive than 1650 and 1850, 1550 is often used as a base for those who work in other resorts. Le Praz (or Courchevel 1300) is a traditional village dominated by the Olympic ski jump in the centre of town. Despite the lower altitude of this seemingly sleepy Savoyard village, Le Praz is almost as expensive and exclusive as 1850. There are some fabulously flashy chalets and the bubble lift in Le Praz takes you right into 1850 so the altitude isn't a problem. Another lift will have you on your way into Meribel in no time. La Tania (1350) is a small friendly resort, set in the middle of a pine forest with great access to Courchevel and Meribel. The traffic-free centre doesn't contain many bars and restaurants but there is still a lively après ski scene at the famous ski lodge.

The mountains

Height: 1850–2740m

Ability	Rating
Expert	❄❄❄❄
Intermediate	❄❄❄❄❄
Beginner	❄❄❄❄

Getting about

There is a vast amount of terrain in Courchevel alone, and even keen skiers may find that it is best to buy a Courchevel lift pass and purchase extensions where necessary. There are 3 bubble lifts in the centre of Courchevel 1850: the Jardin Alpin gives access to good but busy beginners' runs; Verdons connects to the Vizelle and Saulire lifts for some great high altitude red runs, the black Suisse run and some great couloirs from Saulire; Chenus will take you over towards Meribel. In 1650 the Ariondaz lift from the centre of the village takes you up to Bel Air. From here you have a number of options; you can start with the gentle runs down to the Signal chairlift or head straight down the Bel Air red run to the Chapelets chairlift. Chapelets is one of the best red runs in Courchevel and there are some great trees to play in. Pyramide and Mont Russe are some of the best long sweeping blues for the timid intermediate.

The park

The family park can be accessed from the Verdans bubble and contains a couple of small beginner jumps and a number of rails. There is also a skiercross course, and for a few extra euros you can practise your tricks on the airbag. Advanced freestylers should probably try out the superb parks in Meribel and Mottaret. If you want to build your own jump in Courchevel, just off the Pyramide run is a good spot.

Off-piste and backcountry

For finding your feet in the powder, Chapelets has some great areas in between the trees and gulleys and the snow always keeps well. Les Avals Valley is a more substantial adventure. Hike up from the top of the Chanrossa chairlift for breathtaking scenery and wide sections of untracked snow. You can turn this into an overnight escapade – take a warm sleeping bag and food for the evening, catch the last lifts up the Chanrossa, and spend the evening halfway down at a mountain refuge. Early in the morning head back down towards 1650. There is a fair amount of flat terrain that you have to push and walk out of, which will be especially tough for snowboarders. However, it is well worth all the effort and yields sufficient respect when you recount your adventures in the bars later. Research snow conditions and weather fully before you attempt the Les Avals Valley.

The Creux bowl is easily accessible from the Creux chairlift in 1850. Cross right to the end of the bowl to a huge, pointed rock, known as the Needle. Climb around the Needle for fresh powder that usually takes a good week to be tracked out after a snowfall and provides a long run down to the bottom of the Chanrossa chairlift.

The best couloirs are to be found at the top of the Saulire cable car. Directly under the cable car is the easily accessible Télépherique couloir, which is perhaps slightly less challenging than the rest. Further along the path is the Grand Couloir, which is marked as a black run on the piste map but is far more difficult than the average black. It is wider than most couloirs, but has the tendency to transform into a mogul field in the absence of fresh powder. A 5-minute hike up from the Grand Couloir is the Petit Couloir, where incredible conditions can be unearthed because the short hike, though fairly easy, puts a lot of people off. A 30-minute hike will take you to Croix de Verdons. This has the advantages of a wide, open face, very few tracks and a long run down. Be aware of the drop-off on the right-hand side (from the riders' point of view) as it's a long fall to the rocks below.

All the couloirs arrive at the Saulire piste, which leads you straight back to the cable car so you can head back up and try another. Some of the finest powder in Courchevel can be found on the Roche de Loze. From the end of the 2-person chair, Col de la Loze, the Roche de Loze is the towering face on your left. It takes a good 45 minutes to hike to, but the ride down is well worth it and your mum will appreciate the pictures from the top. Manu Gaidet, a world champion freeskier, declares it to be his favourite place to train in Courchevel.

Lift passes

Check the latest prices at www.courchevel.com

Instruction

ESF

The ESF is a well-respected association and there are some fantastic instructors but it's a bit of a lottery.
0033 (0)4 79 08 07 72
www.esfcourchevel.com

Magic in Motion

Magic employs fun and charismatic instructors, both French and British, but all are English speaking. They have garish jackets and a big mouse mascot who skis around to entertain the kids. The kids' fun factory begins on Sunday or Monday with 4 hours of lessons every morning – Tuesday and Thursday are

special adventure days with a full day on the mountain and lunch in a mountain restaurant.
0033 (0)4 79 08 11 99
www.magicinmotion.co.uk

Mountain Guides Office

A number of activities are on offer including off-piste, ski touring and heliskiing.
0033 (0)4 79 01 03 66
www.guides-courchevel-meribel.com

New Generation

New Gen teaches all levels of skier and boarder and all lessons are in English. They also do gap year courses and BASI instructor's courses with impressive pass rates.
0033 (0)4 79 01 03 18/0844 484 3663 (UK)
www.skinewgen.com

RTM snowboarding school

The way forward when it comes to snowboard instructors, RTM employs passionate and professional snowboarders who provide the best service in town.
0033 (0)6 15 48 59 04
www.rtmsnowboarding.com

Rob Sewell

Rob is a private ski instructor who has lived in Courchevel for many years and is now one of the most respected instructors in Les Trois Vallées. He is known for teaching the unteachable and tuning up advanced skiers.
0033 (0)4 79 08 04 17.

Ski Supreme

Ski Supreme has a friendly and professional team with a great reputation. They are the longest-serving British ski instructors in Courchevel and have led the way for those who followed. All instructors have lift queue priority. The directors are the parents of Alan Baxter, Britain's most successful alpine racer. Lessons are guaranteed to be in English.
0033 (0)4 79 08 27 87 (France) or 01479 81 0800 (UK)
www.supremeski.com

Other activities

Bowling: There are 8 bowling lanes at the Forum in 1850 (0033 (0)4 79 08 23 83), which are open every day 11am–2am.

Cinema: The cinema in 1850 often shows films in English.

Climbing wall: There is a 13m-high wall with 7 ways up at the Forum. For booking contact the Mountain Guides office on 0033 (0)4 79 01 03 66.

Hot air ballooning: Take a 1-hour trip above Courchevel and you get champagne and a diploma on landing. Call Aéro Action Aventure (0033 (0)6 07 48 16 79) or Ski Vol (0033 (0)4 79 08 41 72/0033 (0)6 83 97 53 26, www.skivol.com).

Ice climbing: This takes place on the ice tower in between 1850 and 1650. It can be quite challenging and is dependent on conditions and temperatures.

Ice go-karting: Literally go-karting on ice – you can do this in 1550 (0033 (0)6 08 73 70 58). Really good fun but fairly expensive.

Ice skating: The ice skating rink (0033 (0)4 79 08 33 23) at the Forum is open every day 3–7pm and until 11pm on Wednesdays and Fridays.

Massage: Pamper Off-piste (0033 (0)6 17 60 89 02, www.pamperoffpiste.com) provides a large range of massage and beauty treatments. They visit you in the comfort of your chalet to relieve tired, aching bones.

Parapenting: Ski off 1 of the top peaks with an instructor, gliding for around 15 minutes and landing in Le Praz where you catch the lift back up. The best schools are the legendary Pascal Piazzalunga (0033 (0)6 09 76 50 40, www.directicime.com) and Craig's Paragliding (0033 (0)4 79 08 43 65, www.paraglide-alps.com).

Plane trips: See the Trois Vallées circuit from the air (0033 (0)4 79 08 31 23, www.aeroclub-courchevel. com).

Skidoos: Skidoos can be hired for an afternoon of fun from Chardon Loisirs (0033 (0)4 79 08 39 60, www.chardon loisirs.com) or Ski Vol (0033 (0)6 83 97 53 26, www.skivol.com). A guide takes you along the marked tracks.

Tobogganing: Grab a sledge, available at most ski shops, and head down the specially made luge track in front of the Kalico in 1850 to the bottom of 1550.

Events

New Year's Eve Party on the Piste is a great event in the centre of 1850. Huge numbers of people turn up to dance on the snow to the live music and wonder at the fireworks. All the bars serve drinks in plastic cups so you can wander round with them and most places stay open until the last people fall over. The **Three Valleys X Wing Rally** takes place in April and is open to everyone. Teams of 3 make their way around the ski area, choosing their own itinerary. There is a Derby, Speed Skiing, Freeride, Giant Slalom, Super Combo, Family Schuss and Ski Style. The **Columbia Ride Week** takes place in March. Over 4 days each team of 2 riders and a cameraman create a freeride film. The final day is for editing and production and there is a presentation and awards ceremony in the evening. In 1650, the legendary **Derby** takes place at the end of March; contestants start at the top of the Pyramids run and have to race to the bottom of the resort to claim their prize.

Accommodation

In 1850, luxury chalet accommodation is provided by **Flexiski** (020 8939 0862, www.flexiski.com), **Kaluma** (0870 442 8044/0208 789 6100, www.kalumatravel.co.uk) and **Ski Scott Dunn** (020 8682 5450, www.scottdunn.com/ski), so why not bankrupt yourself for a week of sheer indulgence? In similar fashion, there are some amazing, top-of-the-range hotels with seriously high prices. **Le Lana** (0033 (0)4 79 08 01 10, www.lelana.com) is a luxurious but cosy hotel. Mid-range hotels include the **Hotel de la Croisette** (003 (0)4 79 08 09 00, www.hoteldelacroisette.com), which is well placed for the main lifts and town centre and contains the popular Bar le Jump. It's a good, 3-star hotel and rooms on the first floor are slightly cheaper because of the noise from the bar, so you could take advantage of the good rate and go out and join in the fun. **Courcheneige** (0033 (0)4 79 08 02 59, www.courcheneige.com) is a 2-star on the Bellecotte piste, very handy for the slopes but not for going out at night. There is a huge terrace that is busy at lunch. **Hotel Olympic** (0033 (0)4 79 08 08 24, www.courchevelolympic.com) is a good budget option with competitive rates and a small bar that is popular at happy hour. It's handy for town and good value but not much to look at.

Most of the accommodation in 1650 is in chalets, run by tour operators. **Ski Olympic** (www.skiolympic.co.uk) and **Le Ski** (www.leski.com) have good chalets and chalet hotels. There is a beautiful 3-star hotel bang in the centre of 1650, **Le Seizena** (0033 (0)4 79 08 26 36, www.hotelseizena.com), which has 20 rooms, a hot tub, fitness centre and internet terminals. The **Hotel du Golf** (0033 (0)4 79 00 92 92) is another great 3-star with the best position in the valley; you can ski to the door and you're right in the centre of town. It has 47 rooms and a number of self-catering apartments. The 2-star **Edelweiss Hotel** (0033 (0)4 79 08 26 58, www.courchevel-edelweiss.com) is good for those on a budget and is also in a superb position.

In Le Praz, the traditional and charming 3 star **Les Peupliers** (0033 (0)4 79 08 41 47, www.lespeupliers.com) is the place to stay. It's in a great location just opposite the ski lifts and right next to the bus stop. The hotel bar is also a local meeting point and there is a sauna, steam room and Jacuzzi to help you relax.

Eating out

On the mountain

The **Cap Horn** (0033 (0)4 79 08 33 10, www.le-cap-horn.com), next to the Altiport in 1850, is a favourite of the rich and famous for the ultimate exclusive lunch. You'd never believe you were in the mountains. It has a cosy but luxurious feel and fabulous food that includes seafood and Savoyard specialities. Reservations are essential. The **Bouc Blanc** (0033 (0)4 79 08 80 26) just below the Col de Loz chair has fantastic views, a huge open deck and a great Beaufort cheese tart. It's fantastic value compared to most of the restaurants on the mountain and the food and service is excellent. **The Jump** (0033 (0)4 79 08 09 00) at the bottom of the slopes in 1850 serves lunch 12am–3pm and the chilli and chips is highly recommended.

Kalico (0033 (0)4 79 08 20 28, www.lekalico.com), the nightclub on the piste just below 1850 centre, serves good value and tasty food in massive portions (burgers, salads, fajitas, etc).

In 1650, try the very popular **Bel Air** (0033 (0)4 79 08 00 93) restaurant, which serves omelettes, salads, pasta and snails – the food is fantastic. It is advisable to book. There's a terrace on 3 levels with deckchairs on the bottom level and it's a great place to chill and watch the world ski and board by. **L'Ours Blanc** (0033 (0)4 79 00 93 93), at the base of 1650's slopes, serves huge burgers, and for a cheap panini, the **Bubble Bar** (0033 (0)4 79 01 14 21, www.lebubble.com), just round the corner from L'Ours Blanc is a good bet.

In town

1850 is home to the gourmet options. The **Chapelle** (0033 (0)4 79 08 19 48) has a fabulous, cosy, candlelit atmosphere, focused around an open wood fire on which all the meat is cooked – great for red meat lovers, not so much for vegetarians. The **Via Ferrata** (0033 (0)4 79 08 02 07) is stylish and funky, and while you can pay top dollar for some dishes and for drinks, the pizzas are surprisingly reasonable. They may have loud music but this somehow manages to remain unobtrusive and adds to the chic, cosmopolitan environment

'Stylish and funky with a chic environment'

The **Mangeoire** (0033 (0)4 79 08 02 09) is a restaurant/bar with an ambience second to none. Magnums of Moet and platefuls of caviar are the norm here. Those with a poor sense of humour need not apply as it is not unknown for the barmen to open up the fancy dress box and pop a hat on your head. **La Bergerie** (0033 (0)4 79 08 24 70) serves some of the best food on the mountain and often has live music and theme nights. It is just by the side of the piste so you can stop in for lunch or book dinner, in which case a car will come and pick you up.

Le Petit Savoyard (0033 (0)4 79 08 27 44) is the best restaurant in 1650 with a cosy atmosphere and the menu, traditional food and service are second to none. It is always busy and booking is recommended. **L'Eterlou** (0033 (0)4 79 08 25 45) serves tasty pizzas and also does takeaways and **L'Alberon** (0033 (0)4 79 08 24 87) has a great selection of salads, meats and Savoyard specialities. In Le Praz, **La Table de Mon Grand-Père** in hotel Les Peupliers (0033 (0)4 79 08 41 42) is atmospheric and popular. If you are in a self-catering chalet or apartment, have a look at **Extreme Cuisine** (0033 (0)6 32 91 84 56, www.extreme-cuisine.co.uk) who can cook you a 3-course meal in your chalet or can even deliver an Indian, complete with Naan breads and poppadoms (0033 (0)6 81 54 32 90)!

Bars and clubs

Make sure your wallet's looking healthy if you're after a big night in 1850 – the drinks can be pricey. **The Jump** (0033 (0)4 79 08 09 00) has a great atmosphere and is busy all day – for mid-morning stops, lively après ski and 10.30pm–1am, when people are getting going for the evening. The **Mangeoire** (0033 (0)4 79 08 02 09) has similarly extortionate prices but the work that is put into the cocktails is impressive. It serves as a fine dining restaurant in the early evening, but when dinner is over you are, surprisingly, actively encouraged to jump on to chairs, tables and any other available surfaces. After the bars have shut, **Kalico** (0033 (0)4 79 08 20 28, www.lekalico.com) is the only place to be and is jam packed with hedonistic young people. DJs play every night, and top quality bands twice a week. Those still wishing to shed some weight from their wallets should head on to **Les Caves** (0033 (0)4 79 08 12 74) with its neon strip lighting and funky dance atmosphere. In these clubs thousands of euros are shelled out for bottles of vodka or champagne that are lit by sparklers and brought to your table (if you are a mere mortal who drinks by the glass you're not allowed a table).

In the heart of 1650 is **Rocky's bar**, which is popular with holidaymakers. Its recent revamp has made it much more modern. **Bubble Bar** (0033 (0)4 79 01 14 21, www.

lebubble.com) is the main meeting point in 1650 for seasonaires and holidaymakers alike. It's open from 8am for a morning coffee, serves a mean panini at lunchtime and live music is often playing for après or in the evenings. The Bubble kicks on until 1am. Le Schuss is another great après night spot with a traditional chalet feel. It also serves food and has internet terminals, which is handy. For late-night dancing and drinking, the **Moriond Lounge** (0033 (0)4 79 08 23 75) is the way to go. It has great live bands playing until the early hours and drinks are much cheaper than in 1850. In Le Praz, the **brasserie/pizzeria** is a huge bar that serves great snacks, has good games tables and has great live music – just what you want from an après ski bar.

Getting there

By car

From Calais, the drive takes about 10 hours. Directions can be found at www.courchevel.com

By plane

Geneva (145km) From here there are a number of different options to get to Courchevel. The bus takes about 3.5 hours (www.alpski-bus.com). It's best to book in advance. Alternatively, take a taxi or a helicopter.

Lyon (180km) is also 3.5 hours away by bus. Contact Satobus (0033 (0)4 37 25 52 55, www.satobus.com). Alternatively, take a taxi or a helicopter.

Chambéry (115km) is closer. Transfer takes 1.5 hours.

By train

Take the Eurostar from London St Pancras to Paris; then an overnight train to Moutiers, and then a bus (45 minutes – 1650; 55 minutes – 1850) to the resort. Contact Rail Europe (0870 830 4862, www.raileurope.co.uk) or European Rail (020 7387 0444, www.europeanrail.com). Bus tickets can be purchased in advance from Altibus (0033 (0)4 79 68 32 96, www.altibus.com) or bought at the station.

Useful facts and phone numbers

Tourist office

T: 0033 (0)4 79 08 00 29
F: 0033 (0)4 79 08 15 63
W: www.courchevel.com

Direct reservations

T: 0033 (0)4 79 08 14 44
W: http://reservation@courcheval.com

Emergency services

- In a medical emergency dial 15, for the fire brigade call 18, or 112 for either from a mobile.
- Police: 0033 (0)4 79 08 34 69/04 79 08 26 07

Doctors

- Blanc Alexandre: 0033 (0)4 79 08 26 40
- Cabinet Médical du Forum: 0033 (0)4 79 08 32 13
- Chedal Marc: 0033 (0)4 79 08 20 14
- In 1650, Maalej Adnène: 0033 (0)4 79 08 04 45
- Physiotherapy clinic: 0033 (0)6 68 57 00 99 (Siân and Chris are definitely the best in town)

Taxis

- Courchevel Taxi Association: 0033 (0)4 79 08 23 46
- Abatrans Taxi: 0033 (0)4 79 00 3000, www.courchevel-taxi.com
- Taxi Jack: 0033 (0)6 12 45 11 17
- Luxury taxi service: Poirel Thibaut, 0033 (0)6 09 40 19 10, www.courchevel-prestige.com
- Helicopter-Taxi: 0033 (0)4 79 08 00 91, www.saf-helico.com

Les Deux Alpes

The heart of the European freestyle community.

On the slopes	Rating
Snow reliability	❄❄❄❄
Parks	❄❄❄❄❄
Off-piste	❄❄❄
Off the slopes	
Après ski	❄❄❄❄
Nightlife	❄❄❄❄
Eating out	❄❄❄
Resort charm	❄❄

The resort

Les Deux Alpes is situated where the Northern and Southern Alps meet, in the heart of the Oisans. The nearest town is Grenoble, 79km away. The town centre is focused along the main street, which is more than 1km long. It's not exceptionally beautiful, but the mountains, slopes and the flawless snowpark more than make up for it. It also has a strong community atmosphere, as the resort is open year-round and has a large number of permanent residents.

'It has a strong community atmosphere'

Les Deux Alpes was built on a marshy plateau between 2 villages: Mont de Lans (Les Deux Alpes 1300) and Venosc, a more traditional craft village at the far end of the resort. There is also the 'Village' area (Les Deux Alpes 1800), known to the locals as the 'ghetto'. This area has been known to attract some dubious characters and isn't particularly close to the lifts or local amenities, but if you're looking for a bargain it could be worth checking out.

The pistes are superb for all abilities and the high altitude glacier allows skiing and snowboarding almost all year round. In the summer there are a number of freestyle camps here as the park on the glacier is fantastic.

The mountains

Height: 1650–3600m

Ability	Rating
Expert	❄❄❄❄
Intermediate	❄❄❄❄
Beginner	❄❄❄❄

Getting about

There are over 200km of marked runs in Les Deux Alpes, 59 ski lifts, a superb snowpark, and an abundance of alternatives for the budding freestyler or freerider. There are a little more than 700ha of off-piste. Sixty per cent of on-piste runs are designated for beginners and intermediate skiers and boarders and 40 per cent for the more competent and experienced riders. Les Deux Alpes also has the advantage of guaranteed snow year round due to high altitude and the use of 105 snow cannons.

The Jandri Express cable car takes you up to 3200m and then the funicular up to 3425m. At the top you are greeted with a 360-degree panoramic view of the French and Italian Alps: la Meije, le Mont Blanc and many others. The Diable gondola heads up to the Tête Moute at 2800m and gives access to steep on-piste runs, including a challenging 1200m vertical mogul field.

The park

Les Deux Alpes was 1 of the first resorts to passionately adopt New School riding. It costs around £500,000 per winter to maintain the New School riding zones. In winter the resort's snowpark is situated at 2600m, on the Toura area which can be reached by the Jandri cable car. In the summer, the park is shifted up to the glacier.

The snowpark consists of: a beginners' zone, created for freestyle debutantes, and containing 6 small kickers; a half pipe zone 120m long and 4m high; a slopestyle zone with a series of hips, gaps and quarters leading to rail zones of almost 400m; BBQ; music; DJ's turntable and deckchairs.

There is a boardercross area at 2600m where official boardercross competitions are held. The length of the boardercross is 1000–1230m and there is also a new, smaller boardercross for beginners, which is situated parallel to the old one.

The Jumping Training System (JTS) or the 'snow air bag' was set up by Les Deux Alpes ESF snowboarding school. The air bag is 14m by 28m and allows both beginners and experienced freestylers to up the level of their tricks in complete confidence as there is less chance of injuries if you land badly. Each week there is a JTS competition where competitors battle for the biggest air.

Off-piste and backcountry

Les Deux Alpes benefits from significant heights with reliable snow. Therefore, although the resort is not known for its off-piste terrain, there are many excellent spots for off-piste freeriding, such as Chalance, La Fee, Les Vallons du Diable, Les Posettes, Bellecombes and La Selle. There are also the legendary descents to La Grave.

> 'A big playground of open powder fields, small couloirs and cliffs'

In the centre of the mountain is the Clot de Chalance, a big playground of open powder fields, small couloirs and cliffs. You need to be there first thing in the morning after a fresh snow fall to get first tracks – by the afternoon it's tracked out. It is often blasted by the pisteurs and is relatively safe from avalanching, but there are stories of a couple of fatal slides. If you're feeling slightly more daring, it is possible to carry on all the way down to the Lac du Chambon, located below the base of the resort. It concludes with a lengthy tree run, but this should only be done with a guide and in the right conditions.

The Diable (at 2400m) has some top quality runs after a big powder storm. Starting from the top of the Télécabine du Diable, you can ride all the way back to town. The terrain isn't too challenging but great for getting freshies.

For couloirs, make your way to the Lac du Plan, which can be seen as you're heading up the mountain in the Téléphériques Debrayables and can be reached by taking the Télésiège de la Fee chair lift. Just below the lake is a variety of options, including a long, narrow, challenging couloir that is held in high regard amongst the top riders in the resort.

Make your way to the top of the glacier by catching the Funiculaire Dome Express. The Dome, nicknamed the Ice Wall, is ideal for getting fresh powder and a perfect place for building backcountry kickers. From here you can see all the terrain leading to La Grave, which has some of the best off-piste riding in the world (see the chapter on La Grave, page 99). A guide is recommended if you fancy attempting this terrain.

Lift passes

Check the latest prices at www.les2alpes.com

Instruction

ESF

0033 (0)4 76 79 21 21
www.esf2alpes.com

European Ski School

This ski school comes highly recommended by the locals due to the quality of instruction. They limit the size of groups to 8 or 9 and all the instructors speak good English. They also offer a 'Natural Born Skiers' course with a maximum of 4 per group, lift queue priority and video analysis (you must be a good skier).
0033 (0)4 76 79 74 55
www.europeanskischool.co.uk

St Christophe International Ski and Snowboard School

0033 (0)4 76 79 04 21
www.esl2alpes.com

Ski Privilège

This school offers group and private ski or snowboard lessons by the hour or half day. Anne Millet is an ex-member of the French Ski Team and offers competitive prices.
0033 (0)6 09 69 78 87
www.skiprivilege.fr

Stages Damien Albert

This school teaches only freeride, off-piste and 'bump' courses. Students need to be able to ski black runs.
0033 (0)4 76 79 50 38
www.abc-skifreeride.com

Mountain Guides Bureau

The bureau offers training in avalanche rescue and snow awareness, as well as off-piste guiding and the opportunity to climb frozen waterwalls.
0033 (0)4 76 11 36 29
www.guides2alpes.com

Other activities

On the mountain

Unless otherwise stated, contact the tourist office (see Useful facts and phone numbers) for more information.

> 'Ski down a drop in altitude of 1300m with only the moon to see by'

Full moon parties: Combining night riding and drinking sounds pretty dangerous but it is great fun. Take the last lifts up the mountain at around 4.30pm, ski/board as the sun sets on the glacier and enjoy a lively meal in a mountain restaurant. Then, after nightfall, ski back down towards the resort, over a drop in altitude of 1300m with only the moon to see by.

Ice cave: Found at 3400m, this is the longest and highest in the world. The grotto was dug entirely by pickaxe, there was no use of machines, and it now contains many ice sculptures. Open winter and summer.

Night in an igloo: In the Pied Moutet area, at 1700m, in a wild mountain setting, the Kanata igloo village offers the chance to spend a night in an igloo. Access is on snowshoes in the evening or on skis during the day. Call 0033 (0)6 12 29 49 03 for more information.

Night skiing and boarding: This takes place 3 times a week on the Piste de Lutins in the middle of the resort – and it's free! For more information call Deux Alpes Loisirs (0033 (0)4 76 79 75 01).

Paragliding: Call Ecole de Parapente Air 2 Alpes (0033 (0)6 81 44 38 31, www.air 2alpes.com) for tandem flights. Or Ecole de Parapente des 2 Alpes (0033 (0)4 76 79 21 21 or 0033 (0)6 07 72 26 60) for tandem flights.

Quad motorbikes: Night-time treks run from 5.30pm. Take your driving licence. (0033 (0)6 81 31 64 01).

Snowmobiles: 2 Alpes Motoneige (0033 (0)6 08 63 07 40, www.2alpesmotoneige.com) organise trips from Lutins draglift from 6pm.

Tobogganing: The Alpette lift is open for tobogganing until 10pm 2–3 times a week. There are 2 runs: 1 fast and 1 slow.

In the town

Bowling: There are 2 bowling alleys and lots of games arcades. Bowling Le Strike (0033 (0)4 76 79 28 34) and Bowling Les 2 Alpes 1800 (0033 (0)4 76 79 25 64, www.clubforme1800.com) each have 6 lanes.

Cinema: The local cinema has 2 screens and shows films at 6pm and 9pm.

Fitness activities: The health and fitness activities available include squash, jacuzzi, hammam, sauna, tanking, fitness circuits, slimming courses, massages, relaxation, gym, body building, cardio-training, aqua gym, solarium, UVA, spa and shiatsu.

Ice skating: There's an open-air Olympic ice rink (0033 (0)4 76 79 22 73). You can either ice skate or try out the dodgem cars on ice.

Swimming: Club forme has a heated outdoor pool and wellness facilities (0033 (0)4

76 79 25 64, www.club forme1800.com).

Wellness: Aquaflorès wellbeing centre (0033 (0)4 76 80 56 90, www.chalet-mounier.com) has an indoor pool plus spa days: physiotherapy, massages, diet advice, seaweed treatments, aromatherapy, etc. Shiatsu Santé (0033 (0)6 07 60 03 50, www.shiatsu2alpes.com) offers shiatsu and reflexology.

Events

The **Rock on Snowboard Tour** celebrates the start of the winter season in October/November with product testing, partying and competitions.

In January, Les Deux Alpes holds a poker week everyday from 6pm to midnight.

Other events include the **Snowzone** event (mid-March), which combines riding and music. The day starts with sounds on the slopes that gradually make their way down to the resort, and then carry on into the bars and clubs. Popular DJs will be playing house, techno and electronic sounds in an extraordinary atmosphere at the bottom of the Deux Alpes slopes.

Accommodation

Farandole (0033 (0)4 76 80 50 45, www.hotel-la-farandole.com), one of the only 4-star hotels in town, is a traditional chalet, with 60 bedrooms and apartments. There is a smart restaurant, fitness club, indoor pool, sauna and jacuzzi.

There are 8 3-star hotels, 1 of the best being **Chalet Mounier** (0033 (0)4 76 80 56 90, www.chalet-mounier.com), which has a great atmosphere in an authentic chalet. There is a billiard room, spa and indoor pool with a wave machine. It is handy for the Diable gondola and the main bar scene.

There is also an enormous choice of apartments, but it is very important to check their location as Les Deux Alpes sprawls over a large area.

One good-value company that is definitely worth checking out is **Scuba-Ski** (0033 (0)4 76 11 03 14 (Oct–April), 0033 (0)668 868 988 (any time), www.scuba-ski.com), which offers both catered and self-catered apartments, for between 2 and 10 guests. All their accommodation benefits from a great location, right in the middle of the action (just a few minutes' walk from the ski lifts) and is priced at a very competitive rate. They have 1 10-bed chalet (comfortably fits 7), which really is home away from home with hundreds of classic videos to watch, and board games to play. It's more homely than luxurious but highly recommended. They will even arrange for your lift passes, ski/board hire and/or ski/board school to be booked and ready for you on arrival, with a 10 per cent discount! If you're looking for apartments of good standard, the **Le Prince des Ecrins** residence (0033 (0)4 76 80 53 53) is situated 500m from the nearest shops and within immediate proximity of the slopes. It contains 28 apartments for 4–10 people that have a magnificent view over the Veneon valley and the Venosc and Muzelle peaks. All apartments have south-facing balconies.

Eating out

On the mountain

There are nine mountain restaurants in Les Deux Alpes. **Le Panoramic** (0033 (0)6 86 81 67 26) is a popular meeting point, at the heart of the action at 2600m. Choose between the restaurant or self-service. **Chalet La Fée** (0033 (0)4 76 80 24 13) has a friendly atmosphere, simple food and good views from the terrace.

> 'More than 60 restaurants with a wide variety of cuisines'

In town

There are more than 60 restaurants in Les Deux Alpes with a wide variety of cuisines. Fast food joints and crêperies can be found all through town and offer decent burgers, kebabs, paninis and steak sandwiches. Don't expect a bargain though.

Most of the restaurants in the area serve traditional French cuisine – fondues, raclettes, tartiflette, pierres chaudes, etc. **Cellier** (0033 (0)4 76 79 08 79) has a charming wooden interior with a roaring fire. It is located at the end of town; follow the main road to the Place de Venosc and it's just opposite. **Crêpes à GoGo** (0033 (0)4 76 79 29 61, www.lescrepesagogo.com) is a stunning restaurant, with not bad prices for such a gorgeous place. The huge fire and cushioned benches create a very cosy and alpine atmosphere. **Le P'tit Polyte** at the Chalet Mounier (0033 (0)4 76 80 56 90, www.chalet-mounier.com) has a strong reputation for serving traditional Savoyard dishes.

La Spaghetteria (0033 (0)4 76 79 05 77) has good-value pasta dishes. **Smokey Joes** (0033 (0)4 76 79 28 97, www.smokeyjoes.fr) and The **Red Frog** (0033 (0)4 76 79 23 28) serve good, classic bar food all day until 11pm.

Bars and clubs

There are 30 bars, open until 2am and 3 clubs that are open until about 5am.

Smokey Joes (0033 (0)4 76 79 28 97) is right in the heart of Les Deux Alpes, a second's walk from the lifts and town centre. It is British run and is open 8am–2am every day. The food is fantastic and is served all day until 11pm. Choose from full English breakfasts until midday, bacon sandwiches, paninis, fajitas, ribs and many more tasty morsels. Smokeys also has internet access, DJs and regular theme nights. The **Red Frog** (0033 (0)4 76 79 23 28) is run by an Englishman, Irishman and Scotsman and always has a good busy atmosphere. Located at the Venosc end of town, it is open 7am–2am, serving food until 11pm. The Frog serves legendary, all-day, full English breakfasts as well as burgers, pasta, steaks and salads. They show all the footie on plasma TVs and have opened a sitting room at the back of the bar with comfy sofas. There is also has a pool room and wireless laptops.

'The Frog serves legendary, all-day, full English breakfasts'

Smithy's (0033 (0)4 76 11 37 76, www.smithystavern.com) is open 5pm–2am and is located next to the Avalanche club at the Venosc end of town. It's a huge, open-plan pub on 2 floors, the ground floor being the pub and the top floor the restaurant. Its popularity is due to regular DJs and live bands and (allegedly) the longest vodka bar (with over 20 flavours of vodka shots) in the Alps, although we think the Couloir in Tignes has stolen this title. The music is an eclectic mix (anywhere from cheesy pop to hip hop, rap and house), and is usually adapted to suit the crowds. Pool and table football tables pass the time. The restaurant (open 5–11.30pm) serves steaks, fresh fish and vegi dishes and, in the summer, BBQs are held on the outside terrace, which is used as an après ski terrace during the winter.

The **Boardroom** (0033 (0)4 76 79 08 89) benefits from a very central location on the main street and a sunny terrace. It opens 11am–2am and serves food all day. At happy hour, usually 7–9pm, free tapas is available. Its plasma TVs show videos during the day, as well as all the major sporting events. Among the variety of drinks and cocktails available, they also have an interesting range of absinthe cocktails for the more courageous drinkers. **Mezzanine** (0033 (0)6 15 10 55 65) is a small bar, towards the Mont de Lans end of town, that does great cocktails and is the only place in town to serve the lethal 'Mutzig' beer.

There are a few clubs that are open until 5am, the best being the **Brésilien** (0033 (0)4 76 79 04 98) and the **Avalanche** (0033 (0)4 76 80 52 44). The Avalanche, towards the Venosc end of town, isn't huge but has plenty of atmosphere and regularly has DJs playing to keep the crowds entertained. It's a funky club and is right next door to Smithy's, so there's no need to get cold – just stumble on over.

Getting there

By car

Take the motorway direct from Paris (643km) or Lyon (170km/2-hour drive approximately) to Grenoble (turn off N8 Briançon, Vizelle, stations de l'Oisans), then RN 91 in the direction of Briançon via Bourg d'Oisans. Turn right at Barrage du Chambon (Chambon dam) and take the D213.

If you are driving from the UK, it's about 950–1130km from the channel ports.

By coach

Eurolines run a bus from London to Grenoble, where you can pick up the VFD/Satobus connection to Les Deux Alpes.

By plane

Geneva (220km) Connect to Les Deux Alpes by VFD coaches via Grenoble – 3-hour drive.
Lyon (170km) Connect to Les Deux Alpes by Satobus (0033 (0)8 20 32 03 68, www.altibus.com) – 2-hour drive.
Grenoble (110km) is closer but is no longer serviced by a schedule airline, although charter flights still operate – 1.5-hour drive. Transfers are available from Bensbus (www.bensbus.co.uk) or VFD (0033 (0)4 76 80 51 22, www.vfd.fr).

By train

Take the Eurostar from London St Pancras to Paris; then by TGV to Grenoble, then a bus (100 minutes) to the resort. Contact Rail Europe (0870 830 4862, www.raileurope.co.uk) or European Rail (020 7387 0444, www.europeanrail.com). Bus tickets must be purchased in advance from VFD coaches (0033 (0)4 76 60 46 37, www.vfd.fr).

Useful facts and phone numbers

Tourist office

T: 00 33 (0)4 76 79 22 00
F: 00 33 (0)4 76 79 01 38
W: www.les2alpes.com

Direct reservations

T: 0033 (0)4 76 79 24 38
F: 0033 (0)4 76 79 51 13

Emergency services

- In a medical emergency dial 15, for the fire brigade call 18, or 112 for either from a mobile
- Police: 0033 (0)4 76 80 58 57
- Ambulance: 0033 (0)4 76 80 52 39
- Weather information: 0033 (0)8 92 68 02 38

Doctors

- Centre Clinique des 2 Alpes: 0033 (0)4 76 79 20 03
- Centre Médical du Lauvitel: 0033 (0)4 76 80 52 48
- Dr Bron: 0033 (0)4 76 79 28 96

Taxis

- Trans'Oisans Taxis: 0033 (0)4 76 80 06 97/ 06 09 38 38 38, 5–9 seater taxis
- Autocars Rouard: 0033 (0)4 76 80 04 21, www.rouard.com

La Grave

Freeriding heaven.

On the slopes	Rating
Snow reliability	❄❄❄❄
Parks	–
Off-piste	❄❄❄❄❄
Off the slopes	
Après ski	❄❄
Nightlife	❄❄
Eating out	❄❄
Resort charm	❄❄❄½

The resort

You shouldn't come here if…

- you like cruising round between mountain restaurants
- the idea of a steep red run sets you panicking
- you place great importance on a resort's provision of late-night drinking holes
- you won't stay in hotels that have fewer than 4 stars
- you are a snowpark junkie
- you can't fathom the thought of skiing (if applicable) on skis that are shorter than 195cm – they'd call you a pussy.

And, to be honest, we hope this includes most people because if you all came, you'd spoil it. However, if you are still interested, you'll have the most amazing time of your life on this mountain. It takes the mountains back to how they used to be, and how they should be, completely opposite to the crowded, motorway-style runs that now shroud most resorts. You will not see lifts (apart from the one Old School bubble that takes you to 3200m); you will not see coloured poles marking nicely groomed runs (as there aren't any); you will not see ski patrols (there is only the great Jean-Charles who starts the morning at the bottom of the lift to provide you with invaluable info about the avalanche risk, etc – then he's off skiing); you won't see anything to warn you about rocks, cliff drops or crevasses (of which there are many); you probably won't even see other skiers or boarders; you will simply see the majestic, imposing and commanding mountains – and they're all yours. With a vertical drop of 2150m from top to bottom, the devoted freerider will be in heaven.

If you do come to La Grave you will need, without question, all the avalanche-safety gear (probe, shovel and transceiver) and enough money to invest in a guide, or know someone who knows the mountain well. It's not that it's not safe to be without one – it's no different to anywhere else, you just won't have a clue where you're going and you will, for definite, get completely lost, which would be a shame as no one's there to come and find you. You also need to be in pretty good physical condition.

The mountains

Height: 1400–3550m

Ability	Rating
Expert	❄❄❄❄❄
Intermediate	❄❄
Beginner	❄

Getting about

The whole mountain is available to ride, depending on your ability. There are some set itineraries but they are pretty much impossible to follow without a guide, never mind if you want to explore the couloirs and hidden areas. If, for some unknown reason, you do want to leave this beautiful mountain, La Grave is also connected with Les Deux Alpes, although there is a walk involved. If you are a beginner and you somehow end up in La Grave, La Chazelet is nearby and a good place to learn. (If you need lessons contact the ESF: 0033 (0)4 76 79 92 86, www.esf-la-meije.com.)

The 1 and only cable car takes you right to the top of the mountain and takes around 30 minutes in total. There are a few stops, and the usual course of action is to take the lift right to 3200m first thing and then ride down to P1 (the first stop) and take the lift back up. You'll probably manage this 3 to 4 times in 1 day. At first you may think the cable car is too slow but after a couple of runs you'll welcome the break and, if it went any quicker, it would allow more people to be on the mountain at once, which is against the philosophy of La Grave.

Be sure that you prepare yourself with sufficient safety equipment and knowledge. For example, for some couloirs you need ropes and climbing equipment to lower yourself in – do your homework before you set off. If you have any questions, make sure you seek out the patrouilleur, who usually resides in the wooden chalet by the lift pass office.

Backcountry

From the moment you step on the lift you know that you're about to start an amazing adventure. As you step off the lift at the top of the mountain (3200m), you can tell in an instant that you are somewhere special and unique. There are no marked pistes, no ski/board schools and no ski patrol. Therefore, it is 100 per cent certain that you need a guide, especially if you have not been here before. People who don't take a guide tend to look confused, lost and a little scared. Without a guide, you will also miss out on some of the best areas.

'You're about to start an amazing adventure'

One of the first places to check out for your warm-up run is the classic itinerary: les Vallons (turn left as you exit the lift). There is challenging and fun terrain and you can really let yourself go. It's a long-lasting run and the likelihood is that you won't bump into a single person on your way down. Your guide can also show you some great couloirs if you're up for it. Our favourites are the Triffides couloirs; Triffide 1 is at the top of Les Ruilliains. Your guide will rope you in and then it opens up into 1 nice shoot.

If you turn right on exiting the lift, you can set out along the Chancel, another classic itinerary, with some exciting deviations. One such digression is over to English Man Valley (nicknamed by the locals). The Banane couloir is approximately 150m long. It's quite steep at the top but it's easily accessible and a good ride down to a beautiful lake called Lac de Puyvachier. If the conditions are bad, and there's too much wind for them to open the top lift, panic ye not, as there are some great tree runs at the bottom of the mountain, some with good mogul lines.

There are some amazing riders in La Grave and all have a great deal of knowledge about the mountains. La Grave, we salute you!

Lift passes

Check the latest prices at www.lagrave-lameije.com

Guiding

There are 28 guides in La Grave, ranging from former ski champions to locals who've lived here forever.

You can register for a 'Discovery Descent' day at the guides' office or at the cable car. You pay for your lift pass and a single descent at either 10.30am (meet in La Grave) or at 2.30pm (meet at 3200m) with a mountain guide.

Bureau des Guides

On a 1-day tour you will discover the classic off-piste descents of Vallons de la Meije and Chancel in a group of 1–8 people. They can also take you to couloirs and the steeper, secret spots, depending on the level of the group. Other courses include off-piste awareness courses, ice climbing, winter mountaineering, heliskiing, ski touring and paragliding.
0033 (0)4 76 79 90 21
www.guidelagrave.com

Handiski

The ESF in La Grave offers adaptive skiing for disabled children and adults.

0033 (0)4 76 79 92 86
www.esf-la-meije.com

Snow Legend Camps
0033 (0)6 81 97 03 25
www.snowlegend.com

Events

The Ultimate Test Tour (www.ultimatetesttour.com) is a weekend of ski and board testing in January.

The **Big LePlowSki** gathers backcountry riders to test out the latest gear with special groups for women, beginners, photographers and advanced skiers (www.thebigleplowski.com).

Derby de la Meije (www.derbydelameije.com) takes place around the end of March/beginning of April. It comprises the longest vertical drop of any race in the world: 2150m. There are over 1000 participants, on snowboard, skis or telemarks, dressed up or not, alone or in a team and each one chooses their own line down the mountain. For a few days La Grave really kicks off with loads of music, partying, drinking and riding, after which it returns to its idyllic state.

Accommodation

There aren't many places to stay in La Grave but there are some great ones, and nothing's too expensive. **L'Edelweiss** (0033 (0)4 76 79 90 93, www.hotel-edelweiss.com) is a lovely, 2-star hotel offering a great standard of accommodation in a beautiful location. There are 23 rooms that are all en suite and can house 2–4 people. The atmosphere is cosy, friendly and homely with loads of facilities: a TV room, Jacuzzi, sauna, library, games and videos. Robin and Marlon, the Scottish/Dutch couple that run the hotel, will make sure you are very well looked after. Robin can provide you with good advice about the mountain – he's had many years of experience and was the British freestyle champion (in the days of hotdogging). The food's great, there's a good bar, they have free WiFi internet and often have live music events – all the staff play instruments as do loads of the locals!

The Castillan (0033 (0)4 76 79 90 04, http://perso.wanadoo.fr/castillan) is another 2-star in the centre of town. If you're looking for self-catering accommodation, the 3-star **Les Enfetchores** (0033 (0)4 38 37 13 60, www.les-enfetchores.com) offers good apartments with dishwasher, washing machine and TV. You can book accommodation through the central reservation office, **Meije Tours** (0033 (0)4 76 79 92 46, www.meijetours.com), who will advise you on accommodation for your budget and requirements, and put you in contact with private apartment owners if necessary. They will also offer you good prices for mountain guides.

Eating out

On the mountain

There are 3 good restaurants up the mountain. At 3200m is a self-service restaurant, **Le Haut-Dessus** (0033 (0)4 76 79 23 08), that serves excellent pizzas, steaks, pork and all sorts. The staff are all really friendly. At full moon, there has been known to be the occasional party after everyone else has gone down the mountain. The locals congregate at 3200m, have a fair few shots and ride down the mountain in the bright moonlight – not recommended unless you know the mountain like the back of your hand. The **Evariste Chancel** (0033 (0)4 76 79 97 05, www.refuge-chancel.com) at 2508m, just off the Chancel route, is a great restaurant and, for an experience not to be missed, try staying there overnight. The other restaurant, at the middle station, also serves good quality food. There's nothing you'll be disappointed with in La Grave.

In town

There are 2 restaurants in town that are fantastic. The **Edelweiss hotel** (see Accommodation) serves a delicious, home-made 4-course set menu at a very good price and if you don't fancy what's on the menu, they also have an à la carte selection with a great 3-cheese fondue. The other restaurant is the **Le Vieux Guide** (0033 (0)4 76 79 90 75), down a small alleyway, which is fabulously cosy and serves fantastic, traditional Savoyard food. We loved the raclette and left feeling very content. **Le Bois des Fées** (0033 (0)4 76 11 05 48) bar also serves superb food if you fancy a simple but tasty pizza or gratin. It is themed in a kind of *Midsummer Night's Dream* fashion.

Bars and clubs

There isn't much in the way of bars in La Grave. **Le Bois des Fées** (0033 (0)4 76 11 05 48) is 1 of the most popular bars with a pool table, internet access and good food (see Eating out). The **Edelweiss** bar, with WiFi (free with a drink) after 5pm, is a popular choice with the locals and a really friendly place. It stays open as long as Robin and Marlon feel they want to keep it open and they often arrange music nights; the locals all seem to be top musicians as well as exceptional riders.

Whatever you do, don't brag about the 30m cliff you dropped off or the couloir you straight-lined – the 80-year-old local sat next to you probably went 10 times faster yesterday and wouldn't even bother to mention it.

Getting there

By car

It will take nearly 10 hours to drive from Calais. Head towards Grenoble and then take the RN91 towards Briançon. La Grave is around 80km from the motorway exit and is easily accessible.

By plane

Lyon (150km) Transfer takes around 2 hours.
Geneva (220km) Transfer takes around 3 hours.
Grenoble (100km) Transfer takes just under 2 hours.

By train

Take the Eurostar from London St Pancras to Paris; then the TGV to Grenoble, then a bus (90 minutes) to the resort. Contact Rail Europe (0870 830 4862, www.raileurope.co.uk) or European Rail (020 7387 0444, www.europeanrail.com). Bus tickets must be purchased in advance from VFD coaches (0033 (0)4 76 60 46 37, www.vfd.fr).

Useful facts and phone numbers

Tourist office

T: 00 33 (0)4 76 79 90 05
F: 00 33 (0)4 76 79 91 65
W: www.lagrave-lameije.com

Direct reservations

T: 00 33 (0)4 76 79 97 72

Emergency services

- In a medical emergency dial 15, for the fire brigade call 18, or 112 for either from a mobile.
- Police: 0033 (0)4 76 79 91 02
- Mountain rescue: 0033 (0)4 92 22 22 22
- Snow and avalanche bulletin: 0033 (0)8 92 68 10 20

Doctors

- 0033 (0)4 76 79 98 03

Taxi

- Taxi de la Meije: 0033 (0)6 79 53 45 67, www.taxidelameije.com
- Meije Autocars: 0033 (0)4 76 79 92 09

Meribel

Trendy, with a great atmosphere (and great parks), if you don't mind feeling like you are in a pub on the King's Road.

On the slopes	Rating
Snow reliability	❄❄❄
Parks	❄❄❄❄
Off-piste	❄❄❄½
Off the slopes	
Après ski	❄❄❄❄
Nightlife	❄❄❄½
Eating out	❄❄❄
Resort charm	❄❄❄

The resort

Meribel is a friendly place, dominated by the Brits. It's a purpose-built resort but much more attractive than others such as Tignes, Les Arcs and Val Thorens as everything has been built in chalet style. Meribel 1450 contains most of the bars, restaurants and shops – not to be confused with Meribel Village, which is 2km away. Meribel prides itself on being funky and trendy, with some really smart bars and a good atmosphere. It can feel like you're in a bar in London, so your perception of Meribel will relate to whether you think this is a good or bad thing. Either way, the riding is fantastic, and the links to Courchevel, La Tania and Val Thorens make this ski area cruising paradise. There is a reservoir that holds 60000m^2 ensuring better snow cover. Meribel should be especially praised for its 2 superb parks. Mottaret is not as charming (it's ugly), and doesn't have much in the way of nightlife. It does have good access to the slopes, however – and it's a great place for families.

The mountains

Height: 1450m

Ability	Rating
Expert	❄❄❄❄
Intermediate	❄❄❄❄
Beginner	❄❄❄

Getting about

There are 150km of trails in Meribel; 76 runs in total. Of these, 9 are black, 23 red, 36 blue, and 8 green. There are also 650 snow guns, which assure snow coverage for 37 per cent of the ski area. This is a great help in Meribel as the resort is pretty low so the snow at the bottom is often fairly poor. The lift system is very quick and efficient.

The park

At 1800m is the Meribel Moonpark, which has it all. It has 10 table-top jumps, 10 rails, 2 pipes (1 competition level pipe, 145m long and a 125m pipe for novices), a massive hip and a 1000m boarder/skier cross course. It is always kept in tiptop condition and is the main meeting point in Les Trois Vallées. There's a group of enthusiastic shapers taking care of the park every day and experimenting with different ideas. Check out www.moonpark.net for pictures and videos.

Meribel's little brother Mottaret, also has a great park at 2400m; the Plattières Park. It has 5 table tops, 1 hip, 3 rails, 2 pipes and a skier/boardercross. Having all this in the same area has to make Meribel one of the best places for freestyle in Europe. We love it!

Off-piste and backcountry

From the top of Saulire, which is famous for having amazing couloirs leading to Courchevel, you have the couloirs to Meribel. There is the central Meribel couloir, and just along from this is death couloir, which is great when the snow's right, and first thing in the morning before the sun does too much damage.

Look out for Super Mario Land, Rock Garden and the Spot – local favourites around the Bartavelle area that you can get to by going up the Roc de tougne drag lift. The Bartavelle also has one of the best mogul fields in Les Trois Vallées, which has hosted events like the Meribel Shaker Bump competition. A great adventure is the Gébroulaz. It's best to take a guide or you might not find it. It's a good 1-hour hike via Val Thorens and has to be done early in the morning. Once you're at the top you can look forward to a 14km run across a stunning glacier untouched by the masses.

Lift passes

Check the latest prices at www.meribel.net

Instruction

ESF

The ESF offers freeride, freestyle and off-piste tuition as well as the usual private and group lessons.
0033 (0)4 79 08 60 31
www.esf-meribel.com

Magic in Motion

Magic in Motion is well respected and loved in the local community. The Magic team consists of both British and French instructors who are a fantastic choice for all, from beginners to those who want to hook back flips in the park. Disciplines taught include skiing, snowboarding, monoski, telemarking and ski-touring. There are a lot of characters within the team! Some of France's top freestyle skiers work for Magic in Motion and have set up their own 'Team Magic' who now do the freeride and freestyle competition circuit as well as doing demos. This school is perfect for children.
0033 (0)4 79 08 53 36
www.magicinmotion.co.uk

New Generation

New Generation offer all levels of ski and snowboard instruction from the usual lessons to gap year and instructor courses.
0033 (0)4 79 01 03 18/0844 484 3663 (UK)
www.skinewgen.com

Other activities

Cinema: The tourist office publishes a cinema guide each week. There is 1 cinema just up the road from the Meribel tourist office and another inside the Mottaret tourist office complex.

Climbing: The Bureau des Guides (0033 (0)4 79 00 30 38, www.guides-courchevel-meribel.com) offers climbing classes – either on a frozen waterfall or on a climbing wall.

Dogsledding: For more information contact Traineau Evasion on 0033 (0)6 80 63 15 72/ 0033 (0)4 79 08 81 55.

Hot air ballooning: Take a 1 or 2-hour flight with Ski Vol (0033 (0)4 79 08 41 82).

Ice skating, swimming and bowling: The Parc Olympique (0033 (0)4 79 00 59 96) is home to a number of amenities, such as an ice skating rink, a climbing wall (free for experienced climbers), a huge swimming pool with spa facilities (sauna, Jacuzzi) and a 6-lane bowling alley (0033 (0)4 79 00 36 44).

Mountain flying: Courses in mountain flying are available with coaching for the mountain pilot qualification from the Méribel Air Club (0033 (0)4 79 08 61 33).

Paragliding: From the top of Saulire or La Loze pass. Contact either Aero-Dynamique (0033 (0)6 09 92 25 80, www.parapentemeribailes.com), A Parapente (0033 (0)6 80 11 86 77, http://aparapente.free.fr) or Tandem Top Saulire (0033 (0)4 79 00 45 67, www.tandemtop.com).

Skidoos: These can be rented in Meribel-Mottaret from Snow Biker (0033 (0)4 79 00 40 01, www.snow-biker.com).

Snowshoeing: Snowshoeing for children is offered by the ESF (see Instruction). Overnight expeditions with mountain-hut accommodation are available. Raquett'Evasion (0033 (0)4 79 24 10 40, www.raquettevasion.com) offers a number of trips and lessons.

Events

The **MoonCrew Invitational** is a ski and snowboard slopestyle/rail jam in March. There is an amateur freestyle contest and a pro rider demonstration. Finals and demos take place in front of the Rond Pont terrace. Thc 3 Valleys **X-Wing Rally** also comes to Meribel.

Magic in Motion (see Instruction) holds a competition dedicated to 1 of its friends who died in an avalanche in Courchevel a few years back. It's called the **Magic Dedern** competition, consists of a big air and a quarterpipe and is open to anyone. If you're around Meribel in April, check it out. Contact adam@adamj.net for more details.

It's also worth looking out for the **ice hockey** battles in Meribel at the Parc Olympique (0033 (0)4 79 00 58 21).

Accommodation

The best 4-star hotel in Meribel (another in Mottaret): **Le Grand Coeur** (0033 (0)4 79 08 60 03, www.legrandcoeur.com). This impressive hotel manages to be very welcoming and grandiose at the same time.

Most tourists arrive on package holidays and there are tons of luxury chalet companies to cater for them, for example **Meriski** (www.meriski.co.uk) and **Kaluma** (0870 442 8044 (UK), www.kalumatravel.co.uk). The accommodation tends to be 'ski-in, ski-out' or minibuses are provided to shuttle you about – so not too much room for concern. Look out for chalets with outdoor hot tubs.

Le Roc (0033 (0)4 79 00 48 29, http://hotelleroc.mountainpub.com), above the lively Taverne bar and restaurant (see Bars and clubs), is 1 of the only really good-value hotels with a fantastic location in the centre of town. The 12 rooms are comfy and homely and the staff are friendly and helpful.

Eating out

On the mountain

The **Rond Point** (see Bars and clubs) is a great place for lunch and the place for après ski, with loads of live bands. If you want to chill on a good sun terrace, head to the **Chardonnet** (0033 (0)4 79 00 44 81), at the mid-station of the Pas du Lac gondola.

In Mottaret there are loads of fast food joints that have easy access from the slopes. The **Plan des Mains** (0033 (0)4 79 07 31 06) mountain restaurant (2100m) is at the foot of Mont Vallon. There is a sandwich bar, a brasserie and a gastronomic restaurant. There is also a shop and free ski lockers. Cruises to Courchevel for lunch are pretty good if you've got a few quid in your pocket. Check out the Courchevel chapter for more info (see page 87).

In town

Meribel is packed full of lovely restaurants. Gourmet food is on offer at the plush hotels, such as **Le Grand Coeur** (see Accommodation). The **Fromagerie** (0033 (0)4 79 08 55 48), next to the Board Brains shop, has a great atmosphere and particularly good fondues, and the **Refuge** (0033 (0)4 79 08 61 97) is a cosy, central restaurant serving great pizzas. **La Taverne** (www.tavernemeribel.com, 0033 (0)4 79 00 32 45), in town offers simple food such as sandwiches, cheesy chips, etc and are often really busy as they are popular with the locals.

If you are in a self-catering chalet or apartment, have a look at **Extreme Cuisine** (0033 (0)6 32 91 84 56, www.extreme-cuisine.co.uk) who can cook you a 3-course meal in your chalet or can even deliver an Indian, complete with naan breads and poppadoms (0033 (0)6 81 54 32 90)!

Bars and clubs

For après ski, the **Rond Point** (0033 (0)4 79 00 37 51, www.rondpointmeribel.com) is the place to be. It's packed from 4pm with live music and lots of dancing on the terrace. **Jack's Bar** (0033 (0)4 79 00 30 94, www.jacksbarmeribel.com) is also hugely popular at après ski as it's close to the slopes and also kicks off later on, until 2am. It has 'pitcher hours' and a cocktail hour 10–11pm. As well as TVs, it has a 42in plasma screen for showing all the big sporting events and DJs or live music each evening. Next door is Evolution (0033 (0)4 79 00 44 26, www.evolutionmeribel.com), owned by the same company. It serves food all day (with a variety of culinary influences), including a great full English brekkie in the mornings. Evolution has internet terminals that double up as sports TVs for crucial matches. There is a massive plasma screen for films and you can even while away a few hours on the Xbox.

Le Pub (0033 (0)4 79 08 60 02, www.doronpub.com) has pool tables and is a good place to watch sports. It's a bit big and characterless though, and they don't provide much in the way of seating in order to try and cram in as many people as possible. The **Barometer** (0033 (0)4 9 00 41 06, www.meribelbarometer.com) is a stylish place on the main street and has a number of pool tables, free wi-fi and a good ambience. The **Taverne** (www.tavernemeribel.com, 0033 (0)4 79 00 36 18), right in the centre of town is the hub of the local (British) community. It's a really cool bar with a good atmosphere and does decent food too. It also has a few internet terminals downstairs.

Dicks Tea Bar (0033 (0)4 79 08 60 19, www.dicksteabar.com/meribel) is the place to go later on. It's always got a good line-up of DJs, and it's jam packed full of Brits up for a good laugh, although be aware that this can result in a bit of trouble now and again. The music varies from pop to house music, it depends on the night.

Getting there

By car

Take the autoroute A43 to Albertville, then the N90 to Moutiers, then follow the D90 for 18km. Meribel is 1070km from London.

By plane

Lyon (185km) Transfers take 3.5 hours by Satobus (0033 (0)4 37 255 2555, www.satobus.com).

Chambéry/Aix les Bains (95km) Transfers take 1.5 hours by Cars Transavoie (0033 (0)4 79 54 49 66, www.altibus.com).

Geneva (135km) Transfers are by Touriscar bus and should be booked in advance (0033 (0)4 50 43 60 02, www.alpski-bus.com). Helicopter and plane transfers are also available with SAF (0033 (0)4 79 08 00 91 (www.saf-helico.com).

By train

Take the Eurostar from London St Pancras to Paris; then an overnight train to Moutiers, and then a bus (45 minutes) to the resort. Contact Rail Europe (0870 830 4862, www.raileurope.co.uk) or European Rail (020 7387 0444, www.europeanrail.com). Bus tickets can be purchased in advance from Altibus (0033 (0)4 79 68 32 96, www.altibus.com) or bought at the station.

Useful facts and phone numbers

Tourist office

T: 0033 (0)4 79 08 60 01
F: 0033 (0)4 79 00 59 61
W: www.meribel.net

Direct reservations

T: 0033 (0)4 79 00 50 00
W:www.meribel-reservations.com

Emergency services

- In a medical emergency dial 15, for the fire brigade call 18, or 112 for either from a mobile
- Police station: 0033 (0)4 79 00 58 92 or 17
- Moutiers Hospital: 0033 (0)4 79 09 60 60
- Weather information: 0892 68 02 73/32 50 (www.meteo.fr)

Doctors

- Cabinet medical – Mottaret: 0033 (0)4 79 00 40 88
- Dr Schamash: 0033 (0)4 79 08 60 41
- Dr Mabboux: 0033 (0)4 79 08 60 41
- Dr Vabre: 0033 (0)4 79 08 65 40

Taxis

- Meribel: 0033 (0)4 79 08 65 10
- Meribel-Mottaret: 0033 (0)4 79 00 44 29

Morzine

A great resort for weekend trips, with masses of riding potential.

On the slopes	Rating
Snow reliability	❄❄❄½
Parks	❄❄
Off-piste	❄❄❄❄
Off the slopes	
Après ski	❄❄❄
Nightlife	❄❄❄❄
Eating out	❄❄❄
Resort charm	❄❄❄

The resort

Morzine is a fantastic example of how a French resort should be. You can certainly see why Morzine attracts so many of Britain's leading boarders and skiers; you have access to the impressive Portes du Soleil circuit, including some of Europe's best parks (see Champéry and Avoriaz chapters, pages 170 and 78), a great night scene, a picturesque village and easy accessibility from Geneva.

Morzine's altitude is a bit of a setback, with many European resorts providing runs above 3000m, even the 2275m peak in the Portes du Soleil may be enough to put off the most snow-cautious.

The nearby town of Les Gets is a traditional Savoyard village and a lovely base for families escaping the busy night scene in Morzine.

The mountains

Height: 975–2275m

Ability	Rating
Expert	❄❄❄❄
Intermediate	❄❄❄❄
Beginner	❄❄❄½

Getting about

From Morzine town centre you can access 2 very different areas. The official Morzine slopes are on the Le Pléney side of town and from here you can ride over to Les Gets via some nice blues and reds. This area has a park and some good off-piste of its own, although more proficient riders should head to the Super Morzine lift on the other side of town to gain easy access to the superb terrain of the Portes du Soleil (see also pages 78 and 170) or take the cable car from Les Prodains.

The park

On the Le Pléney side of Morzine is a beginners' park with a selection of rails and intermediate kickers. Some fantastic parks are accessible via the Portes du Soleil circuit including those in Avoriaz (see Avoriaz chapter, page 78), and Les Crozats (see Champéry chapter, page 170).

Off-piste and backcountry

The best off-piste on the Le Pléney side of town can be found off the back of the Pointe de Nyon – you really need a guide to be able to explore this area properly. Alternatively, head to the top of the Chamossière, from which you will find an accessible bowl on the left. There is some good tree skiing around the Le Pléney area, too, so it's a good place to head towards in bad weather. The Portes du Soleil circuit has some fantastic terrain to unearth (see also the Avoriaz and Champéry chapters, pages 170 and 78).

Lift passes

Check the latest prices at www.morzine-avoriaz.com

Instruction

ESF

0033 (0)4 50 79 13 13
www.esf-morzine.com

Easy2Ride

This ski, snowboard and adventure school offers freeride, freestyle and backcountry lessons, as well as the usual.
0033 (0)4 50 79 05 16
www.morzineski.fr

The Guidance Office

Off-piste, helicopter trips and skiing the Vallée Blanche can be arranged through the Guidance Office.
0033 (0)4 50 74 72 23/06 86 95 43 74
www.easy2ride.fr

The Snow School

This ski and snowboard school sets a maximum group size of 6. Its unique range of courses includes skills clinics in expert secrets, freeride and freestyle and special day or half-day trips, including a girls' day out, heliskiing, torchlit descents and telemark try-outs.
0033 (0)4 86 68 88 40
www.the-snow-school.com

Other activities

Unless otherwise stated, contact the tourist office (see Useful facts and phone numbers) for more information.

'Try a tandem parapente flight or a course'

Horse-drawn sleigh rides: You can take a short tour of Morzine or a longer tour of Montriond.

Hot air balloon: Contact the Cameleon Organisation (0033 (0)4 50 75 94 00) about flights.

Ice diving: This takes place under the ice of Lake Montriond. Contact the Cameleon Organisation (0033 (0)4 50 75 00 59).

Massages: Contact Cocon au Pays des Flocons (0033 (0)4 50 75 81 29) or Massages du Monde (0033 (0)4 50 74 61 97).

Night skiing: This popular activity takes place on Le Pléney.

Parapente: Try a tandem flight, with an instructor, a discovery lesson or a course to take you from a beginner to a proficient flier, with pilot licence. Morzine has a well-established parapenting scene. Contact Ecole de Parapente des Portes du Soleil (0033 (0)4 50 75 76 39 or 0033 (0)6 12 55 51 31, www.morzineparapente.com) or Airéole (0033 (0)6 07 63 16 25 or 0033 (0)4 50 74 71 01, www.aireole.fr).

Snowmobiles: Guided tours are available for either half an hour (10km) or 1 hour (20km).

Snowshoe: Contact Alpi'raquettes (0033 (0)6 19 2 95 57), Frank Herbron (0033 (0)6 85 74 17 58), Relief (0033 (0)6 77 77 74 64) or Traces directes (0033 (0)4 50 74 70 40).

Sports centre: Facilities include a skating rink, ice hockey, climbing wall and fitness centre (0033 (0)4 50 79 08 43).

Tobogganing: This can be organised from 6pm onwards from Le Pléney cable car. Contact Indiana'ventures (0033 (0)4 50 49 48 60, www.indianaventures.com).

Accommodation

When choosing your accommodation in Morzine it is advisable to take into account the slopes on which you will spend most of your time, as cable cars set off from opposite sides of Morzine and the slopes are not connected by lifts. On one side of the valley the Le Pléney cable car takes you up to the Morzine and Les Gets slopes and on the other side of the valley the Super Morzine cable car takes you to Avoriaz and the Portes du Soleil. The street of bars, known as 'the strip', is pretty much midway between the 2 cable cars.

At the Le Pléney side, you couldn't get closer to the lifts than the logis **L'Equipe** (0033 (0)4 50 79 11 43, www.hotelequipe.fr) or the 3-star **Tremplin** (0033 (0)4 50 79 12 31, www.hotel-tremplin.com). The Tremplin's dining room is basic but the lounge is comfortable with books, chess and a piano. It also has a large outdoor terrace at the bottom of the slopes that's great in good weather. The **Hotel Sporting** (0033 (0)4

50 79 15 03, www.hotelsporting-morzine.com), a minute or so's walk from the lift to Le Pléney, is a gorgeous and great value hotel with homely rooms. In the centre of town, 1 of the friendliest and cosiest hotels is **La Bergerie** (0033 (0)4 50 79 13 69, www.hotel-bergerie.com). The **Farmhouse** (0033 (0)4 50 79 08 26, www.thefarmhouse.co.uk) is a superb chalet with amazing food (see Eating out) but requires a decent budget!

Eating out

On the mountain

On the Le Pléney slopes **Chez Nannon** (0033 (0)4 50 79 21 15) is definitely 1 of the best restaurants. It has a beautiful chalet atmosphere, excellent food and a good terrace. At Super Morzine, **les Cretes des Zorre** (0033 (0)4 50 79 24 73) is 1 of the best mountain restaurants on the way back to Morzine from Avoriaz. Both food and service are fantastic.

In town

Restaurant la Chamade (0033 (0)4 50 79 13 91, www.lachamade.com), in the centre of Morzine, is a gourmet restaurant, but also does basic pizzas. It's really cute and cosy inside, with loads of cow-bells and other paraphernalia. **L'Atelier d'Alexandre** (0033 (0)4 50 79 00 79, www.hotel-lesamoyede.com) is another great gourmet restaurant. The **Farmhouse** (0033 (0)4 50 79 08 26, www.thefarmhouse.co.uk) is a famous chalet above the Dixie bar, down the hill. It is possible to call up and book in for dinner – the chalet can accommodate 15/16 guests, but they usually cook for around 40 people. The best pizzeria in town is **L'Etale** (0033 (0) 04 50 79 09 29), on the strip. It has great staff and serves fantastic food: massive salads and good meat dishes, as well as the wood-fired pizzas. At the other end of town is the very pleasant pizzeria **Le Tyrolien** (0033 (0) 04 50 79 13 15) with a terrace and a wood-fired oven.

For a good panini or hot dog before you hit the slopes, check out the little hut **L'Anka,** just in front of the Super Morzine télécabine.

If you get the munchies in town you'll want to head to the **Burger Place** (0033 (0)4 50 74 71 30) at the end of the strip, near the Le Pléney cable car. They do great burgers, hot dogs and bacon sandwiches. It's a little wooden hut with a good terrace.

Bars and clubs

For après ski you will want to be hitting 1 of 2 bars down the hill. **Bar Robertson**, a favourite with all Morzine residents, is 1 of the most popular après venues – largely due to the supply of very strong beer (Mutzig). If you are staying on the other side of the river to Morzine town centre you should check out the **Ridge bar** (500m from the bridge, part of the Ridge Hotel), with big TVs for sports, friendly staff, hip-hop nights and a games room with free table footie.

'As the night moves on, you will no doubt find yourself on the strip'

As the night moves on, you will no doubt find yourself on the strip, a great row of bars and clubs that always end up packed. The best are the **Cavern** (0033 (0)4 50 74 22 79, www.cavernbar.com), an atmospheric bar full of seasonaires and great for a drunken dance, and **Tibetan Café** (was the Buddha Bar), with some superb interior design going on (the owner makes his own furniture and it is for sale at his shop in town). As far as clubs go, you have a choice between **L'Opera** (cheesy, with cages) (0033 (0)4 50 79 16 65) and **Paradis** (0033 (0)4 50 74 69 79) with a dancefloor that lights up, black and pink zebra print chairs and neon lighting. If you're drunk, it could be hilarious. If not, we wouldn't recommend it.

Getting there

By car

On the Autoroute Blanche motorway, take the Bonneville or Cluses exit.

By plane

Geneva (75km) Transfer takes only an hour, (www.altibus.com).
Helicopter transfers can be arranged for 2993 (0033 (0)4 50 92 78 21).

By train

Take the Eurostar from London St Pancras to Paris; then an overnight train to Cluses, and then a bus (55 minutes) to the resort. Contact Rail Europe (0870 830 4862, www.raileurope.co.uk) or European Rail (020 7387 0444, www.europeanrail.com). Bus tickets must be purchased at least 7 days in advance from Altibus (0033 (0)4 79 68 32 96, www.altibus.com).

Useful facts and phone numbers

Tourist office

T: 0033 (0)450 747 272
F: 0033 (0)450 790 348
W: www.morzine-avoriaz.com

Direct reservations

T: 0033 (0)4 50 791 157
F: 0033 (0)4 50 747 318
W: www.resa-morzine.com

Emergency services

- Police: 0033 (0)4 50 79 13 12
- Ambulance: 0033 (0)4 50 26 26 02/ 0033 (0)4 50 75 93 09
- Thonon Hospital: 0033 (0)4 50 83 20 00
- Fire: 18

Taxis

A full list of taxis is available from the tourist office/website.

- Cheraiet Momo: 0033 (0)4 50 79 03 40
- Heritier Eric: 0033 (0)6 11 95 02 26
- Laury's France Taxi: 0033 (0)4 50 74 69 77, www.laurys.com.

La Plagne

You won't have a problem finding virgin snow on this huge mountain.

On the slopes	Rating
Snow reliability	❄❄❄½
Parks	❄❄❄❄
Off-piste	❄❄❄
Off the slopes	
Après ski	❄❄
Nightlife	❄❄❄
Eating out	❄❄½
Resort charm	❄❄

The resort

La Plagne consists of about 10 villages, all of varying degrees of attractiveness, from the sleepy, quiet beauty of the small village resorts of Montchavin and Les Coches to the ugly, but functional and well-placed Bellecôte and Aime la Plagne. The resorts also have varying numbers of services (bars, restaurants, facilities, etc). Plagne Centre is a functional resort that has great access to the slopes (you'll be at the top of Grande Rochette in minutes) and attractive on-piste restaurants. However, the run-down indoor centre that contains the bars (all 2 of them), restaurants and shops needs a good face lift. Bellecôte is excellently placed for the half pipe but it is not aesthetically pleasing, to say the least. If we were staying in La Plagne, we would choose to stay in Belle Plagne as it is very central in the Paradiski area (that consists of La Plagne and Les Arcs), it's attractive and has a few good bars and the best club. Therefore, whilst we might refer to other areas, Belle Plagne is being referred to if we don't specifically say otherwise.

The location of your accommodation in Paradiski is very important as getting to the main ski area from the lower villages can take a long time. Belle Plagne is a great base in this respect.

The mountains

Height: 1250–3250m

Ability	Rating
Expert	❄❄❄
Intermediate	❄❄❄❄
Beginner	❄❄❄❄

Getting about

The Paradiski area (combining La Plagne with Les Arcs) is one of the largest in Europe with a total of 293 pistes over 425km (225km in La Plagne). Even the most competent riders would struggle to make it from 1 end of the Paradiski area to the other. Most of the runs are pretty cruisy (well over half the pistes are blue runs) but, with 2 accessible peaks over 3000m, there is a lot to keep the fervent backcountry rider happy.

The park

As well as the main park, there is another in the Champagny valley, consisting of hips, rails, table tops and a skier/boardercross. This is by the Télésiège de la rossa at 2300m, so the snow is always pretty good and there is no excuse for them not to keep it well maintained. The main park is the 7 cube snowpark, in which you may spot the likes of Julien Regnier, Marie Martinod and Matthieu Crepel hanging out. This is the place to really push yourself. It contains 3 skier/boardercross courses, rails, hips, table tops, a pipe, and a step up and quarter pipe! There is also a great 90m long, 5.5m high pipe at Bellecote.

Off-piste and backcountry

There are loads of good faces and couloirs in La Plagne if you know where to look. Although you may think you can see plenty of powder bowls from Plagne Centre, some are a bit flat for the advanced freerider – they can be good to practise a few powder turns for the freeriding newcomers though. From the top of the Bellecôte, the highest point of Paradiski at 3417m, there are exploits in all directions. For a good long powder run, take the glacier chair from the top of the Bellecôte bubble and hike for 20 minutes straight up to the backside of the glacier. From here you can ride right down the back to Champagny, which should take between an hour and an hour and a half. There is a lot of flat terrain at the end, so not a great one for boarders – skiers will be poling for about half an hour. You should take a guide, as there is a 20m drop into a river at 1 point, which you may not see if you don't know where it is. From the Bellecôte bubble you can also take the Trevasse chair, from which you can either hike up to tackle the challenging terrain from the Glacier de Bellecôte and end up in Nancroix (from where you will have to take a bus to Peisey and catch the Vanoise express), or you can come down to the Pointe de Friolin and ride down to the Bauches chair. Alternatively, the north face of the Bellecôte has some good lines but it is prone to sliding. From the Roche de Mio cable car, come back on yourself and you will find a few great couloirs off to the right, just below the Roche de Mio restaurant. This will bring you back down to the Bauches chair. Couloir fanatics can also head up the Funiplagne cable car from Plagne Centre, go straight ahead (under the barriers) and there are loads to choose from. You even have an easy out – you will come to a blue run that brings you down to the Verdons Sud chair. Take care though as this is prone to avalanches. A 45-minute hike from the Fornelet lift above Montalbert leads you to a number of faces, although this area can get a bit sun trapped.

From Aime la Plagne you can set off on a momentous quest – head up the Becoin chair and the Crêtes poma, where a traverse followed by an hour and a half hike will allow you to ride all the way down to the sleepy little village of Notre Dame du Pre. You might have to place your car there strategically before you do it though – not much passes through here and the locals don't look kindly on wandering skiers and boarders.

Lift passes

Check the latest prices at www.la-plagne.com

Instruction

Ecole El Pro Belle Plagne

This school also organises guiding, bobsleigh, snowmobiling, quads on ice and parapenting (see Other activities).
0033 (0)4 79 09 11 62
www.elpro.fr

ESF

As well as skiing and snowboarding lessons, ESF also has mountain guides that offer a mix between ski touring and off-piste skiing. It offers freeride and freestyle training.
0033 (0)4 79 09 06 68 (Belle Plagne)
www.esf-belleplagne.com

Evolution 2 (Montchavin-Les Coches)

0033 (0)4 79 07 81 85
www.evolution2.com

Oxygéne (Plagne Centre)

0033 (0)4 79 09 03 99
www.oxygene-ski.com

Other activities

Unless otherwise stated, contact the tourist office (see Useful facts and phone numbers) for more information.

Bobsleigh: Between the beginning of December and mid-March you can ride the bobsleigh course built for the Albertville Winter Olympics. Choose from a Bob Raft (a self-steering bobsleigh with automatic braking, at about 80kph), a Taxi Bob (a 4-person sleigh, driven at 100kph by a professional driver) or a Mono Bob (on your own in a self-steering bobsleigh at almost 90kph). Book at the ESF schools in resort or in advance (0033 (0)4 79 09 12 73, www.bobsleigh.net).

Bowling alley: This is located in Belle Plagne.

Cinema: Aime la Plagne, Plagne Centre, Plagne Bellecôte, Champagny en Vanoise and Montchavin-Les Coches all have local cinemas that often show films in English.

Dog sledding: In the nearby resort of Montalbert you can sign yourself up to dog sledding – call Mathias Bernal on 0033 (0)6 12 78 50 05.

Ice climbing wall: You can climb on the 22m high artificial wall (with or without supervision) in Champagny. There are three levels of difficulty and you will be given equipment as part of the package. It is also the venue of the Gorzderette tournament (see Events). Call 0033 (0)4 79 55 06 55 for more details.

Ice rink: Bellecôte has a outdoor ice rink.

Library: The library in Plagne Centre stocks books in English.

Paintball: This can be played in Bellecôte.

Paragliding: From the top of the Grande Rochette, the Roche de Mio and Les Verdons, tandem paragliding flights can be booked. There are a number of schools to contact. For take off from Grande Rochette or Les Verdons call Plagn'Air on 0033 (0)6 12 73 66 56, or the ESF on 0033 (0)4 79 09 06 68. For take off from the Roche de Mio call Ecole El Pro on 0033 (0)4 79 09 11 62.

Relaxation centres: These can be found in Belle Plagne (0033 (0)4 79 09 26 88), Plagne Centre (0033 (0)4 79 09 03 45) or Plagne Bellecôte (0033 (0)4 79 09 22 48) and have a variety of facilities, such as relaxation, spa treatments, beauty care, massage, multi-treatment courses, physiotherapy, saunas and Jacuzzis.

Snow bike circuit: Biking can be booked at Belle Plagne from the Ecole El Pro (0033 (0)4 79 09 11 62).

Snow quad biking, adventure trail, snowmobiling: To zip round the circuit in Belle Plagne call Ecole El Pro (see above). El Pro can also book you on to the adventure trail in Belle Plagne and organise snowmobiling.

Snowshoeing and cross-country skiing: These can be booked through the ESF schools (see above).

Sports hall, weight training, snow skating: These are all available in Plagne Centre.

Swimming pool: Bellecôte has a heated, open air swimming pool.

If you want to try an activity in another resort, the shuttle bus or gondola lift will take you between most of the resorts.

Events

A **World Cup Mogul event** takes place in late December in Plagne Centre, where they also hold **World Cup Slalom** and **Telemark events** throughout the season. Champagny le Haut village is host to the **Gorzderette Trophy** (www.gorzderette.com) that brings together big air freestyle, cross-country skiing, the Mont de la Guerre derby and an ice climbing contest.

Accommodation

There is loads of ski-in ski-out accommodation in La Plagne, although you should check your location carefully to be sure. Apartments take up most of the visitor beds in La Plagne, although there are some good hotels to check out if you prefer. If you wish to take an apartment it's best to go to the direct reservations office (see Useful facts and phone numbers) and let them know your specific requirements.

In Belle Plagne there are 2 main hotels. **Les Balcons de Belle Plagne** (0033 (0)3 84 86 15 51) is by far the best, in a good location with authentic wooden-chalet-style charm, great views, a cosy restaurant and bar with comfy seats and games to play. There is also a pool, sauna and gym as well as underground car parking. **Mercure Belle Plagne** (0033 (0)4 79 09 12 09, www.mercure.com) is also pretty good but bigger and less personal. It's in a great position to ski to the door and is popular with families.

In Plagne Centre, the **Hotel Terra Nova** (0033 (0)4 79 55 79 00, www.hotel-terranova.com) is the only 1 in town and not a bad looking place. It has a fairly smart but simple restaurant serving a basic menu. There is also a bar, fitness and sauna rooms, sunny terrace and a good location for riding to the door and for the town 'centre'.

In Plagne Montalbert, a small friendly resort, at the far end of the Paradiski area, there are some great chalets to stay in. **Chalet Genepy** (0033 (0)4 79 09 80 50 – or 01937 581287 (UK) – www.cgski.co.uk), run by a British couple, Giles and Claire, is a fab place for either families or a group of friends (there are only a few bars and 1 club in Montalbert, but it's a giggle if you've got a good group). The chalet sleeps 12 and there is a cosy lounge area with a bar (the monkey bar) in which you could happily chill out all night.

In the tiny village of Montvilliers, less than 10 minutes' drive from Montalbert (which gives access to the Paradiski area), is **Maison Astier** (0033 (0)4 79 09 26 03, sharplespaul@hotmail.co.uk), a huge family-run guest house that accommodates 12 guests. The open plan living/dining area has a large fireplace and a cosy, homely atmosphere. This is the perfect place for families and those seeking an authentic, peaceful mountain village atmosphere. You will need to bring/rent a car as you will need to drive to the lifts in Montalbert. Next door you can find the **Gite de Montvilliers** (0033 (0)4 79 09 75 43, www.gite-de-montvilliers.com), another cosy place with great food.

Eating out

On the mountain

On the mountain itself there are some great options. If you head towards Champagny you will find a beautiful restaurant at the bottom of the Verdons Sud chairlift, called **Verdons Sud** (0033 (0)6 21 54 39 24), which can be accessed from the hara-kiri or kamikaze runs. This restaurant has a great terrace, deckchairs in which to soak up the sun and, most importantly, the best toilets on the mountain! **Le Forperet** (0033 (0)4 79 55 51 27, www.forperet.com), at the bottom of the Forpelet lift, above Montalbert, is an excellent, traditional log-cabin-style restaurant with a log fire, nice terrace and lovely views. **Au Bon Vieux Temps** (0033 (0)4 79 09 20 57), next to the Golf lift, just below Aime la Plagne, is a cute little chalet-style restaurant with open log fires and lots of character. Finally, in the middle of the Paradiski area, just above Les Coches by the Pierres Blanches lift is **Le Sauget** (0033 (0)4 79 07 83 51, www.le-sauget.com), a traditional Savoyard restaurant with an open fire and lots of atmosphere.

If you fancy just grabbing a sandwich, pop inside the indoor shopping centre to **Bar La Cheminee** for a panini, sandwich or hot dog. In Belle Plagne, **Le Matafan** (0033 (0)4 79 09 09 19) is on the piste and serves delicious food and great portions. **Face Nord** (0033 (0)4 79 09 01 73), is also popular and equally good.

In town

In Belle Plagne, the restaurants mentioned above: **Le Matafan** (0033 (0)4 79 09 09 19) and **Face Nord** (0033 (0)4 79 09 01 73) are open at night and all have a great atmosphere. The **Cheyenne** (0033 (0)4 79 09 20 72) serves great Tex Mex (see Bars and clubs).

In Plagne Centre, the **Métairie** (0033 (0)4 79 09 11 08) is cosy and traditional with checked table mats, Savoyard bits and pieces on the walls and tables, and serves pizzas, salads, meat and the traditional fondues, raclettes and pierres chaudes. **L'Etable** (0033 (0)4 79 09 04 82), opposite, is another cosy, traditional Savoyard restaurant serving similar fare with tables tucked into alcoves. **Le Vega** (0033 (0)4 79 09 00 61) and **Chaudron** (0033 (0)4 79 09 23 33), mentioned above, are also popular in the evenings, serve good food and have a great atmosphere. Le Vega has fantastic fish. Also in Plagne Centre is **La Galerne** (0033 (0)4 79 07 73 37), a wooden restaurant with a range of tasty crêpes as well as the usual fare, and it has a nice, small terrace to sit on at lunchtime.

In Bellecôte, the best restaurant is **Colosses** (0033 (0)4 79 09 28 70), offering unusual cuisine for a resort – the chicken curry is fantastic.

Bars and clubs

In Belle Plagne, the **Tête Inn** (0033 (0)4 79 55 10 85), also referred to as Mat's bar, has loads of character and is atmospheric and wooden. There are big barrels to sit on, a good happy hour 4–6pm every day and live music from 5.30pm. They serve a few sandwiches at lunchtime. The **Cheyenne** (0033 (0)4 79 09 20 72) is a cool, unassuming bar with memorabilia hung up all over the place and fantastic Tex-Mex food. The **Saloon** (0033 (0)4 79 09 06 98, www.lesaloon.com) is a funky club that everyone goes to later on and is definitely worth checking out. It's open 4pm–4am and often has live music and a great atmosphere. Out of the centre of town, next to the Balcons de Belle Plagne hotel is another bar/restaurant, **Maitre Kanter** (0033 (0)4 79 55 76 70) that has a big and slightly impersonal bar, but has a few cocktails and the restaurant is great for big groups. If you're staying nearby it would be worth popping in at happy hour (4–6pm).

In Bellecôte, **Spitting Feathers** (0033 (0)4 79 06 61 28, www.spitting-feathers.com) is popular with the Brits.

In La Plagne 1800, there is 1 (and only 1) bar, the **Mine** (0033 (0)4 79 09 24 89), but it is very cool, and has bar tables set out like a train.

Getting there

By car

La Plagne is 645km from Paris and will take around 10 hours from Calais. Head towards Lyon/Albertville on the A43 and A430 then follow signs to Moutiers, Aime, Macot and La Plagne. If you are driving from Geneva, take the N201 (Cruseilles) then A41 to Chambéry, then A43 and A130 to Albertville then N90 to Moutiers and head towards Aime, Macot and La Plagne.

By plane

Geneva (149km) Take the bus with Transports Berard (0033 (0)4 79 09 72 27) or go by taxi.
Lyon (200km) Take the Satobus (0033 (0)4 72 22 71 27, www.satobus.com) or taxi or the A43 autoroute if you're in a hired car.

By train

Take the Eurostar from London St Pancras to Paris, then an overnight train to Aime la Plagne, and then a bus (40 minutes) to the resort. Contact Rail Europe (0870 830 4862, www.raileurope.co.uk) or European Rail (020 7387 0444, www.europeanrail.com). Bus tickets are purchased at the station.

Useful facts and phone numbers

Tourist office

T: 0033 (0)4 79 09 02 01 (Plagne Centre)
0033 (0)4 79 09 85 91 (Belle Plagne)
F: 0033 (0)4 79 09 27 00
W: www.la-plagne.com

Direct reservations

T: 0033 (0)4 79 09 79 79
F: 0033 (0)4 79 09 70 10

Emergency services

In a medical emergency dial 15, for the fire brigade call 18, or 112 for either from a mobile.

- Police: 0033 (0)4 79 09 04 57/04 79 55 61 17
- Medical surgery, Belle Plagne: 0033 (0)4 79 06 93
- Ambulance: 0033 (0)4 79 55 58 17/0033 (0)4 79 24 38 11

Doctors

- Belle Plagne: 0033 (0)4 79 09 06 93
- Plagne Centre: 0033 (0)4 79 09 04 66
- Hospital Bourg St Maurice: 0033 (0)4 79 41 79 79

Taxis

- Christian Bouzon (Plagne Centre) has a number of minibuses (0033 (0)4 79 09 03 41, www.taxi-bouzon.com) and will transfer between stations in La Plagne, as well as to stations and airports.
- Allo Bic Taxi: 0033 (0)4 79 06 33 71

Ste Foy

Clever use of 4 lifts opens up masses of terrain.

On the slopes	Rating
Snow reliability	❄❄❄
Parks	–
Off-piste	❄❄❄❄❄
Off the slopes	
Après ski	❄
Nightlife	❄
Eating out	❄❄
Resort charm	❄❄❄½

The resort

Ste Foy is a beautiful, traditional and authentic alpine resort. There are none of the big, ugly buildings that plague many of the big European resorts; all of the buildings are nestled amongst the trees, and built in the traditional chalet-style, using local wood and stone. Don't come here if you are looking for crazy nights out though, as it won't happen.

Ste Foy has some of the best freeriding terrain around; there are some superb, day-long itineraries with very little time spent on lifts.

The mountains

Height: 1550–2620m

Ability	Rating
Expert	❄❄❄❄
Intermediate	❄❄❄
Beginner	❄❄❄

Getting about

Unless you're staying right by the lifts, you'll need to get the free shuttle bus from the main village to the slopes. Ste Foy is a small area that, until recently, had only 3 charlifts. The handful of chairlifts now provide access to the 15 slopes, and what the resort lacks in marked runs, it more than makes up for with long off-piste descents. At the top of the Col de l'Aiguille at 2612m the backcountry adventures begin. Ste Foy is also on the road to Val d'Isère and Tignes, so day trips are possible if you want to explore some different terrain.

The park

There is far too much amazing terrain for the lack of a park to worry you – there are loads of great areas for building backcountry kickers if your heart is set on freestyle.

Off-piste and backcountry

Ste Foy is 1 of our favourite places for venturing out into the backcountry or off-piste. The resort rarely has lift queues. It does, however, attract the powder hounds from Val, Tignes and La Rosière on a bluebird powder day.

As you are slowly making your way up the chairlifts, it's fairly easy to see the area's potential and spot some good lines. A guide can take you from the top of the Col de l'Aiguille through lots of little derelict villages, coming out on the main road between Val d'Isère/Tignes and Ste Foy (you can come back to the bottom of the resort if you know where you're going). One of the most spectacular routes takes you through the deserted farming hamlet of Le Monal, with amazing views of Mont Pourri. It is also worth employing the services of a guide in order to explore the infamous 1700m vertical descent of the north face of Fogliettaz, which retains a good quality of snow long after other routes have been skied out. Lower down there are some superb tree runs. This route will take you a full day. La Marquise lift provides access to some great tree runs.

Generally, the terrain is challenging so you should make sure that you know what you're doing. It's also advisable to hire a guide to make the most of this area.

There have been many reports of avalanching in Ste Foy so be careful, be aware of the conditions and check with the pisteurs before attempting anything you're not sure about.

Lift passes

Check the latest prices at www.saintefoy.net

Instruction

ESF

0033 (0)4 79 06 96 76
www.esf-saintefoy.com

Mountain Guides

The local mountain guides in Ste Foy organise off-piste trips and heliskiing.
0033 (0)6 14 62 90 24
www.guide-montagne-tarentaise.com

Other activities

Dog sledding: Drive your own sled pulled by a team of dogs, under the leadership of a professional guide. Trips are available for half a day, a whole day or over 2 days, with a night in a refuge. For more information contact Stéphane and Véronique Lépine (0033 (0)4 79 06 18 68/0033 (0)6 16 48 60 47, stephanemush@aol.com).

Heliskiing: As Ste Foy is so close to Italy, where heliskiing is allowed, it is one of the few places in France where it is possible, with the potential for virgin descents from 3400m right back to Ste Foy. Contact the tourist office for more details.

Parapente: This can be booked with David Bicheron, a paragliding instructor (0033 (0)6 12 90 10 62).

Ski biking: Initiation lesson are offered, after which you can hire a ski bike. Contact Alistair Platt: 0033 (0)4 79 06 68 45, www.skibike.net.

Spa: Les Balcons de Sainte Foy (0033 (0)4 79 06 68 47, www.spa-conference.com) has a pool, sauna, Jacuzzi and fitness room. Les Fermes de Ste Foy (0033 (0)4 79 06 14 61) has the above, plus beauty treatments.

Accommodation

Accommodation is available at the ski resort itself, in the main village, and in many of the surrounding small farming hamlets. The chalets are often the most attractive and cosy places to stay and there are loads to choose from. Check out the list of chalets on the tourist office website (www.saintefoy.net).

> **'In the village of Villaroger is a beautiful, cosy chalet'**

We particularly like **Gite de Sainte Foy Station** (0033 (0)4 79 06 27 20, www.ste-foy.fr) with Jacuzzi, sauna, heated ski room and DVD home cinema. In the small village of Villaroger, is a beautiful and cosy chalet, **Tarentaise** (0131 208 1154 (UK), 0033 (0)4 79 06 91 26 (FR), www.optimumski.com), owned by the lovely Martin and Deirdre Rowe. There are 9 bedrooms, all done out beautifully and all with en-suite facilities, and a sauna and in-house masseur. From Villaroger you have direct access to the slopes of Paradiski (Les Arcs and La Plagne), as well as easy access to Ste Foy, Val d'Isère and Tignes.

The Auberge (0033 (0)4 79 06 95 83, www.auberge-montagne.co.uk) is a lovely wood-beamed chalet/hotel in the small hamlet of La Thuile, run by a really friendly British couple. The chalet has a cosy lounge with big fire, and an outdoor hot tub and sauna. If you completely book out the hotel (8 rooms), they will run it as a private chalet for you. **Hotel Le Monal** (0033 (0)4 79 06 90 07, www.le-monal.com) has 24 rooms. **Auberge Le Cret Folliet** (0033 (0)4 79 06 97 47) is a traditional inn with only 3 rooms.

Eating out

On the mountain

The mountain restaurants in Ste Foy are superb and we happily stop anywhere, in the knowledge that we will not be disappointed. All of the huts are in true, rustic, alpine style. Two of our favourites are at Plan Bois at the top of the first chair lift: **Chez Leon** (0033 (0)6 09 57 23 88 or 0033 (0)4 79 06 90 83) and **Les Brevettes** (0033 (0)6 76 35 21 70). Both have excellent Savoyard food and sunny, south-facing terraces. At the top of the Arpettaz chair is **Chalet La Foglietta** (0033 (0)6 17 36 10 88), a little hut where you can pick up a hot drink and a tasty panini to munch on the lifts.

In town

There are few restaurants in Ste Foy, so here we would recommend staying in a catered chalet, and choosing a restaurant to sample on your host's day off. **La Grange** (0033 (0)4 79 06 97 30) is a good typical Savoyard restaurant/wine bar, popular for its wood-fired grills and **La Maison à Colonnes** (0033 (0)4 79 06 94 80), at the base of the first lift, is another excellent traditional farmhouse restaurant (see Bars and clubs).

La Bergerie (0033 (0)4 79 06 25 51) is a stunning, wood-beamed and candlelit restaurant with a warm and cosy fireplace. You can book the private room for a group of family or friends (16 people max.). **Chez Merie** (0033 (0)4 79 06 90 16), in the nearby village of Miroir, is one of the best restaurants in the area. Reservation is absolutely essential.

Bars and clubs

As après ski goes, there's not too much going on in Ste Foy. There are a couple of local bars that are cosy and relaxed, but that's about it. **La Maison à Colonnes** (0033 (0)4 79 06 94 80), at the base of the first lift, is a cool little bar for a beer at the end of the day. **La Pitchouli** is the liveliest bar around, with live music several times a week. There's table football, and the drinks are a good price. **L'Iceberg** (0033 (0)4 79 04 14 86) is a piano bar that also has live music.

Getting there

By car

Take the motorway A43 (dir. Lyon/Albertville) and then the main road N90 to Bourg St Maurice. From here there are signs to Tignes and Val d'Isère and on this road you will soon come to Ste Foy.

By plane

Lyon (215km)

Geneva (160km) Both Geneva and Lyon are approximately 2.5 hours away from Ste Foy.

By train

Take the Eurostar from London St Pancras to Paris, then an overnight train to Bourg St Maurice, and then a bus (15 minutes), followed by a free shuttle bus (10 minutes) to the resort. Contact Rail Europe (0870 830 4862, www.raileurope.co.uk) or European Rail (020 7387 0444, www.europeanrail.com). Bus tickets (from Autocars Martin) are purchased at the station.

Useful facts and phone numbers

Tourist office

T: 0033 (0)4 79 06 95 19
F: 0033 (0)4 79 06 95 09
W: www.saintefoy.net

Central reservations service

T: 0033 (0)4 79 06 95 22
F: 0033 (0)4 79 06 95 09

Emergency services

- Police: 17 or 0033 (0)4 79 07 04 25
- Fire: 18 or 0033 (0)4 79 06 91 03

Doctors

- Dr Régis Gobert: 0033 (0)4 79 06 92 22

Taxis

- Altitude Espace Taxi: 0033 (0)6 07 41 11 53, www.altitude-espace-taxi.com
- Papillon: 0033 (0)6 08 99 93 96

Serre Chevalier

A good mountain for cruising and for freeride with 4 main areas

On the slopes	Rating
Snow reliability	❄❄❄
Parks	❄❄❄
Off-piste	❄❄❄❄½
Off the slopes	
Après ski	❄❄❄
Nightlife	❄❄½
Eating out	❄❄½
Resort charm	❄❄❄

The resort

Serre Chevalier, more affectionately known as 'Serre Che', comprises 4 main areas/towns, on the main road from Gap to Grenoble, all of which have access to the massive ski area of Grand Serre Che. These towns combine traditional rustic French ambience, with new, purpose-built (and sometimes ugly) buildings. There are 9 other smaller villages, too, but, while charming and pretty to look at, there's not much going on in most of them.

From Grenoble, the first town you will get to is Le Monêtier (1500), a spa town that is more beautiful, charming and quiet than the others, but far less convenient. Next are the 2 main towns, Villeneuve (1400) and Chantemerle (1350), collectively referred to as 'Le Serre Che'. Villeneuve is the hub, with some purpose-built architecture by the slopes, and a much more charming village centre. Chantemerle is a popular town and a good place to look for a cheap apartment. Briançon is a very large town and the highest in France. The old town isn't convenient for the slopes, but it's traditional and pleasant to walk around. The resorts are really spread out; the closest are the 'Serre Che' resorts but these are still a half-hour walk from each other.

There is a free bus service within the resorts for those with a valid lift pass, but they stop running at night. A car is not essential but we think it's worth it; there are some fantastic resorts nearby and the strange climate in this area means that if there is bad weather in Serre Che, it is more than possible that you will find decent snow within an hour of the resort. Les Deux Alpes is a good start or La Grave, one of our favourite spots in Europe for freeriding (check out these chapters for more information, pages 93 and 99). Sestriere (Italy) and Risoul (France) are also under an hour away.

The mountains

Height: 1200–2850m

Ability	Rating
Expert	❄❄❄
Intermediate	❄❄❄❄
Beginner	❄❄❄❄

Getting about

The massive 250km of pistes covers 4445 hectares and comprises 114 runs: 25 green, 32 blue, 42 red and 15 black. These slopes provide well for all levels of skier and boarder; there are good slopes for learning, travelling through the various sectors will please the cruisy intermediates and the experts can pick from some good challenging black runs, especially the steep run back to Chantemerle, which is great fun when it's quiet. Freeriders will also be more than satisfied.

The park

There are 3 areas to the snow park in Villeneuve – for beginners, intermediates and advanced. There are about 30 features to the park, includig boxes, rails, table top and hip jumps. There is also a boardercross at Chantemerle.

Off-piste and backcountry

Riding through the trees is Serre Che's speciality, although it's not that steep if that's what you're after. One of the best off-piste tree runs is under the Prorel chair above Chantemerle, where there are some good lines. The trees next to the piste in Briançon are worth checking out too. You have to be careful when you are riding through the trees in Serre Che as it's pretty easy to get stuck or end up at the main road with a long walk home. Stick by the piste, or make sure you're with someone who knows where they're going.

Villeneuve and Monêtier are home to the best big mountain runs. There is a great open powder field in between the 2, under the Cucumelle peak. Head up the Cucumelle chair and go for a ride. The best powder is on Monêtier, on La Montagnole. If you are very nice to the locals and buy them a beer or 2, they might show you where to go within this area; it's a big secret. Avalanching is a problem here, too, so you really do need a guide.

Lift passes

Check the latest prices at www.serre-chevalier.com

Instruction

ESF

0033 (0)4 92 24 17 41 (Chantemerle), 0033 (0)4 92 24 71 99 (Villeneuve), 0033 (0)4 92 24 42 66 (Monetier), 0033 (0)4 92 24 17 41 (Briançon)
www.esf-serrechevalier.com

Instruction in Chantemerle

Génération Snow
0033 (0)4 92 24 21 51
www.generation-snow.com

Montagne Aventure

0033 (0)4 92 24 74 40
montagne@aol.com

Instruction in Villeneuve

Axesse

0033 (0)4 92 24 27 11 or 0662 765 354
www.axesse.com

Ecole de Ski Buissonnière

This school consists of both British and French instructors and mountain guides. Advanced and off-piste groups are limited to 6 people. Freeride and freestyle ski and snowboard courses for teenagers are also available.
0033 (0)4 92 24 78 66
www.esi-serrechevalier.com

Instruction in Monêtier

Ecole de Ski et de Snowboard Internationale

0033 (0)6 83 67 06 42
www.esi-monetier.com

Montagne et Ski

This company offers ski touring costs, heliskiing and a snowmobiling tour with a meal in Italy.
0033 (0)4 92 24 46 81
www.montagne-et-ski.com

Other activities

Unless otherwise specified, contact the tourist office for more details.

Cinemas: There are cinemas in each resort.

Drive on ice: Learn how to drive a kart on ice using. Contact 0033 (0)4 92 52 60 60.

Horse-drawn carriage/sleigh rides: These take place on the roads or in the snow. Attelage Montagne (0033 (0)6 07 57 34 04) departs from Pontillas gondola base. Club Hippique (0033 (0)4 92 24 78 61, www.clubhippique-serreche.com) also do tours.

Ice climbing: Climb on gorges, chutes and waterfalls. Contact 0033 (0)4 92 24 75 90, www.guides-serrechevalier.com for more information.

Natural hot pools: These can be found in Monêtier.

Paragliding: Introductory flights are available. Contact Les Aigles du Briançonnais (0033 (0)4 92 24 02 71) or Axesse (see Instruction).

Ski jöring: Get a horse to pull you on skis. Contact 0033 (0)4 92 24 78 61, www.clubhippique-serreche.com for more information.

Snowkiting: The school is located at the Col du Lautaret (0033 (0)6 70 46 53 88).

Snowmobiling: Sun Scoot (0033 (0)4 92 24 21 70) offer snowmobile trips in which you can either be a passenger or a pilot.

Events

See the sky speckled with kites during the **snowkite festival** in Col du Lautaret at the end of December. Towards the end of the season there is a **mountain bar crawl**, with only 1 day to visit 15 bars. It finishes in the Grotte du Yeti and you should expect some seriously drunken behaviour on the slopes. Few, if any, make all 15 bars.

Accommodation

Chantemerle

The **Plein Sud** (0033 (0)4 92 24 17 01, www.hotelpleinsud.com) is 1 of the best bets, well placed for the centre of town and 250m from the lifts and pistes. It has mini bars and dressing gowns in the rooms and a heated swimming pool open both summer and winter. There is also a steam room and parking, if necessary. The rooms are lovely and the restaurant is good, too.

Villeneuve

The **Christiania** (0033 (0)4 92 24 76 33, www.hotel-lechristiania.com) is a really cute and cosy hotel, recognised by the dependable *Logis de France*. **Hotel Mont Thabor** (0033 (0)4 92 24 74 41, www.mont-thabor.com) is a great and attractive hotel in the centre of town, with minibars and TVs in rooms, and a solarium, sauna and hammam. It is also home to the Baïta nightclub. There are 24 standard rooms and 3 luxury suites.

Monêtier

The **Auberge du Choucas** (0033 (0)4 92 24 42 73, www.aubergeduchoucas.com) tries to market itself as the most exclusive place in town. The reality is a decent 3-star but nothing more. You can explore the charming and quiet town of Monêtier from here, but you won't be having any crazy parties.

It's pretty easy to find apartments in any town – the Serre Che tourist office will help you out and you can book on the website.

Eating out

On the mountain

Bachas (0033 (0)4 92 24 50 66) above Monêtier (at the top of the Bachas chair) has good sandwiches and hot dogs, but it's not the place for a long relaxing lunch; for this you should head to **Peyra Juana** (0033 (0)6 81 11 40 26). This restaurant is on the blue slope Rochamout and has table service inside or on the lovely terrace. For a smart meal, with full-on main courses, book a table at **L'Echaillon** (0033 (0)4 92 24 05 15) on the Fangeas piste from the summit of the Casse du Bœuf chairlift. Sit on the sunny terrace or inside by the fire.

In town

In Chantemerle, the **Triptyque** (0033 (0)4 92 24 14 94) is a small French restaurant where you can get a fantastic meal.

In Villeneuve the **Refuge** (0033 (0)4 92 24 78 08) has the best French specialities such as fondues and pierrades (cooking meat at your table on a hot stone). **Marotte** (0033 (0)4 92 24 77 23) is a gorgeous and tiny place, that has the best atmosphere in town. If you're desperate for a **McDonald's**, there's one in Briançon.

'A gorgeous and tiny place that has the best atmosphere in town'

Bars and clubs

It's a bit of a nightmare going out in Serre Che because everything is so far apart. If you are in Briançon or Monêtier you are pretty much stuck there as buses don't run at night, and taxis are pretty expensive. Travelling between the Serre Che resorts Villeneuve and Chantemerle is half an hour walk or a taxi ride.

The best place to go is the **La Grotte** in Villeneuve, unless you don't like being stuck with all the other Brits. There are advantages to this, however; they serve a great English breakfast, or pie, chips and gravy, until 8pm every day. There's usually a live band playing – look out for the Harper Brothers, a really good English rock band. They offer wi-fi internet access. The French clubs are easy to see on the main street, but the main partying happens in the bars. The **Baïta** nightclub is open 11pm–5am and has themed evenings every Wednesday.

If you do happen to end up in Monêtier, the **Rif Blanc** is the place to be, especially to watch sports, and in Briançon the **Saloon** is a lively après ski bar at the bottom of the lifts and the **Gotcha** bar is good for a cheep beer.

Getting there

By car

From Paris, Lyon, Turin or Nice take the A43 motorway (via the Frejus tunnel from the north) and exit at Oulx, Montgenèvre, 35km from Serre Che. From Marseille, and Montpellier, take the A51 motorway via Aix en Provence, and Sisteron. Exit at La Saulce, 90km from Serre Che. From Grenoble, Lyon or Paris, take the A51, and exit at Pont de Claix, 80km from the resort via the Lautaret Pass.

By plane

Turin (108km) Transfer takes just 1 hour. BA, Easy Jet and RyanAir all fly to Turin from London airports.

Grenoble (110km) Transfer takes 1.5 hours. Buses and trains regularly run to Serre Che. Buzz fly to Grenoble from London Stansted.

Lyon (200km) Transfer by bus (www.satobus.com)

By train

Take the Eurostar from London St Pancras to Paris, then an overnight train to Briançon, and then a local bus (20 minutes) to the reosrt. Contact Rail Europe (0870 830 4862, www.raileurope.co.uk) or European Rail (020 7387 0444, www.europeanrail.com). Bus tickets (from Autocars Rignon) are purchased at the station.

Useful facts and phone numbers

Tourist office

T: 0033 (0)4 92 24 98 98

F: 0033 (0)4 92 24 98 84

W: www.serre-chevalier.com

Unofficial website: www.skiserreche.com

Emergency services

- Police: 0033 (0)4 92 24 00 56
- Mountain rescue: 0033 (0)4 92 22 22 22
- Briançon Hospital: 0033 (0)4 92 25 34 56

Doctors

- Drs Annie and Roger Assor (1500): 0033 (0)4 92 24 42 54
- Dr Cuvilliez (1400): 0033 (0)4 92 24 71 02
- Dr Varziniak (1400): 0033 (0)4 92 24 71 37
- Dr Revalor (1350): 0033 (0)4 92 24 28 73
- Dr Triantaphylides: 0033 (0)4 92 24 28 73

Taxis

Villeneuve

- Jacques Caillaud: 0033 (0)6 13 51 17 66, www.taxi-serre-chevalier.com
- M Turco: 0033 (0)6 08 61 20 63

Chantemerle

- Allo Taxi Serre Chevalier: 0033 (0)4 92 24 05 58 or 0033 (0)6 09 32 22 81
- Blanchard Phillippe Taxi: 0033 (0)6 87 82 21 21
- Abeille Taxi: 0033 (0)4 92 21 31 81

Monêtier

- Taxi Aschettina: 0033 (0)6 62 12 31 15

Tignes

Some of the best skiing and boarding in Europe, with stunning mountains and a fun, albeit unattractive town.

On the slopes	Rating
Snow reliability	❄❄❄❄❄
Parks	❄❄❄
Off-piste	❄❄❄❄½
Off the slopes	
Après ski	❄❄❄
Nightlife	❄❄❄
Eating out	❄❄❄
Resort charm	❄

The resort

There are loads of reasons to love Tignes, which is why we can forgive the unsightly architecture – and government grants are bringing about aesthetic improvements. The slopes are the main attraction; the Espace Killy is one of the best areas in Europe for all abilities. The nightlife is good too, and the people are friendly. The self-catering accommodation can be a little hit and miss but many apartments have been improved in recent times.

There are a number of areas to Tignes, which can be confusing at first. Initially you will see Tignes Le Brévières (at 1550m), a traditional and peaceful town with a beautiful Baroque church.

You will then arrive in Tignes Les Boisses (at 1850m). This area is quiet at present but it has the advantage of having a few pretty chalets (comparatively speaking) and you can ski to and from it fairly easily on some nice runs (weather permitting). If you fancy some peace and quiet and maybe only 1 or 2 nights out up the hill, this may be worth a look.

The hub of Tignes is focused at 2100m, which is split into another 3 areas: Lavachet, Le Lac and Val Claret. Lavachet and Le Lac are next to each other and it's easy to walk between them. Val Claret is a bus/car journey away from the other 2. Both areas have quite a lot going on, although Val Claret has better access to the slopes and good parking next to the pistes.

The mountains

Height: 1550–3455m

Ability	Rating
Expert	❄❄❄❄
Intermediate	❄❄❄❄
Beginner	❄❄❄

Getting about

There are 150km of pistes in Tignes alone. If you add this to the accessible area of Val d'Isère, the whole of the Espace Killy has 300km of pistes. There are 90 lifts and 131 pistes: 16 blacks, 35 reds, 60 blues and 20 greens. With the height of the resort at 2100m you can almost guarantee good snow all the way down to the resort.

The Grande Motte Glacier has a height of 3656m, from which you can ski a number of really good red runs in summer (mid-June to September) as well as winter (October to May).

Access to this area is speedy; the underground funicular from Val Claret takes only 7 minutes. The Tovière area is the way to head over to Val d'Isère, and there are some good cruisy runs back to Val Claret from here. Le Palet and Pramecou are in the shade of the Grande Casse mountain and the freeriding potential here is huge. Finally, there are the quieter, east-facing slopes on L'Aiguille Percée, from which you can ride all the way down to Les Boisses or Le Brévières.

The park

The Swatch snowpark offers 'Shoot My Ride' where you film your efforts on the park and then have them displayed on a giant screen at the bottom of the park. You can also land your jumps on an air mattress called the Big Air Bag. Val d'Isère has a good park that is easily accessible from Tignes.

The Winter X-Games is the highlight of the European freeski calendar and has people flocking from all over in March.

Off-piste and backcountry

In Tignes, safety is an extremely important consideration because the avalanche risk here and in Val d'Isère is 1 of the highest in Europe. It is advisable to ski or board with a guide or very knowledgeable local.

Tignes has excellent and extensive back-country for the experienced freerider. As you drive into Tignes you will see the lake to your left. Overlooking this is a massive face named the Tignes Fingers due to the appearance of the rocks and couloirs. Some of the couloirs are a lot more challenging than others; ask your guide to recommend 1 for your ability. Tignes Fingers are popular amongst the locals and seasonaires, and you can pretty much stick to the area all day long and not get bored. Remember to check out the conditions though, as there have been rumours of slides taking riders right down into the lake.

Just above Le SPOT is the Pramecou. The 45-minute hike up to Dôme de Pramecou will give you access to some challenging off-piste and this will lead you to the Grande Balme just below – another area with some superb powder. Chardonnet can be hiked to from the Col du Palet in which you are faced with a range of couloirs. There is 1 that is always tracked out so shop around. If you are after tree runs, the Brévière is definitely worth a look. Alternatively, from the top of the Chaudannes, you can ride off-piste all the way back to Les Boisses through some great trees.

Lift passes

Check the latest prices at www.tignes.net

Instruction

ESF

The ESF offers instruction and off-piste guiding.
Tignes Le Lac:
0033 (0)4 79 06 30 28
www.esftignes.com
Tignes Val Claret:
0033 (0)4 79 06 31 28
www.esfvalclaret.com

Evolution 2

Ask anyone in Tignes: these guys are definitely the best. They offer any kind of instruction/coaching for skiers and boarders, including the bumps, race training, freestyle, avalanche awareness, off-piste training or they can simply provide a guide to help you explore on and off-piste (as well as loads of other things – see Other activities). You can even opt to test next year's skis!.
Tignes Le Lac: 0033 (0)4 79 06 43 78
Tignes Val Claret: 0033 (0)4 79 40 09 04/ (0)4 79 06 65 92
www.evolution2.com

Snocool

Snocool has initiated a 'push to talk' backpack system so clients are in constant contact with their instructor.
0033 (0)4 79 24 30 94
www.snocool.com

Other activities

For all the activities mentioned below (unless otherwise stated), Evolution 2 are the people to call (0033 (0)4 79 06 43 78). They also organise corporate events.

Winter

Aqua Centre 'Le Lagoon': (Call the Tourist Office for information, 0033 (0)4 79 40 04 40). This centre is on the lakeside in the heart of the resort at 2100m. Some of the facilities in the 5000m^2 spa include a 25m pool, a fun pool with 4 30m water slides, a leisure pool with swimming against the current, hydro-massage and a fitness room.

Full Moon descent: Once a month in the light of the full moon there is a torchlit descent from Les Boisses.

Gastronomic Espace Killy Tour: This usually takes place on a Friday (9am–4.30pm) so that you can treat yourselves at the end of the week. Ski the best pistes in the Espace Killy and eat in a beautiful and traditional Savoyard farm restaurant.

Helicopter flights: Choose between a 5-minute discovery flight and a 45-minute flight over Mont Blanc, among others.

Horse riding: An hour and a half riding excursion with a vin chaud break.

Husky driving and rides: These take place on 2 days a week (book as far in advance as you can). You can either be a passenger or drive the pack yourself on the Ste Foy Husky Experience.

Ice climbing: The keen mountaineers can use ice axes and crampons to scale a frozen waterfall. You can even do it floodlit at night if you so desire.

Ice diving: This basically involves dropping through a hole cut into the ice and swimming under the ice to check out the ice formations. It is available from mid-December until early April and you don't need any prior experience. The school is also an ice diving training centre.

Paragliding: Longer flights are available in the summer when you can also learn to fly solo (check out www.parapente.biz or Evolution 2).

Skidoo trips: There are a variety of options, at night or during the day, and you can be a passenger or the driver.

Ski jörring: Here the skier is pulled along the snow by a riderless horse – looks kind of dangerous, but lots of fun.

Torchlit descent, Les Nocturnes du Panoramic: Have dinner on the Grande Motte glacier and ski back down the Double M piste with a flaming torch.

Events

The **Winter X Games Europe** takes place in March and gives you the opportunity to watch the experts on the slopestyle course and the superpipe. Also look out for the **Full Moon Freeride**, where the best freeriders in France ride the Tufs couloirs in the light of the moon.

Le Grand Raid is a long-standing event organised by Evolution 2. The idea is that, in teams of 2 (any combination of boarder/skier, male/female and pro/amateur), you hike to the chosen face to compete against other teams for the fastest times. The competition takes place at the weekend, and the competitors sleep in a mountain refuge. Around 60 teams compete (it is advisable to book around a month in advance) and the price includes all food and the non-luxury refuge accommodation! Check out www.grandraidgortex.fr

Accommodation

Do some research – you have the choice of peace and quiet, easiest access to the lifts, the centre of the night-time action or budget. You can get some great self-catering deals if you don't mind a slightly pokey apartment. However, apartment standards are improving as the resort has initiated a scheme to encourage landlords to update their apartments. Contact Tignes Reservations for more information (see Useful facts and phone numbers).

The **Dragon Lodge** (0870 068 0668 – UK, 0033 (0)870 068 068 – FR, www.dragonlodge.com) is run by a fun and friendly group.

Les Campanules 3-star Hotel (0033 (0)4 79 06 34 36, www.campanules.com) in Tignes Le Lac is a good option with the Altitude Spa, which is open only to hotel guests. It includes a sauna, a Turkish bath, a Jacuzzi and a heated outdoor swimming pool with a clear view of the Grande Motte Glacier. There are also a number of specialised treatments such as hydromassage baths and chromotherapy.

The **Alpaka Lodge** in Le Lac (0033 (0)4

79 06 45 30, www.alpaka.com) has a cosy chalet feel and an open fire. Everyone in Tignes loves chilling out at the Alpaka bar for a coffee during the day or a cocktail in the evening. Free wi-fi is a bonus too.

The **Hotel L'Ecrin des Neiges** (www.pv.holidays.com) is a beautiful hotel in Tignes Val Claret, at the entrance to the resort.

Eating out

On the mountain

The **Alpage** (0033 (0)4 79 06 07 42, www.restaurant-tignes.com) self-service restaurant at the top of the Chaudannes chairlift has fantastic views. **L'Armailly** (0033 (0)4 79 06 41 82, www.armailly.com) in Tignes Les Brévières is an ideal lunch stop for some traditional Savoyard cooking.

In town

In Val Claret, the **Petit Savoyard** (0033 (0)4 79 06 36 23) has a great atmosphere and range of food, from meat dishes to salads and pizzas. **Daffy's Tex Mex** (0033 (0)4 79 06 38 75) in the centre has good fajitas, burritos and ribs. For a fairly smart night, try **Le Caveau** (0033 (0)4 79 06 52 32), a highly recommended French restaurant with live music.

In Le Lac we suggest eating at the popular **Loop Bar** (0033 (0)4 79 09 15 89). **Le Clin d'Oeil** (0033 (0)4 79 06 59 10) is a tiny restaurant that seats about 20 people. There isn't much choice but it's all very fresh and very good. **Le Bagus Café** (0033 (0)4 79 06 49 75), above the Angels bar, is a funky eatery serving traditional Moroccan dishes. **Croq' Burger** (0033 (0)4 79 06 38 80) is the perfect place to pick up a burger or American (baguette with burger and chips in it) – great with or without a hangover.

In Le Lavachet, **La Ferme des 3 Capucines** (0033 (0)4 79 06 35 10) is a farm and traditional family-run restaurant – so traditional that you can watch the cows while you eat.

Bars and clubs

There are more than 50 bars in Tignes. Here is a selection of the best in each area.

In Lavachet go to Harri's (0033 (0)4 79 06 63 20), a cosy, sometimes so crammed it's a bit too cosy, wooden bar in the centre of town. It's been re-named **Censored** but everyone still calls it Harri's. **TC's bar** (0033 (0)4 79 06 46 46, www.tcsbar.com) is a small, English-run bar, open around 3pm–1am. They serve snacks such as ribs and curly fries, and on Saturdays they offer full English brekkies all day long. They host a number of parties including fetish nights and the night of 1000 shots (in which TC will give away the first 100 shots, then sell the next 500, then give away 100, etc). It gets messy.

In Le Lac, the **Loop Bar** (0033 (0)4 79 09 15 89, www.loopbartignes.com) is a very popular bar for a game of pool and a bite to eat at lunch (12–2.30pm) or at night (7–9.30pm). During happy hour (4–6pm) all wine and draft beers are 2 for 1 and later on you might be able to take part in some dancing on tables. For a chilled-out night, with masses of cocktails, try the **Alpaka Lodge** (0033 (0)4 79 06 45 30, www.alpaka.com). It has a big, cosy fire and 2 massive Irish Wolfhounds to make you feel at home.

In Val Claret, **Le Saloon** (0033 (0)4 79 01 04 98) is a great party bar. The **Couloir** bar is another strong favourite, not just because of the 60 flavours of vodka shots, but also due to the friendly staff, ample space and well-chosen live bands.

For a late night boogie, **Jacks** (0033 (0)4 79 06 54 84) in Le Lac is a small, hilarious club that you are bound to end up in if you have a night out in the area. The **Blue Girl** (0033 (0)4 79 06 51 53) in Val Claret is a French club, with a dodgy mirrored ceiling, zebra skin upholstery and a dancing cage to accompany the long-standing pole. The **Melting Pot** (0033 (0)6 10 82 67 83) is the seasonaire hangout with good DJs but overpriced drinks.

Getting there

By car

Bourg St Maurice is accessible by Eurostar and the snow train. From Bourg drive up the road towards Val d'Isère and Tignes (takes about 30 minutes). Look out for the painting of Hercules holding back the water as you cross over the spectacular dam. Under the water in the dam is the old village of Tignes, which can actually be seen when the dam is drained. From Calais it will take you around 12 hours (995km). Book your car into the car park by calling 0033 (0)4 79 40 04 40 or e-mail parkings@tignes.net.

By plane

Lyon (235km) Transfer takes 2.5–3 hours by car.

Geneva (179km) Transfer takes around 2.5 hours.

By train

Take the Eurostar from London St Pancras to Paris; then an overnight train to Bourg St Maurice, and then a bus (75 minutes) to the resort. Contact Rail Europe (0870 830 4862, www.raileurope.co.uk) or European Rail (020 7387 0444, www.europeanrail.com). Bus tickets (from Autocars Martin) are purchased at the station.

Useful facts and phone numbers

Tourist office

T: 0033 (0)4 79 40 04 40
F: 0033 (0)4 79 40 03 15
W: www.tignes.net

Direct reservations

T: 0033 (0)4 79 40 03 03
W: www.tignesreservation.net

Emergency services

In a medical emergency dial 15, for the fire brigade call 18, or 112 for either from a mobile.

- Police: 17 (Emergency)
  0033 (0)4 79 06 32 06 (Gendarmerie)
  0033 (0)4 79 40 04 93 (Municipal police)
- Ambulance: 0033 (0)4 79 06 59 18/ 0033 (0)4 79 06 43 00
- Piste safety: 0033 (0)4 79 06 32 00
- Doctor's surgery: 0033 (0)4 79 06 50 07

Taxis

- Diane Taxis, Les Brévières: 0033 (0)6 07 06 30 32
- AA Anémone, Val Claret: 0033 (0)6 09 41 01 46, www.taxitignes.com
- Delta Taxi: 0033 (0)6 11 45 67 01, www.deltataxis-tignes.com

Val d'Isère

Val gets top marks all round; it's the place to come for a week of hedonistic riding and partying.

On the mountain	Rating
Snow reliability	❄❄❄❄
Parks	❄❄❄❄
Off-piste	❄❄❄❄½
Off the slopes	
Après ski	❄❄❄
Nightlife	❄❄❄❄
Eating out	❄❄❄
Resort charm	❄❄❄

The resort

Val d'Isère is one of Europe's most famous resorts and the hype is well deserved. The village stretches down the valley from La Daille up to Le Fornet, with the focus of the nightlife and village life in the centre, Val Village. Created for the 1992 Olympics, Val Village is attractive and bustling with activity. The few not-so-pretty buildings are well hidden.

The only problem with having your base in Val Village is that the runs back to resort aren't great, with the choice of the challenging black run, Face, or Piste M, which is packed with all the others who didn't fancy the black. This results in mass carnage. Purpose-built La Daille is a very convenient base for the slopes but is lacking in character and not great for going out in the evenings. The free buses are efficient during the day but not so regular in the evenings.

The Espace Killy ski area is legendary to piste bashers, freeriders and jibbers. The immense backcountry should be treated with respect – too many ignorant riders visit Val d'Isère and head off piste with no regard to local advice. Too often this ends in tragedy – there are fatalities here on a regular basis. Take notice of avalanche warnings and always ride with a guide.

The mountains

Height: 1785–3300m

Ability	Rating
Expert	❄❄❄❄❄
Intermediate	❄❄❄❄½
Beginner	❄❄❄

Getting about

Val has 300km of marked runs: 20 green, 60 blue, 35 red and 16 black. There are 90 ski lifts that are a credit to Val d'Isère.

There are 3 main sectors:

Bellevarde is easily accessed by the funicular at La Daille or L'Olympique gondola in town and is the route over to Tignes. The Bellevarde area contains the legendary Face run, often completely bumped up. The World Cup downhill is held on the OK run at La Daille.

Solaise is a sunny area that's really good for intermediates, although there are some challenging runs back to the village.

Col de l'Iseran can be accessed from Solaise or from Le Fornet in the main valley. The runs are pretty easy and the views beautiful. From here you can also access some of the best off-piste terrain.

The park

The Val Park (www.valdiserevalpark.com) has always been a favourite amongst the pro boarders and skiers and all the locals are at such a high level that they have to make sure this park rocks. It has various hips, jumps, high and low rails, a fun box, a rainbow and a bordercross. There is also a recreational area with music and a barbecue.

Off-piste and backcountry

Le Fornet is the backcountry mecca, with access to huge areas of off-piste. The trees are fantastic and there are loads of shoots, gullies and cliffs; a great playground, especially when there's too much wind on top. The Grand Vallons, Col Pers and Pointe Pers are awesome but take care on Pointe Pers as it's steep – approaching 50° at the top. Grand Vallons is easily accessible from the Signal drag lift; for the others a guide is recommended.

From Solaise, take the Cugnai 'antique' chairlift and, rather than taking the St Jacques red run down, head over the back of the mountain to the Cugnai off-piste run. This run has some of the best back drops, especially if you keep left under the epic cliff face. This can warm you up for Lorès, some of the best off-piste in Val. For this though, do take a guide as it can be dangerous. To reach it, once you have skied the first half of Cugnai, hang a left and ski tour up to the Refuge des Fours. From here it's about an hour's walk to Lorès ridge, where you should stop to check out the stunning views and then head down the best powder field you'll find in Val.The Bellevarde is another huge playground with countless couloirs and bowls. Couloir des Pisteurs is a firm favourite. When looking from the top of the funicular, you are faced with a flat-topped mountain that forks into 3 halfway down. You can take any route, but the left fork (from the rider's point of view) has some of the best powder. Another great run is the Face du Charvet; there are many routes down but it is often best in treacherous snow conditions, so be warned and take a guide. To the rider's right is the most adventurous and encompasses great mini-bowls and couloirs; just don't get stuck or go over any cliffs!

Lift passes

The lift pass for Val d'Isère seems fairly expensive but it does cover the whole Espace Killy area. Your lift pass will also give you bad weather insurance and free access to the swimming pool. You can buy your lift pass on-line (7 days or more) and it will be delivered to your holiday home in Val. Reserve your pass at www.stvi-valdisere.com or write to STVI, Gare Centrale, 73 150 Val d'Isère. Check the latest prices at www.stvi-valdisere.com

Instruction

There are tons of ski and snowboard schools to choose from, so you'll easily be able to find something to suit you.

ESF

This is the largest and oldest school in town with over 400 instructors. Some of the best skiers in town work for the ESF, but you'd be lucky to get one. It can be great, but it's a bit of a lottery.
0033 (0)4 79 06 02 34
www.esfvaldisere.com

Evolution 2

A wealth of variety and programmes are available on and off your skis.
0033 (0)4 79 41 16 72
www.evolution2.com

Misty Fly

This snowboard school has a great reputation for all aspects of boarding, including off-piste and freestyle. The shop is also pretty cool.
0033 (0)4 79 41 95 77
www.mistyflyvaldisere.com

Mountain Masters

The French and British ski instructors and guides have a great depth of experience. They are extremely popular and perhaps the best guarantee of quality coaching whether for on-piste cruising, heliskiing or racing, etc.
0033 (0)4 79 06 05 14
www.mountain-masters.com

Snow Fun

Best for kids and intermediates. The first school to insist on small group sizes: max. 8 people.
0033 (0)4 79 06 19 79
www.valfun.com

Top Ski

Pat Zimmer, an ex-French-team skier, heads up a team of around 20 excellent guides and

instructors, many of whom have a strong background as competitive skiers. Eric Bertan, the ex-World-Champion mogul skier is based with Top Ski.
0033 (0)4 79 06 14 80
www.topskival.com

Other activities

Driving on ice: Have a go at this using karts, quads, snowmobiles or a car (0033 (0)4 79 06 21 40, www.circuitvaldisere.com).

Health and relaxation spa: Hotel Christiania (0033 (0)4 79 06 08 25, www.hotel-christiania.com) has a health and relaxation spa that offers massages, whirlpool baths and a very expensive slimming treatment. Yoga lessons are available in English and French (0033 (0)6 03 10 63 95). The spa at the luxury Les Barmes de l'Ours (0033 (0)4 79 41 37 00, www.hotel-les-barmes.com) is the biggest in the Alps, and is open to the public at certain times.

Husky driving: If you've got a spare evening you could always have a go at driving a team of huskies (0033 (0)4 79 06 18 68/06 16 48 60 47, stephanemush@aol.com).

Ice skating: The rink (0033 (0)4 79 22 09 96) has 1 late-night session per week.

Scenic flights: If you fancy it, take a scenic flight over the Espace Killy (0033 (0)4 79 41 15 07/00033 (0) 07 22 43 97, www.marine-air-sport.com).

Shop shop shop: The shops are far better than the usual resort rubbish, and form a great way to while away a bad weather day.

Sports and aquatic centre: The new leisure centre has a swimming pool, leisure pool, climbing area, fitness suit, gym, squash court and spa. Call 0033 (0)4 79 04 26 01 for more information or visit www.oxygen-valdisere.com.

Events

Val hosts the **Criterium de la Première Neige** in December, which includes 6 Alpine World Cup Alpine Ski events and loads of entertainment. **The White Battle** in March takes over from the X-Box Big Day Out as the freestyle ski and snowboard competition to watch.

Accommodation

The main lift stations are linked by efficient, free shuttle buses. During the day they are up and down all the time, but at night it might get a bit nippy waiting at the bus stop. It's worth looking around to find the best location for you. There is a huge range of accommodation available from budget to luxury.

The 5-star, luxury **Les Barmes de l'Ours** (0033 (0)4 79 41 37 00, www.hotel-les-barmes.com) is super expensive and also contains the biggest spa in the Alps. The 4-star **Blizzard** (0033 (0)4 79 06 02 07, www.hotelblizzard.com) is cosy and civilised with a great bar but has prices to match. It has a swimming pool, Turkish bath and Jacuzzi. The restaurant is good quality but expensive and lacks inspiration for the price.

Hotel Kandahar (0033 (0)4 79 06 02 39, www.hotel-kandahar.com) has 3 stars, is mid ranged and has a great location, smack in the centre of town. It has a comfortable, modern alpine décor, a great bar and a tavern downstairs that is a favourite with the locals.

Chalethotel Moris (0033 (0)4 79 06 22 11, www.markwarner.co.uk) is a favourite of the Brits. The food and accommodation are pretty good and the pub below is a well-liked watering hole. A popular choice, especially for those who don't place pampering high up on their priority list.

Eating out

On the mountain

The mountain restaurants in Val are surprisingly good value. Obviously we're not talking cheap but, compared to other resorts of a similar standard, Val scores very highly for value for money on the mountain.

Le Fornet

Le Signal (0033 (0)4 79 06 03 38, www.lesignalvaldisere.com), at the summit of the Signal cable car, is on the top floor of the building with a cheap and cheerful self-service below. The staff are attentive and friendly and the hearty portions have an excellent reputation. The **Edelweiss** (0033

(0)6 10 28 70 64, www.chalet-edelweiss-73.com) is a beautiful chalet halfway down the Mangard blue run, with great food, ambience and service.

Solaise

Le Bar de l'Ouillette (0033 (0)4 79 41 94 74) is a bustling little self-service restaurant that is a huge sun trap. It is popular with instructors and has very friendly staff.

Bellevarde

La Folie Douce (0033 (0)4 79 06 01 47, www.lafoliedouce.com) and **La Fruitière** (0033 (0)4 79 06 07 17) are at the top of the La Daille bubble. The self-service Folie is OK for food, but better for après beers. La Fruitière, set in a restored dairy farm, is the place to be seen on the hill in Val d'Isère. It's often over crowded and fully booked but worth it. The best tables and service are on the upper tier inside; reservations are a must. **Marmottes** (0033 (0)4 79 06 05 08) is a well-positioned meeting place by the lift of the same name, overlooking the park. It is a great self-service restaurant with good portions and good value for money. Outside is a fab hot dog stand and a couple of rows of deckchairs. **Le Trifollet** (0033 (0)4 79 41 96 99) serves the best pizzas on the hill. If you want a good table it's best to reserve and the upper terrace is fantastic in the spring.

In town

Reservations are essential, especially in high season. **The Lodge** (0033 (0)4 79 06 02 01, www.lodgebar.net), up by Dicks Tea Bar, is a funky and cosy little restaurant that is fantastic for groups of mates, families and also for romantic dates. They do great food at good prices (pizzas, steaks, etc). **La Perdrix Blanche** (0033 (0)4 79 06 12 09), right in the centre of town, is popular with the locals. It's atmospheric and serves good food. **La Taverne d'Alsace** (0033 (0)4 79 06 48 49) has good rustic food, a great atmosphere and good service, but it's pricey. **La Grande Ourse** (0033 (0)4 79 06 00 19) is expensive and kitsch. **Chez Paolo** (0033 (0)4 79 06 28 04) has the tastiest pizzas and Italian fare in town. It can get really busy though, so it's best to pick your times. **Bananas** (0033 (0)4 79 06 04 23, www.bananas.fr), just by the slopes, is a Tex-Mex restaurant upstairs that is really busy when people come in from the slopes and has a great bar downstairs. **Bar Jacques** (0033 (0)4 79 06 03 89) combines quality, service and price, and **L'Atelier d'Edmond** (0033 (0)4 79 00 00 82, www.atelier-edmond.com) is a gastronomic restaurant in the style of an ancient carpenter's shop.

Bars and clubs

La Folie Douce (0033 (0)4 79 06 01 47, www.lafoliedouce.com) is the place to be for après ski. From lunch onwards you will often find people dancing on the tables and/or roof. There's always loud music, and sometimes a DJ, that you can hear from the top of the mountain. When you're suitably hammered you can ski/board back down (which we obviously don't condone) or take the lift.

'There's loud music you can hear from the top of the mountain'

Café Face (0033 (0)4 79 06 29 80, www.cafeface.com), opposite Dicks Tea Bar, is a packed après ski bar with a fab atmosphere and an inspired happy hour (from about 4pm) during which the beers are amazingly cheap; the prices get steadily more expensive as time passes. **Pacific Bar** (0033 (0)4 79 06 29 19, www.pacificbar.co.uk) is the place to watch sports as it has plasma screens pretty much in front of every table. The **Moris Pub** (0033 (0)4 79 06 22 11, www.morispub.mountainpub.com), at the end of town, is a massive pub that has great live music, happy hours and theme nights.

The **Saloon Bar** (0033 (0)4 79 06 01 58, www.saloonbar.com) has a fab atmosphere, loads of seating and is great at any time of day or night. The 2 for 1 cocktail hours are a plus point too! It also has a dance floor on which to strut your stuff. **Bananas** (0033 (0)4 79 06 04 23, www.bananas.fr) is a small bar with a good atmosphere and good cocktails. Upstairs is a popular Tex-Mex restaurant (see Eating out). **Petit Danois** (0033 (0)4 79 06

27 97, www.lepetitdanois.com) is a cool late-night bar that has some good DJs and is often hectic and crowded but fun.

Dicks Tea Bar (0033 (0)4 79 06 14 87, www.dicksteabar.com) is the main club and gets absolutely packed. Despite Val's reputation for being a hive of late-night entertainment, if you want a boogie this is pretty much the only place to go (or at least where all the Brits go). It's worth a visit, but it is ridiculously expensive to get in and the queues are often massive. Once inside, it's full of little alcoves and can be fun but the drinks aren't cheap! **Le Graal** (0033 (0)6 16 79 52 90, www.graalclub.com) is Dicks' only real competition.

Getting there

By car

Drive via Bourg St Maurice and take the N90 towards Tignes and then Val d'Isère. Around 10.5 hours from Calais.

By plane

Geneva (180km) Transfer 3–3.5 hours.

By train

Take the Eurostar from London St Pancras to Paris; then an overnight train to Bourg St Maurice, and then a bus (60 minutes) to the resort. Contact Rail Europe (0870 830 4862, www.raileurope.co.uk) or European Rail (020 7387 0444, www.europeanrail.com). Bus tickets (from Autocars Martin) are purchased at the station.

Useful facts and phone numbers

Tourist office

T: 0033 (0)4 79 06 06 60
F: 0033 (0)4 79 06 04 56
W: www.valdisere.com

Direct reservations

T: 0033 (0)4 79 06 18 90/
0033 (0)4 79 06 06 60 (hotel/apartment)

Emergency services

In a medical emergency dial 15, for the fire brigade call 18, or 112 for either from a mobile

- Police: 17 or 0033 (0)4 79 06 03 41
- Ambulance: 0033 (0)4 79 06 43 00
- Slope rescue/Ski patrol: 0033 (0)4 79 06 02 10

Doctors

- MédiVal Medical Centre: 0033 (0)4 79 40 26 80
- Val Centre Medical Centre: 0033 (0)4 79 06 06 11
- Val Village Medical Centre: 0033 (0)4 79 06 13 70
- Hospital in Bourg St Maurice: 0033 (0)4 79 41 79 79

Taxis

- Taxis Bozzetto: 0033 (0)4 79 75 03 75, www.taxis-bozzetto.com
- ABC taxis: 0033 (0)6 18 19 20 00, www.valdiseretaxi.com
- Taxi Nicolas: 0033 (0)4 79 41 01 25, www.taxi-nicolas.com
- Altitude Espace Taxi: 0033 (0)6 07 41 11 53, www.altitude-espace-taxi.com
- Taxi Papillon: 0033 (0)6 08 99 93 96, http://taxi-papillon.wifeo.com
- Etoile des Neiges Taxi: 0033 (0)6 25 89 40 53, www.etoiledesneiges.com

Val Thorens

If you're looking for good nightlife and great snow and can ignore the concrete jungle, you're sorted.

On the slopes	Rating
Snow reliability	❄❄❄❄
Parks	❄❄❄
Off-piste	❄❄❄
Off the slopes	
Après ski	❄❄❄
Nightlife	❄❄❄❄
Eating out	❄❄
Resort charm	❄

The resort

Val Thorens is the highest resort in Europe at 2300m, making the snow as reliable as it can be. The blocks of dreary flats seriously damage the 'resort charm' factor, but it's not all ugly: the cluster of newer developments at the top of the resort contains much prettier, traditional chalets. Val Thorens is also very compact so many hotels and residences have the ski-in ski-out facility and you are never too far from the bars, restaurants and lively nightlife.

The skiing and snowboarding is great for all standards and Val Thorens is one of the best places anyone can find themselves after a fresh snowfall.

The resort is car-free – you can unload but must park in one of the surrounding car parks.

The mountains

Height: 2300–3200m

Ability	Rating
Expert	❄❄❄❄
Intermediate	❄❄❄
Beginner	❄❄❄

Getting about

Val Thorens' mountains are far more appealing than the town. There are 170km of pistes (66 pistes), with access to the 600km of Les Trois Vallées (328 pistes). Of the 66 pistes in Val Thorens, 5 are black, 28 red, 25 blue and 8 green. It is therefore more suited to intermediates and experts, although a new 10ha of beginners' ski area improves this situation. The more challenging pistes are towards the top of the glacier with some motorway pistes that are great for intermediates. There is also plenty to keep the backcountry explorer entertained. The snow is virtually guaranteed and the lift systems are pretty modern and quick. The disadvantages are that there is nowhere to escape to in bad weather as the trees are non-existent, and the runs can get busy due to people coming over from Courchevel and Meribel. If you fancy a pretty view, head up to the Cime de Caron (at 3200m) for a panoramic view of hundreds of French, Swiss and Italian summits.

The park

Just above the 2 Lacs piste, at the bottom of the resort and accessible from the 2 Lacs chairlift, is the snowpark (www.snowparkvalthorens.com), which is always kept in really good condition. The jumps are not the most fierce, but are perfect for practising your latest tricks. There are lots of rails to jib on which are changed throughout the winter so the locals don't get bored and a 115m half pipe that can be pretty good after it's been shaped.

Off-piste and backcountry

Val Thorens has a huge quantity of off-piste, and the snow stays in good condition as the mountain is one of the highest in the Alps, so you can pretty much always find some tempting powder. The Cime de Caron is 1 of the most popular places and has 1 of the best views in Les Trois Vallées. Some of the riding on the glaciers of Péclet and Chavière can be totally mind blowing, and this is where to go after a snowstorm (with someone who knows the place). If steeps and couloirs are your bag, head to le Plein Sud; these get tracked out pretty quickly but the snow's always wicked and they don't get boring. Our favourite place is the long ride over the Gébroulaz glacier down towards Meribel. You can get to this by hiking up from the top of the Col chairlift.

> 'Some of the riding on the glaciers can be totally mind-blowing'

Lift passes

Check the latest prices at www.valthorens.com

Instruction

ESF

The ESF provides a variety of courses, including group, private, freeride, freestyle and heliriding, and also organises torchlit descents.
0033 (0)4 79 00 02 86
www.esf-valthorens.com

Prosneige

Prosneige offers all-inclusive packages (lessons plus lift pass and equipment), as well as private tuition, guiding and heliskiing on Italian summits. Prosneige is great for adaptive skiers.
0033 (0)4 79 01 07 00
www.prosneige.fr

Ski Cool

Ski Cool offers carving and freestyle courses for both boarders and skiers, and 3-hour ice-climbing courses.
0033 (0)4 79 00 04 92
www.ski-cool.com

Other activities

Unless other contact details are given, call the tourist office for more information (0033 (0)4 79 00 08 08).

Beauty and well being: Institut des Neiges (0033 (0)4 79 01 04 81) offers loads of treatments (1–5 day packages). Le Spa (0033 (0)4 79 22 99 62, www.lespa-valthorens.com) has rooms for facials and other treatments, a spa, a sauna and a hamman.

Bowling Leisure Centre: This centre (0033 (0)4 79 22 25 57, www.bowlingvalthorens.com) in the heart of the resort is open every day between 2pm and 2am. There are 8 bowling lanes, pool halls (7 pool tables and 1 snooker), an internet café, games room, bar and TV.

Flying: Take a microlight flight from the base on the Moutière plateau (2500m). Call 0033 (0)6 60 66 73 00.

Ice climbing: You can take a 3-hour introduction or improvers' lesson on a natural waterfall. Contact Ski Cool (0033 (0)4 79 00 04 92).

Ice driving: The Val Thorens Ice Driving Academy (0033 (0)6 74 78 25 13) gives lessons on general ice driving through to competition level.

Paragliding: Tandem paraglides are available over Les Trois Vallées (0033 (0)6 81 55 74 94, www.libre-envol.com).

Snowmobiling: This is a popular activity in Val Thorens. Valtho Motoneige (0033 (0)6 08 58 21 71) has 42 snowmobiles for hire.

Sports centre: This centre (0033 (0)4 79 00 00 76) combines fitness, sport and relaxation. The Aquaclub has an island theme and includes a swimming pool, in which you can swim against the current. There are also several saunas, Jacuzzis and a heated solarium. The fitness centre contains a 170m^2 weight/circuit training room and a 110m^2 fitness room. Leisure activities include tennis, volleyball, football, squash, ping pong, badminton, roller skating, hockey, and a kids' play room with trampolines and ball pools. Aquaclub is open 2–10pm and in the morning in bad weather.

Tobogganing: The highest toboggan run in Europe is situated in the Tête Ronde sector. At the foot of the Péclet glacier, this run drops 700m during its impressive 6km descent and will take around 45 minutes. It is accessible during the day via the Funitel of Péclet in just 8 minutes.

Events

Popular current events include: **Ski and Boarder Week**, with equipment testing, parties and concerts; the **ATR (Agence To Ride) session**; and many more.

Accommodation

Most accommodation is well located, either near town and/or the slopes.

For exclusive, self-catering accommodation try the 4-star **L'Oxalys** chalet complex (0033 (0)4 79 10 49 15, www.loxalys.com). Prices depend on time of season and whether you require a VIP chalet (contains whirlpool bath, video recorders, slippers…). The other glam option is the 4-star **Fitzroy** (0033 (0)4 79 00 04 78, www.hotelfitzroy.com) which is very posh and beautiful. For slightly less expensive beautiful apartments in a big, cosy, wooden chalet, try **Les Chalets du Soleil** (0033 (0)4 75 75 45 75, www.chaletsdusoleil.com).

If you are looking for a less expensive visit, try the **Mercure hotel** (0033 (0)4 79 00 04 04, www.mercurevalthorens.com) which has 104 rooms. It's right on the slopes, and the spa has lots of treatments on offer. The Mercure appeals to a large range of clients, but mostly families, attracted by the nightly entertainment for children, and family rooms; and corporate clients, who can take advantage of the 500m^2 of conference and meeting facilities that the hotel offers.

If you prefer an inexpensive apartment, rather than a hotel, try **Le Chamois D'Or** (0033 (0)4 79 01 34 34, www.lechamoisdor.fr) in the centre of town, offering studios or apartments.

Eating out

On the mountain

There are many restaurants overlooking the mountains on the slopes by the town centre. **Le Galoubet brasserie** (0033 (0)4 79 00 00 48, www.le-galoubet.fr) is one of the best traditional restaurants on the mountain; it has a big terrace and you can either have a quick panini or opt for a fancy main meal. **Le Scapin** (0033 (0)4 79 00 05 94), just behind Le Galoubet, has very friendly service and more simple food such as pizzas, pastas and steak.

On the slopes, **Chalet des 2 Lacs** (0033 (0)4 79 00 28 54, www.chaletsdes2lacs.com) has a snack bar outside for hot dogs, chips and crêpes to enjoy on deckchairs in the sun. It also has a very cute wooden restaurant with an open fire and serves good pizzas and big chunky chips. **Chalet le Caribou** (0033 (0)6 11 18 06 71) is another cosy chalet with a big fire.

In town

There are lots of places to eat in town, including a number of fast-food options and kebab houses. For British pub grub (fish and chips, burgers and the like), try the **Frog and Roast Beef** (0033 (0)6 84 12 87 16, www.thefrogandroastbeef.com). **El Gringos** (0033 (0)4 79 00 01 61, www.restoleil.com) serves fab Tex-Mex food and the staff are a hoot. There are long wooden benches, perfect for large groups. For a pizza or traditional Savoyard cuisine, **La Paillotte** (0033 (0)4 79 00 01 02) in the town centre is very cosy and serves excellent food. Pizzas and salads are also available at Le Scapin with a good atmosphere and affordable prices. If you want something less affordable but definitely memorable, try **L'Oxalys** (0033 (0)4 79 00 12 00, www.loxalys.com). The restaurant is run by Jean Sulpice, who has been awarded the 'highest' Michelin star in Europe, at 2300m. Make sure you book well in advance.

Bars and clubs

The row of bars at the top of the resort is where your night should begin. Choose an end and work your way along, picking your way through bars such as the **Frog and**

Roast Beef (see In town), **Saloon** (www.saloonbar.com), **O'Connells** (0033 (0)4 79 01 05 05) and **Le Viking** (0033 (0)4 79 04 27 65). All of them have various happy hours and some offer tasty meals too. The Frog Challenge at the Frog and Roast Beef bar is to down a yard of lager – if the yard is drunk (without spillage) in under 45 seconds it's free and if under 30 seconds beer is free until closing time. O'Connells happens to be the highest Irish pub in the world and was the fastest built in France – it took just 4 weeks to build it, ship it to the Alps and install it. **Le Chantaco** (0033 (0)4 79 08 38 13, www.restoil.com) in the centre of town is another option with table football and somewhere you can usually sit for a chat.

Later on the place to be is the **Malaysia cellar bar** (0033 (0)4 79 00 05 25, www.malaysia.com). It's right by the piste and looks like it's just a little wooden hut but, once inside, you walk down into a large club that has live bands all the time, and at about 1.30am the second part of the club opens up. Another option is **Dicks Tea Bar** (www.dicksteabar.com) in Place de Péclet.

Getting there

By car

From Calais (209km), drive time is around 11 hours. You can't park your car in town, so either make sure your hotel/apartment has a car park or book into 1 (0033 (0)4 79 00 02 49, www.valthoparc.com); it's cheaper than paying on arrival.

By plane

Lyon (193km) Transfer time is around 3 hours. For bus transfers contact Altibus on 0033 (0)4 79 68 32 96 or www.altibus.com. *Geneva* (160km) Transfer takes about 3 hours.

By train

Take the Eurostar from London St Pancras to Paris; then an overnight train to Moutiers, and then a bus (75 minutes) to the resort. Contact Rail Europe (0870 830 4862, www.raileurope.co.uk) or European Rail (020 7387 0444, www.europeanrail.com). Bus tickets can be purchased in advance from Altibus (0033 (0)4 79 68 32 96, www.altibus.com) or at the station.

Useful facts and phone numbers

Tourist office

T: 0033 (0)4 79 00 08 08
F: 0033 (0)4 79 00 00 04
W: www.valthorens.com

Direct reservations

T: 0033 (0)4 79 00 01 06
F: 0033 (0)4 79 00 06 49

Emergency services

- In a medical emergency dial 15, for the fire brigade call 18, or 112 for either from a mobile
- Police station: 0033 (0)4 79 00 08 50
- Medical centres: 0033 (0)4 79 00 00 37/0033 (0)4 79 00 74 39 (rue du Soleil)
- Clinique des Trois Vallées: 0033 (0)4 79 24 01 76
- Hospital: 0033 (0)4 79 09 60 60 (Moutiers)

Taxis

- Station de taxis: 0033 (0)4 79 00 69 54
- Favre, Pascal: 0033 (0)4 79 00 64 59
- Legay, Eric: 0033 (0)4 79 00 28 74/06 80 36 34 31

Italy

Italy has some of the most incredible scenery in Europe

Alagna

This tiny town remains largely undiscovered but provides access to some of Italy's finest freeriding.

On the slopes	Rating
Snow reliability	❄❄❄½
Parks	❄½
Off-piste	❄❄❄❄½
Off the slopes	
Après ski	❄
Nightlife	❄
Eating out	❄❄
Resort charm	❄❄❄½

The resort

'Freeriding Paradise' is written all over the lifts and town of Alagna, and for good reason. Alagna is 1 of the 3 valleys in the Monterosa area (with Champoluc and Gressoney – see Gressoney chapter, page 150), which encompasses a massive range of backcountry escapades. There are plenty of pistes for other levels of rider (except complete beginners), but it's the freeriders who really reap the benefits of the Monterosa ski area.

The jagged, striking mountains provide a stunning backdrop to your explorations of the surrounding peaks. If you should get bored of this magnificent area you can try heliskiing or a backcountry quest to Zermatt. Alagna's town is beautiful, centred round an eye-catching church. Beauty aside, there's not too much going on, although you can find a good glass of wine or bite to eat if you know where to look. Like its neighbouring Gressoney, Alagna is probably more suited to a weekend of intense riding, followed by a couple of relaxing evenings, than a week's holiday.

The mountains

Height: 1200–3550m

Ability	Rating
Expert	❄❄❄❄
Intermediate	❄❄❄
Beginner	❄

The Monterosa area is best known for its off-piste and this extends throughout the three valleys. Now that the connecting lift between Gressoney and Alagna is completed, it makes no sense to separate them, as the Gressoney lifts lead to the Alagna off-piste and vice versa. Therefore, for information on the Alagna mountains (including lift pass prices, the park, off-piste and general info), see the Gressoney chapter, page 150.

Instruction

Corpo Guide Alagna (Scuola di Alpinismo)

A number of freeride and heliski trips are available.
0039 0163 913 10
www.guidealagna.com

Guide Monterosa

Guide Monterosa comprises 25 guides who can take you on heliskiing trips or just guide you round the mountain. They also offer a service of organising your accommodation, taxis, the works. The company is based in Gressony, so see page 150.
0039 0125 366 019 or 0039 3493 674 950
www.guidemonterosa.com

Lyskamm 4000

This adventure travel group offers heliskiing, freeriding, winter mountaineering, ski mountaineering and other adventure excursions as well as organising hotels and taxis if required.
0039 3468 077 337 or 0039 3472 264 381
www.lyskamm4000.com

Scuola Sci and Snowboard Alagna

0039 0163 922 961
scuolascialagna@tiscali.it

Other activities

Apart from heliskiing and guiding, the only other activity is to stroll around town.

Events

In mid-February, Alagna is home to the **Telemark Karnival** (www.telemark.it) to which many budding telemarkers will flutter.

Accommodation

There is a stunning 4-star hotel in Alagna called the **Hotel Cristallo** (0039 0163 922 822, www.hotelcristalloalagna.com), with top notch service and a luxurious feel. You have the choice of the lovely and colourful classic room, the more roomy Prestige room or the ultimate, multi-level suite. The Wellness suite, lounge and restaurant are also divine. This hotel would be a wonderful place for a romantic weekend.

> ‘Wonderful place for a romantic weekend’

The 3-star hotel **Monterosa** (0039 0163 923 209, www.hotelmonterosa-alagna.it) was the first to be opened in Alagna in 1865. It is bang in the centre of the village, opposite the church and 100m from the cable car. There are 14 rooms with en-suite facilities, and an old restaurant (La Stube) with magnificent high ceilings and chandelier, although there is a feeling of eating in an archaic school dining room.

Indren Hus (0039 0163 911 52, www.indrenhus.it) has rooms or apartments on offer, as well as some ‘panoramic attics’ that boast spectacular views. All rooms have satellite TV and most have a deck or balcony. The bar and restaurant are friendly and great and there is a small fitness centre, as well as a sauna and whirlpool shower. Half-board accommodation means that you eat at the Dir und Don Brasserie (see Eating out) or at the Indren Stube inside the hotel. The hotel is also in association with the local wine bar (see Bars and clubs) and guests are occasionally invited to wine tastings.

Eating out

On the mountain

Rifugio Guglielmina (0039 0163 914 44/ 0039 03472 732 082, www.rifugioguglielmina.com) has a traditional restaurant as well as accommodation. **Rifugio Grande Halte** (0039 0348 875 2203, www.grandehalte.it) on path no. 5, is a relaxing hut with restaurant and hotel – there are 10 rooms with either 2, 4 or 6 beds. Check out the Gressoney chapter for more options (see page 150).

In town

Most of the hotels have restaurants attached, for example **La Stube** at the Monterosa (see Accommodation) is the place to go if you fancy a fondue or raclette. Indren also has a good restaurant. There is also a surprisingly stylish bistro in the centre of town called the **Dir und Don Brasserie** (0039 0163 922 642). This has a terrace with outside heaters and bar, and a cosy wooden interior. They serve meat, pasta, risotto and pizzas. **Unione** (0039 0163 922 930) is a friendly, informal restaurant and it has a good terrace.

Bars and clubs

As you will have guessed there's not too much going on and most people are tucked up in bed early preparing themselves for the next day. The best bar in town is the **Bacher Wine Bar** (0039 0163 91301), which is really cosy and has wine bottles covering the walls. Apart from this, the best bet is to infiltrate a local crowd and suggest that they throw a party.

Getting there

By car

From Milan or Turin, take the motoway A4 or A26 and turn off at Biandrate for Gravellona Toce and Romagnano-Ghemme. Then take the main road S299 to Alagna.

By plane

Milan Linate (137km)
Milan Malpensa (98km)
Turin Caselle (170km)
All information about buses linking Alagna with Milan and Turin can be obtained by calling 0039 0163 922 988.

By train

Take the Eurostar from London St Pancras to Paris, then an overnight train, changing at Milan and Novara, to Varallo Sesia, and then a local bus (58 minutes) to the resort. Contact European Rail (020 7387 0444, www.europeanrail.com). Bus tickets are purchased on the bus.

Useful facts and phone numbers

Tourist office

T: 0039 0163 922 988
F: 0039 0163 912 02
W: www.atlvalsesiavercelli.it

Emergency services

- Call 118

Cervinia

Not over-challenging, but great for Sunday afternoon cruisers and regulars love it.

On the slopes	Rating
Snow reliability	❄❄❄❄
Parks	❄❄❄
Off-piste	❄
Off the slopes	
Après ski	❄❄❄½
Nightlife	❄❄❄½
Eating out	❄❄❄½
Resort charm	❄❄

The resort

Cervinia is a strange resort but regular visitors love it. The pedestrian centre is great; everything's really handy and within a few minutes' walk, there are some top bars, decent restaurants and you can ride over to Zermatt without paying Zermatt prices. Cervinia also benefits from superb altitude, with slopes reaching 3883m, ensuring good snow cover. On the other hand, the buildings outside of the centre are mostly pretty ugly, and the slopes aren't challenging for anyone above an intermediate level. But if you're not an expert, it will probably do you just fine.

The mountains

Height: 1525–3883m

Ability	Rating
Expert	❄
Intermediate	❄❄❄❄
Beginner	❄❄❄❄

Getting about

Cervinia has 200km of pistes of its own, and connects to the lower valley, Valtournenche, and over the Swiss border to Zermatt; in total providing 350km of accessible terrain. Most of this area is great for cruisy intermediates, but can be dull for gutsy intermediates and experts. The base station of the gondolas isn't particularly well located for most of the accommodation, but you can always work your way up from the nursery slope drag lifts. The Plateau Rosa (3480m) is the gateway to Switzerland or you can return back to Cervinia via another of Cervinia's pleasing red runs. The cable car link in Zermatt between Furi and Riffelberg connects the Klein Matterhorn and Gornergrat areas; a great bonus for anyone travelling over from Cervinia as it opens up areas of Zermatt that were previously unreachable without a trek through town.

The park

Cervinia's Indian Park (www.indianpark.it) is well shaped and there is a fairly good variety of kickers. The jumps are graded, with 2 blues, 4 reds, and 1 black – a good 12m table with perfect transition. At the bottom of the park is a hip that you can hit from either side. Jibbers will be happy with the few rails and fun boxes. We had heard that it was only for boarders, but in fact there are just as many skiers and it has a great atmosphere. Sometimes there's a mediocre pipe, if the conditions are right. A great park for all, from learning your first jumps to pulling crowd pleasers off the big bertha.

Off-piste and backcountry

Cervinia is not the place to come if all you want to do is ride off-piste. The resort gets loads of snow due to its high altitude, but it also gets strong winds, which can wreck the fresh powder. There are not many easily accessible areas and virtually no steeps. Your best bet is to get a guide, and maybe head over towards Zermatt, where you will find some of the best riding in Europe. There's also some amazing heliskiing and boarding that can be done with a guide. Check out the Zermatt chapter (page 215) for the backcountry terrain on the Swiss side of the glacier.

'There's some amazing heliskiing and boarding'

Lift passes

There is a pass that can only be used in the snowpark and 1 for those who only use the mountains in the mornings or in the afternoons.

Check the latest prices at www.cervinia.it

Instruction

Breuil Ski School

0039 0166 940 960
www.scuoladiscibreuil.com

Cervinia Ski School

As well as skiing and boarding lessons, the school also organises heliskiing on the Monte Rosa and on the downhill from Château des Dames on the Grandes Murailles mountains.
0039 0166 949 034/ 0039 0166 948 744
www.scuolacervino.com

Heliski Company

0039 0166 949 267
www.heliskicervinia.com

Other activities

Horse riding: Bepe, at the Hotel Hermitage, can take you out horse riding on the slopes (0039 0166 948 998).

Ice skating: The natural ice skating rink is open day and night, and hockey matches are also organised here.

Night skiing: Every week guides organise a night trip in a snowcat followed by skiing/ boarding down by torchlight.

Paragliding: A half-hour paragliding flight can be organised by Fans de Sport (0039 0335 457 155 or 0039 0347 359 2304, www.fansdesport.it). They also arrange quad biking on specially laid track, kite-skiing and airboarding.

Skidoos: These can be driven across the snow at night. (Contact MotoSlitte on 0039 0166 940 127 or 0039 0335 565 0635, www.motoslittecervinia.it).

Sports centre: Situated in Valtournenche, the Centro Polivalente (0039 166 926 98) has a gym, swimming pool, volleyball, tennis, 5-a-side football, a climbing wall, a sauna and a Turkish bath.

Accommodation

Cervinia doesn't come across as an upper-class place, but there are loads of 4-star hotels to choose from. For the ultimate in luxury, head to the **Hotel Hermitage** (0039 0166 948 998, www.hotelhermitage.com), an elegant and beautiful hotel that also manages to be welcoming and friendly. The 34 luxurious rooms and suites have fireplaces and spa baths. Facilities include a transfer service to the lifts that are 300m away, a beauty spa and swimming pool. Another 4-star treat is the **Hotel Europa** (0039 0166 948 660, www.htl-europa.com). There's a beautiful bar and a luxurious hotel lounge.

'For the ultimate in luxury, head to the Hotel Hermitage'

The **Excelsior Planet** (0039 0166 949 426, www.excelsiorplanet.com) is a lovely hotel with 35 suites and 11 rooms and is a decent price for a 4-star.

For a 3-star option, check out the **Hotel Edelweiss** (0039 0166 949 078, www.matterhorn.it), right in the centre of town and 300m from the slopes (they have a transfer service). The bar is good, as are the prices.

For 2-star hotels, **Marmore** (0039 0166 949 057, www.hotelmarmore.com) is a decent small hotel that is close to the action. **Castelli** (0039 0166 949 183, www.castelli.

ao.it) is an apart-hotel with 12 flats and 2 rooms, 300m from the slopes. **Petit Tibet** (0039 0166 948 974, www.petit-tibet.com) has some really cheap deals for apartments, but it is incredibly inconvenient at the top of town and you can't easily access the town centre.

Eating out

On the mountain

The **Rifugio Guide del Cervinio** (0039 0166 948 369, www.rifugioguidedelcervino.com), right at the top of the Plateau Rosa, is a cute and small self-service restaurant. **Les Skieurs D'Antan** (0039 0166 940 250) is a nice restaurant right at the bottom of the mountain, just above the main cable car where you can get pasta, fish, steak or raclette. It's also open at night.

'In the basement is the cosy tavern, complete with pool table and candles'

In town

The **Copa Pan** (0039 0166 940 084) (see Bars and clubs) has a beautiful restaurant downstairs. The pizzas are a bargain in such gorgeous surroundings. The **Hotel Punta Maquignaz** (0039 0166 949 145, www.puntamaquignaz.com) serves steaks and fondues in comfortable surrounds, as long as you're not put off by all the bear skins and heads in the lobby. The **Capanna Alpina** (0039 0166 948 682, www.capannaalpina-cervinia.com) has a great, atmospheric pizzeria on its top floor, overlooking the bar. In the basement is the cosy tavern, complete with pool table and candles. The **Matterhorn** (0039 0166 948 518) is an informal but welcoming place, and serves some of the best pizzas in town. For a memorable night, try the **Baita Cretaz** (0039 0166 949 914, www.hotelbaitacretaz.it), just up the slopes from town – they will come into town on skidoos to pick you up. One again, the food is traditional and the atmosphere relaxing.

Bars and clubs

There are some great bars in Cervinia and all are a few minutes' walk from each other to save you getting chilly in-between beers. Facing the slopes are the Yeti and the Dragon pubs. The **Yeti** (0039 0166 949 196, www.yeticervinia.it) is a dark but cosy bar with loads of big screens showing sports, internet access and good-value sandwiches, burgers and hot dogs. The Thistles pub at the **Dragon Hotel** (0039 0166 940 255, www.hoteldragon.it) is like a big British pub. It is open 10.30am–12/1am upstairs and 2.30am downstairs. Food is served 12–3pm and 7.30–9.30pm, and the happy hours are good. It's busy at après and then again from about 9.30pm. Watch out for theme nights.

'A cute and cosy wine and cocktail bar'

Our favourite bar for après is the **Ymeletrob** (0039 0166 949 145, www.puntamaquignaz.com), a cute and cosy wine and cocktail bar at the end of the town centre that has chips, dips and more free snacks dotted around the bar. The prices are inflated because of the free snacks but it's worth it. The cocktail of the day tends to be a reasonable price. The **Copa Pan** (0039 0166 940 084) has a stunning restaurant (see Eating out), a bar and a club. The bar is open 4pm–1am, and the club 10pm–3/4am. The Copa Pan attracts a mix of seasonaires and tourists and has theme nights about once a month where they really go to town; for example, on Woodstock night they laid the floor with grass and brought in tepees.

Out of town, past the cable car, towards the big apartment blocks at the top of town, there are a few shops and restaurants. There is also a fab bar and restaurant where an old cinema used to be, called the **Taverna di Gargantua** (0039 0166 940 167). There's a massive screen that usually shows concerts and, instead of a pool table to entertain you, you can practise your golf putting.

Getting there

By car

From France go through the Mont Blanc tunnel and take the main road 26 from Courmayeur to Châtillon. At Châtillon, take the regional road (SR) 46 and follow signs for Valtournenche and Breuil-Cervina.

By plane

Milan (170km) Fly to either Milano Malpensa or Milano Linate.
Turin (118km)
Geneva (180km)
Transfer details can be obtained from the Consortium-Consorzio per lo Sviluppo Turistico del Comprensorio del Cervino (0039 0166 949 136). Alternatively call a taxi transfer (see right). Car rental services, minibuses and buses can be obtained from C.A.A.R.P. (0039 0112 472 072, www.caarp.it).

By train

Take the Eurostar from London St Pancras to Paris, then an overnight train, changing at Milan and Chivasso, to Chatillon, and then a local bus (60 minutes) to the resort. Contact European Rail (020 7387 0444, www.european rail.com). Bus tickets are purchased on the bus.

Useful facts and phone numbers

Tourist office

T: 0039 0166 949 136
F: 0039 0166 949 731
W: www.cervinia.it/www.montecervino.it

Emergency services

- Police: 0039 0165 279 111/948 103
- In a medial emergency call 118

Doctors

- Medical centre: 0039 0166 940 175
- Dr Salvatore Bongiorno: 0039 0339 54 17 321

Taxis and airport transfers

- Paolo Giannini: 0039 0166 62 220/0039 0335 565 3189
- Giuseppe Pession: 0039 0166 925 62/0039 0348 312 3036
- Riccardo Ferraris: 0039 0166 61 874/0039 0339 13 96 490
- Sergio Meynet: 0039 0166 92 723/0039 0333 23 74 523, www.cervinia-taxi.it

Cortina d'Ampezzo

Stunning scenery, spoilt by the pretentious town.

On the slopes	Rating
Snow reliability	❄❄❄
Parks	❄❄
Off-piste	❄❄
Off the slopes	
Après ski	❄
Nightlife	❄
Eating out	❄❄
Resort charm	❄❄❄½

The resort

Cortina is home to some of the most stunning scenery that Europe has to offer. From the quaint, olde worlde village centre you can witness the dramatic scene at sunset when the Dolomitic limestone mountains turn a beautiful shade of pink. But you'd have to rate scenery at the top of your wish list to visit Cortina; as a ski resort it's a pretty strange place.

Most of the visitors jet in from Rome or Milan, and spend their time eyeing up this season's fur coats in the ritzy boutiques or getting themselves seen in the exclusive bars and expensive restaurants. Only very occasionally might they venture up the mountain and only then to recline on a deckchair for an hour or 2. Cortina is great for celebrity spotting and for awe-inspiring views, not so good for baggy-panted freestylers looking for some dancing-on-the-bar style après ski.

The mountains

Height: 1224–2939m

Ability	Rating
Expert	❄❄
Intermediate	❄❄❄
Beginner	❄❄❄❄

Getting about

The 115km of pistes in Cortina are a nightmare to get to – no wonder half the Cortina visitors don't bother trying. There are 2 main cable cars leaving Cortina town, from opposite ends of the town's fringes. It's so disjointed that you would be best off with a car, but the 1-way system is so stressful and confusing that driving around is not fun. The Mandres cable car takes you up to the Faloria area, where you can find your way across to the few red runs under the spectacular Cristallo. Just underneath here is the separate, inconvenient Mietres that only has a few runs. From the other side of town is the cable car to Tofana, from which you can make your way over to the Socrepes area, the largest area full of cruisy blues. Cinque Torri and Passo Falzarego are 2 small areas that can only be accessed by car or bus, but they have the best freeride potential.

The park

This park used to be 'boarders only' but is now little more skier-friendly. The park is located in the Faloria area, which you can get to by catching the Vitelli chairlift. There are up to 4 kickers (depending on the amount of snow), rails and a small half pipe. You wouldn't catch the experts and pros hanging out here, but it's good for starting off in or just having a jib.

Off-piste and backcountry

We weren't particularly inspired by this mountain as a freeride destination (apart from the incredible views, which are hard to beat). There are places to check out, but the best bits aren't all that great, and are often inconvenient. A guide will be able to show you the areas worth visiting, which include a decent couloir at the top of Forcella Staunies (2930m), under Son Forca chair, or the narrow gorges of Bus Tofana and Canalino del Prete. Alternatively your guide could take you to the Cinque Torri or Passo Falzarego, respectable freeriding areas that can only be accessed by car or bus.

Lift passes

Check the latest prices at www.dolomitisuperski.com

Instruction

Guide Alpine Scuola d'Alpinismo

This school can guide you round the pistes of the Sella Ronda or can teach and/or guide you in off-piste and freeride.
0039 0436 868 505
www.guidecortina.com

Scuola Sci Snowboard Cortina

0039 0436 2911
www.scuolascicortina.com

Other activities

Contact Cortina Adrenalin (www.adrenalincenter.it) for more information about the activities.

Bobsleighing: Have a go on the bobsleigh (December–February), and reach speeds of up to 120kph. If the mood takes you, you can throw yourself down the sheet ice without the aid of a bobsled, just on a crazy sledge.

Ice skating and curling: The ice rink is open for skating, curling, and a crazy ice disco once a week.

Sledging: There are loads of sledging runs but most aren't that easy to get to.The handiest one can be reached by the first stage of the Mietres chairlift. This is 1km long, pisted, and reserved for sleds. You can also sledge from Rifugio Ra Stua (1668m), after an hour's walk from the car park. This 3km run has a vertical drop of 200m. The enthusiastic tobogganists should head to the Croda da Lago (2046m). The walk up is 3 hours, but you can contact the Croda da Lago refuge (00 39 0436 862 085) and see if they will get the motorsled out for you. A 4km run (550m vertical drop), starts out at the Rifugio Scoiattoli (00 39 0436 867 939). The walk up is an hour and a half or you can take the chair from Bai de Dones, although you wind up 3.5km from where the chairlift sets off. Moonlight sledding is available, too, and you get to wear a helmet with a light on it!

'Moonlight sledding is available, too, and you get to wear a helmet with a light on it!'

Snowrafting: Sit in a large rubber dinghy and fly down pretty steep snow/ice at 90kph.

Events

Cortina Winter Polo, **bobsleigh races** and the **Sleddog European Championships** are about as exciting as it gets.

Accommodation

There are 2 5-star hotels: the **Cristallo** (0039 0436 881 111, www.cristallo.it) and the **Grand Hotel Savoia and Spa** (0039 0436 3201, www.grandhotelsavoiacortina.com). Both are beautiful big buildings but they are pretty inconvenient. The best hotel in town, in our opinion, is the 4-star **Ancora** (0039 0436 3261, www.hotelancoracortina.com), a beautiful and traditional hotel that has won a number of awards, as well as a tribute in the *Hip Hotels Ski* book. The 2-star **Hotel Montana** (0039 0436 862 126, www.cortina-hotel.com) is right in the pedestrianised centre of town and is simple but cheap.

Eating out

On the mountain

There are lots of lovely mountain huts to stop off at for lunch, and the fur-clad contingent will head straight to them. The beautiful **Rifugio Tondi** (0039 0436 5775) is 1 of the best places to lunch. You'll find it on the Tondi Normale piste (61) in the Faloria area at the top of the Vitelli chairlift. Under Cristallo, the **Rifugio Son Forca** (0039 0436 866 192) has great big terraces with beautiful views. On the other side of the valley, under Tofana, the **Pomedes** restaurant (0039 0436 862 061) is 1 of the best places to stop for a bite to eat.

In town

Ra Stua restaurant (0039 0436 868 341) in Hotel Regina do the standard pasta, risotto and meat dishes. For pizza, **Rotondo** (0039 0436 867 777) on the main square is cosy and **Al Passetto** (0039 0436 2254, www.alpassettoghedina.it) is good.

> 'Michelin rates many restaurants around Cortina'

Michelin rates many restaurants around Cortina: **Tivoli** (0039 0436 866 400) has a star and **El Toulá** (0039 0436 3339, www.toula.it), in a converted barn, has 3 Michelin forks. We liked **Restaurant Zoco** (0039 0436 860 041), on the edge of town, as it's really cosy and serves good, smart food.

Bars and clubs

The après ski scene wasn't really our cup of tea, but there are a couple of fun places to go. The **Enoteca** wine bar is the best; it's cosy and usually packed. For dancing the night away, head to the **VIP club** at Hotel Europa.

Getting there

By car

There is a route planner on Cortina's website that will help you to plan your route.

By plane

Venice (162km)
Treviso (168km) Ryanair.
On Saturdays and Sundays there is a transfer service from Venice and Treviso airports to Cortina for the guests of Cortina Hotels. Journey time is 2 hours. You can book it on the tourist office website.
Innsbruck (156km)

By train

Take the Eurostar from London St Pancras to Paris, then an overnight train, changing in Padova and Belluno, Calalzo di Pieve, and then a local bus (58 minutes) to the resort. Contact European Rail (020 7387 0444, www.europeanrail.com). Bus tickets are purchased at the station.

Useful facts and phone numbers

Tourist office

T: 0039 0436 866 252
F: 0039 0436 867 448
W: www.cortina.dolomiti.org
www.dolomitisuperski.com

Emergency services

- Police-public service: 113
- Police emergency services: 112
- Town police: 0039 0436 866 200
- Alpine First Aid: 0039 0436 2943

Doctors

- Doctor for tourists: 0039 0436 883 111
- Croce Bianca Ambulance Aid: 0039 0436 862 075

Taxis

- Piazza Rome: 0039 0436 2839
- Piazza Venezia: 0039 0436 4619
- Lucio Sgobbi: 0039 0436 890 669

Courmayeur

Beautiful scenery and a gorgeous village – one of Italy's best.

On the slopes	Rating
Snow reliability	❄❄❄
Parks	–
Off-piste	❄❄❄❄½
Off the slopes	
Après ski	❄❄❄
Nightlife	❄❄❄
Eating out	❄❄❄❄
Resort charm	❄❄❄❄

The resort

Courmayeur is only 10 minutes away from the Mont Blanc Tunnel; a charming and picturesque village, with a maze of cobbled streets and some stylish and chic bars and restaurants. The slopes aren't extensive but are good for cruising and posing. It's a great place for people-watching too; top-end designer clothes – and fur – abound. If you want to parade around in the latest designer clothes, sip cocktails in classy bars and don't need a massive challenge on the slopes, this could be the resort for you.

The mountains

Height: 1210–2755m

Ability	Rating
Expert	❄❄❄
Intermediate	❄❄❄❄
Beginner	❄❄

Getting about

The slopes aren't the easiest to get to; the cable car on the edge of town takes you across the river to the mountains and most choose to take this lift down at the end of the day rather than to come down across the river and face the wait for the bus back to town. There are only 36km of slopes that are mostly cruisy runs, a few challenging pistes for the expert and no park, but there is some decent off-piste. Check out some of our favourite runs below and contact Società Guide Alpine for more information (see Instruction).

The park

Courmayeur's snow park is at the top of the Plan De la Gabba lift. It has a few jump, a rail and a box, but no half pipe.

Off-piste and backcountry

There's tons of good backcountry around Courmayeur. As well as loads of wicked tree riding, you will find routes to La Thuile, and to La Rosière and Chamonix in France.

The Valley Blanche Descent is one not to miss. It starts at Punta Helbronner (3462m) and ends in Chamonix (1037m); a 24km descent in the heart of the Mont Blanc Massif on the glaciers of the Colle del Gigante descending into the Valley of Chamonix. This is an amazing adventure across the Mar de Glace sea of ice, through crevasses and ice tunnels. A guide is essential.

The Toula Glacier is a great place to go in the right conditions. From Helbronner point (3462m) you can get to the Toula pass (3450m) in a few minutes. Then you have to make your way up a metal staircase to get to the Toula Glacier, after which you have a 2000m descent back down to La Palud Courmayeur. You don't have to be a pro to do this – as long as you feel comfortable off-piste you should be fine, though it is recommended to take a guide.

We rate the guides from the Società Guide Alpine Courmayeur centre for the routes we have described, plus heliskiing and boarding.

Lift passes

Check the latest prices at www.courmayeur-montblanc.com

Instruction

Courmayeur Ski/Snowboard School

0039 0165 848 254
www.scuolascicourmayeur.it

Guide Alpine del Monte Bianco

0039 347 435 0182/0165 809469
www.guidealpinemontebianco.it

Monte Bianco Ski and Snowboard School

This ski and snowboard school offers freeride, freestyle, tours and camps.
0039 0165 842 477
www.scuolascimontebianco.com

Società Guide Alpine Courmayeur

Skiers and snowboarders can discover more of the Courmayeur ski area through backcountry and freeride guides, ski-touring, heliskiing, mountaineering and ice-fall climbing.
0039 0165 842 064
www.guidecourmayeur.com

Other activities

When not on the mountain, most people choose to wander round town in their best designer kit, elegantly sipping cocktails and looking gorgeous, but there are a few other things to entertain you.

Forum sports centre: Most of the sporting activities can be found at this huge sports centre (0039 0165 844 096) with ice skating, ice hockey matches to watch, indoor tennis, squash, gym and climbing wall. It's across the river and contains the Planet bar (see Bars and clubs).

Ice-fall climbing: See Società Guide Alpine details above.

Mountain guide museum: This is worth a look if you're interested in guiding and mountaineering in the olden days.

Paragliding, snow-biking and dog-sledding: Contact the tourist office for more details (see Useful facts and phone numbers).

Spa: Just a few kilometres from Courmayeur and easily accessible using the skibus is the stunning spa centre of Pré-Saint-Didier (0039 0165 867 272, www.termedipre.it). The water of Pré-Saint-Didier is famous for its soothing properties (due to its low mineralisation), regenerating properties (due to the iron content) and anti-rheumatic qualities (due to moderate radioactivity).

Accommodation

There are some seriously swish and swanky hotels in Courmayeur, as you would expect, as well as a few cheaper options. The **Royal and Golf Hotel** (0039 0165 831 611, www.hotelroyalegolf.com) is smart and luxurious. There are 86 elegant rooms, all kitted out with internet connection, satellite TV and mini bar. There is also a fitness centre, gym, sauna, steam room and massage facilities. It's exactly what you would expect of a smart hotel, but it's pretty impersonal. We would rather stay at the **Hotel Mont Blanc** (0039 0165 846 555, www.hotel-montblanc.it), a traditional and elegant place with a welcoming and cosy atmosphere. All rooms have video recorder and mini bar. You will find the Hotel Mont Blanc on the left of the main square as you drive into town. At the time of writing it is closed for renovation.

Less than a minute's walk from the cable car is the retro-looking **Le Grand Chalet** (0039 0165 841 448, www.legrandchalet.it). This apart-hotel consists of 33 apartments, including 13 studios, 17 1-bedroom flats and 3 2-bedroom flats. Also close to the lifts is the cosy **Hotel Courmayeur** (0039 0165 846 732, www.hotelcourmayeur.com), which is full of character. Rooms can only be rented for a full week, Sunday to Sunday. Try to get a room with a balcony.

Eating out

On the mountain

There are loads of choices in Courmayeur when it comes to eating on the mountain, from snacks to delicious bites in rustic huts – the most well known of which is **Maison Vieille** (0039 328 058 4157, www.maisonvielle.com), famous for its homemade pasta, wood-fired oven and friendly service.

For sunny terraces and snack bars, head over to the Val Veny side of the valley and try the **Grolla** (0039 0165 869 095). For an exquisite treat of foie gras and wild boar, head to Chiecco (0039 338 700 3035, www.chiecco.com).

In town

Cadran Solaire (0039 0165 844609) is a gorgeous, romantic and rustic restaurant. **Pierre Alexis** (0039 0165 84 3517) is a smart restaurant, renowned for being an expensive place but not everything will cost you a fortune.

For a quick snack at après ski, head to the **Petit Bistrot**, where you can sit in a small, cosy and busy atmosphere tucking into a tasty crêpe. **Coquelicot** (0039 0165 846789) is one of the few places that still does beef fondues, as well as cheese fondues and lots of fish. **Pizzeria du Tunnel** (0039 0165 841705, www.pizzeriadutunnel.it) is a good-value and cute snack bar that serves homemade pastas, pizzas, omelettes and steaks. They also do massive pizzas for sharing and heart-shaped pizzas on request!

Mont Frety (0039 0165 841786, www.ristorantemontfrety.net), on the road that leads from the town to the gondola, is a good pizzeria that is less pricey than most of the other options and not at the expense of quality. **Poppy's Bar** (see Bars and clubs) also serves great wood-fired pizzas for lunch and at night.

Bars and clubs

The **Roma** is the best bar in town, especially for après ski. It's beautiful and cosy and there is a huge amount of food out for you to munch on whilst you drink. The **Café Della Posta** (0039 0165 842272) looks like a regular café but if you sneak through to the room at the back you will find a huge stone fireplace with a roaring fire, a few tables and some snug sofas and chairs. **Cadran Solaire** (see Eating out) has a gorgeous, but expensive bar attached. **Ziggy's** is the place to go to check your e-mails. Down one of the winding backstreets, this dark, basement bar opens at 3pm. **Poppy's Bar** (bar/restaurant/club) is convenient, big, good value and fun. **Planet**, at the sports complex in La Villette across the river, is a huge open bar/club that has a big stage for live music and DJs; it also has pool tables and table football. It's open 11am–2am and looks very much like a student union bar with long wooden tables and a lived-in feel. It's inconvenient if you're staying in town but is a good night out and good value.

Getting there

By car

Courmayeur is easy to get to from France as it is only 10 minutes' drive from the Mont Blanc Tunnel. Make sure you don't speed while you're in the tunnel – they'll catch you on the other side.

By plane

Geneva (100km)
Turin (150km)
Transfer from both takes around 2 hours.

By train

Take the Eurostar from London St Pancras to Paris, then an overnight train, changing at St-Gervais-Les-Bains, to arrive in Chamonix station at 09.25 (this is 4 hours faster than the alternative with fewer changes). Then take a taxi (30 minutes) to Courmayeur. Contact Rail Europe (0870 830 4862, www.raileurope.co.uk) or European Rail (020 7387 0444, www.europeanrail.com).

Useful facts and phone numbers

Tourist office

T: 0039 0165 842 060
F: 0039 0165 842 072
W: www.aiat-monte-bianco.com

Emergency services

- Police: 0039 0165 890 720/0165 831 334/0039 0165 842 225
- Medical emergency: 118

Doctors

- Dr Bahren: 0039 335 6367 959
- Dr Di Cesare: 0039 340 979 5327
- Dr Mannu: 0039 0165 809 853
- Dr Rocchio: 0039 0165 841 113

Taxis

- P.le Monte Bianco Courmayeur: 0039 0165 842 960

Gressoney

The heliskiing capital of Europe and a quiet, unspoilt town.

On the slopes	Rating
Snow reliability	❄❄❄
Parks	–
Off-piste	❄❄❄❄
Off the slopes	
Après ski	❄
Nightlife	❄
Eating out	❄❄
Resort charm	❄❄❄❄

The resort

Gressoney, in the Monterosa ski area at the north-east end of the Aosta valley, is a beautiful, quiet and unspoilt village; many of the local families have lived here for over 500 years. There's little to do in the evenings in this idyllic community, although this is probably for the best in order for you to keep your strength up for the next day on the mountain, as Gressoney has access to extensive backcountry terrain and some of the finest heliskiing in Europe. Like its neighbour, Alagna, and La Grave in France, Gressoney would not be the model resort for most. However, for the earnest skiers (Gressoney is less suitable for boarders) who value their time on the mountain more than in the pub, and would take pleasure in tranquil, yet spectacular surroundings, a long weekend of heliskiing and mountain exploration would be a first-rate trip.

Gressoney consists of 2 separate villages. Gressoney La Trinité is at the end of the valley where the lifts to the Monterosa ski area are located. Here you will find a number of convenient hotels, and a couple of local facilities. Gressoney St Jean is further from the lifts (it does have a few of its own, but the reason you're here is to experience the Monterosa area so we wouldn't bother too much with these) but is larger and has more hotels, restaurants and facilities. However, this part of town does extend over a few kilometres and the restaurants and hotels require a certain amount of travel between them. Although the bus service isn't bad, we wouldn't come here without a car.

The mountains

Height: 1200–3550m

Ability	Rating
Expert	❄❄❄❄
Intermediate	❄❄❄
Beginner	❄

Getting about

There are 200km of pistes in Monterosa, and a landscape that consists of almost endless off-piste. Snowboarders are advised to go elsewhere – there is a fair bit of traversing on most of the off-piste itineraries. The piste map is pretty shocking, but the signs on the mountain are good so just decide where you're headed and follow the signs. From anywhere on the mountain you can also be guaranteed stunning views, not least of the striking Monte Rosa glacier.

The Monterosa area tends to remain in good condition until the end of April and the later half of the season is usually the best time to visit.

The park

In between Gressoney and Alagna there is a small park that consists of 2 rails, 1 of which is kinked, 1 table top over a 6m gap and a pretty wicked hip jump. There are also 2 fun boxes at the bottom. You wouldn't come here if riding the park was all you wanted to do, but it's still good for a change.

Off-piste and backcountry

Gressoney has fantastic access to massive backcountry areas, being right in the centre of the Monterosa area, which is renowned for its backcountry expeditions. There are a number of off-piste itineraries marked on the map – we had a great long run down from the Punta Indren on the way back from Alagna to Gressoney. These routes are fairly easy to explore without a guide if you are a confident off-piste rider.

'Gressony has fantastic access to massive backcountry areas'

Understandably, many people come to Gressoney and Alagna for the heliskiing on the Monte Rosa. We highly recommend the Guide Monterosa (see Instruction), which offers guiding, touring and heli-trips, with 4 different drop-offs. If you are splashing out on a heli-trip try the descent down the huge Alexandra couloir or the descent right down to Zermatt. This trip usually involves a helicopter flight to the Col du Lys (4270m) and descent towards the Swiss side of the Monte Rosa (Grenz glacier) to Furi, a hamlet of Zermatt. The cable car will take you to the Matterhorn with a descent to Frachey near Champoluc and from here you will return to Gressoney using the Monte Rosa lifts.

Heliskiing is by no means the only way to get the best out of the mountain; the day, weekend or week-long excursions planned by the Guide Monterosa are a fantastic way to explore. If couloirs are your thing, head to the Balma area, which can be reached from the Gressoney lift, or the Salza Valley, which has a huge area of powder and several couloirs. The Lost Valley and the Bettolina area in-between Gressoney and Champoluc (which involves 1.5 hours with skis on) are 2 vast and astonishing areas that are worth a look.

If you would like to explore the off-piste but are lacking in confidence you can ask for a special package in which you spend 3 days with an Instructor and 3 days with a guide (see Instruction).

To learn how to use your avalanche equipment, visit the Ortovox training ground at the Passo dei Salati.

Lift passes

Check the latest prices at www.monterosa-ski.com

Instruction

Guide Monterosa

This guiding association has been in existence for over 10 years and its guides know the mountains better than anyone. There are 25 guides who speak a number of languages and can cater for any level of experience. They offer days for experienced riders from short freeride courses to day tours and heliskiing. If you wish, they can arrange an airport to airport service, including your hotel, taxis, lift pass, skis/board, guiding – the lot.

0039 349 367 4950/0039 0125 366 019
www.guidemonterosa.com

Scuola Sci Gressoney Monte Rosa

Lessons are offered in skiing, boarding, carving and freeriding
0039 349 366 265/0039 0125 366 015
www.scuolascigressoney.it

Scuola Sci Gressoney St Jean

0039 0125 355 291
www.scuolascigressoney.net

Other activities

There's not a huge amount to do in Gressoney, although there is a toboggan run in Gressoney St Jean and a popular cross-country skiing track (contact the tourist office).

Events

Once every 2 years the **Mezzalama Trophy** (www.trofeomezzalama.org) occurs; a 45km race from Cervinia to Gressoney La Trinité over snow, rock and ice at an average altitude of 4000m.

Accommodation

There are 23 hotels in Gressoney and 1800 beds. There should be something for most tastes, be it moderately priced, romantic or convenient.

Gressoney St Jean

Situated in a small hamlet is the 2-star **Hotel Villa Tedaldi** (0039 0125 355 123, www.villatedaldi.com) that is more like a stately home than a hotel. It's a charming, old-fashioned building, with 8 large rooms that each have private bathroom, TV, phone and great view. The hotel offers only B&B accommodation.

The stunning **Lyshaus** (0039 0125 356 644, www.lyshaus.com) has the most incredible rooms and suites – we have no idea why it has only a 3-star rating. Many of the rooms have separate lounges, hydromassage showers and a luxurious and romantic feel. And the bedrooms aren't the best feature of the hotel – this prize would have to go to the remarkable billiard room with panelled walls lined with expensive old wines and a small wooden bar with racks of champagne glasses and dusty bottles of champagne. It also has a beautiful, candlelit restaurant (Carducci) serving dishes such as fondues, risottos and a variety of meats.

If you like to cater for yourself you could try the 4-star **Residenza del Sole** (0039 0125 357 400, www.residenzadelsole.it) that has a number of facilities, including a pool, sauna, gym, billiard room, beauty salon, cocktail bar and restaurant.

Gressoney La Trinité

If you like hopping out of bed straight on to the lifts you'll want to stay in this part of the resort. The 3-star **Hotel Jolanda Sport** (0039 0125 366 140, www.hoteljolandasport.com) is about as close to the slopes as you can get and is a lovely hotel. However, you can only book for the whole week and half-board accommodation is essential. Also close to the slopes is the friendly **Hotel Dufour** (0039 0125 366 139, www.hoteldufour.it), with a homely feel and a large, comfy bar area in which you can curl up with a book.

If you're on a budget there are a number of other options. In Issime (approximately a 10-minute drive away), for example, you can stay at the friendly **Albergo Posta** (0039 0125 344 204, www.hotelpostaissime.com).

Eating out

On the mountain

The **Bedemie** (0039 0125 366 429) is a cute little restaurant with a big terrace, serving simple food such as slices of pizza, sandwiches, pasta, soup and lasagne. Our favourite restaurant is the **Morgenrot** (0039 0125 366 410), just below the Bedemie on the way back down into Gressoney. From the outside it looks like a rowdy bar with music playing and Carlsberg banners, but inside it is a beautiful restaurant with great food (homemade pastas and chunky chips) at reasonable prices and lots of character. The **Gabiet** (0039 0125 366258, www.rifugiogabiet.it) is a good, simple establishment with a terrace overlooking the snowpark and the **Rifugio Guglielmina** (0039 0163 914 44, www.rifugioguglielmina.com) has a traditional restaurant as well as accommodation, which can only be accessed off-piste. Finally the **Alpenhütte Lys** (0039 0125 366 057), by the side of the chair from Gabiet to Passo Salati, has a stunning terrace with hand-built wooden loungers looking out on to the pistes and the mountains. A great place to watch the sun fade after a run down the Punta Indren.

'A stunning terrace with hand-built wooden lounges looking out on to the pistes'

In town

In St Jean there are a few standard restaurants. The **Flora Alpina** (0039 0125 355 179) has a big and bright restaurant with lots of plants. The **Genzianella** (0039 0125 355 178) is cute, rustic and good value (if you can understand the Italian menu) and **Marmotta** (0039 0125 355 197/357 400, www.residenzadelsole.it) at the Residenza del Sole looks smart but is, once again big and bright with little atmosphere. **Carducci** (0039 0125 356 644) at the Lyshaus hotel is one of the finest restaurants in town (see Accommodation). Another is the **Nordkapp** (0039 0125 355 096, www.nordkapprestaurant.com) in the centre of the cobbled square. This charming restaurant has a great couple in charge, and the chefs met working at Mal Maison in Glasgow. They mix local specialities with their own culinary ideas and experiences and create beautiful food. There's also a cute bar downstairs with a little fire. In La Trinité there are only a handful of places to eat, most of them in the hotels. One great, atmospheric pizzeria is the **Walserchild** (0039 0125 366 025).

Bars and clubs

There isn't a huge choice of bars; a lot of the hotels claim to have bars but there is rarely anyone in them. In La Trinité there is pretty much only the **Schnee Blume**, opposite the Jolanda Sport hotel, that's a simple cosy bar, aimed at the local trade. The bar at the **Dufour** (0039 0125 366 139, www.hoteldufour.it) is big and comfy. In St Jean, the olde worlde **Bierfall** in the centre of town is a cute, local place. The **Castore Lounge** (0039 0125 366 809, www.castorelounge.com) is a firm favourite – great food and atmosphere.

Getting there

By car

Take the A5 motorway from Turin to Aosta, exit at Pont-Saint-Martin and take the highway for the Valle di Gressoney.

By plane

Turin (100km) has the quickest and easiest access to Gressoney.
Milan (165km)

By train

Take the Eurostar from London St Pancras to Paris, then an overnight train, changing in Milan and Chivasso, to Pont St Martin, and then a local bus (65 minutes) to the resort. Contact European Rail (020 7387 0444, www.europeanrail.com). Bus tickets are purchased on the bus.

Useful facts and phone numbers

Tourist office

T: 0039 0125 366 143 (La Trinité)/
0039 0125 355 185 (St Jean)
F: 0039 0125 366 323
W: www.aiatmonterosawalser.it/
www.monterosa-ski.com

Emergency services

- Police: 0039 0125 355 304 or 112
- In the case of medical emergency call 118

Doctors

- Dr Chiara Marandino: 0039 339 128 54 48
- Dr Aldo Mignini: 0039 339 435 13 58
- During the day there is usually at least 1 doctor available; at any other time call 118

Taxis

- Taxi Gressoney: 0039 347 578 7132/ 0039 0125 355 957
- Taxi Monterosa: 0039 348 264 7285

Selva in Val Gardena

The breathtaking landscape will strike you first, then the extensive terrain.

On the slopes	Rating
Snow reliability	❄❄❄
Parks	❄
Off-piste	❄❄❄
Off the slopes	
Après ski	❄❄❄
Nightlife	❄❄❄
Eating out	❄❄❄
Resort charm	❄❄❄

The resort

Selva Gardena is just one of the villages within the Val Gardena valley. The alternative towns of Ortisei and S. Cristina are just as charming, but Selva has the best access to the slopes and the best selection of restaurants and bars. The Dolomite landscape is absolutely breathtaking and the extent of the slopes is equally impressive. Intermediate cruisers will be in heaven with the far-reaching Sella Ronda circuit, that takes you on a spectacular journey round the Gruppo Sella – a magnificent limestone massif.

'A spectacular journey'

At first you will probably be confused by the language, no matter how good your skills are, as many locals still speak the age-old dialect of Ladin. Fortunately all speak Italian and German as well and English is also pretty widespread.

The mountains

Height: 1250–2520m

Ability	Rating
Expert	❄❄❄
Intermediate	❄❄❄❄❄
Beginner	❄❄❄❄

Getting about

The 510km of pistes will more than satisfy the adventurous intermediate, but the experts and beginners are also pretty well catered for. The serious experts should give heliskiing a go or perhaps try the more demanding Porta Vescovo trail from Arabba.

The Sella Ronda circuit is a satisfying route that anyone who is happy on red runs can have a go at. Speedy riders will whizz round in a morning, but it could take up to 6 hours. Make sure you give yourself plenty of time or you might end up paying for a very expensive taxi back. You can set off clockwise or anticlockwise. The Hidden Valley of Falzarego is definitely worth a trip.

The park

The Piz Sella park has boxes, rails, kickers and jumps, as well as a boardercross. There is a natural half pipe by the Sotsaslong Chair and a little park for kids by the euro chair.

Off-piste and backcountry

Despite most of the terrain being fairly flat, there are some easily accessible bowls that are great after a snowfall. Exploration requires a guide here, or you will get lost. Ask them to show you the Mezdi Valley or the 'Grand Canyon' of the Dolomites, a freerider's heaven with enough terrain for a whole day's riding in untracked snow (in good conditions).

Lift passes

Check the latest prices at www.dolomitisuperski.com

Instruction

Ski and Boarders Factory

0039 0471 795 156
www.ski-factory.it

Ski and Snowboard School '2000'

0039 0471 773125
www.skischool-valgardena.com

Val Gardena Mountain Guide Association

This guiding school offers everything from guiding, touring, ice climbing, off-piste and freeride, to glacier hiking.
0039 0471 794133
www.guidegardena.com

Other activities

Climbing: There are 2 climbing walls. The Iman Sports Centre in S. Cristina (0039 0471 777 800) has a climbing wall but you cannot hire climbing equipment.

Horse-drawn sleigh rides: On the top station of the cableway Alpe di Siusi there are horse-drawn sleighs.

Ice climbing and glacier hiking: Val Gardena Mountain Guide Association offers ice climbing and glacier hiking as well as many other exhausting activities. For contact details see Instruction.

Ice skating: There's an ice stadium in Selva (0039 0471 794 265).

Nativity: The biggest nativity in the world is exhibited in the Sport Centre Iman of S. Cristina. Each year new figures are added.

Night skiing: Every Tuesday, Thursday and Friday at 7.30pm Taxi Gardena (0039 0335 560 6141, www.taxigardena.com) organises night skiing on floodlit slopes followed by après ski at Richy's Igloo. Transfer back to the hotel is included (at about 11pm).

Shooting: At the Pranives sports stadium.

Sleigh rides by night: Taxi Gardena (see Night skiing) organises sleigh rides by night. They take you to the Alpe di Siusi, where you make an ascent by snowcat to the Dialer Lodge and then have dinner at 2145m. Depart at 7pm and return to your hotel at 11pm.

Swimming: There is an outdoor and indoor pool with wellness facilities in Ortisei.

Tennis: The massive tennis centre incorporates 6 tennis courts, 2 squash courts, billiards, bowling and a fitness centre.

Tobogganing: There is a 6km sled run from the Rasciesa chairlift in Ortisei. The middle station allows you to go down the first part as many times as you like. You can hire sleds when you get there.

Events

The **FIS World Cup (Super G and Downhill)** is held in Val Gardena in December. The **Skijöring** event in February is a good 1 to watch: 16 ski instructors, pulled by horses, compete for the champion's title. The 6km giant slalom, at the end of the season, **Sudtirol Gardenissima**, is the longest in the Dolomites.

Accommodation

The 5-star **Alpenroyal Sporthotel** (0039 0471 795 555, www.alpenroyal.com), on the outskirts of town, is a large and smart complex, although it does have a slight '80s tinge to it. There is a swimming pool and a games room with a pool table and table footie. It's not too handy for town but they do have a shuttle service. The lovely **Hotel Aaritz** (0039 0471 795 011, www.aaritz.com) has a fantastic location in the centre of town and right opposite the lift. The pool, sauna and gym are another advantage.

We loved the beautiful **Hotel Freina** (0039 0471 795 110, www.hotelfreina.com), a stunning chalet hotel just a couple of minutes from town and right next to the lifts. The rooms are huge and the whirlpool and sauna are great places to relax. **Hotel Laurin** (0039 0471 795 105, www.hotel-laurin.it) is the place to stay if you want to be right in the middle of town. This hotel contains the popular bar and restaurant Laurinkeller as well as a sauna, steam bath, Turkish bath, whirlpool and gym.

Eating out

On the mountain

There are tons of cosy huts dotted all over the Sella Ronda circuit. The **Baita Vallongia** (0039 0471 794 071, www.baita-vallongia.com) on the route from Ciampinoi to Plan de Gralba is a stunning spot to relax outside. The food is superb and there is Italian folk music. Other favourites are the **Piz Setëur** (0039 335 6139 112, www.pizseteur.com), especially for an après ski beer, and the **Panorama** (0039 0471 795 372) for its cosy and rustic atmosphere. For value, you can't beat the restaurant at the top of the cable car from Selva.

In town

Pizzas, pasta and local dishes are the staple food of the restaurants in Selva. **L'Medel** (0039 0471 795 235), on the outskirts of town, has loads of character, and is well worth a short taxi ride or drive. It has a cute little bar and the restaurant serves hundreds of fantastic pizzas. Another stunning place to enjoy a pizza is the **Stübele** in Hotel Sun Valley (0039 0471 771 508, www.hotelsunvalley.it). Its classic wooden feel creates a superb, cosy atmosphere. For more casual surroundings, head to **Rino's** (0039 0471 795 272), **Laurinkeller** (0039 0471 795 004) for ribs, steaks and snacks or **La Bula** (0039 0471 795 208), a pizzeria/club at the Hotel Stella. The restaurant at **Hotel Freina** (0039 0471 795 110) is lovely and serves a huge range of tasty food.

Bars and clubs

One of the great things about Val Gardena compared to many other European resorts is the prices. For après, the liveliest haunt is the **Luislkeller** (0039 0471 794109), which you may never leave. Both the Luislkeller and **Laurinkeller** are kicking at all times of the evening. Other options for après ski are the cosy **La Stua** (0039 0471 795072), where you will often find live folk music, or the **Goalies Irish Pub** (www.goaliespub.com) that also has live music, plus a proper pub feel, and serves Guiness, Carling and Murphy's. Those looking for a dance should boogie on to **La Bula** (0039 0471 975298, www.la-bula.com), the pizzeria-turned-club at the Hotel Stella. **Yello's Music Lounge Bar** (0039 0471 795255, www.yellosbar.com) has great cocktails and a nice atmosphere.

Getting there

By car

Use the Brenner Motorway (A22) and take the Chiusa/Val Gardena exit. You should reach Selva after 20–30 minutes.

By plane

Bolzano (40km)
Innsbruck (120km)
Verona (190km)
Airport transfers run to Val Gardena from Milano–Bergamo and Verona–Brescia. More information on www.flytovalgardena.com

By train

Take the Friday Eurostar from London St Pancras to Brussels, then the Bergland Express overnight skitrain, changing in Innsbruck, to Bolzano, and then a local bus (80 minutes) to the resort. Contact European Rail (020 7387 0444, www.europeanrail.com). Bus tickets are purchased on the bus.

Useful facts and phone numbers

Tourist office Selva

T: 0039 0471 777 900
F: 0039 0471 794 245
W: www.valgardena.it

Tourist office Val Gardena

T: 0039 0471 777 777
F: 0039 0471 792 235
W: www.valgardena.it

Emergency services

- In an emergency call 118
- Police: 113
- Avalanche information: 0039 471 271 177
- Medical Services Selva: 0039 0471 794 266

Taxis

- Autosella: 0039 0471 790 033
- Bauer Martin: 0039 335 560 6141, www.taxigardena.com
- Wienen Schmalzl M: 0471 796 543

Norway

Small, quiet resorts that perk up at the weekend

Hemsedal

The best riding in Norway, with reliable snow.

On the slopes	Rating
Snow reliability	❄❄❄❄
Parks	❄❄❄❄
Off-piste	❄❄❄½
Off the slopes	
Après ski	❄❄❄½
Nightlife	❄❄
Eating out	❄❄
Resort charm	❄❄

The mountains

Height: 625–1920m

Ability	Rating
Expert	❄❄❄
Intermediate	❄❄
Beginner	❄❄❄

The resort

Hemsedal is the best place for riding in Norway; there is plenty of off-piste (including a few nice couloirs), a great park and the snow is really reliable. It's also good for beginners, but mileage-hungry intermediates might find the on-piste terrain limited. At the weekends the après ski scene is fun and lively but during the week families outnumber party-goers. The ski area is a few kilometres from the village centre, but the free bus service isn't bad and there are vague plans for a gondola link between the 2.

Getting about

Hemsedal has the highest alpine point in Scandinavia, at 1500m above sea level and a vertical drop of 810m. There are 43km of slopes with the longest slope at 6km. The terrain is limited, and not the best for cruisy intermediates (although the long red runs from Tinden are nice), but the beginners' slopes are pretty good and experts can amuse themselves on the 8 black slopes, off-piste or in the fantastic park. Make sure you get wrapped up: it's cold.

The park

Hemsedal is very proud of its freestyle park, and rightly so. Each year money is pumped into expanding and developing it, ensuring that it is up there as one of the very best.

In the main park they have catered for all standards of rider. They have a red line for advanced skiers and boarders, and a black line for the experts and pros. The 600m-long park contains 2 half pipes, jumps, table tops, quarter pipe, big air, boxes and rail slides.

The Blue Park is designed for beginner freestylers and those looking for a gentle jib. This has a blue line with the same sorts of jumps, table tops and rails as the main park, only smaller. There's also a new rail park, Olaparken.

The parks are groomed every day and the pipes are reshaped 2 or 3 times a week. On top of this, the elements are painted and outlined every day to make them visible.

Off-piste and backcountry

Off-piste conditions are usually pretty decent as Hemsedal gets a good share of snow. The top of the Totten summit (1450m) is the best place to head for freeriding, where you are more than likely to find some fresh snow, and fun cliff drops. There is also a popular couloir that is fairly steep and long, but it's not over-fierce. There's no shortage of trees and there are some good routes amongst them. You can also find some off-piste just to the side of the pisted areas, from the top of Hamaren.

Lift passes

Check the latest prices at www.skistar.com/hemsedal

Instruction

Hemsedal Ski School

0047 32 05 53 90
www.skistar.com/hemsedal

Kruse Topptur

0047 41 41 96 82/57 67 22 91
www.topptur.com

Norske Opplevelser

Each day there is a different activity, from ice climbing to off-piste guiding or an avalanche course.
0047 32 06 00 03
www.norskeopplevelser.no

Other activities

Bowling, pool, darts and games: The activity centre, Experten Sportsbar (0047 32 05 54 10), has 4 bowling lanes, pool, darts, games and a big TV for sports.

Drive a pack of dogs: A great drive over 16km of frozen lakes and forest. Book at Hemsedal tourist office 1 day in advance (0047 32 05 50 30).

Horse-drawn sleigh rides: Flaget Farm (0047 91 51 70 82, www.hestesenter.no), Gjedokk Hestesenter (0047 95 73 40 44) or Hemesedal Hestesenter (0047 32 06 02 02, www.hemsedalhestesenter.no) all offer sleigh rides. Most will take you through the forest and some provide food and drink round a camp fire.

Ice climbing: Norske Opplevelser (0047 32 06 00 03, www.norskeopplevelser.no) offers lessons for beginners. Hemesedal tourist office (0047 32 05 50 30) offers two-and-a-half-day beginners' courses and instruction on more advanced ice waterfalls for those with experience.

Kiteskiing: Wintersteiger Norge (0047 952 99 999, www.kiteaction.no) will teach you how to fly a kite on your skis/board. Bring your own board/skis and helmet.

Night skiing: For 4 days a week the slopes of Hemsedalsløypa (red no.10), Såhaugløypa (black no. 8) and the children's and beginners' area are open for night skiing 6–9pm. Contact Hemsedal Skisenter (0047 32 05 53 00).

Overnight stay in a lavvo (wigwam): Take a horse-drawn sleigh ride into the forest and have supper around an open fire. Have a warm bath in a hot tub and sleep on a reindeer skin around an oven in the centre of the lavvo. Book through Flaget Farm (0047 0047 32 06 24 00/ 0047 0047 91 51 70 82).

Paragliding: Oslo Paragliderklubb (0047 99 44 75 54, www.opk.no) organise tandem flights and courses over 4–5 weekends or in 1 intensive week.

Snowmobile: You can either drive a snowmobile behind a guide on the mountain for 45 minutes (0047 32 05 53 90) or drive on the big race track in Lykkja forest and over fields (0047 32 06 02 02, www.hemsedalsnoscooterutleie.no).

Events

Hemsedal hosts its own freeride (**Hemsedal freeride**) and **Big Air** jump competition.

Accommodation

The best hotel around is the **Skarsnuten**

Hotel (0047 32 06 17 00, www.skarsnutenhotel.no/eng). There are 37 rooms and a superb restaurant, fitness room and sauna. The only problem is that it is at 1000m altitude, on the slopes at Skarsnuten, which obviously has its benefits but it's not too convenient for Hemsedal centre. In Hemsedal village the **Skogstad Hotel** (0047 32 05 50 00, www.skogstadhotell.no) has a spa, bar and nightclub.

If you want to be right in the centre of the action, the **Hemsedal Café Skiers' Lodge** (0047 32 05 54 10) is in the same building as the very popular Hemsedal Café. There are 4 apartments for 4–6 people and 4 apartments for 7–9 people. **Hemsedal Fjellandsby** (0047 32 05 50 60) have a number of apartment blocks (Alpin, Staven, Tinden and Trotten) next to Hemsedal Ski Centre. Up on the slopes you can stay at **Harahorn Hyttegrend** (0047 32 05 51 10), next to Solheisen Ski Centre, or **Lykkja Feriesenter** (0047 32 06 18 20, www.lykkja.net), well placed for cross-country skiing.

Tour operators include Ski Norway (020 7917 6044, www.ski-norway.co.uk), Neilson Ski (0844 879 8155, www.neilson.co.uk/snow) and Thomson (0871 231 5612, www.thomsonski.co.uk).

Eating out

On the mountain

There is 1 self-service restaurant and a few huts, which are better for picking up a snack rather than relaxing over a nice lunch.

In town

There's not a huge choice of restaurants and many of them are in the hotels (see Accommodation). The **Bistro** at Skogstad Hotel (0047 32 05 50 00) is good. **Peppes** (0047 32 06 06 00 or 0047 22 22 55 55 for takeaway) serves tasty pizzas. The food at the **Hemsedal Café** (0047 32 05 54 10) is popular. The restaurant at the **Skarsnuten Hotel** on the slopes (see Accommodation) is smart with great views.

Bars and clubs

The best bar for après ski is the packed **Hemsedal Café** (0047 32 05 54 10). The bar and club at the Skogstad Hotel, and the bars at the **Oxen** (0047 32 05 58 50) and the **Garasjen** are all popular. Expect strange age restrictions – the club at the **Hemsedal Hotel** is only open to those over 23. The **Experten Sportsbar** is good for games (bowling, darts, etc, see Other activities) and for watching sports.

Getting there

By car

From Oslo take the E-16 to Sandvika, then the E-16 to Hønefoss, the R-7 to Gol and finally the R-52 to Hemsedal.

By plane

Oslo (220km) Oslo Airport Gardermoen is the main airport. There are direct buses to Hemsedal on Fridays and Sundays. Book online at www.hemsedal.com Ryanair flies to Oslo Torp from Glasgow or London. Torp is 280km from Hemsedal.
Lavik (290km)

Useful facts and phone numbers

Tourist office

T: 0047 32 05 50 30
F: 0047 32 05 50 31
W: www.hemsedal.com

Ski centre

T: 0047 32 05 53 00
W: www.skistar.com

Direct reservations

T: 0047 32 05 50 60
F: 0047 32 05 50 61

Emergency services

- Police: 0047 32 05 55 11
- Ambulance: 113
- Emergency: 112
- Emergency at night time or weekends: 0047 32 02 95 00
- Red Cross: 0047 32 06 04 77

Doctors

- 0047 31 40 89 00
- Night time or weekends: 0047 32 06 07 88

Taxis

- Hemsedal Taxisentral: 0047 32 06 01 80
- Løken Taxiservice: 0047 32 06 07 50
- Partybussen: 0047 32 06 21 12

Sweden

A mecca for party-going Swedes, who will welcome you as if you were one of their own

By far the best Swedish resort, with great riding, park, events and nightlife.

On the slopes	Rating
Snow reliability	❄❄❄
Parks	❄❄❄❄
Off-piste	❄❄❄
Off the slopes	
Après ski	❄❄❄
Nightlife	❄❄❄❄½
Eating out	❄❄
Resort charm	❄❄❄

The resort

Åre is awesome. It's popular with everyone, from families and couples to groups of young party people. There aren't too many Brits around, but the Swedes are fun, speak good English and know how to party. Åre is a popular destination for the Scandinavian jetset. The centre of town has a great atmosphere and it's a charming and beautiful place, made up of stylish wooden buildings. Some awesome talent has originated in this area too, such as Jon Olsson who perfected his tricks in the awesome snowpark.

The mountains

Height: 380–1270m

Ability	Rating
Expert	❄❄❄
Intermediate	❄❄❄❄
Beginner	❄❄❄❄

Getting about

Åre has around 100km of groomed runs, which are split over 4 areas: Åre and Åre Björnen (a fairly big area with the main slopes and off-piste) and Duved and Tegerfjäll (connected, but not massive). The variety of riding is good and should suit most, although experts won't find many steeps. Darkness shrouds the resort for most of the days in early winter; the best time to come is March or later.

The park

We expected Åre's Land Park to rock as so many of the world's best riders grew up here, and we weren't disappointed. Everything is well set up, with the kickers organised like a slopestyle course. The jumps were in tiptop condition and there were hits for all abilities. There are also some big-ass hip jumps and quarter pipes and a wicked half pipe, all well maintained by the shapers. The ideas tank is pretty good, too, with locals designing their own rails and bringing them to the park. There's a boardercross, but it's not as popular as the rest of the park. It's located in the Bräcke area. Join 'Åre Snow Park' on Facebook for the latest pictures.

Off-piste and backcountry

Åre is a pretty good freeriding destination. There are wind lips and cornices to play on that are pretty obvious from the pistes or you can explore more uncharted terrain. One popular local adventure is to hitch a ride with a piste basher or skidoo to the top of Åreskutan and go exploring. There is some amazing backcountry terrain that you can reach from here (and a 1000m vertical drop), but it is very easy to get lost, so watch out or check it out with a mountain guide first. If everything goes to plan you will come out at the bottom of the resort.

> 'There are wind hips and cornices to play on or you can explore more uncharted terrain'

As in Riksgränsen, the heliskiing is mind-blowing, but it's not cheap. It's a good idea to get a group of 3 or 4 of you together and do a deal with your heli guide.

Lift passes

Check the latest prices at www.skistar.com/are

Instruction

Åre Skidskola

0046 (0)771 840 000
www.skistar.com

Other activities

Contact Åre tourist information for more information on any of these activities (0046 (0)647 177 20).

Åre Sleddog Adventures: A fantastic company with over 50 well-trained Alaskan Huskies (0046 (0)647 303 81, www.aresleddog.se).

Gyms: A few of the hotels have gyms that are open to the public including Hotell Årevidden (6km east of Åre). Åre also has a training centre.

Horse riding: Try horseback riding on an Icelandic horse. One-hour or half-day trips are available (0046 (0)647 250 80).

Ice fishing: There are good ice fishing grounds at Åresjön, Froåtjärn in Åre Björnen, Greningen above Duved and Hensjön in Edsåsdalen. A fishing permit is required and can be bought at tourist information or at an agent in any of the villages.

Indoor climbing: Indoor climbing is available in the sports hall in Duved (book though the tourist office) or at the Lokalen in Åre. At Ristafallet you can climb the frozen waterfall.

Snowmobiling: This can be combined with ice fishing or dinner. Evening, half-day and full-day trips can be taken on Ottsjö mountain. Call 0046 (0)647 340 77.

Tobogganning: A toboggan course runs from Hotel Fjällgården down to the square. You can toboggan at night 6–9pm (open 1 day a week).

Events

There is a big end of season finale in April, when the elite New School riders, photographers and film-makers all meet up in Åre, with sessions, DJs and great après ski in the square.

Accommodation

The **Holiday Club** (0046 (0)647 120 00, www.holidayclub.se) is one of the best hotels in town, and a short 5-minute walk from the town centre and the lifts. It is a huge complex that has everything including a great restaurant and bar, games room, free internet, a bowling alley, spa and sauna world and an awesome water world complete with a horizon pool with views of the mountains and 67m of waterslide! All rooms have TV, mini-bar, internet and views of the peak or lake.

If you would prefer to stay in the centre of the resort the **Hotel Diplomat Åregården** (0046 (0)647 178 00, www.diplomathotel.com) is the best and most popular. It's a beautiful and stylish place, with good rooms and friendly staff. The breakfasts are worth getting up for and the smart restaurant is popular in the evenings.

Eating out

On the mountain

Buustamons (0046 (0)647 531 75, www.buustamonsfjallgard.se), a hut in the woods with an outdoor heated tub, is the best restaurant. Contact them to book an evening meal, to arrange to be picked up on a skidoo or to book the hot tub for your group. You help yourself to beer and champagne from the fridge and then pay when you leave. There is accommodation too so you can stay the night.

In town

The **Karolinen** (0046 (0)647 320 90, www.karolinen.se) is one of the best restaurants in town, cosy and intimate with good traditional food and a nice hot tub. They can arrange a private dining room for a group booking and can also arrange collection by dogsled or snowmobile. **Villa Tottebo** (0046 (0)647 506 20) is the place to try a reindeer steak. **Broken** attracts a younger crowd for burgers and steaks and has plasma screens playing the latest ski and snowboard movies. The hotel restaurants (see Accommodation) are good and the burger huts in the centre of town serve fantastic fast food.

Bars and clubs

The après ski rocks on from 4pm and most people head straight to the **Wallmans Dippan** in Hotel Diplomat Åregården (see Accommodation) where there is a dinner show and leading DJs. This gets really crowded and it's great fun but not the place for a quiet drink. You can also pick up snacks; the burgers and chips taste superb after a few beers. Around 10–11pm the night really starts. The **Bygget Club** (0046 (0)647 123 45, www.bygget.se) is one of the best clubs ever, and it's the place to rub shoulders with the Scandy jetset. It's absolutely massive, and includes a restaurant serving great sushi, and loads of rooms playing different types of music: live bands, '60s and '70s music, techno, hip hop... The atmosphere is completely crazy. It's definitely worth putting up with the long queues and extortionate drinks' prices to get in. Another club that is worth checking out is the **Country Club** in Hotel Diplomat Åregården (see Accommodation), which has live bands.

Getting there

By plane

Östersund (100km) There are regular bus services from Östersund to Åre.
From Stockholm you can reach Östersund by air or you can take the sleeper train, which brings you almost right into Åre.

Useful facts and phone numbers

Tourist office

T: 0046 (0)647 177 20
W: www.skistar.com/are
See also www.are360.com

Direct reservations

T: 0046 (0)771 840 000

Emergency services

- Police station in Järpen (22km from Åre): 0046 (0)647 105 55 or 112 in an emergency

Doctor

- Hälsocentralen: 0046 (0)647 166 00

Riksgränsen

Heliski in the Midnight Sun, but don't expect much from the resort – it's all in 1 hotel

On the slopes	Rating
Snow reliability	❄❄❄❄
Parks	❄❄❄
Off-piste	❄❄❄❄❄
Off the slopes	
Après ski	❄
Nightlife	❄
Eating out	❄
Resort charm	❄

The resort

Riksgränsen is in Lapland, 300km north of the Arctic Circle and most visitors are there for the seemingly endless heliskiing. If you can, take your trip in May, when the sun never sets, and hit the mountain at midnight. The mountains are more majestic than most resorts in Scandinavia, with the jagged landscape you would expect to see in the Swiss or French Alps.

'The mountains are majestic'

Back in resort, there is simply the Riksgränsen Hotel, which contains the shops, restaurants, bars and nightclub. This is the resort; there is nothing else.

The famous ice hotel (and the world's biggest igloo) is in Jukkasjärvi, about half an hour from Kiruna, the closest airport to Riksgränsen. We definitely recommend a little stop off on the way there or the way back, for a quick drink in the Absolut Ice Bar, and maybe a night stop for the full experience.

The mountains

Height: 520–910m

Ability	Rating
Expert	❄❄❄❄❄
Intermediate	❄❄❄
Beginner	❄

Getting about

The ski season doesn't actually start when the winter does; nothing happens in the first winter months as Riksgränsen is in complete darkness. Only in February are there sufficient daylight hours to kick off the season. The hours of sunshine gradually increase until midsummer's day, when the sun never goes down. It's pretty difficult to sleep when the sun's pouring through the window but there is another alternative – you can get your skis or board out and head up the mountain to ride the powder at midnight. At these times, lifts are open 10pm–1am; check with the tourist office for exact dates.

On piste there are 34 descents, but if you are looking for cruisy pistes you should really be elsewhere.

The park

The freestyle scene in Riksgränsen is pretty big. Dedicated freestylers are up on the hill each day spending hours building huge gap jumps and crazy hips. Jon Olsson (X Games gold medallist) is often in the park working hard and helping all the up-and-coming rippers. There's a selection of rails that are moved around to different spots, as well as a half pipe and a quarter pipe that are used for the Swedish Snowboard Cup and for all the freestyle camps that are held here.

Off-piste and backcountry

When the conditions are right (the weather is a tad unpredictable), this crazy mountain becomes a freerider's heaven. The whole mountain is geared towards freeride and there are loads of really accessible steeps, cliffs and shoots, on which they hold the Scandinavian Big Mountain Champs.

'This crazy mountain can become a freerider's heaven'

A good route to explore is called Lilla Ölturen, or 'The Little Trip for a Beer' (there used to be a nice place for a beer at the end). You start from the summit of Riksgränsen and head down to the bottom of the Norwegian Björnfjell railway station. You will return to Riksgränsen by train and the excursion takes about 1.5 hours. The full 'beer tour' is an 18km classic trip that requires touring skis. The tour starts by heading toward Katterjåkk, turning off towards Katterjaure and carries on into Norway and down towards Björnfjell Station before heading back towards Riksgränsen

You should definitely take a guide to show you the best spots to find untracked powder. If you embark on a half-hour trek from the top lift station you can get to the fantastic Mörkhåla snow bowl. There are also some marked trails on the map: Branten, Ravinen and Gränsängarna.

'Take a guide to show you the best spots to find untracked powder'

To get the most out of these amazing mountains you definitely need a guide and a helicopter. The heliskiing here is out of this world and you are dropped off in areas that look like man has never touched them. Krister from Alpine Madness takes his avalanche-trained dog who can keep up with anyone down some steep faces in 2m of powder. Superb.

Lift passes

Check the latest prices at www.riksgransen.nu

Instruction

Book instruction, off-piste guiding, and heliski trips at the Riksgränsen Hotel (0046 (0)980 400 80, www.riksgransen.nu).

Other activities

All activities can be booked at the hotel (0046 (0)980 400 80).

Driving dog sleds and ice climbing: Both of these are fun options at Riksgränsen.

Snowmobiles and ice fishing: You can either rent snowmobiles and go off on your own or combine the outing with ice fishing in a frozen mountain lake.

Spa: If your bones are aching, visit the spa, which has massage, treatment pools, sauna, Tai Chi, yoga, Qi gong, facials and body treatments. They also offer Lappish Zen, a unique treatment that involves cleansing, deep relaxation, hot stone massage, birch oils and stones from the Torneträsk river bank. The hotel offers good ski and spa packages.

Events

At the **Scandinavian Big Mountain Championships** (SBMC, www.bigmountain.se) the best freeriders fight it out to become national champion. It is one of the oldest extreme competitions in the world. Contact the tourist office for other freeskiing competitions in Riksgränsen.

Accommodation

The one and only **Hotel Riksgränsen** (0046 (0)980 400 80) isn't amazing, but it's comfortable and cosy, and you're handy for everything. Stay in a hotel room, a very basic skiers' room or a self-catering apartment. There are 2 types of apartment – the old apartments that are very dated and the new 8-bed apartments that are very swanky with leather sofas, saunas and underfloor heating. The **Meteorologen** (0046 73 503 24 17, www.meteorologen.se) is in a separate 100-year-old timber building that has been rebuilt and restored to make it both comfy and stylish.

Eating out

In town

Restaurant Lapplandia is the smartest restaurant in the Riksgränsen Hotel, and has won awards for food and service. There is also **Café Lappis** at the foot of the lift system, a pizzeria with a wood-fired, Italian stone-oven. For a quick hot dog or burger, head to the **Café Lappis** or the **Nordalskiosken**.

Bars and clubs

Grönan is a fairly decent après ski bar and club; it's a casual place, but can get pretty nuts. They often have live music at après, and the place kicks off properly from about 11pm.

Getting there

By car

From Kiruna, take the Nordkalott Highway (E-10) for about 3 hours.

By plane

Kiruna (130km) Domestic flights from Stockholm fly to Kiruna.
Stockholm (1500km) Fly to Kiruna or take the 18-hour overnight train.

Useful facts and phone numbers

Tourist office

T: 0046 (0)980 400 80
F: 0046 (0)980 431 25
W: www.riksgransen.nu

Emergency services

- Call 112

Doctors

There is a ski doctor in the hotel during the winter season.

Switzerland

Swiss tourism have their finger on the button – fault them if you can!

Arosa

A good, intermediate mountain, and a great town for everyone – from families to party people.

On the slopes	Rating
Snow reliability	❄❄❄½
Parks	❄❄
Off-piste	❄❄
Off the slopes	
Après ski	❄❄
Nightlife	❄❄❄
Eating out	❄❄❄
Resort charm	❄❄❄

The resort

Arosa has a certain charm that we really fell for. The town is quite pretty, but it's the atmosphere that we loved: the people, the restaurants, the bars, everything. Most of the action is around the Obersee/Untersee area. It seems to attract all sorts of people – families, a few fur coats, some trendies and some party people (Arosa has a great night scene if you know where to look). The mountain's not bad either; it's a wide, open area, perfect for blue and red run riders but not challenging enough for the expert.

The mountains

Height: 1800–2653m

Ability	Rating
Expert	❄
Intermediate	❄❄❄
Beginner	❄❄❄

Getting about

Arosa's 100km of pistes (60km of prepared pistes, 40km of freeride trails) are great for beginner and intermediate riders. There are lots of gentle slopes to get you started and then you'll be cruising all over the mountain. However, if you are a good intermediate or expert you will probably cover the terrain in a couple of days. There is the same number of hiking trails as there are pistes so get used to sharing the mountain with walkers.

The park

The park is in a small area near to the Sit hütte restaurant at the top of the Tschuggen-Ost chairlift. It is OK for beginner freestylers but there isn't much choice. There's an obstacle kicker, jibs and rails, but the 150m long half pipe is the main incentive for freestylers to hit Arosa.

Off-piste and backcountry

In the right conditions, there are some easily accessible and good spots for freeriding. A favourite place of the locals is towards the resort Lenzerheide by the Hornli area, where you can often find fresh tracks. Avalanching is a problem though, so do take a guide.

Lift passes

Check the latest prices at www.arosaberg bahnen.com

Instruction and equipment

ABC

0041 (0)81 356 56 60
www.abcarosa.ch

Swiss Ski School and Bananas Snowboard School

0041 (0)81 378 75 00
www.sssa.ch

Other activities

Balloon trips: At weekends these trips are available over Arosa, the Grisons alps or in the low-lying hills. Call Walter Vollenweider on 0041 (0)52 214 37 14.

Ice skating: You can ice skate on the open air rink (0041 (0)81 377 17 45) until 5pm (night skating on Mondays and Wednesdays) and on the natural ice rink at Inner Arosa (0041 (0)81 377 29 30). You can rent the whole ice rink if you fancy your own ice hockey match, or you can learn how to curl.

Moonlight skiing: Takes place 7–10pm on 1 day each month and is free with a season pass.

Paragliding: Call Jogi Engewald (0041 (0)79 449 88 13). You can buy a gift certificate at the Swiss Ski and Snowboard School by the bottom of the cable car.

Sleigh rides: By the station you will find horses and sleighs all ready to take you for a ride.

Sunrise on Weisshorn summit: The trip includes breakfast at the Weisshorngipfel.

Sunset and fondue nights: Take place on the Weisshorn twice a month in January, February and March. For reservations call 0041 (0)781 378 84 84.

Tobogganing: There are a number of toboggan runs in Arosa, with a variety of lengths, and one that is floodlit (Prätschli-Scheiterböden-Obersee). You can take the bus from Postplatz.

Tuesday night skiing: Takes place in Inner Arosa (Tschuggen chairlift) 4.30–10pm.

Events

Arosa seems to hold a fair number of music events, from rock concerts, to popular DJs and hip hop events. The **Alpine Hot Air Balloon week** and **humour week** are popular, and the **horse racing on snow** is worth seeing.

Accommodation

If money was no object, there would be no question of where we would stay in Arosa; the **Hotel Eden** (0041 (0)81 378 71 00, www.edenarosa.ch) is by far the best place in town. From the outside the hotel looks fairly standard, but take a look inside and you will find yourself at the cutting edge of interior design. The bar is gorgeous, and 1 of the best clubs in town, the **Kitchen Club**, resides in the hotel's basement (see Bars and clubs).

> **'The rooms range from the slightly odd to the completely absurd'**

The individually designed rooms range from the slightly odd to the completely absurd. The Garden Eden room has a tree above the bed and rocks and gorges around the whirlpool. For an interesting Valentine's Day why not book yourself into the Lilly Tiger room, complete with velvet, fur, a cage bed and an open bathroom. It's not cheap, but it is an experience. The auction room is a good opportunity to grab a last-minute bargain – 4 rooms are on offer each week to bid on and auctions end on Fridays at 6pm, 9 days before arrival. Get bidding...

Another smart and more classic hotel is the **Hotel Cristallo** (0041 (0)81 378 68 68, www.cristalloarosa.ch) on the main road. It has a smart restaurant and you can hire DVD players and films for a quiet night in. The large **Post Hotel** (0041 (0)81 378 50 00, www.posthotel-arosa.ch) is in a good location and has a spa as well as a range of different restaurants in the same building including a pizzeria, the Mexicalito Mexican, and a classic eatery. It's pretty '70s, but in an endearing way.

The 5-star **Tschuggen Grand Hotel** (0041 (0)81 378 99 99, www.tschuggen.ch) is all very plush, but it's the breathtaking spa that is really worth visiting. Designed by the famous architect and designer Mario Botta, the spa, Tschuggen Bergoase, is set within a mountain and is linked to the hotel by a glass bridge. The £15 million investment in 2007 was used to create four floors and 4000m^2 with numerous pools, saunas and treatment rooms.

'The breathtaking spa is really worth visiting'

More exotic features include a grotto where guests can enjoy a programme of seasons – summer rain, a winter storm or pure sunshine – and a Kneipp Path where guests can walk over natural stones through a knee-deep stream of ice cold and hot spots, stimulating their blood circulation and nervous system. The spa treatment menu has no less than 23 pages and contains every treatment under the sun. Not content with 1 of the most uniquely designed spas, the pioneers at Tschuggen have developed the coolest lift system to transport their guests to the slopes. The guest summons the 'Tschuggen Express' as you would a lift and it then flies you to the Tschuggen mountain hut in the heart of the ski area in a comfy 6-seater cabin. Awesome!

If you're looking for a bargain, your best bet is to get an apartment. The tourist office has a good selection on the website.

Eating out

On the mountain

Our favourite bar on the mountain on a sunny day is the very accessible bar on the **Brüggerstuba** (0041 (0)81 378 84 25) at the top of the cable car from Obersee. This is a great place to sit and have a few beers after a hard day on the mountain. If you're peckish, they also cook up a tasty hot dog. In bad weather, a big umbrella-type cover keeps you out of the snow. The **Sit hütte** (0041 (0)79 407 89 38, www.sit-huette.ch), at the top of the park is the place to sit back and look cool. There are big, loungy cushions on the snow and a palm tree with sofas round it. There's also table football and good snack food. At **Tschuggenhütte** (0041 (0)81 378 84 45, www.tschuggenhuette.ch), by the colourful, tented Mickey Mouse club, there is a raclette bar, snack bar, ice cream hut, massive terrace and huge double loungers to relax on. If you're a bit knackered, take a good book and chill out here. **Restaurant Weisshorngipfel** (0041 (0)81 378 84 02) lacks atmosphere inside but has amazing views from the outside. Surprisingly the food isn't too expensive. As well as traditional dishes, they serve the simpler sausage and chips or spag bol.

In town

There are some great restaurants around town. In the centre 1 building contains 3 of the best (www.grottino.ch). On the middle floor, the pizzeria **Grottino** (0041 (0)81 377 17 17) is a cosy and friendly place with a busy atmosphere. The restaurant below it, **Schnüggel** (0041 (0)81 377 17 17), is small and romantic. Order one of the house meat spits, where you can choose 2 sauces and 3 side dishes to accompany it. On the top floor is a raclette/fondue restaurant: **Alpträumli** (0041 (0)81 377 06 06), also under the same ownership. The cheese fondue is absolutely superb and the raclettes good, although you don't have the satisfaction of melting the cheese yourself, which is a shame; they do it in the kitchen and bring it out to you.

For Thai, head to **Chilli's** (0041 (0)81 377 13 66) at the top end of town, and for a smart meal, try the Italian in the **Casino** building, the traditional **Le Bistro** restaurant in the Cristallo (0041 (0)81 378 68 68, www.cristalloarosa.ch) or the funky restaurants at the Hotel Eden (0041 (0)81 378 71 00, www.edenarosa.ch), where you can choose between a fondue at the **Roggenmoser** or a Spanish meal at the **Tapa' bar**.

Bars and clubs

Good places for après ski are the **Sitting Bull** (0041 (0)81 378 70 20) and **Bellini's** café bar (0041 (0)81 377 06 06) for a chilled out glass of wine. The Casino building may have you reaching for your poker chips, but hold your horses; there's no blackjack or roulette, just a few slot machines. There is a really nice smart bar though, and the **Nuts Club** (0041 (0)81 377 39 40, www.disconuts.ch) for dancing later on.

Our absolute favourite bar is the **Eden Bar** in the Hotel Eden (see Accommodation), a smart place where it's great to chill out and chat in the midst of candlelight and sushi. On 1 night there was a massive bed adorned with Egyptian sheets, and a glam crowd smoking a sheesha pipe. Downstairs is the unique **Kitchen Club**, which looks just like an old kitchen with a couple of bars put in. The drinks are really expensive but it has a great atmosphere and music, and the hip hop nights are superb.

Getting there

By car

The road to Arosa is pretty dreadful. It takes almost an hour from Chur on a windy and narrow road and accidents are not uncommon. Best avoided if possible.

By plane

Zürich (163km)
Friedrichshafen (around 170km) for Ryanair flights.
Transfer from Zürich and Friedrichshafen will take around 1.5 hours. Your best bet is to avoid the awful road and take the efficient and beautiful Rhaetian Railway up to Arosa from Chur.
Milano (217km)

By train

Take the Eurostar from London St Pancras to Paris, then an overnight train, changing at Chur to arrive at Arosa station in the resort. Contact Rail Europe (0870 830 4862, www.raileurope.co.uk) or European Rail (020 7387 0444, www.europeanrail.com).

Useful facts and phone numbers

Tourist office

T: 0041 (0)81 378 70 20
F: 0041 (0)81 378 70 21
W: www.arosa.ch

Emergency services

- Police: 117 or 0041 (0)81 377 19 38/ 0041 (0)81 378 67 17
- If you have an accident on the piste call 0041 (0)81 378 84 05
- Snow reports: 0041 (0)81 378 84 50

Doctors

- Drs V Meyer and M Walkmeister: 0041 (0)81 377 27 28
- Dr M Röthlisberger: 0041 (0)81 377 14 64

Taxis

- Taxi Koller: 0041 (0)81 377 35 35
- Taxi Obersee: 0041 (0)81 377 11 33

Champéry

Part of the Portes du Soleil circuit, Champéry has extensive terrain and a fantastic park.

On the slopes	Rating
Snow reliability	❄❄❄
Parks	❄❄❄❄❄
Off-piste	❄❄❄
Off the slopes	
Après ski	❄❄❄
Nightlife	❄❄½
Eating out	❄❄❄½
Resort charm	❄❄❄❄½

The resort

Champéry is the main Swiss resort in the Portes du Soleil and sits at the foot of the Dents du Midi and the Dents Blanches peaks. The resort is fairly quiet and charming, with a real sense of community among the locals. It is well suited to families and couples, but not to those looking for a wide variety of bars and clubs. The ski area of the Portes du Soleil has something to suit most standards of skier and snowboarder, with seemingly endless runs and easy access to snowsure slopes. The freestyle park in Les Crozats is a jibber's dream.

The mountains

Height: 975–2466m

Ability	Rating
Expert	❄❄❄❄
Intermediate	❄❄❄❄
Beginner	❄

Getting about

The slopes have a lot going for them. Intermediates and experts will have a whale of a time, whether exploring the 650km of pistes in the Portes du Soleil, tackling the more challenging steep and mogully Swiss wall or attacking the massive kickers in the incredible Superpark. However, Champéry is not suited to beginners; there are very few slopes gentle enough. The other disadvantage is the fact that you cannot ride back into the centre of town; you can come all the way back down into Grand Paradis (there are free buses all day to the village), but to get straight to the centre of Champéry you will have to take the cable car down and then possibly a bus if you're not staying near the lift.

The park

Les Crosets is home to one of the best parks in Europe. The park is high and has a huge selection of kickers for all standards of riders ranging from small table tops to 30m gap jumps. There are 4 hip jumps, at a variety of heights, 10 rails, including a massive rainbow rail and a couple of flat-downs. A big bonus is the gap jump to a big snow block to drop off, then a quarter pipe with a rail on top to finish off. A jibber's paradise. World-famous pro boarders Travis Rice and Romain di Marchi have been spotted filming for their latest flick. If parks are your thing, check this place out, it's arguably the best park in Europe. At least visit the website www.superpark.ch – if your French isn't up to scratch, you'll have to settle for the pictures.

Off-piste and backcountry

Though not its strongest feature, Champéry does have something to offer in the off-piste sector. Les Crosets and Chavanette are good places to start. The sun can kill the lovely powder, so if there is an area that you spot and want to ride, check it out first thing. Also at Chavanette is the legendary Swiss wall: a marked black run that gets the best moguls on the mountain. This is a pretty steep face and can be amazing after a big snowfall. You may want to seek out some spots in Avoriaz, Chatel and Morzine for the off-piste.

Lift passes

Check the latest prices at www.champery.ch

Instruction

Freeride Co.

0041 (0)24 479 10 00
www.skichampery.com

Swiss Ski and Snowboard School

Ski, snowboard, telemark, racing, freeride and heliskiing.
0041 (0)24 479 16 15
www.esschampery.ch

Other activities

Unless other contact details are given, call the tourist office for more information (0041 (0)24 479 20 20).

Night skiing: This takes place twice a week and is really good fun; 5km of ski runs are open until 10pm.

Paragliding: Tandem flights, training flights or initiation courses can all be arranged. Contact Vincent Marclay (0041 (0)79 478 92 66) or Simon Wiget (0041 (0)79 306 46 67).

Snow-kiting: To try your hand at this call 0041 (0)79 409 22 75.

Sports centre: The Champéry Palladium (0041 (0)24 479 05 05, www.palladiumde champery.ch) has a pool, fitness room, curling rink and ice rink.

Tobogganing: The 200m sledding slope is on the Grand Paradis. Rent your toboggan from Berra Sports (0041 (0)24 479 13 90) or Borgeat Sports (0041 (0)24 479 16 17). A 500–800m toboggan run departs from the Relais Panoramique in Les Crosets.

Events

In the first week of February is the **Chavanette Session**, a race that takes place on the densely moguled Chavanette piste, also known as the Swiss wall. As part of this festival is the **Derby**, a great competition in which teams of 3 race to finish the 5km course from Pas de Chavanette (2180m) to Grand Paradis (1055m). There is also **The Wall**, an individual race on the Chavanette. The snowpark hosts events all winter long – check with the tourist office for the latest information. At the end of the season is the **Happy End festival**, with a big air ski/ snowboard comp. The après ski and party scene is great, with a number of good DJs.

Accommodation

The charming chalet-hotel **Auberge de Grand-Paradis** (0041 (0)24 479 11 67, www.grandparadis.ch) is right on the slopes with ski-in ski-out accommodation. This does mean that it's a 20-minute walk into the centre of town, but avoiding the après-ski jostle to catch the cable car and bus more than makes up for this. There are 10 spacious bedrooms (which share 5 bathrooms).

In town, the newly refurbished **Beau-Sejour** (0041 (0)24 479 58 58, www. bo-sejour.com) is a great option, with some beautiful rooms and a games room with PlayStations. The **Hotel Suisse** (0041 (0)24 479 07 07, www.hotel-champery.ch) is right in the centre of town and has charming rooms. It also contains the Bar des Guides and Les Mines D'Or (see Bars and clubs).

Eating out

On the mountain

Restaurant Chez Coquoz (0041 (0)24 479 12 55) at Planachaux is one of the best places to stop for a bite to eat. **Les Marmottes** (0041 (0)79 691 07 00) is a cosy alpine chalet towards Chavanette and Ripaille. On the French side, Avoriaz has some great places for lunch (see Avoriaz chapter, page 78).

In town

The best restaurant in town is, without a doubt, **Mitchell's** (0041 (0)24 479 20 10, www. champery-mitchells.com). Tree trunks grow through the restaurant, and the lighting is perfect, with well-placed spot lights and candles. The menu is beautifully composed. For lunch, choose between a homemade burger, grilled sandwich (big or small), wrap, beef or fish noodle wok, or delicious salad. In the evening you will have a really tough time choosing between the mouth-watering dishes. If you go to Champéry, you must eat here at least once.

Another good restaurant is **Café du Centre** (0041 (0)24 479 15 50), which is open all day. The top floor serves only their gourmet menu, but downstairs serves just as delicious dishes, such as Thai green curry, Indonesian stew, fish and Cajun Chicken. The **Gueullhi** (0041 (0)24 479 35 55, www.legueullhi.ch) café-restaurant, by the cable car station is a decent place to stop for lunch or dinner. The menu and food is fantastic but the service a bit slow at peak times.

Bars and clubs

Champéry isn't massively into its boozing, but the bars there are, are good. In the Hotel Suisse (see Accommodation) is the **Bar des Guides**, full of locals enjoying après ski, and the **Mines D'Or**, a wicked bar, with cavernous hideaways – a great place at all times of night for a cosy pint and live music. **Mitchell's** restaurant (see Eating out) also has a great bar, with massive comfy sofas and it is a popular meeting point for the Champéry community. After hours, you will find the locals at **Le Farinet** (0041 (0)76 525 72 61) and the riders at **La Crevasse** (www.la-crevasse.com).

Getting there

By car

From Geneva take the Lake Geneva motorway past Lausanne to Monthey and follow signs to Champéry.

By plane

Lausanne (62km)
Geneva (126km) Transfer around 1.5 hours.
Zürich (250km)

By train

Take the Eurostar from London St Pancras to Paris, then an overnight train, changing at Zürich, Lausanne and Aigle to arrive at Champéry station in the resort. Contact Rail Europe (0870 830 4862, www.raileurope.co.uk) or European Rail (020 7387 0444, www.europeanrail.com).

Useful facts and phone numbers

Tourist office

T: 0041 (0)24 479 20 20
F: 0041 (0)24 479 20 21
W: www.champery.ch

Emergency services

- Police: 0041 (0)24 479 09 18
- Ambulance/mountain rescue: 144
- Medical centre: 0041 (0)24 479 15 16
- Hospital de Monthey: 0041 (0)24 473 17 31
- Hospital d'Aigle: 0041 (0)24 468 86 88

Taxis

- Serge Rey-Bellet: 0041 (0)79 430 15 15
- Closillon Tours: 0041 (0)79 622 22 24, www.taxi-bus-closillon.ch

Crans Montana

Sunny cruising on the slopes, stunning mountains and a town you'll want to come back to.

On the slopes	Rating
Snow reliability	❄❄❄
Parks	❄❄❄
Off-piste	❄❄❄
Off the slopes	
Après ski	❄❄
Nightlife	❄❄❄½
Eating out	❄❄❄
Resort charm	❄❄❄

The resort

The 2 resort centres of Crans and Montana have a definite charm about them; the town doesn't have the 'chocolate box' feel of a number of Swiss resorts but the mountains are stunning, and the resort has a certain character and warmth. Crans is full of Paris-style boutiques, and has some top-class restaurants and hotels. Most of the good bars and clubs are in Crans too, although there are a couple in Montana, as well as the massive Casino. It's not too British either; we make up only 3.5 per cent of visitors to Crans Montana giving it a cosmopolitan feel that many resorts lack. The slopes are dominated by fur-clad skiers searching for a nice restaurant before cruising back down to town for a massage. However, the area does have more to offer.

The mountains

Height: 1500–3000m

Ability	Rating
Expert	❄❄
Intermediate	❄❄❄❄
Beginner	❄❄❄

Getting about

The Crans Montana mountains have some truly stunning views. They are, however, geared to the cruisy intermediate with a preference for pretty paths through the trees rather than steep and challenging terrain. Saying this, there are a few slopes for the expert skier/boarder and there are a number of options for the enthusiastic powder hounds, and these areas rarely get tracked out as few Crans Montana regulars are interested in exploring the surrounding backcountry.

The park

The Aminona Snowpark is a good size, with a good range of jumps and rails for all standards of rider. There are several small kickers in different lines, according to the level of the rider and a reasonable range of rails, including a rainbow rail and C-rail. There's a fairly easy skier/boardercross course, a quarter pipe and 2 huge big-air jumps in the centre of the park, which are very well looked after. The shapers and designers are enthusiastic and do a great job. There is also a snack bar and BBQ hang-out spot.

Off-piste and backcountry

There aren't loads of backcountry areas to explore in Crans Montana, but there is a lot of really easily accessible off-piste to be had. Just off the side of the pisted runs are some sweet faces. There are a couple of narrow couloirs (experts only) and a steep face by the Bella-Lui area. We recommend that you only do this with a guide or knowledgeable local. Some easier spots can be found beneath La Tza and Chetseron. Beware of the sun; most of the mountain is exposed to the sun and the snow can get very heavy by lunchtime, resulting in some nasty slides.

Lift passes

Check the latest prices at www.mycma.ch

Instruction

Crans Montana official guide office

The Swiss ski school is also the official mountain guides' office. They can take you ski touring, off-piste skiing, on avalanche courses, and heliskiing. They also offer semi-private lessons (min. 4 people, max. 6) in ice climbing and freeride.
0041 (0)27 481 14 80
www.essmontana.ch

Ecole Swiss de Ski de Crans

0041 (0)27 485 93 70
www.cranskischool.ch

Ski and Sky

This company can teach you skiing, boarding, snowbiking and telemarking. They also organise tandem paragliding.
0041 (0)79 385 10 47
www.skiandsky.ch

Swiss Mountain Sports

This company can organise all-in-one packages including accommodation, activities, transport and meals. Tandem paragliding, paintball, telemarking, free ride, heliski and sledging are also available.
0041 (0)27 480 44 66
www.swiss-mountain-sports.ch

Other activities

4x4 snowbikes: Take the 10km descent from Crans to Sierre. Contact Adrenatur (0041 (0)27 480 10 10, www. adrenatur.ch).

Casino: The large casino has blackjack, roulette and slots (see Bars and clubs).

Curling: There are a few curling rinks, on which you can have lessons (0041 (0)27 225 88 73).

Heliskiing: Trips can be organised by some of the ski schools and also by Air Glaciers SA (0041 (0)27 329 14 15, www.air-glaciers.ch) and Eagle Helicopters AG (0041 (0)27 327 30 60, www.eaglehelicopter.ch).

Hot air ballooning: Flights can be arranged by the Club Aérostatique de Crans-Montana (0041 (0)27 483 50 00).

Husky driving: Adrenatur (see above) run excursions sledding with dogs in the day and in the evening.

Ice climbing and snow kiting: Also offered by Adrenatur.

Ice skating: There are 2 ice skating rinks – the Ycoor in Montana (0041 (0)27 481 30 55) and Sporting in Crans (0041 (0)27 485 97 95).

Indoor bowling: Another great way to while away an evening (0041 (0)27 481 50 50).

Internet cafes: There are a number of places to check your e-mails and surf the web – Avalanche (which also has a wireless hotspot), Café 'Au Garage', Club 360, Restaurant Le Farinet and Bar Number Two, Hotel Olympic, and the New Pub.

Night skiing: This takes place on Friday nights on the floodlit slope of Verdets (via the cable car Grand Signal), 7–10pm.

Paintballing: This can be arranged with Para-look (0041 (0)79 606 46 28, www.paralook.ch).

Paragliding: Tandem paragliding flights can be booked with Ski and Sky (see Instruction), or Paralook (see above).

Shopping: For shopaholics with cash to splash, there are some seriously chic boutiques to mosey around. Not the place to pick up the slope fashions though – it's more Prada and Chanel than Oakley.

Squash: There are 2 squash courts (0041 (0)27 481 16 15, www.leregent.ch).

Swimming: A number of hotels have swimming pools available to the public – Hotel Aïda-Castel (Montana), Alpina and Savoy (Crans), Hôtel Etrier (Crans) and Hôtel de la Forêt (Montana).

Tennis: Crans Montana has the largest tennis centre in the Swiss Alps (0041 (0)27 481 50 14) with 5 indoor courts and 6 outdoor courts.

Tobogganing: There is a 6km toboggan run from Petit Mt-Bonvin (2400m) to Aminona (1500m).

Torchlit descent: Organised by Ecole Swiss de Ski de Montana and Swiss Mountain Sports (see Instruction).

Wellness centres: There are a number of centres offering treatments, swimming pools, etc. Dabliu Beauty Farm (next to Hotel du Golf, 800 690 409, www.dabliu.com), Centre thérapeutique 'Medica' (0041 (0)27 480 40 40) and Centre de 'Bien-être' (0041 (0)27 481 26 12).

Yeti Adventure: Organised by Adrenatur (see above). From Aminona you will take the gondola to 2400m and begin the challenges of rope bridges above deep gorges, climbing frozen waterfalls, snowshoeing and other obstacles.

Events

Crans Montana has a number of good events, from the **Crans Montana Snowgames** (www.cransmontanasnowgames.ch), which combines a big-air jam session, a water slide contest and a sumo contest, to **Caprices**, the music festival (www.capricesfestival.ch) in which 60 concerts are scheduled over 9 days with some genuinely good artists. The main stage is in a huge marquee with 3200 places.

Accommodation

Crans

If price isn't an issue, the best place to stay is the **Hostellerie du Pas de L'Ours** (0041 (0)27 485 93 33, www.pasdelours.ch), which has 9 suites, including junior suites, that are all individually decorated and absolutely stunning. Each suite has a fireplace, mini bar and Jacuzzi. There is 1 restaurant in the hotel and another beside the main building, Bistrot des Ours, which is as stunning as it is expensive.

The larger **Hôtel de l'Etrier** (0041 (0)27 485 44 00, www.hoteletrier.ch) next door shares the newly built spa, massage and pool complex. It's slightly less expensive.

Montana

Montana has some more reasonable hotels. **Hôtel Olympic** (0041 (0)27 481 29 85, www.amadays.ch) is a simple hotel in the centre of Montana, right next to loads of the bars and the casino and only 300m from the slopes. **Hotel Mirabeau** (0041 (0)27 480 21 51, www.mirabeau-hotel.com) is well placed, pretty nice and not too expensive.

Slightly more off the beaten track is the **Grand Hôtel du Parc** (0041 (0)27 481 41 01, www.parc-hotel.ch). It's a big ugly building on the outside but inside it's really nice, the staff are friendly and the views are incredible. The **Bella Lui** (0041 (0)27 481 31 14, www.bellalui.ch) is in a quiet area in the trees but it's not too far from everything. Again it's not beautiful, but the views are.

The 4-star **Alpina and Savoy** (0041 (0)27 485 09 00, www.alpinasavoy.ch) is bang in-between Crans and Montana, but close to the lifts. There's a spa centre, a pool and comfy rooms.

You can book your accommodation directly on the Crans Montana website (www.crans-montana.ch) and they give you cheaper prices for booking earlier (December).

Eating out

On the mountain

The **Plumachit** (0041 (0)27 481 25 32) is tucked away in the trees on the path to Aminona with a huge terrace and stunning views. The service can take a while on busy, sunny days, but once you've managed to get your order in, the food arrives fairly quickly. The run down is a very flat path so it attracts a lot of walkers too. Other favourites of ours with outdoor bars and terraces are the restaurant at **Merbé** (0041 (0)27 481 22 97), at the first stop of the gondola from Crans Montana, and the **Amadeus** (0041 (0)27 481 24 95), above Montana.

In town

In Crans, **Le Chalet** (0041 (0)27 481 05 05, www.lechaletcransmontana.ch) is a stunning restaurant in the centre of town that serves a fantastic raclette and other tasty treats. **Raphaele** (0041 (0)27 480 31 50, www.leraphaele.ch) is the best pizzeria in town, opposite the post office. It has a beautiful interior and a large wine cellar. **La Channe** (0041 (0)27 480 41 38) is one of our favourite restaurants in town. It serves fantastic Mexican food in a romantic, candlelit atmosphere. Alternatively, you can also sit at or near the bar and have some tapas, which is great if you get sick of big meals. For gourmet cuisine you should head to the **Bistrot des Ours** at the Hostellerie du

Pas de L'Ours (see Accommodation) and get your favourite credit card ready.

The **Mayen** (0041 (0)27 481 29 85, www.amadays.ch), under the Hotel Olympic, is similarly traditional and has an alpine feel. Rostis are their tasty specialities. At the end of town, the **Michelangelo Pizzeria** (0041 (0)27 481 09 19, www.lemichelangelo.ch) is simple and cheery, with checked tablecloths. The **Gerber** (0041 (0)27 481 62 47), on your left as you come into Montana from Crans, has a large terrace that gets the sun at lunchtime and is also beautiful inside. A great place for lunch or dinner. There is also a café area and patisserie.

Bars and clubs

In Crans head to the lively **Le Pub** (0041 (0)27 481 54 96), also known as George and Dragon – the busiest bar, open 4pm–2am. **La Channe** (see Eating out) also has a cosy bar where you can snack on some tapas as you drink. From 11pm there are a number of lively options to choose from: the **Xellent club** (0041 (0)27 481 65 96), **Le Barocke** (0041 (0)79 221 16 35) and the very funky **Leo's Bar** (0041 (0)27 481 98 00, www.leosbar.com). The best thing about all the bars in Crans is that they are only a few steps away from each other.

Most of the good bars are in Crans, but there are a couple in Montana that are worth checking out. The **Amadeus** bar (0041 (0)27 481 29 85) has concerts on Sundays and a jam session every Thursday (days may change). It's open 4.30pm–1am. The **Grange** is a bar to stay away from – it's pretty dingy, amazingly smoky and full of old locals. One of the best places to while away an evening in Montana is the **Casino** (0041 (0)27 485 90 40, www.casinocm.ch) with roulette, blackjack and slot machines as well as a great restaurant and a bar open 3pm–3am. Remember to take your passport for ID.

Getting there

By car

From Geneva/Lausanne, take the A9 motorway to Sierre, then follow signs to Crans Montana

By plane

Geneva (180km)
Milan (260km)
Zürich (300km)

By train

Take the Eurostar from London St Pancras to Paris, then by train, changing at Lausanne, to Sierre, and then a funicular train to the resort. Contact Rail Europe (0870 830 4862, www.raileurope.co.uk) or European Rail (020 7387 0444, www.europeanrail.com). Funicular train tickets are purchased at Sierre station. (For people booking through European Rail to Swiss resorts, the rail fare includes the funicular connection to resort at no extra cost, so there is no need to pay for a bus ticket.)

Useful facts and phone numbers

Tourist office

T: 0041 (0)27 485 04 04
F: 0041 (0)27 485 04 60/61
W: www.crans-montana.ch/www.mycma.ch

Direct reservations

T: 0041 (0)27 485 04 44
F: 0041 (0)27 485 04 60

Emergency services

- Fire brigade: 118
- Police: 117
- Police cantonale: 0041 (0)27 486 65 60
- Police municipale: 0041 (0)27 481 81 81
- Medical centre: 0041 (0)27 480 40 40
- Medical emergency: 144

Doctors

- Dr Bonvin Louis: 0041 (0)27 481 35 35
- Dr Kunz Ariane: 0041 (0)27 481 32 32
- Dr Vouilloz Patrick: 0041 (0)27 481 42 74

Taxis

- Emery, Jean: 0041 (0)27 481 19 19
- Morard, Jaques: 0041 (0)27 481 53 65
- Pott, César: 0041 (0)27 481 13 12
- Pott, Michel: 0041 (0)27 481 71 71
- Taxi Philippe: 0041 (0)79 422 29 85, www.goroutair.ch

Davos

Incredible mountains, with stacks of opportunities, and a city where the resort should be.

On the slopes	Rating
Snow reliability	❄❄❄½
Parks	❄❄❄❄
Off-piste	❄❄❄❄
Off the slopes	
Après ski	❄❄❄
Nightlife	❄❄❄½
Eating out	❄❄❄½
Resort charm	❄½

The resort

There's no doubt about it, Davos is a bizarre place. On the plus side the mountains are incredible. There are 5 main mountains in the Davos-Klosters area that present stacks of opportunities for all sorts of riding, from unlimited on-piste opportunities to masses of freeriding and the best pipes around. Travelling from, to and between the mountains can be a bit of a laborious task though and you really have to make use of the mountains to make it worthwhile. You certainly wouldn't visit Davos to experience resort charm. It's not ugly, but its city feel doesn't create a particularly endearing atmosphere. There are loads of restaurants, bars and clubs, as well as the kind of designer shops, museums and other facilities that you expect in a large town or city, but the lack of people creates an eerie atmosphere.

The mountains

Height: 1124–2844m

Ability	Rating
Expert	❄❄❄❄½
Intermediate	❄❄❄❄½
Beginner	❄❄❄

Getting about

There are 103 pistes (310km) in the Davos-Klosters region. There are 4 different mountains to be accessed from Davos, each with its own clientele. Parsenn, accessible from Davos Dorf (also from Klosters) is the best mountain for cruising around on well-groomed slopes and checking out the stunning scenery. The restaurants are great, there's some fantastic off-piste and it's generally a great place. The only run back down, though, is to the outskirts of Dorf.

From the centre of Davos Platz, you can get to Jakobshorn mountain, home of the park, fun restaurants and good, wide pistes. Rinerhorn and Pischa both take a bit of travelling to get to from Dorf or Platz. Rinerhorn is good for cruising around in the sun. Pischa is purely a freeride mountain; 2 ski lifts and the cable car are open, but the pistes will not be prepared.

The park

Jakobshorn is the main hangout spot for the freestylers. It has 2 superb pipes; 1 super pipe is located in the village in the Bolgen area and is floodlit for night-time riding, the Nidecker monster pipe is at the top of Jatz with the park. There are a lot of world-class riders who hang out in the area and these guys make sure that the pipes are always perfectly shaped. There's a good range of kickers, from small table tops to big booters and plenty of rails to jib. The Rinerhorn and Pischa mountains each have a park and there's supposed to be a kicker at Parsenn, but they need the right conditions in order to build it. Davos rocks for freestyle.

Off-piste and backcountry

On Pischa, the freeride mountain, you have a choice. You can hit the accessible, unpisted runs, but if you are prepared to hike for 2 hours maximum you can drop down the back of the mountain and have access to everything: cliffs, bowls and couloirs. From there you end up in the middle of nowhere though so a car is handy. Parsenn has some of the best off-piste; you can pretty much access powder from every lift. There's not much hiking involved and plenty to do. The Totalphorn area, between the Meierhoftäli and Totalp chairlifts, is superb, but does get sketchy if the snow isn't great and bad accidents have been known to happen in these conditions. Don't let that put you off: on a perfect powder day it's definitely worth checking out. If the visibility is bad, there are loads of tree runs to play in on the Gotschna side and on Madrisa.

'Parsenn has some of the best off-piste'

The Weissfluh, a north-facing slope, is one of the most famous off-piste runs. It's around a 500m drop with a 15-minute hike out. You can also take a guided tour to Arosa and Lenzerheide from the Weissfluh – there is no walking involved, although you do have to buy different lift tickets. Definitely take a guide with you for this one. We recommend contacting Lukas Dürr at Swiss Freeride (www.swissfreeride.ch).

There is an avalanche training centre at the top of the Carjöl lift (Fuxägufer) on the Jakobshorn. You can practise using your avalanche equipment under realistic conditions.

Lift passes

Check latest prices at www.davosklosters.ch

Instruction

Snow and You

Reto Cahenzli is a local ski teacher who offers carving, guiding and powder skiing.
0041 (0)79 636 70 30
snowdesign1@bluewin.ch

Swiss Snowsport-School Davos

This school offers the usual lessons as well as off-piste touring, telemarking and freestyle boarding.
0041 (0)81 416 24 54
www.ssd.ch

Top Secret Ski and Snowboard School

Freestyle, freeride and off-piste courses are available and include video coaching.
0041 (0)81 413 73 74
www.topsecretdavos.ch

Other activities

Remember to get a guest card from your hotel as it entitles you to a number of discounts on activities, as well as unrestricted use of the Landschaft Davos public transport network.

Non-sporting activities

Casino: This is located at the Hotel Europe in Davos Platz, offering blackjack, American roulette and 70 slot machines. Remember to take your passport for ID.

Cinema: Four or 5 films are shown daily (www.kino-arkaden.ch).

Museums: There is a choice of visiting a cultural museum, a doll museum, a folk museum, a winter sports museum, a mining museum or a museum of medicine. Don't exhaust yourself with all that culture.

Wellness and pool centre: Eau-là-là (0041 (0)81 413 64 63, www.eau-la-la.ch) has a range of swimming and adventure pools including a diving area with 1m and 3m-high diving boards, a heated outside pool and a giant 80m long 'black hole' slide. The wellness areas include saunas, hydrotherapy, massage and solarium.

Sporting activities

Hang-gliding and paragliding: Choose from tandem flights, passenger flights or a weekly course over Jakobshorn or Parsenn from a number of schools: Luftchraft Paragliding School (0041 (0)79 623 19 70, www.luftchraft.ch); Flugcenter Grischa (0041 (0)81 422 20 70, www.gleitschirm-schule.ch); Paragliding Davos (0041 (0)79 236 19 70, www.paragliding-davos.ch).

Horse riding: Lessons and treks can be booked for both beginners and advanced riders. Call either Hans Lenz (0041 (0)81 413 19 55) or Andreas Stiffler (0041 (0)81 416 46 82).

Ice skating: In Davos Platz, Europe's largest natural ice rink (over 18 000m^2), an outdoor ice rink and an ice stadium are all top venues for ice hockey, ice skating, speed skating, curling and Bavarian curling (0041 (0)81 415 36 00).

Tennis and squash: Phone to book courts on 0041 (0)81 413 31 31.

Tobogganing: There are toboggan runs on Schatzalp, Rinerhorn, Madrisa and Parsenn (totalling 22km of runs – the longest at 8.6km).

Swissraft (0041 (0)81 911 52 50, www.swissraft.ch) offer a range of activities to try, from balloon trips to canyoning and hydrospeeding.

Events

The **Spengler Cup Ice Hockey Tournament** is the most important ice hockey event on the international calendar, and is held annually in Davos between Christmas and New Year (www.spenglercup.ch). The **O'Neill Evolution** (www.oneilleurope.com/evolution) is also held at New Year in Davos on the Bolgen area at Jakobshorn. It has become one of the major events on the freestyle snowboarding calendar and is now part of the Ticket To Ride (TTR) World Snowboarding Tour.

For further information regarding events in Davos contact the tourist office (see Useful facts and phone numbers).

Accommodation

In Davos Platz, the 4-star **Hotel Europe** (0041 (0)81 415 41 41, www.europe-davos.ch) is a great place to stay – just to be near all the action. With restaurants, bars and a casino in 1 place, as well as a pool and a fitness centre, who'd want to go anywhere else? The 2-star **Alte Post** (0041 (0)81 417 67 77) is good value, simple, cosy and handy for Jakobshorn.

In Davos Dorf, **Hotel Parsenn** (0041 (0)81 416 32 32, www.hotelparsenn.ch) is an attractive, 3-star hotel, right opposite the Parsenn railway, so in a perfect position for the slopes. The **Snowboarders' Palace** (0041 (0)81 413 07 63) provides the cheapest, dormitory style accommodation and is handy for the Schatzalp funicular.

Eating out

On the mountain

The restaurant at the **Höhenweg** (0041 (0)81 417 67 44, www.gourmetdavos.ch), just up the Parsennbahn train from Davos Dorf, has a massive terrace and bar and it's a great place to chill out with some top nosh. The **Alte Schwendi** (0041 (0)81 332 13 24, www.alteschwendi.ch) is the best mountain restaurant in which to hang out, due to the great music and atmosphere. It's located at Chesetta, just above the Schifer. There's a massive terrace, great traditional food, a cosy chalet inside and really friendly staff. If you just fancy grabbing a good burger, the restaurant on the Weissfluhjoch (0041 (0)81 417 66 44) has the best in town.

On Jakobshorn, the **Bolgen Plaza** (0041 (0)81 413 58 18, www.bolgenplaza.ch) is where the après ski dancing is to be found and **Jatzhütte's** (0041 (0)81 413 73 61, www.jatzhuette.ch), near to the terrain park, is pretty funky and madly themed with fake palm trees and other paraphernalia.

In town

There is a great variety of cuisine in Davos if you know where to look. **Bistro Angelo** (0041 (0)81 247 97 79) is a simple but cool restaurant. In Davos Platz there are lots more opportunities to track down a decent meal. If you have a taste for some oriental cuisine you will not be disappointed with **Zum Goldener Drachen** in the Hotel Bahnhof-Terminus (0041 (0)81 414 97 97, www.bahnhof-terminus.ch). Hotel Europe also has a stylish Chinese eatery, **Zauberberg** (0041 (0)81 414 42 00), and the same building houses another restaurant, **Scala** (0041 (0)81 414 42 20), which serves some good-value and tasty dishes until midnight. If you're peckish in the early hours of the morning try **After Hours** (0041 (0)81 413 63 76), for 24-hour takeaway munchies including pizzas, sandwiches and hot dogs. If you're too lazy to move from your room, **Hotel Albana** (0041 (0)81 413 58 41) deliver pizzas with beers, wine and champagne.

Bars and clubs

Pick the right bars and clubs, and you can have a great night out in Davos. The crowd is young and there is a good mix of tourists and locals around. **Bolgenschanze** (0041 (0)81 413 71 01, www.bolgenschanze.ch) is the snowboard hangout. It has great deals on pitchers and shooters and plays a range of music: hip hop, rock and the like. It's a big place, gets pretty busy and has a young, hip atmosphere. They also offer accommodation. **Chämi Bar** (0041 (0)81 413 55 55) is one of the most popular bars in Davos Platz and tends to be fairly hectic and jam-packed. **Ex Bar** (0041 (0)81 413 56 45, www.ex-bar-davos.ch) is a good late-night bar, especially if you have the munchies, as you can eat until 6am. The Hotel Europe is right in the centre of the action and comprises a number of restaurants and cafés (see Accommodation), the **Casino**, a comfy and chilled out piano bar, **Tonic** (0041 (0)81 413 59 21) where the top people tinkle out their tunes, and the 2 main clubs: **Cabanna Club** (0041 (0)81 415 42 01, www.cabanna.ch) and **Cava** (0041 (0)81 413 23 57, www.cava-davos.ch).

Getting there

By car

It takes about 12–13 hours to get to Davos from Calais, so it's probably easier to fly unless you're going to take a few days over the drive.

By plane

Zürich (150km) is the easiest place to fly to and it takes under 3 hours to get from the airport to Davos by train or car. You can get the train straight to Davos Dorf or Platz but you will have to change trains a couple of times. For more info contact the railway on 0041 (0)81 288 32 50, www.rhb.ch

By train

Take the Eurostar from London St Pancras to Paris, then an overnight train, changing at Landquart to arrive at Davos station in the resort. Contact Rail Europe (0870 830 4862, www.raileurope.co.uk) or European Rail (020 7387 0444, www.europeanrail.com).

Useful facts and phone numbers

Tourist office

T: 0041 (0)81 415 21 21
F: 0041 (0)81 415 21 00
W: www.davos.ch/www.davosklosters.ch

Emergency services

- Fire brigade: 118
- Police (emergency): 117
- Local police: 0041 (0)81 414 33 11
- Cantonal police: 0041 (0)81 413 76 22
- Rescue and ambulance: 144
- Hospital: 0041 (0)81 414 88 88, www.spitaldavos.ch
- Snow and avalanche report: 187
- Weather information: 0041 (0)81 415 21 33/162

Doctors

There are nearly 30 doctors and dentists in Davos so we shall name only a few.

- Dr P Flurry: 0041 (0)81 413 71 28
- Dr B Knöpfli: 0041 (0)81 415 70 70
- Dr R Stocker: 0041 (0)81 416 61 62
- Dentist – Dr A Bader: 0041 (0)81 413 34 30

Taxis

- Angelo's Taxi: 0041 (0)81 416 73 73 or 0041 (0)79 416 59 05
- Express Taxi: 0041 (0)81 410 11 11, www.expresstaxi.ch

Engelberg

A great freeriding destination.

On the slopes	Rating
Snow reliability	❄❄❄❄
Parks	❄❄❄½
Off-piste	❄❄❄❄
Off the slopes	
Après ski	❄❄
Nightlife	❄❄
Eating out	❄❄❄
Resort charm	❄❄❄½

The resort

Engelberg is renowned for its freeriding potential, with the rideable vertical drop allegedly the longest in Switzerland. Recent years have seen a growth in interest due to a good snow record and investment in the lift system, and the resort is aiming its revival at young freeskiers in particular. The pisted runs are aimed at competent riders but there is something for everyone. Unless you're exploring the off-piste, keen riders will cover the mountain in a few days.

Engelberg is a fairly large town, with some grand old hotels and beautiful views. If it's clear enough you can see the magnificent views of Lake Lucerne. Some of the hotels are an inconveniently long way from the slopes so be careful where you stay. Due to the proximity to Zurich and Lucerne, Engelberg is popular with weekenders, resulting in beautifully quiet weeks. Spring is popular as the whole mountain is open until mid May.

The mountains

Height: 1020–3028m

Ability	Rating
Expert	❄❄❄❄
Intermediate	❄❄
Beginner	❄❄❄

Getting about

There are 82km of pistes split into 2 areas, inconveniently on opposite sides of the valley. On 1 side is sunny Brunni, most suitable for families and accessed by a cable car from just above town. The towering peak of Titlis on the other side is where all the steeps, moguls and freeriding can be found, although the Gerschnialp (accessed from the gondola station at Trübsee) is a good isolated area for beginners, and Untertrübsee has a couple of good beginners' runs. Titlis can be reached either by funicular and cable car or by gondola. At Trübsee you can divert to Jochstock and the terrain park or you can carry on to the summit of Titlis via the Rotair – a unique, revolving cable car with stunning views. Titlis is a challenging mountain with steep reds and a good mogully black run from the peak down to Stand, best for the advanced and strong intermediate riders rather than for easy cruising. Less confident riders should stick to the wider reds below Stand down to Trübsee and those from Jochstock down to Alpstübli and Untertrübsee.

The park

The Jockpass terrain park is on the Titlis glacier next to the Jochstock Xpress. It's not a bad park but it's not great. There are a couple of OK kickers and 5 or 6 rails, including boxes and an S-rail.

Off-piste and backcountry

Engelberg is one of Europe's top freeriding destinations and is an awesome place to visit after a big dump of snow. There is so much powder that you can find fresh tracks days after a big snowfall. The off-piste isn't just for the serious freeriders, there are some great sections close to the pistes. Laub is the classic off-piste itinerary with a 1000m vertical drop and superb views. This memorable powder bowl is between Titlis and the Ritz restaurant. The Galtiberg run is another unforgettable run with a 2000m drop.

Lift passes

Check the latest prices at www.engelberg.ch

Instruction

Active Snow Team

Active offer off-piste guiding (3–7 hours) and also have a VIP service where your instructor/guide will meet you at your hotel.
0041 (0)41 630 45 49
www.active-snow-team.ch

Boardlocal

Just for the boarders, Boardlocal offers private and group lessons and freestyle and freeride camps.
0041 (0)41 637 00 00
www.boardlocal.ch

Prime Ski School

The focus here is on children and families.
0041 (0)41 637 01 55
www.prime-engelberg.ch

Schweizer Ski and Snowboard School

0041 (0)41 639 54 54
www.skischule-engelberg.ch

Other activities

Full moon on the Joch Pass: Full moon evenings (5–10pm) include a beer or 2 in the Jochpass restaurant and then a moonlit descent to Engelberg (0041 (0)41 637 11 87, www.jochpass.ch).

Hiking: Winter hiking is a popular activity in Engelberg with a 49km network of winter footpaths. The routes take from 25 minutes to 3 hours 15 minutes.

Horse-drawn sleigh rides: Take a half-hour ride round the village, a 1-hour valley round trip, a 2.5-hour trip with a stop or a night-time trip (0041 (0)41 637 33 29, www.hufe.ch).

Igloo village: With whirlpools and an ice bar, the igloo village on the Trübsee is a great place to visit or have a conference. Rooms range from dormitory-sized igloos to romantic igloos (0041 (0)41 612 27 28/0800 11 33 55 (in Switzerland), www.iglu-dorf.com).

Sports centre: The sports centre has indoor and outdoor ice skating, indoor tennis courts, a fitness centre, a curling competition area, billiards, darts and table tennis.

Tobogganing: The toboggan path at Brunni is a 2.5km run for families from the Brunni hut via Hütismatt to Ristis. The run at Gerschnialp is a more interesting 3.5km run and can also be done at night on Fridays and Saturdays. The 1km path at Fürenalp is a gentle run suitable for young children.

Events

The **FIS world ski jumping** takes place in December (www.weltcup-engelberg.ch) and the **Swiss Snow Walk and Run** in March (www.swisssnowwalking.ch). At the end of the season in April there is a **waterslide contest** on the Jochpass right by the Berghaus Jochpass. The aim is to cross the 25 x 25m pool on skis, snowboard or with some homemade vehicle. If you fall in, you're out of the competition; if you make it, you go on to the next round. The run-up distance is made shorter each time, which makes the crossing more difficult. See www.titlis.ch

Accommodation

Hotel Terrace (0041 (0)41 639 66 66, www.terrace.ch) is a traditional and charming 3-star hotel in a great location, just above the main street. There is a funicular that takes you down in to the village and there is a free 4-minute shuttle ride to the mountain. The location of the hotel provides wonderful views of both Engleberg town and the stunning mountains. There is a wellness centre with a sauna and a steam room. The public rooms are all grand with high ceilings and the bedrooms are clean and modern. **Hotel Schweizerhof** (0041 (0)41 637 11 05, www.schweizerhof-engelberg.ch) is in the middle of town, and the Bruni cable car is a short walk away. Built in the early 20th century in Belle Epoque style, the remodelled rooms are clean and well furnished with great views across the mountains. To be the first on the mountain in the mornings stay at the **Berghotel Trübsee-Hof** (0041 (0)41 639

50 92, www.truebseehof.ch), which is in a beautiful setting halfway up the Titlisbahn. The cafeteria is open to the public during the day. **Garni Sunnmatt** (0041 (0)41 637 20 45, www.sunnmatt-garni.ch) is a lovely and good value B&B that is a short way from the Titlis cable car and town centre. Apartments are available through the tourist office.

Eating out

On the mountain

At Titlis station, **Titlis-Stübli** (0041 (0)41 639 50 80) serves gourmet cuisine and fine wines and there is also **Mamma Mia** pizzeria, a self-service restaurant, sandwich bar and ice-cream boutique. **Untertrübsee**, (0041 (0)41 637 12 26, www.untertruebsee.ch) serves rösti, pastas and other cheese-covered dishes. **Ritz** (0041 (0)41 637 22 12, www.gasthaus-gerschnialp.ch) at Gerschnialp is one of the most popular mountain restaurants. You can also stop in the **Igloo village** for a cheese fondue (see Other activities).

In town

Axels (0041 (0)41 637 09 09) is a smart, modern restaurant serving traditional, though fairly fancy, French cuisine. They are also very proud of their wine cellar. **Hotel Waldegg** (0041 (0)41 637 18 22, www.waldegg-engelberg.ch) has one of the finest gourmet restaurants and **Restaurant Spannort** (0041 (0)41 639 60 20, www.spannort.ch) serves fancy local food.

The rustic restaurant in the **Alpenclub** (0041 (0)41 637 12 43, www.alpenclub.ch) is popular for its cheese fondues, raclette and hot stones to cook your own meat, plus a pizzeria. There are 2 Chinese restaurants (chinarestaurants.belfortnetwork.org): **Moonrise** (0041 (0)41 637 15 56) and **Sunrise** (0041 (0)41 637 17 10), which also offers takeaway. **Yucatan** (0041 (0)41 637 13 24) has great Mexican.

Bars and clubs

The chalet at the valley station of the Titlis is a great place to start the après ski fun. **Yucatan** in Hotel Bellevue is the place to go for lively drinks and late-night dancing. They have happy hours every day and great music. **Spindle** in the Alpenclub Hotel (www.spindle.ch) is another popular club. The contemporary **CCBaR Musicbar** (0041 (0)41 637 40 00) is a stylish place to sip a cocktail or a whisky. For a more chilled out après ski, **Dream Life** at the Central Hotel (www.central-engelberg.ch) is modelled on a British pub.

Getting there

By car

There are motorways from Geneva via Bern, or from St Gallen via Zurich to Lucerne. Leave the A2 motorway at the Stans-Süd exit (16km after Lucerne) and it's about a 20-km drive to Engelberg.

By plane

Zürich (100km) You can drive to Engelberg in around 1 hour or take a train, which will take an hour and a half.

Basel (130km) Transfer by car takes about an hour and a half.

By train

Take the Eurostar from London St Pancras to Paris, then an overnight train, changing at Zurich and Luzern to arrive at Engelberg station in the resort. Contact Rail Europe (0870 830 4862, www.raileurope.co.uk) or European Rail (020 7387 0444, www.europeanrail.com).

Useful facts and phone numbers

Tourist office

T: 0041 (0)41 639 77 77
F: 0041 (0)41 639 77 66
W: www.engelberg.ch

Emergency services

- Police: 117 or 041 666 68 00
- SOS Titlis: 0041 (0)41 639 50 61
- SOS Brunni: 0041 (0)41 639 60 60

Doctors

- Dr Hansjörg Bucher: 0041 (0)41 637 00 30
- Dr Christoph Ehrat: 0041 (0)41 637 40 60
- Dr Matthias Müller: 0041 (0)41 637 33 33

Taxis

- Taxi Hans Flückiger: 0041 (0)41 637 21 21/ 0041 (0)79 422 61 61
- Taxi Häcki: 0041 (0)41 637 33 88/ 0041 (0)79 668 07 07
- Taxi 57: 0041 (0)78 666 57 57, www.taxi57.ch

Flims

A freestylers' mountain and a pretty Swiss resort, spoilt by a constant flow of traffic.

On the slopes	Rating
Snow reliability	❄❄❄
Parks	❄❄❄❄½
Off-piste	❄❄❄
Off the slopes	
Après ski	❄❄❄
Nightlife	❄½
Eating out	❄❄
Resort charm	❄❄

The resort

The Flims-Laax-Falera mountains are fantastic. They are particularly perfect for the budding freestyler, and there's some good off-piste into the bargain that you can find with or without guidance. It's a little flat, but you'll forgive that when you see the park. The town, however, is not for the fun-crazed freestyler; there are a couple of very cool après ski bars but little to entertain you later on.

'Perfect for the budding freestyler'

It is quite attractive in the way that all the buildings have an appealing, chalet-style look, but the resort is hugely disadvantaged by the endless traffic that runs through the centre of the town at all hours of the day. Also many of the interiors of hotels and restaurants look like they need bringing into the 21st century. If you want to ride these mountains you should also look at Laax Murschetg (see Laax Murschetg chapter, page 192); it has easier access to the park, and the best bars and places to stay.

The mountains

Height: 1100–3018m

Ability	Rating
Expert	❄❄❄
Intermediate	❄❄❄❄
Beginner	❄❄❄½

Getting about

Flims is located at the far end of the Alpenarena (which combines Flims, Laax and Falera), providing access to 220km of slopes. The mountain is pretty flat so it's great for cruisy intermediates, though there is a fair bit of fresh powder that you can see from many of the pistes. The park is located at Crap Sogn Gion and there are some freeride routes marked on the piste map. As the mountains in the Alpenarena are the same, the details on the park and the off-piste can be found in the Laax Murschetg chapter, page 192.

Lift passes

Check the latest prices at www.alpenarena.ch

Instruction

Mountain Fantasy

These are the best mountain guides in town for skiers, boarders and anyone else who wants to explore. They also do private lessons.
0041(0)81 936 70 77
www.mountain-fantasy.ch/www.bergsportflims.ch

Ski and Snowboard Schools

0041 (0)81 927 77 77
www.laax.com

Other activities

Curling: There is a curling stadium in Flims (0041 (0)81 911 19 50) with 4 rinks and a heated spectator stand. You can pay to rent the stadium or for lessons.

Full-moon skiing: In January, February and March you can ski under the full moon; contact the tourist office for more details and exact dates.

Golf: There is an indoor driving range at the Park Hotel Waldhaus (0041 (0)81 928 48 48, www.waldhaus-flims.ch) if you can't stand a week away from your golf clubs.

Helicopters: These can be hired for pleasure trips or as a taxi from Air Grischa (0041 (0)81 322 57 57, www.airgrischa.ch).

Ice skating: There are 2 ice skating rinks at the sports centre (0041 (0)81 920 91 91); the natural rink can be skated on from December until February and the other until the end of March.

Paragliding or delta flying: Training and trial days paragliding or delta flying can be arranged by a few companies including Swissraft (0041 (0)81 911 52 50, www.swissraft.ch) and X-Dream Fly (0041 (0)79 291 45 12).

Sports centre: The sports centre Prau La Selva (0041 (0)81 920 91 91, www.sportzentrum-flims.ch) has an ice rink (see above), fitness room, basement shooting range, solarium, table tennis, outdoor ice rink, Bavarian curling and an interestingly named 'Vibra bed'.

Tobogganing: There is a 3km tobogganing run from Foppa to Flims (0041 (0)81 927 70 73).

Wellness centres: There are loads of wellness centres to check out, with the best 2 being La Mira at the Hotel Adula (0041 (0)81 928 28 28, www.adula.ch) with an outdoor hot tub, and the 2500m^2 of facilities at Delight at the Park Hotel Waldhaus (0041 (0)81 928 48 48, www.waldhaus-flims.ch). Other hotels with wellness facilities include Cresta (0041 (0)81 911 35 35, www.cresta.ch), Sunstar Hotel Surselva (0041 (0)81 928 18 00, www.sunstar.ch/flims) and the Romantik Hotel Schweizerhof (0041 (0)81 928 10 10, www.schweizerhof-flims.ch).

Events

The best events are in the park, such as the **Burton European Open**, **British Championships** and **Orage European Freeski Open**. These are detailed in the Laax Murschetg chapter, see page 192.

Accommodation

Waldhaus

The **Park Hotel Waldhaus** (0041 (0)81 928 48 48, www.parkhotel-waldhaus.ch) contains the stunning Delight spa and beauty wellness centre. The 'water world' area is made up of 3 different pools with a total of 355m^2 of water. The hotel (which is really more like a self-contained village) is massive, with acres of long corridors. It is fairly impersonal, despite being impressive. We would prefer to stay in the beautiful **Hotel Adula** (0041 (0)81 928 28 28, www.adula.ch), for a more friendly and cosy kind of luxury. The spa (La Mira) has a gym, pool and outdoor spa (beware of naked areas) and the restaurants are the best in town (see Eating out). The spa facilities in both the Park Hotel and the Adula are open to the public.

'Stay in the Hotel Adula for a friendly kind of luxury'

For a slightly less expensive alternative try the pleasant and comfortable **Arvenhotel Waldeck** (0041 (0)81 928 14 14, www.waldeck.ch) or **Hotel Garni National** (0041 (0)81 928 14 74, www.national-flims.ch).

Flims Dorf

The best hotels are in Waldhaus but there are some in Dorf that are worth a look, and they do have the advantage of being closer to the lift station. The best hotel in Flims Dorf is the **Arena** (0041 (0)81 920 93 93, www.arenaflims.ch). It is in a fantastic position for the après ski bars, and the hotel's own bar is a popular après ski venue as is the nightclub.

This can create some noise, so families may be better off staying in the hotel's annex. For those who will be joining in the noise, the hotel has some great value deals. The 'backpacker rooms' have 4 beds and a bathroom. Eight rooms have been specially designed around major snowboarding brands, for example, Nitro, Nikita, Vans and O'Neill (a personal favourite, with palm trees painted on the walls and an umbrella over the bed).

'If you enjoy the tranquility of isolation, the Fidazerhof has spectacular views'

If you enjoy the tranquillity of isolation, 1 of the best places to stay is the **Fidazerhof** in the nearby town of Fidaz (0041 (0)81 920, 90 10, www.fidazerhof.ch). It is a short bus ride from the town and slopes (the buses run every half hour during the day) and has a spectacular view from the terrace. It's really friendly, has great rooms and a restaurant, and a wellness suite that offers a large variety of treatments.

Eating out

On the mountain

If you're hitting the park and pipe you will be eating and drinking at the popular bars at Crap Sogn Gion: **Rock Bar** (0041 (0)81 927 73 73) and **Café No Name** (0041 (0)81 927 73 44). These bars are just above the half pipe and they are great places to hang out. For a beer, hit the terrace of Café No Name right at the top of the park and for a great cheeseburger head upstairs to the café **Capalari** (0041 (0)81 927 73 73). There are tons of deckchairs and comfy outdoor seating at the **Rock Bar** so you'll always be able to find a place to relax with a beer. There's even a free games room in the basement with an Xbox and table football. The restaurant at **Foppa** (0041 (0)81 911 16 50) is a good place for lunch, just above Flims, and can be reached by foot or on skis or a board. If you like small, family-run chalet-restaurants, turn off the route from Startgels to Flims to **Runcahöhe** (0041 (0)81 911 15 88).

'You'll always be able to find a place to relax with a beer'

In town

Most of the decent restaurants in Flims are in hotels and take a little searching for. In Waldhaus, the **Hotel Adula** (0041 (0)81 928 28 28, www.adula.ch) has 2 of the best restaurants in town. **La Clav** is a small and smart Italian restaurant that serves top quality pasta and risotto (no pizza). The cream of the crop is the **Barga**, a very beautiful and quaint French restaurant with 14 Gault Millau points and a log fire; perfect for a smart celebration. There are 2 restaurants in the Hotel Bellevue, the most atmospheric of which is the **Caverna-Keller** (0041 (0)81 911 31 31, www.bellevueflims.ch), a 425-year-old cavernous basement perfect for a romantic candlelit dinner. If you tire of the traditional cuisine, try the fantastic **Little China Restaurant** (0041 (0)81 928 48 27, www.parkhotel-waldhaus.ch). If you fancy a pizza, you can head to the **Pomodoro** (0041 (0)81 911 10 62) in Waldhaus for a wood-fired pizza or the cheery Pizzeria Veneziana (0041 (0)81 929 90 10, www.hotelvorab.ch) in Flims Dorf.

A 5-minute drive away in Fidaz is the **Fidazerhof Hotel** (0041 (0)81 920 90 10, www.fidazerhof.ch) that has a pleasant restaurant with stunning views from the terrace. For something unusual, take a trip up the slopes to the **Startgels Alpenrose** (0041 (0)81 911 58 48, www.startgels.ch); when you book they will arrange to come and pick you up in a piste basher from outside the Legna Bar on the slopes. On certain nights, the **Foppa** restaurant (see Eating out On the mountain) is open; enjoy a raclette or fondue and then a sledge ride back to town.

Bars and clubs

The best bars are the après ski bars in Flims Dorf. The stylish **Legna Bar** is right on the slopes in Flims Dorf and has a great après ski vibe. Moving on down a few stairs you will come to **The Iglu** bar (0041 (0)81 927 99 76, www.theiglu.ch), a small dome that is very cool and cosy. Hotel Arena has a great bar (formally the Stenna bar) and a club. The **Livingruhm** (www.livingruhm.ch) nearby, has a lounge with a fireplace and offers good food all day.

If you want to hear some top class DJs in action, take a taxi to Laax Murschetg, where you can find the über-cool **Riders Palace** lobby bar and club complete with neon lighting (see Laax Murschetg chapter, page 192).

Getting there

By car

Don't try to drive from Geneva via Andermatt; we did and it became a 4-hour detour – halfway along the road it stopped; it's only completely open in summer. Your best bet is to fly to Zürich or Friedrichshafen. From there you can hire a car or catch a bus.

By plane

Zürich (150km)
Friedrichshafen (140km) for Ryanair flights.

By train

Take the Eurostar from London St Pancras to Paris, then an overnight train to Chur, and then a local bus (42 minutes) to the resort. Contact Rail Europe (0870 830 4862, www.raileurope.co.uk) or European Rail (020 7387 0444, www.europeanrail.com). Bus tickets are purchased at the station. (For people booking through European Rail to Swiss resorts, the rail fare includes the bus connection to resort at no extra cost, so there is no need to pay for a bus ticket.)

Useful facts and phone numbers

Tourist office

T: 0041 (0)81 920 92 00
W: www.alpenarena.ch

Emergency services

- Police: In an emergency call 117, if not call 0041 (0)81 928 29 40/0041 (0)81 911 11 64
- In an emergency on the mountain call 144 or 1414 for Swiss Air Rescue
- Hospital in Chur: 0041 (0)81 256 61 11
- Fire brigade: 118

Doctors

- Dr B Durschei: 0041 (0)81 911 26 66
- Dr A Lötscher: 0041 (0)81 911 10 55
- Dr H Michel: 0041 (0)81 911 12 07
- Dr P Reiser: 0041 (0)81 911 13 13

Taxis

- Taxi Mario: 0041 (0)81 941 22 22 or 0041 (0)79 544 50 00, www.taximario.ch
- Taxi Flims: 0041 (0)79 517 70 01 or 0041 (0)79 315 44 44

Klosters

Klosters has an impressive returning population, and it's not hard to see why.

On the slopes	Rating
Snow reliability	❄❄❄
Parks	–
Off-piste	❄❄❄½
Off the slopes	
Après ski	❄❄❄
Nightlife	❄❄
Eating out	❄❄❄❄½
Resort charm	❄❄❄❄

The resort

Klosters has a distinguished reputation as the choice of the rich, royal and famous, but while it obviously does attract an opulent clientele, there are few signs of pretention. It still resembles an alpine farming village. Klosters Platz is the main village centre. Dorf is focused at the base of the separate Madrisa mountain. Klosters is relaxing, welcoming and fairly quiet, making it the perfect choice for families. The nightlife isn't at all bad, but it is expensive and exclusive.

The mountains offer a great variety of skiing and boarding, particularly if you include the nearby slopes of Davos, although travel between these disjointed areas can be tiresome. Parsenn is the main mountain, but experts will cover it quickly and may then need to look further afield.

The mountains

Height: 1124–2844m

Ability	Rating
Expert	❄❄❄½
Intermediate	❄❄❄❄
Beginner	❄❄❄❄

Getting about

There are 2 mountains that can be accessed from Klosters: Parsenn, a large ski area connected to Davos, and Madrisa, a smaller, family-orientated zone that has some fantastic off-piste potential.

The Parsenn mountain is beautiful, the acres of pistes are always well groomed and it is the perfect place for intermediates to cruise around. The runs back down from Parsenn to Klosters and the surrounding areas are not the easiest runs (beginners should catch the lift back down), but they are great. Alternatively, you could embark on the 12km-long run down to Küblis. You'll need to catch the train back to Klosters, but the transport system is superb so it shouldn't pose too much of a problem. The only disadvantage with skiing on Parsenn is that the mountain can only be accessed from the Gotschnabahn lift from Klosters, which can mean really big queues in busy holiday periods.

Madrisa is a smaller mountain, but has a lot to offer and it has the added benefit of being far quieter than Parsenn. Madrisa could almost be classed as a separate resort as there are locally based ski and snowboard schools, a great restaurant and different play areas for the kids. Madrisa is filled with T-bar lifts, which can be a little hard for beginners. There's something for everyone; for starters it's perfect for learning to ride using the magic carpet and special beginners' lifts, there are also some great groomed slopes for carving and loads of untracked areas for freeriding. Madrisa is the perfect area for young families. Mum and dad can leave their child in the care centre (for a small charge) and go off for a bit of on or off-piste action. There is also a room in which you can supervise your own child that is free of charge.

The 3 further mountain regions of Davos (Jakobshorn, Rinerhorn and Pischa) are fairly easily accessible from Klosters (see Davos chapter, page 177).

The park

There is a park near the Selfranga lift, which is open during the day and is also floodlit for 2 nights of the week. The park contains 3 kickers ranging from 6 to 14m, a flat down box, an up box and 2 flat boxes. Check out www.duty.ch.

Off-piste and backcountry

The off-piste in Klosters is fantastic. You can almost always find good snow, even if there has been no snow for a month, due to the large numbers of north-facing slopes and countless tree runs. Disadvantages include more often than not having to catch a bus, train or taxi from wherever you end up as few of the runs actually end up in Klosters.

On a sunny day Madrisa is the place to hit the backcountry. From the top of the mountain is the long run down to San Antonien that is superb. A 5–10-minute walk takes you to a big open powder field. It's not too hard (although there are some steeps if you fancy it) and can be done with the whole family if you feel confident. However, it should be done with a guide so you don't get lost. Once in San Antonien there is a beautiful restaurant to sample and then you'll need to take a taxi back.

On Parsenn you can pretty much access powder from every lift. The Totalphorn area, between the Meierhoftäli and Totalp chairlifts, is superb but does get sketchy if the snow isn't great. Don't let that put you off completely; on a perfect powder day it's definitely worth checking out. If the visibility is bad, there are loads of tree runs around. The Weissfluh, a north-facing slope is 1 of Klosters' most famous off-piste runs. It's around a 500m drop with a 15-minute hike out. You should take a guide with you for this one. We recommend contacting Lukas Dürr at Swiss Freeride (www.swissfreeride.ch).

Lukas can also take you on a guided tour to Gargellen, a village in Austria, starting from the top of Madrisa. The tour involves about 2 hours of walking in total, but the terrain isn't too challenging and the scenery is incredible. Don't forget your passport if you do go.

Lift passes

Check latest prices at www.davosklosters.ch

Instruction

Boardriding

0041 (0)81 420 26 62
www.boardriding.ch

Duty Board and Bananas Head Office

Swiss Snowboard School, Klosters
0041 (0)81 422 66 60
www.duty.ch

Swiss Ski and Snowboard School Klosters

0041 (0)81 410 28 28
www.sssk.ch

Swiss Ski and Snowboard School Saas

0041 (0)81 420 22 33
www.sss-saas.ch

Other activities

Horse-drawn sleigh rides: Popular destinations are Monbiel, Garfiun or Schifer. Contact Christian Flütsch-Aebli (0041 (0)81 422 18 73, www.pferdekutschen.ch) or Johannes Marugg (0041 (0)81 422 24 29).

Paragliding: Flugcenter Grischa (0041 (0)81 422 20 70/079 336 19 19, www.gleitschirm-schule.ch).

Sports centre: The sports centre (0041 (0)81 410 21 31) has artificial ice rinks for skating and ice hockey, skating lessons, curling for beginners and ice stick shooting (Bavarian curling).

Tennis and badminton: There are several courts (you can play for 1 hour a day free with the guest card).

Tobogganing: There are a number of runs: 8.6km from Saaseralp (Madrisa) to Saas, 3.5km from Gotschnagrat to Klosters, 2.5km from Melcheti to Aeuja (free) and 2.5km from Alpenrösli to Klosters Platz (free).

Wellness: A number of hotels have wellness facilities: Alpina (0041 (0)81 410 24 24, www.alpina-klosters.ch), Bad Serneus (0041 (0)81 254 32 00, www.badserneus.ch), Pardenn (0041 (0)81 423 20 20, www.pardenn.ch), Silvretta Parkhotel (0041 (0)81 423 34 35, www.silvretta.ch), Vereina (0041 (0)81 410 27 27, www.vereinahotel.ch). There is also an indoor spa in Davos (see Davos chapter, page 177).

Events

Klosters doesn't have too many fixtures organised in town. In mid-March the popular and highly entertaining **Wild Girls on Snow** (www.wildgirlsonsnow.com) charity spectacle takes place. Celebrities, models and local stars are invited for a 3-day event involving lots of dressing up, larking around and looking gorgeous. Each year the event is run for different charities with different themes, for example 007, Sherlock Holmes and Wild West. The event includes a ski race with past and present racers from the Swiss National Ski Team so there's loads to watch on the mountain, but at night the partying tends to happen behind closed doors.

Contact the tourist office for more information about the events in Klosters.

Accommodation

Klosters isn't huge on the whole tour operator thing; you're better off booking directly with hotels and organising your own transfer. Renting apartments is also popular in Klosters; there are 6600 beds in rented and privately owned flats and houses and 1900 in hotels. Contact the tourist office for specific information about renting.

The 4-star hotel **Alpina** (0041 (8)1 410 24 24, www.alpina-klosters.ch) has everything that anyone would want from a hotel. It has the best location in town and is stunning. The pool and wellness area contains sauna, steam bath, solarium, beauty salon and fitness area. The rooms are beautiful and if you want to splash out there are some great suites. Apartments are also available.

Hotel Rustico (0041 (0)81 410 22 88, www.rusticohotel.com) has 11 rooms (10 rooms and 1 junior suite) and is a 3-star hotel. All of the rooms have a really cosy, alpine feel. The guys who run the hotel, Al and Renee Thöny, will bend over backwards to make sure that your stay is enjoyable. The restaurant is also superb (see Eating out).

The **Hotel Vereina** (0041 (0)81 410 27 27, www.hotelvereina.ch) is a top quality 4-star establishment in a majestic and splendid building. Everything about the hotel is superb, from the gourmet restaurant to the amazing views, to the wellness area and spa. If you want to splash some serious cash, ask for the queen's or president's suite with their balconies, fire places, office areas, etc.

Silvapina (0041 (0)81 422 14 68, www.silvapina.ch) in Klosters Dorf is a family-run hotel and it's a lovely place for families. Breakfast and dinner are provided so it's more like a chalet. It's good value, but it's quite far from the town so not for the party animals.

Eating out

On the mountain

On Madrisa, the **Saaseralp** restaurant (0041 (0)81 410 21 80) has tasty traditional Swiss food (especially the homemade rösti). It has a separate restaurant for large parties, usually dominated by ski school groups, and rooms where kids can play around, supervised by you or their staff.

Bruhin's (0041 (0)81 417 66 44) is a fairly fancy restaurant right at the top of the Weissfluhgipfel on Parsenn, (via the Gipfelbahn cable car). It's a smart restaurant with stunning views but there is no terrace, which is a bit of a shame on a sunny day. Book a table by the window to get the best views.

If you're looking for a traditional, chalet-style restaurant, the **Gruobenalp** (0041 (0)81 422 62 30), just down from Gotschnagrat on the other side to Klosters, is perfect, especially on a sunny day as the terrace has a gorgeous view. The **Alte Schwendi** (0041 (0)81 332 13 24, www.alteschwendi.ch) is the best mountain restaurant for hanging out in. It's located at Chesetta, just above the Schifer. There's a massive terrace, great food, a cosy chalet feel inside and really friendly staff. Be careful though, it's pretty easy to end up staying all afternoon; in fact you can even stay overnight if you like! Below the Schifer, on the way back to Klosters Dorf is the **Serneuser Schwendi** (0041

(0)81 422 12 89, www.schwendiserneus.ch), which is now run by locals and serves some great traditional Swiss cuisine. It is also a mountain hostel. If you just fancy grabbing a good burger, the restaurant on the **Weissfluhjoch** (0041 (0)81 417 66 11) has the best in town.

In town

Hotel Rustico (0041 (0)81 410 22 88, www.rusticohotel.com) has a superb restaurant. It manages to create a stylish and luxurious atmosphere whilst remaining cosy and friendly. The staff are charming and the unusual (and tasty) cuisine falls under a Euro-Asian theme with Japanese, Asian and international specialities. It's open for lunch and dinner, but is very popular in the evening so it's a good idea to book a little in advance. In addition to the main restaurant is a cosy Stübli for fondues and raclettes.

The **Alpenrösli** (0041 (0)81 422 13 57) is a beautiful restaurant. You have to walk up to it, which can take about half an hour from Klosters Platz (or catch a cab) and then you toboggan back down after a few drinks. The excellent rösti dishes are their speciality.

The **Chesa Grischuna** (0041 (0)81 422 22 22, www.chesagrischuna.ch) is a chic restaurant with a very smart bar. The funky and stylish hotel attached is featured in *Hip Hotels* magazine, along with only a handful of others throughout Europe.

There are a number of pizzerias. **Pizza Fellini** in Platz (0041 (0)81 422 22 11) also has a takeaway option.

The tourist office provides a great gastroguide that gives a good summary of all of the restaurants in town and shows you exactly where they all are.

Bars and clubs

Gotschnabar (www.gotschnabar.ch) is a convenient and popular après ski bar. The **Brasserie**, in the super smart Vereina Hotel (see Accommodation), is probably the best bar in Klosters. There's often live music, DJs, pianos and lots more. For a classy place it's quite surprising the carnage that goes on! **Chesa** in the Chesa Grischuna (see Eating out In town) is another really smart bar that is great fun. The beers in these bars can be pretty expensive – much cheaper beverages can be found in the local bars such as the Bistro, next to the train station, or the **Rössli** bar (0041 (0)81 422 52 01, www.roesslibar.ch) in the centre of town. Later on, the most famous and prestigious club to be seen at is the **Casa Antica** (0041 (0)81 422 16 21, www.casaantica-klosters.ch), where William, Harry and those boys hang out. Enjoy it but watch out – beer is expensive and spirits and mixers even more so.

Getting there

By car

It takes about 12–13 hours to get to Klosters from Calais, so it's probably easier to fly unless you're going to take a few days over it.

By plane

Zürich (140km) is the easiest place to fly to and it takes under 3 hours to get from there to Klosters by train or car. For more info contact the railway (0041 (0)81 288 32 50, www.rhb.ch).

By train

Take the Eurostar from London St Pancras to Paris, then an overnight train, changing at Landquart to arrive at Klosters Dorf station in the resort. Contact Rail Europe (0870 830 4862, www.raileurope.co.uk) or European Rail (020 7387 0444, www.europeanrail.com).

Useful facts and phone numbers

Tourist office

T: 0041 (0)81 410 20 20
F: 0041 (0)81 410 20 10
W: www.klosters.ch

Emergency services

- European emergency number: 112
- Fire brigade: 118
- Police: 117
- Ambulance: 144/0041 (0)81 422 17 13
- Medical care: 0041 (0)81 422 49 49
- Police station: 0041 (0)81 423 36 80

Laax Murschetg

The best freestyle hangout in Europe.

On the slopes	Rating
Snow reliability	❄❄❄
Parks	❄❄❄❄❄½
Off-piste	❄❄❄
Off the slopes	
Après ski	❄❄❄
Nightlife	❄❄❄
Eating out	❄❄
Resort charm	❄½

The resort

Laax was relatively undiscovered by the Brits until the British Championships came here in 2005, putting it on the map. Laax itself is a small town with several separate areas, and Laax Murschetg contains all of the important bits – lifts, bars and clubs. Laax is a sanctuary for the avid freestyler: the park is second to none in Europe, you can stay here pretty cheaply (although drinks will set you back a fair bit) and the nightlife is cool (as long as you are). You should have second thoughts if you spend much of your time moseying around town (although Flims is a short bus ride if needs be – see page 184) or if you get bored going to the same restaurants and bars every night. If these things don't bother you, you should definitely give Laax a whirl.

The mountains

Height: 1000–3000m

Ability	Rating
Expert	❄❄❄
Intermediate	❄❄❄❄
Beginner	❄❄❄❄½

Getting about

Laax is at the centre of the Alpenarena, providing good access to its 220km of slopes. From Laax Murschetg it is a quick cable car ride to Crap Sogn Gion and you'll be in the park in a matter of minutes. The mountain is pretty flat so it's great for cruisy intermediates, though there is a fair bit of fresh powder to be had, which you can see from many of the pistes, and there are some freeride routes marked on the piste map.

The park

This is one of our favourite parks in Europe. The guys looking after it are keen and park-proud. There are 2 different areas to the park, on either side of the café/bar/hostel at Crap Sogn Gion. The riders love the slopestyle area at the British Championships; it consists of a selection of rails, including 10m down rails, a C-rail and a fun wall ride. You can hit 3 different kickers on the way down, with a choice of sizes at each hit. In total there are 6 jumps (5–25m tables). The other side of the park has a fantastic selection of rails. There's an S-rail, C-rail, rollercoaster, and big gap jumps to a 5m high rail. There are also 6 straight boxes, 1 4-frame rail, 1 kinked box and 4 rainbow rails. To finish it off there are 2 super pipes (1 80m and 1 140m) in mint condition. Visit the website (www.laax.com/snowpark) for information and pictures.

Off-piste and backcountry

Most of the Alpenarena's off-piste terrain is easily accessible and not bad at all considering the shallow gradients of the mountain. Like many other resorts, they now provide 40km of unprepared but marked and avalanche-controlled slopes for freeriders to play on. These runs lead from the summits of the 3 main peaks: Vorab Pign (2897m), La Siala (2810m), above Laax, and Cassons (2675m). Cassons is great, not just for the marked run there, but also for the off-piste terrain surrounding it (which would require a guide). If you do want to hire a guide contact Mountain Fantasy (see Instruction). From Cassons, they can take you into the backcountry to Seghesgkecier or down to Bargis. Alternatively, you can start your trip from the Vorab Gletscher (3018m), above Falera, and skin (hike) to the Bündner Vorab (3028m), from which you can expect a great ride down a big open valley, ending up in Alp Ruschein (1774m).

Lift passes

Check the latest prices at www.alpenarena.ch

Instruction

Mountain Fantasy

These are the best mountain guides in town for skiers, boarders and anyone else who wants to explore. The office is in Flims.
0041 (0)81 936 70 77
www.mountain-fantasy.ch/www.bergsport flims.ch

Ski and Snowboard Schools

0041 (0)81 927 77 77
www.laax.com

Other activities

There isn't too much to do in Laax Murschteg. If you need other activities, such as paragliding and sledging, Flims is your best bet (see Flims chapter, page 184).

Full-moon skiing: In January, February and March there is full-moon skiing (weather dependant) on Crap Sogn Gion (0041 (0)81 927 70 00); from 8pm you can take the gondola lift up and take a guided moonlit tour down.

Ice skating and curling: Both available on Laax lake (0041 (0)81 921 51 53).

Wellness centre, pool and tennis: The Hotel Signina (0041 (0)81 927 90 00, www.signinahotel.com) in Laax Murschetg has a wellness suite, Laguna pool and tennis courts that are open to the public. Hotel Laaxerhof (0041 (0)81 920 82 00, www.laaxerhof.ch) has a public pool and sauna. If you don't mind catching the bus to Flims, the wellness centres at the Park Hotel and Adula are well worth a look (see Flims chapter, page 184).

Events

The superb and well maintained park means that there are a crazy number of events that take place in Laax. See the park's website for more info (www.laax.com/snowpark). Most of the after parties take place later on in the Riders Palace, so if you're competing or watching, this is the place to book into.

In January, there's the **Burton European Open**: 600 athletes compete – pros, amateurs and juniors – in the super pipe and slope style.

In March the **British Ski/Snowboard Championships** kick off, a must for British boarders and skiers. This competition attracts both pros and up-and-coming riders. It consists of skier and boardercross, slopestyle, big air and half pipe. There are cash prizes for the top 3 in each category, but the title is the main trophy. Check it out on www.britishsnowtour.com

Arguably Europe's most prestigious freeski event takes place in March: the **Orage European Freeski Open** showcases the world's finest freeskiers in half pipe and slopestyle.

Accommodation

The **Riders Palace** (0041 (0)81 927 97 00, www.riderspalace.ch), is a funky, glass, neon-lit hotel/bar/club, full of ultra-cool clientele. Rooms vary from basic dorms to stylish multimedia rooms and suites with DVD player, Xbox 360, surround sound and projector screens. It's the best place to stay if you are going to be partying every night, but it's not the place to get a quiet night's sleep. Our choice would be to stay at the futuristic **Rocks Resort** apartments (0041 (0)81 927 9900, www.rocksresort.com) for both location and facilities.

If you really want to be the first to hit the park you can stay in the **Mountain Hostel** on Crap Sogn Gion (0041 (0)81 927 73 73), at 2228m. The **Laaxerhof** (0041 (0)81 920 82 00, www.laaxerhof.ch) is a pretty smart hotel with an elegant restaurant and good pool and sauna. The **Hotel Signina** (0041 (0)81 927 90 00, www.signinahotel.com) is another great traditional hotel with a wellness suite and tennis courts that are open to the public.

Eating out

On the mountain

If you're hitting the park and pipe you will be eating and drinking at the popular bars at Crap Sogn Gion: **Rock Bar** (0041 (0)81 927 73 73) and **Café No Name** (0041 (0)81 927 73 44). These bars are just above the half pipe and they are great places to hang out. For a beer, hit the terrace at the top of the park and for a great cheeseburger, head up to the café. There are tons of deckchairs and comfy outdoor seating.

At Plaun, the old chairlift station has been converted into a bar with deckchairs outside in good weather, and they barbecue sausages and serve good soup.

On the way back down to Laax there are 2 superb restaurants: **Tegia Curnius** (0041 (0)81 927 99 30) and **Tegia Larnags** (0041 (0)81 927 99 10), both with cosy, traditional atmospheres, sun terraces and local foods.

In town

There are very few restaurants in Laax Murschetg, although you can eat in most of the hotels. **Pizzeria Cristallina** (0041 (0)81 921 22 52) is at the bottom of Laax Murschetg on the main road. It cooks superb pizzas on a big open wood fire and also does takeaways. There is a play corner for kids.

If you need something a little more gourmet, you should take a short bus ride to Flims where you will find a few really good restaurants, such as **La Clav** and **Barga** at the Hotel Adula and the **Little China** if you're bored with local food (see Flims chapter, page 184).

Bars and clubs

For après ski, head to the **Crap Bar** (0041 (0)81 927 99 45) at the bottom of the slopes, built with 24 tonnes of granite. The **Indy** bar is another good choice and houses some top class DJs. The neon-lit **Riders Palace Lobby Bar** (0041 (0)81 927 97 00, www.riderspalace.ch), is kitted out with leather sofas, internet and a huge bar. Downstairs is the massive (and expensive) Ministry-of-Sound-run **Palace Club** where the cool kids hang out. Later on the music ranges from hip-hop to trance and house. If you prefer rock and pop try the **Casa Veglia** club (0041 (0)81 927 99 50, www.casaveglia.ch).

Getting there

By car

See the directions to Flims, page 186.

By plane

Zürich (150km)

Friedrichshafen (140km) for Ryanair flights.

By train

Take the Eurostar from London St Pancras to Paris, then an overnight train to Chur, and then a local bus (44 minutes) to the resort. Contact Rail Europe (0870 830 4862, www.raileurope.co.uk) or European Rail (020 7387 0444, www.europeanrail.com). Bus tickets are purchased at the station. (For people booking through European Rail to Swiss resorts, the rail fare includes the bus connection to resort at no extra cost, so there is no need to pay for a bus ticket.)

Useful facts and phone numbers

Tourist office

T: 0041 (0)81 920 81 81
W: www.alpenarena.ch

Emergency services

- Police: In an emergency call 117, if not call 0041 (0)81 928 29 40/0041 (0)81 911 11 64
- In an emergency on the mountain call 144 or 1414 for Swiss Air Rescue
- Hospital in Chur: 0041 (0)81 256 61 11
- Fire brigade: 118

Doctors

- Dr J Bürki: 0041 (0)81 921 48 48
- District nurse: 0041 (0)81 921 55 05

Taxis

- Taxi Mario: 0041 (0)81 941 22 22 or 0041 (0)79 544 50 00, www.taximario.ch
- Taxi Flims: 0041 (0)79 315 44 44 or 0041 (0)79 517 70 01

Mürren

A tiny, picture-perfect village with exceptional scenery.

On the slopes	Rating
Snow reliability	❄❄❄❄
Parks	❄❄
Off-piste	❄❄❄
Off the slopes	
Après ski	❄❄
Nightlife	❄❄❄
Eating out	❄❄❄½
Resort charm	❄❄❄❄❄

The resort

Mürren is part of the dramatic and remote Jungfrau region. There are only 53km of pistes in Mürren but there is enough to keep strong intermediates and advanced skiers and snowboarders entertained and the picture postcard village and striking setting are more than enough of a reason to visit. Mürren's small, car-free village is set on a sunny plateau above the valley and at the foot of the Schilthorn. The backdrop created by the Jungfrau, Mönch and Eiger mountains is the most famous in the Alps, largely due to its role in the James Bond movie *On Her Majesty's Secret Service*, from which the revolving Piz Gloria restaurant has become a prominent attraction. The village is reached either by a funicular and mountain railway from Lauterbrunnen, or by cable car from Stechelberg and Gimmelwald. The other ski resorts in the Jungfrau region, Wengen and Grindelwald, are accessible by train. It isn't the quickest journey but the intermediate skier or boarder might fancy a day or 2 exploring the extensive cruisy terrain. The Jungfrau lift pass covers Wengen and Grindelwald's slopes.

The history of Mürren adds to its quaintness. In 1911 Henry Lunn persuaded the Jungfrau railway to open during the winter and brought the first ski package holidays to Mürren. His son Sir Arnold founded slalom racing here and got both downhill and slalom racing accepted as Olympic sports. Arnold's son Peter Lunn was a member of the British skiing team, took part in 7 world championships and raced in the 1936 Olympics. The family still skis in Mürren today.

The Inferno race is another huge part of Mürren's history. The Inferno was organised for the first time in 1928 by Arnold Lunn and a group of 'ski crazy' Englishmen. When it started, long before ski lifts had been invented, competitors had to walk up to the top with seal skins bound to their skis. In 1928 just 16 skiers took part, all of them British – today the 15.8km race is so popular that participation has to be limited to 'only' 1800 competitors – less than half the skiers who would like to participate.

The mountains

Height: 1650–2971m

Ability	Rating
Expert	❄❄❄❄
Intermediate	❄❄❄½
Beginner	❄

Getting about

Mürren's 53km of pistes are part of the larger Jungfrau region which has 220km of pistes in total. Mürren's slopes aren't the best for beginners; the challenging slopes are best suited to strong intermediates and advanced skiers.

There are 4 options from Mürren village. The funicular from the centre of the village takes you to Allmendhubel, where you will find the nursery slope and a few blues and reds. Other easy and intermediate runs can be found at Schiltgrat (2145m), accessed by a chairlift from the edge of the village. The Winteregg section, with more blue and red runs, can be reached by train from Mürren or via the Maulerhubel chair. In good snow conditions it is possible to ski all the way down to Lauterbrunnen.

Expert skiers and boarders take the cable car to Birg and then the final stage up to the 2970m peak of the Schilthorn where you will find the revolving Piz Gloria restaurant. The descent from the Schilthorn peak is a classic run, a 1300m drop that provides impressive terrain and views. It is known as the Inferno run, as this is where the classic race begins (see Events) or the 007 run. The Inferno begins with a steep black descent that can have some good bumps later in the day. After some wide open skiing at Engetal, is the Kanonenrohr (the gun barrel), a narrow, steep, and often icy, run.

The park

The mountain twister funpark is near the Schiltgrat chair. It has a half pipe, jumps and a quarter pipe. There are other parks at Klein Scheidegg/Männl in Wengen and at the Bärgelegg lift in Grindelwald.

Off-piste and backcountry

There are some great off-piste areas in Mürren. From the Schilthorn there are a number of options, all of which require a guide and good snow conditions. For example, you can descend the northern valley or you can drop into the east bowl and ride down to the start of the Engetal piste. Tschingelkrache is a great run but it's very steep and demanding. Great powder can be found in the hidden valley, which you can get to from the Maulerhubel lift, and there is more superb off-piste at Blumental.

Touring is also an option. Easy 1-day tours include excursions to the Hundshorn (2928m), Sulegg (2412m) or over the Aletsch Glacier to Riederalp in Valais. Two-day tours include Äbeni Flue (3905m) or the Finstaarhorn (4273m) with an overnight stopover in an Alpine mountain hut. Contact Lauterbrunnen Mountain Guides Agency for more information (see Instruction).

Lift passes

Check the latest prices at www.wengen-muerren.ch

Instruction

Lauterbrunnen Mountain Guides Agency

Freeriding with a guide, glacier hikes, heli-skiing and 1–3-day ski tours are available.
0041 (0)33 821 61 00
www.be-je.ch

Swiss ski and snowboard school

As well as skiing and snowboarding, heli-skiing and off-piste guiding and lessons are also available. There is no competition for the Swiss ski and snowboard school, but the instruction is great. The school also organises a kindergarten for younger children.
0041 (0)33 855 12 47
www.muerren.ch/skischule

Other activities

Curling: There are curling tournaments for guests every Tuesday 4–6pm at the Alpine Sports Centre (0041 (0)33 856 86 86, www.muerren.ch/sportzentrum).

Ice skating: There are 2 artificial ice rinks at the Alpine Sports Centre (see above). Ice skates and sporting equipment can be hired from Stäger Sport, opposite the sports centre. Entrance to the ice rink is free if you are staying at one of the following hotels: Eiger, Anfi Palace, Alpenruh, Bellevue, Blumental, Edelweiss, Jungfrau, Alpenblick, Alpina, Eigerguesthouse, Regina.

Tobogganing: The run from Mürren finishes in Gimmelwald. Toboggans and bobs can be hired at local sports shops and night-time tobogganing is organised by the ski school.

Wellness: The Alpine Sports Centre (see above) has an indoor pool, Jacuzzi, sauna and steam bath, massage (for appointments contact the Mürren tourist office on 0041 (0)33 856 86 86) and yoga. There are also fitness rooms and squash courts.

Events

The **Inferno race** (www.inferno-muerren.ch) is a famous race in mid January and it's spectacular to watch. This tradition was started in 1928 by Sir Arnold Lunn, when he and a group of friends hiked to the top of the Schilthorn to race down the next day. The race starts just below the peak of the Schilthorn and ends in Lauterbrunnen (weather permitting). The winner of the 15.8-km. course completes the course in 15 minutes. A competent skier will cover the course in about 45 minutes.

The official documentation for the race explains that it's the all-rounder who will come out on top: 'The upper part of the course demands downhill turning technique and an optimal line. The middle section calls for an ideal downhill position and fast gliding. From the Kanonenrohr to the Höhenlücke technically superior skiers come into their own. Over the stretch from Maulerhubel to Winteregg, skating step and arm power can be all-important. And from Winteregg-Spriessenkehr to Lauterbrunnen optimal equipment, a clean downhill position and – not least – mental stamina can be the key to a fast final time.'

The **Scaramanga** is a fancy dress ski race from the Winteregg chairlift on New Year's Day.

Accommodation

The **Anfi Palace** (0041 (0)33 856 99 99) is a grand old hotel in a great location, with fabulous views of the Eiger. It has direct access to the sports centre, the ice rink is opposite and it's near the funicular to Almendhubel. There is a bar in the hotel, and the Inferno disco bar in the basement. The 3-star **Hotel Alpenruh** (0041 (0)33 856 88 00, www.alpenruh-muerren.ch) is a gorgeous hotel, and it's as close to the Schilthornbahn cable car as you can get. It is a restored chalet with, once again, fantastic views. The **Jungfrau** (0041 (0)33 856 64 64, www.hoteljungfrau.ch) is right in the centre of town, near the sports centre. It looks traditional from the outside but inside it's very modern. Southside rooms have views to the Eiger, Mönch and Jungfrau and northside to the Birg and Schilthorn mountains.

For budget options, **Hotel Regina** (0041 (0)33 855 42 42, www.regina-muerren.ch) is a good value hotel/hostel. **Eiger Guesthouse** (0041 (0)33 856 54 60, www.eigerguesthouse.com) is the other good value option. It's Swiss-Scottish run, and is a cosy and relaxed hotel with a restaurant, bar and games room. It's located near the BLM train station. Some rooms have private bathrooms.

Eating out

On the mountain

The revolving **Piz Gloria** (0041 (0)33 856 21 59) at the peak of the Schilthorn was made famous by the Bond film *On Her Majesty's Secret Service*. The building was part way through construction when the filmmakers found it. They wanted to use it in the movie as Blofeld's hideout (Piz Gloria), and therefore agreed to make a financial contribution towards the completion of the restaurant in return for exclusive use of the building during filming. The restaurant kept the name that it was given in the film and has a James Bond exhibition on the lower floor, showing the clip from the film when James Bond escapes and (a model of) Piz Gloria blows up. The cuisine and ambience isn't anything to get particularly excited about, but it's worth a visit for the incredible views and the novelty of a restaurant that revolves. In an hour you'll do 360 degrees.

The **Schilthorn Hütte** (0041 (0)79 746 58 67) at the top of the Kandahar chairlift is 1 of the best mountain huts, serving traditional Swiss food. **Gimmelen** (0041 (0)33 855 1366) has fantastic cheese fondues. **Suppenalp** (033 855 17 26, www.suppenalp.ch), at the bottom of the Hindenburg run, has a great sunny terrace and tasty food cooked on the wood stove. You can also stay here overnight – there are double and multi-bed rooms, as well as a dormitory with space for 22 people.

In town

Stäger stübli (0041 (0)33 855 13 16) is a great bar/restaurant in Mürren, and one of the few restaurants not connected to a hotel. It serves a generous steak and chips or tasty lamb chops and has a lively bar to boot. **Hotel Eiger Stübli** (0041 (0)33 856 54 54, www.hoteleiger.com) has excellent traditional Swiss food – great fondues. More traditional food can be enjoyed in the rustic atmosphere of the **Hotel Blumental** (0041 (0)33 855 18 26, www.muerren.ch/blumental). For Italian meals **Peppino** (0041 (0)33 856 99 99) at the Anfi Palace is good.

Bars and clubs

Mürren is a peaceful town but there are some good bars around. Start the night with a few cheap drinks in the **Hotel Regina** (see Accommodation) or the small and cosy pub in the **Eiger Guesthouse** (see Accommodation), where the Brits hang out. As well as cheap beer there is a pool table, table football and darts. The rustic **Stägerstubli** has the best atmosphere in town and is popular with the locals for a beer and some food.

'There's cheap beer, a pool table, table football and darts'

The **Balloon Bar** in the Anfi Palace (see Accommodation) is fairly trendy and the bar itself is in a hot-air balloon basket. **Tächi Bar** in the Hotel Eiger is a good meeting place and often has a DJ or live music. The **Blüemlichäller** disco in Hotel Blumental (see Eating out In town) is another good club – if you're drunk – and the **Inferno** disco in the Anfi Palace has a mixed clientele and is a great place for a cheesy dance later on. The DJ booth is in a pink Cadillac.

Getting there

By car

Take the motorway to Interlaken. Take the Wilderswil exit then on to Lauterbrunnen or further on to Stechelberg. There is ample parking space at both resorts. From Lauterbrunnen, the BLM brings you up to Mürren. From Stechelberg the Schilthorn cableway brings you up to Mürren.

By plane

Zürich (148km) Transfer takes around 3 hours.
Geneva (224km) Transfer takes around 4 hours.
The most frequently used international airports are Geneva and Zürich, but you can also fly into Bern or Basle.

By train

Take the Eurostar from London St Pancras to Paris, then an overnight train, changing at Zurich, Interlaken Ost and Lauterbrunnen to arrive at Mürren station in the resort. Contact Rail Europe (0870 830 4862, www.raileurope.co.uk) or European Rail (020 7387 0444, www.europeanrail.com).

Useful facts and phone numbers

Tourist office

T: 0041 (0)33 856 86 86
F: 0041 (0)33 856 86 96
W: www.wengen-muerren.ch

Emergency services

- Police, Wengen: 0041 (0)33 855 47 01
- Police, Lauterbrunnen: 0041 (0)33 855 76 11
- Ambulance, Lauterbrunnen: 0041 (0)33 855 37 00

Doctors

- Dr Rolf Heimlinger: 0041 (0)33 855 17 10

Taxis

- Feuz Markus Transporte: 0041 (0)33 855 18 70
- Stäger Transporte AG: 0041 (0)33 855 24 80

Saas-Fee

The perfect Swiss 'chocolate box' town, this resort is a favourite, especially in summer.

On the slopes	Rating
Snow reliability	❄❄❄❄❄
Parks	❄❄❄½
Off-piste	❄❄❄½
Off the slopes	
Après ski	❄❄❄❄
Nightlife	❄❄❄❄
Eating out	❄❄❄❄
Resort charm	❄❄❄❄❄

The resort

The village of Saas-Fee does not feel, as many do, like a functional resort built purely to support the winter sports; it is a magical place that you can easily fall in love with. The unique atmosphere is traditional and romantic, and the entire town is surrounded by 13 imposing, 4000m peaks, including the highest mountain in Switzerland, the Dom (4545m above sea level).The traffic-free town and the chalet-style buildings contribute to the relaxing pace of this charming glacier village, and it manages to provide a varied and rich nightlife. In the winter the village can be very cold; conditions are best for autumn or spring skiing when there is plenty of sun and snow. Saas-Fee is also the perfect resort for summer skiing on the glacier.

The mountains

Height: 1800–3600m

Ability	Rating
Expert	❄❄❄
Intermediate	❄❄❄❄
Beginner	❄❄❄❄❄

Getting about

Take two Alpin Express cable cars to Felskinn at 3000m. From here you can either enjoy some long, sweeping red runs back to town or take the highest underground funicular in the world, the Metro Alpin to the Mittelallalin glacier (3500m). When visibility is good you can apparently see the lights of Milan. It will take you around 40 minutes to reach the top.

Winter

There are 100km of marked pistes in Saas-Fee in the winter, most designed for the beginner/intermediate skier or boarder. The 32 runs comprise 13 blue trails, 14 red and 5 black. Saas-Fee has a great reputation for maintaining the runs in tiptop condition, allowing the intermediate riders a great base from which to push themselves to the next level. The unprepared mogul piste under the Längfluh chairlift puts those knees to the test.

Summer

The glacier provides 20km of ski slopes for summer skiing, geared to high-standard riding. It is best to get out early, as the glacier closes some time between 12pm (in high summer) and 2pm. The runs are pretty good, but if you're not doing slalom training or hitting the park, you may end up twiddling your thumbs. If you are hitting the park, you will not be disappointed. Get used to the T-bars and draglifts; chairlifts are difficult to manoeuvre and so are not practical with the moving glacier.

The park

There is a park in the winter, but it is far better maintained in the summer. Saas-Fee was one of the first resorts to put real money in to develop the park and skier/boardercross. It is, therefore, renowned for hosting many of the major competitions such as the Rip Curl Challenge and the World Cup Half Pipe events. Professionals often train here in the summer, and ski and board manufacturers are regularly spotted testing their products.

The park is changed regularly but always consists of a super half pipe, 3 big kickers ranging from 6m to 12m gaps and a huge range of rails. There are plenty of table-top jumps for learning and practising new tricks, before stepping it up to the bigger ones. The atmosphere in the park is superb; a DJ often plays at the bottom and photographers and cameramen are frequently spotted filming for the latest movies.

Off-piste and backcountry

It is wise to be cautious when exploring the off-piste around a glacier due to the crevasses and concealed dangers. However, this does not mean that there aren't any off-piste opportunities to be had. There are 3 pistes that are marked as yellow or off-piste runs, but there are a few more. The absence of glacier on the Plattjen makes it a great place to find fresh tracks through the trees. The trees also shelter the snow, so it stays in good condition all day. Be warned though: this area can be quite challenging!

'A great place to find fresh tracks through the trees'

The Maste 4 is another good place to keep you out of the way of crevasse dangers. It is a relatively easy powder run – a perfect place for cruising. From the top of the Alpin Express you can find the Morenia, great if you like the steeps, and it's hardly ever touched. It is very important only to attempt this after a good snowfall and, even then, it must be done early in the morning. The Hannig, at the other side of town to the Alpin Express (used for hill-walking and sledging), is a great place for an early morning hike. There is a lift from the bottom of the resort, but they won't let you on with your board or skis so it is a bit of a trek. If you fancy a backcountry adventure, set off early from Brittania Hutte and enjoy the legendary, 1.5-hour freeride down to Saas-Almagell. This is pretty challenging, especially at the beginning, and is only recommended with a guide.

Lift passes

Check the latest prices at www.saas-fee.ch

Instruction

Eskimos Snowboard School

This is a well-known school with courses that range from basic to freestyle/carving.
0041 (0)27 957 49 04
www.eskimos.ch

Saas-Fee Ski and Snowboard School

This school comes highly recommended by locals – not that there is a huge amount of choice. All instructors speak a variety of languages.
0041 (0)27 957 23 48
www.skischule-saas-fee.ch

British Freeski Camps

These run for 3 or 4 weeks in the summer every year, and are organised by Warren Smith. You can sign up for the whole time or any 1 week. On the camp, you have the choice of hitting the park, perfecting the skier cross course or improving your technical skills. The top professional skiers in Britain gather together for these camps, some coaching (Andy Bennett, Dave Young, Pat Sharples, Paddy Graham and James Woods) and others training, so it's a great place to introduce yourself to the British ski scene.
0044 (0)1525 374757
www.britishfreeskicamps.com

Popcorn shop

www.popcorn.ch
For buying or renting snowboards or freestyle skis we highly recommend this shop/bar, located right in the centre of town near the clock tower. They always have the latest equipment and clothing and are also happy to offer their expert advice.

Other activities

Always ask if there is a discount with a guest card, obtainable from your hotel or apartment landlord.

Winter and summer

Bobsleigh: The Feeblitz Bobsleigh is a 900m long toboggan run – great fun for all the family. It can be adapted to suit the adrenaline junkie – although not 'officially' recommended, it has been known for riders not to apply the brakes and keep their eyes closed. We didn't tell you to do it though.

Ice grotto: Visit the Allain Ice Pavilion – the biggest ice grotto in the world. It can be accessed from the Metro Alpin top station hall at 3500m above sea level.

Mountain climbing: The mountain climbing schools offer a number of activities for keen climbers, or those who fancy giving it a go. Rock and ice climbing, canyoning, glacier trekking and mountaineering are available for both beginners and advanced climbers. For a James Bond-type activity, the 'Alpine Gorge' is an opportunity to be seized. This is a mountain descent from Saas-Fee to Saas-Grund, where you make your way down with the aid of a guide, fixed steel ropes, ladders, 3 Tyroliennes and a suspension bridge. A final option is to conquer 1 of the 3 Via Ferratas (secured climbing routes). The Mittaghorn is fairly easy and good for families, the Jägihorn is pretty difficult and should be undertaken with a guide and the Via Ferrata del Lago is recommended as a 2-day tour.

For further information contact Saas-Fee Guides Climbing School (0041 (0)27 957 44 64 www.saasfeeguides.ch) or Active Dreams (0041 (0)78 825 82 73, www.weissmies.ch).

Tennis and badminton: There are 2 indoor tennis courts and 4 indoor badminton courts available.

Wellness centre: If you're looking for a good way to while away a bad weather day look no further than the Bielen Wellness Centre (0041 (0)27 957 24 75, www.super-dome.ch). There is a 25m swimming pool, as well as a sauna, solarium, whirlpool, steam bath, solar sun bathing, fitness room, table tennis and table football. The 5-star Hotel Ferienart contains the Paradisa wellness centre (0041 (0)27 958 19 16, www.ferienart.ch) where non-residents can pay for a day's spa package. We'd love to tell you what it was like but we couldn't afford it.

Summer only

Adventure forest: You can swing from tree to tree using rope swings and zip wires and walk across hanging bridges.

Crazy golf: A fantastic way to pass an hour or so! Not a course to be sniffed at, it really is quite difficult and should be taken very seriously.

Golf: A 9-hole alpine golf course can be found just behind the Kalbermatten sports field.

Hiking: There's loads of hiking to be had in and around Saas-Fee. Contact the tourist office for all the details.

Mountain biking: Bikers will be in their element in the summer, as there are around 70km of trails. The marked trails suit a range of abilities. Contact the tourist office for a detailed mountain bike map.

Sports: The Kalbermatten sports ground offers football, basketball, volleyball, a mini skate ramp for skateboarding and in-line skating and tennis courts. Pit-Pat (a weird combination of snooker and crazy golf) is located nearby, at the Hotel Waldesruh.

Winter only

Heliskiing and snow touring: These are definitely worth checking out later on in the season. Contact Active Dreams (see Mountain climbing for details).

Husky tours: These run several times a week and can be booked at the tourist office.

Ice skating: The natural ice rink is open 8am–10pm from mid-December to the end of February.

Sledge run: A 5km sledge run can be found at Hannig. On Tuesdays and Thursdays (6–9pm) you can sledge at night. There is also an 11km run in the nearby town of Saas-Grund.

Snow shoe trekking: This is organised daily. Contact the tourist office.

Snow tubing and air boarding: This and occurs several times a week. The snow tube lift in Saas-Grund is open 3–5.30pm and 8–10pm.

Events

Saas-Fee is a very popular venue for a wide variety of events because the height of the glacier pretty much guarantees snow all year round. The **FIS World Cup** in November has been held in Saas-Fee for many years, with disciplines for skiers and boarders in the half pipe and skier/boardercross. The **Dutch and British Championships** have also been held here over the years. The **Saas-Fee Ride** takes place every summer, usually at the end of July, and many of the best freestyle skiers in Europe turn up for the event. If you fancy your chances at entering the competition or if you just want to improve your style, why not book on to the British Freeski Camps (www.britishfreeskicamps.com) that take place in the few weeks running up to the Saas-Fee Ride.

The **Ice Climbing World Cup** in February is one of the biggest events in Saas-Fee. The world's best ice climbers strut their stuff on a 30m high wall of ice in the car park of Saas-Fee. At the end of April is the last event in the famous **TTR** (Ticket To Ride) tour.

> 'The world's best ice climbers strut their stuff on a 30m high wall of ice'

Accommodation

There are a variety of packages available to suit all budgets. Renting an apartment is often a good option. Bear in mind that the north end of the village is a bit of a hike from the lifts, so always make sure you check the location before you book.

For a funky, unique, well-placed and friendly hotel call the **Dom Hotel** (0041 (0)27 957 77 00, www.uniquedom.com). The PS2s in every room and the friendly staff make this hotel our top pick for the younger clientele. The rooms are minimalist and funky with wooden floors, and the balconies have stunning views. The hotel also contains the hugely popular Popcorn bar and the Living Room, a stylish chill-out bar.

If being near the slopes is of utmost importance to you, check out **La Gorge Apart-Hotel** (0041 (0)27 958 16 80, www.lagorge.ch). It has a beautiful location sitting above a deep creek and contains a charming restaurant. It is only 100m from the lifts and is also close to all the facilities of the town. The rooms are fairly basic but contain a little kitchen so you can save money on food.

For a luxury apartment at a decent price check out the 5-star **Shangri-La Apartments** (0041 (0)27 958 15 15, www.rhone.ch/zumlerch). The apartments are huge (47–83m^2) and contain Sky TV, a DVD player, internet connection, a coffee machine, a dishwasher, a washing machine and a massive balcony, and there is a sauna and whirlpool room for the use of guests.

If price is no object and you enjoy fancy hotels, it has to be the 5-star **Hotel Ferienart** (0041 (0)27 958 19 00, www.ferienart.ch). It has all the charm and splendour and prices that you would expect, with 6 restaurants, a piano bar, dance hall and beauty spa. The spa and beauty salon are very nice.

> 'Dramatic views that can be enjoyed from comfy deckchairs'

Eating out

On the mountain

The world's highest revolving restaurant is at the top lift station on the Mittelallalin glacier. It spins all the way round about once an hour. The views are stunning, the food is tasty and we think it's pretty good value too. It's definitely worth doing at least once and you should book if you want a table by the window (0041 (0) 27 957 17 71).

Other restaurants to check out are the popular, rustic **Gletschergrotte**, (0041 (0)27 957 21 60, www.gletschergrotte.ch) halfway down from Speilboden and the more trendy hangout, **Popcorn Plaza** at Längfluh (0041 (0)27 957 21 32), which has dramatic views that can be enjoyed from comfy deckchairs on the huge terrace.

In town

La Ferme (0041 (0)27 958 15 69) is a superb restaurant in the centre of town. It has a traditional, rustic and charming atmosphere and all the staff don the traditional dress. It's not cheap, but is good value as the food is fantastic.

The **Bodmen** restaurant (0041 (0)27 957 20 75, www.waldhues-bodmen.ch) takes 10–15 minutes to walk to along a beautiful woodland path and is well worth the trip. It's a beautiful place to sit at lunchtime in the summer as the huge terrace has marvellous views and goats scuttle in-between the tables. In the evening it's not too formal and has great food, from fondues to fillet steak. If you wish, you can request the table next to a glass panel with views into a barn so you can see lots of chickens and other farmyard animals strutting their stuff while you eat. It's not advisable to ask for this table if you fancy tucking into a chicken dish. To find the restaurant, walk past the Alpin Express lift station, in the opposite direction to town, and you will see a sign pointing you towards the Bodmen.

The **Fletschhorn** restaurant (0041 (0)27 957 21 31, www.fletschhorn.ch) is highly recommended, is highly expensive and has 18 points in the Gault & Millau gourmet guide. **Boccalino's** (0041 (0)27 957 17 31) is a great pizza restaurant on the main street serving pizzas, pasta and risottos. Probably the best value in town, this is a great place to eat if you're on a budget.

'This is a great place to eat if you're on a budget'

Bars and clubs

Saas-Fee has a very good night scene. The laws are such that there is no specific time at which a bar should close; if it's busy they will open until it's time to hit the slopes again. Dangerous stuff.

The **Popcorn bar** in the Dom Hotel (see Accommodation) is definitely at the centre of the action with good après ski, European DJs, live bands and the odd 'Diva Night' when they play all the classic cheesy music. Dressing up is optional. It's not cheap here though. The younger crowd tend to hang out at the **Happy Bar** (0041 (0)27 957 38 96), at the north end of town, where the drinks are cheaper, especially during happy hour.

If you are in the 25+ category you might favour the **Living Room** in the Dom Hotel (see Accommodation), which is more of a chill-out bar with sofas and candles. If the mood takes you later on, you can always head downstairs to the Popcorn for a drunken boogie. **Poison** nightclub (0041 (0)27 957 50 51) is popular and good fun. Again, it's more for the 25+ age group. Opposite the Popcorn is the **Alpen-Pub** (0041 (0)27 957 38 28), which has live music in the winter and on quieter nights is a great place to have a cosy beer and a game of darts.

If you intend to do your partying indoors, watch out for the 'hush police' who parade the streets after 10pm and can collar you into a fine if they think you're making too much noise.

Getting there

By car

From Calais, it will take around 10 hours to drive to Saas-Fee. Enter Switzerland above Lausanne and from there follow signs for Sion, and then Brig, where you are signed to Saas-Fee.

The village itself is car-free, so you will have to use the car park (open air or covered). The car park price per day decreases the longer you are staying and is cheaper if you have a guest card, which can be obtained from your hotel or apartment owner on arrival.

There are free phones in the unloading areas to call your hotel for a free lift or to call a taxi (free phone numbers are by the phone).

By plane

Geneva (234km) Transfer from Geneva is approximately 3 hours by car. If transfer is by train, change in Brig (or Visp) for the postbus, which takes you right to Saas-Fee. There are hourly connections from Brig from 06.15 to 20.05 and from Visp from 06.35 to 20.25. Reservations may be necessary with the post bus (0041 (0)27 958 11 45).

Zürich (246km) There are regular transfers to Brig or Visp. The transfer is approximately 3 hours.

By train

Take the Eurostar from London St Pancras to Paris, then an overnight train, changing at Zürich, to Brig, and then a local bus (57 minutes) to the resort. Contact Rail Europe (0870 830 4862, www.raileurope.co.uk) or European Rail (020 7387 0444, www.european rail.com). Bus tickets are purchased on the bus. (For people booking through European Rail to Swiss resorts, the rail fare includes the bus connection to resort, so there is no need to pay for a bus ticket.)

Useful facts and phone numbers

Tourist office

T: 0041 (0)27 958 18 58
F: 0041 (0)27 958 18 60
W: www.saas-fee.ch

Direct reservations

T: 0041 (0)27 958 18 68
F: 0041 (0)27 958 18 70
W: www.saas-fee.ch

Emergency services

- Police: 117
- Police station (by the car park): 0041 (0)27 958 11 60
- Ambulance: 114
- Breakdown service: 140
- Weather information: 0900 57 30 70 (CHF1.49/min)

Doctors

- Stefan and Stephanie Kuonen, Saas-Fee: 0041 (0)27 957 58 59
- Medical Centre, Saas-Grund: 0041 (0)27 957 11 55
- Pharmacy, Saas-Fee: 0041 (0)27 957 26 18
- Dentist, St Imseng: 0041 (0)27 957 20 52

Electro-taxis

- Ambros: 0041 (0)79 439 10 29
- Taxi Anselm: 0041 (0)79 220 21 37
- Bolero: 0041 (0)27 958 11 35
- Center Reisen: 0041 (0)27 958 11 33
- Imseng: 0041 (0)27 957 33 44

St Moritz

Glitzy, glam and exclusive – and the riding's pretty good too!

On the slopes	Rating
Snow reliability	❄❄❄❄
Parks	❄❄
Off-piste	❄❄❄❄½
Off the slopes	
Après ski	❄❄❄
Nightlife	❄❄❄❄
Eating out	❄❄❄❄
Resort charm	❄❄❄❄

The resort

St Moritz is absolutely fabulous: stunning mountains, fantastic freeriding and a striking resort. Set over the beautiful Lake San Murezzan, St Moritz Dorf is one of the most famous and exclusive resorts in Europe. The majority of the hotels are 5 and 4-star and are frequented by fur-clad guests and small poodles. If you need more evidence of exclusivity than the Versace and Chanel shops, St Moritz is host to the Cartier Polo World Cup on Snow. It was the upper crust Brits who established the style of the resort, and they're never too far away.

'Stunning mountains and a striking resort'

The mountains

Height: 1327–4354m

Ability	Rating
Expert	❄❄❄❄
Intermediate	❄❄❄❄
Beginner	❄❄❄

Getting about

From Dorf a funicular takes you up to the sunny slopes of Corviglia. From St Moritz Bad you can get a gondola up to these slopes and there is the advantage that you can ride back down into town. However, if you place value on nightlife and shopping, we would still recommend staying in Dorf. The other slopes on Corvatsch are a bus or car ride away, which is worth it if you like cruisy reds or a blast in the park. The best time to check out this mountain is for the Snow Night Parties each Friday, during which 5km of pistes are floodlit. The parties carry on until 2am and are more focused on drinking than riding. Diavolezza is also considered to be part of the St Moritz ski area but it's a half hour drive away. The avant-garde lift system and 350km of pistes are impressive, but it is a shame that the areas aren't linked.

The park

The Mellowpark on Corviglia has a total of 30 obstacles and stays open late for those who can't bear to leave.

Off-piste and backcountry

The off-piste possibilities in St Moritz are great, but not obvious, so it's a good place to invest in a guide if you want to make the most of the area. The powder hounds should head straight to the peaks of Piz Nair (3057m) or Piz Corvatsch. There are some tricky spots, but the snow usually stays in good nick. Get there early after snow fall if you're after fresh tracks. Some steep and deep can also be found opposite the Marguns lift.

Lift passes

Check the latest prices at www.bergbahnen engadin.ch

Instruction

Suvretta Snowsports School

0041 (0)81 836 61 61
www.suvrettasnowsports.ch

Swiss Ski School

0041 (0)81 830 01 01
www.skischool.ch

Other activities

Bobsled: Pros can get up to speeds of 136kph on the natural bobsled run. The races and the championships are great to watch and, if you fancy it, you can have a taxi ride driven by a pro or you can have a go yourself with instructions. The bobsled run has seen the Swiss European Championships, Bobsled World Championships and two Olympic Winter Games. Call 0041 (0)81 830 02 00, or check out www.olympia-bobrun.ch.

'Pros can get up to speeds of 136kph on the natural bobsled run'

The 100-year-old unique Cresta Run (www.cresta-run.com) is another chance to reach speeds of 136kph – but only if you're a bloke. Apparently the reason for the 'men only' policy is that the bumps and blows might cause breast cancer in women! Events on the Cresta Run to look out for include the Heaton Gold Cup, Curzon Cup, Grand National and Gunter Sachs Challenge Cup.

Casino: The casino in St Moritz Bad is definitely worth a look (0041 (0)81 837 54 54, www.casinostmoritz.ch).

Curling: Either rent the rink or book a lesson at the Curling Centre (0041 (0)81 833 45 88). Events held here include the Jackson Cup and the St Moritz Grand Prix.

Horse-drawn sleigh rides: Take a romantic horse-drawn sleigh ride over the frozen lake and through the Staz forest. You can find the sleighs in St Moritz Bad, next to the church.

Horse riding: Indoor horse riding and group trail riding are available (0041 (0)81 833 57 33).

Ice skating and hockey: Open air ice skating, hockey and curling takes place on the Ice Arena (0041 (0)81 833 50 30).

Kitesailing at Silvaplana: Beginners and pros welcome (0041 (0)81 828 97 67, www.kitesailing.ch).

Paragliding and hang-gliding: These take place every hour 10am–4pm, from Corviglia mountain top (0041 (0)79 353 21 59, www.luftarena.ch).

Shopping: A favourite activity of visitors to St Moritz – bring your best credit card with you.

Skydiving: Skydive in tandem with Viviane Wegrath (0041 (0)79 405 13 82, www.vivisurf.ch). For 2 weeks in March it is possible to land on the frozen lake.

Sledging: If the boblsed runs all sound a bit too much for you, there is some normal sledging (a 4.2km run) from Muottas to Punt Muragl. Sledges can be rented from the bottom of the Muottas Muragl funicular. It is open every day 9.30am–4pm.

Snow night parties: These Friday night parties on Corvatsch are a great place to go for riding, drinking and partying. Have a bite to eat at the charming Alpetta Hut and a few beers at the Hossa Bar.

Tennis and squash: Courts can be found in the Corviglia Tennis Centre in St Moritz Bad (0041 (0)81 833 15 00).

Wellness: For some pampering, head to the Medical Therapy Centre, Heilbad St Moritz (0041 (0)81 833 30 62, www.heilbad-stmoritz.ch), where you can take a mineral or aromatic bath, beauty treatment, mud bath or pack, massage, physical therapy, stone therapy and a solarium. There is also an indoor pool in St Moritz Bad (0041 (0)81 837 33 33) and the Kempinski High Alpine Spa (0041 (0)81 838 38 38, www.kempinski-stmoritz.com).

Events

Get the latest on the hundreds of events that take place in St Mortiz at www.stmoritz.ch.

Events in St Moritz take a unique slant with a focus on traditional British high society events on the St Moritz frozen lake.

The **Concours Hippique**, an international equestrian jumping tournament on snow (www.stmoritz-concours.ch) is in January. This annual event sees more than 100 horses competing in 15 tests, including ski jöring (with a riderless horse pulling a skier).The amazing **Polo on Snow** (www.polostmoritz.com), in which around 60 polo horses and 24 of the world's best polo players compete also takes place in January.

Cricket on Ice (www.cricket-on-ice.com) in early February, has been played on the lake since 1989 and **Winter Golf** since 1978. Red golf balls and white greens are a unique sight in the Winter Golf Tournament in Silvaplana (www.silvaplana-events.ch). **White Turf Horse Races** take place the first 3 Sundays in February (www.whiteturf.ch). There are short-distance, flat, trotting and ski jöring events and each winter the prize money totals a whopping CHF500000.

The **gourmet festival** at the end of January/beginning of February (www.stmoritz-gourmetfestival.ch) is yet another long-standing tradition, in which the best chefs from all over the world inspire young talented chefs from St Moritz hotel kitchens. The Grand Gourmet Finale once again takes place on the St Moritz frozen lake.

Engadin Cross-country Skiing Marathon is on the second Sunday in March, and 13000 participants will take part in this 4.2km race. Check out www.engadin-skimarathon.ch.

Accommodation

The place to stay is St Moritz Dorf, unless you are happy to sacrifice the atmosphere and nightlife for the benefit of being able to ride back to town, in which case you should stay in St Moritz Bad.

There is a huge range of 5 and 4-star hotels to choose from. Many of the 5-star hotels are very grand and a bit stuffy. The impressive **Badrutts Palace** (0041 (0)81 837 10 00, www.badruttspalace.com) is one of the most distinguished. The **Kulm Hotel** (0041 (0)81 836 80 00, www.kulmhotel-stmoritz.ch) is another imposing one; remarkable to look at, but only the true aristocracy will feel comfortable.

We much preferred the smart, comfortable and friendly 4-stars in the centre of town. The **Schweizerhof** (0041 (0)81 837 07 07, www.schweizerhofstmoritz.ch) is 1 of the best, with amazing staff, a beautiful dining room, and a relaxation room on the top floor where you can chill out in your dressing gown after a nice sauna and read a magazine, looking out at the beautiful river through the windows. It has 1 of the best locations, 1 of the best restaurants and 3 of the best bars in town. The **Steffani** (0041 (0)81 836 96 96, www.steffani.ch), across the road, is another great option and the 4-star **Crystal** (0041 (0)81 836 26 26, www.crystalhotel.ch) is superb, and is as close to the funicular as you can get.

'One of the best locations, 1 of the best restaurrants and 3 of the best bars in town'

The distinctively decorated 3-star **Hotel Arte** (0041 (0)81 837 58 58, www.arte-stmoritz.ch) is one of the least expensive, central hotels but don't expect a bargain. You can also contact the tourist office (0041 (0)81 837 33 99), who are incredibly helpful, and will be happy to help you find a hotel or apartment to suit your budget.

Eating out

On Corviglia

If your parched mouth will sip nothing but champagne alongside a soupçon of caviar, and you managed to squash your platinum credit card into your white fur-lined ski suit without spoiling the lining, swish your way over to the **Marmite** restaurant (0041 (0)81 833 63 55, www.mathisfood.ch), where your palate and wallet are in for an exquisite shock. **Paradiso** (0041 (0)81 833 40 02, www.el-paradiso.ch) and **Trutz Lodge** (0041 (0)81 833 70 30, www.suvrettahouse.ch) are both charming, traditional and have beautiful views.

On Corvatsch

The **Hossa Bar** (0041 (0)81 834 32 32) is a heated tent with music and a packed terrace. This place is perfect on the Snow nights (see Other activities, when it stays open until late. The **Hahnensee** (0041 (0)81 833 36 34), on the run back down to St Moritz Bad, is great for lunch, après and evening meals. The **Alpetta** (0041 (0)81 828 86 30, www.alpetta.ch) is charming and rustic. The owner shoots the game himself.

In town

Secondo (0041 (0)81 834 99 90, www.younic.ch/secondo.htm) is one of our favourite restaurants, and a break from the swanky white tableclothed eateries. It is stylish and colourful, with a busy atmosphere and a wide range of food, from tapas and Mexican to pasta and local dishes. **California Bar** (0041 (0)81 833 61 88) is good for a quick burger or snack, as is **Bobby's Bar** (0041 (0)81 834 42 83, www.bobbys-pub.ch), with hot dogs, burgers and chicken nuggets. You should also pop into the renowned **Hanselmanns** (0041 (0)81 833 38 64, www.hanselmann.ch) at tea time; it's part of the St Moritz history and everyone goes there at least once.

'It's part of the St Moritz history and everyone goes there at least once'

Of the smart places to eat, the **Acla** (0041 (0)81 837 07 07, www.schweizerhofstmoritz.ch) at the Schweizerhof is superb. The **Grissini** (0041 (0)81 836 26 66, www.crystalhotel.ch) at the Crystal (with 13 Gault & Millau points) is not as extortionate as it looks. **Cascade** brasserie (0041 (0)81 833 33 44, www.cascade-stmoritz.ch) serves pasta, meat, salads and risotto. For posh pizza head to the beautiful and cosy **Chesa Veglia** (0041 (0)81 837 26 70, www.badruttspalace.com/chesaveglia). Chesa Veglia is owned by the prestigious Badrutts Palace and is famous due to the Club Privé – apparently the most exclusive club in St Moritz, attended only by appointed lifetime members.

For a night of pure indulgence, take a 5-minute taxi to **Jöhri's Talvo** in Chamfér (0041 (0)81 833 44 55, www.talvo.ch). In a converted hay barn, you will find a beautiful, cosy, candlelit restaurant on 2 levels. If you are planning a romantic night, ask for 1 of the 2 tables on the separate balcony. It is definitely recommended to book, especially in high season. If caviar, foie gras and lobster with black truffles make your mouth water, you're in the right place. Jöhri's Talvo has 18 Gault & Millau points and 2 Michelin stars, making it the highest scoring restaurant in St Moritz.

The **Post Haus** (0041 (0)81 833 80 80) is a restaurant/bar lounge designed by the famous architect Lord Norman Foster and forms part of the Murezzan complex. The restaurant, serving pasta, steaks and fish, is fairly impressive but is still welcoming. The lounge menu includes burgers, club sandwiches and roast beef sandwiches.

Bars and clubs

Après ski is good at the outdoor **Roo Bar** (0041 (0)81 837 50 50, www.hotelhauser.ch) in the main square in good weather. Later, there are loads of bars to choose from, with varying degrees of exclusivity. **Bobby's Pub** (see Eating out In town) has a British-pub feel, with a comfy 'outdoor' area indoors and pool tables. The **Cava** bar in the Steffani (0041 (0)81 836 96 96, www.steffani.ch) is a cavernous bar with a relaxed and friendly feel, and over the road in the Schweizerhof Hotel (see Accommodation), you will often find live music in the packed and great fun **Stübli** bar and the country-style **Muli** bar and live jazz in the **Piano** bar. If you're still going, head to the bar/club **Diamond** (0041 (0)81 834 97 65, www.diamond-stmoritz.ch), opposite the Kulm hotel, or the **Vivai** (0041 (0)81 836 97 23, www.vivai.ch) back at the Steffani. If you have infinite cash, and popped your jacket and tie into your ski or board bag, you could head to the famous **Kings Club** at Badrutts Palace (0041 (0)81 837 26 70, www.badruttspalace.com/kingsclub) or to the **Casino** (0041 (0)81 837 54 54, www.casinostmoritz.ch) down in St Moritz Bad.

Getting there

By car

The road to St Moritz seems to go on forever but it is well maintained. From Zürich the driving time is approximately 3 hours, from Milan about 3 hours and from Munich about 4 hours.

By plane

Zürich (200km) Transfer will take you 3 hours by car, 4 by bus.
Basel (290km) Transfer takes 4 hours by car.
Munich (360km) Transfer takes 4 hours by car.

By train

Take the Eurostar from London St Pancras to Paris, then an overnight train, changing at Chur to arrive at St Moritz station in the resort. Contact Rail Europe (0870 830 4862, www.raileurope.co.uk) or European Rail (020 7387 0444, www.europeanrail.com).

Useful facts and phone numbers

Tourist office

T: 0041 (0)81 837 33 33
F: 0041 (0)81 937 33 77
W: www.stmoritz.ch

Direct reservations

T: 0041 (0)81 837 33 99

Emergency services

- Police: 117
- Medical emergency: 144
- Heli-rescue:1414

Doctors

- Dr P R Berry: 0041 (0)81 833 79 79
- Dr P Hasler: 0041 (0)81 833 83 83
- Dr F Kuthan: 0041 (0)81 833 18 48
- Dr C Riederer: 0041 (0)81 833 30 30
- Dr P F Signotell: 0041 (0)81 833 69 43
- Dr P O Steiner: 0041 (0)81 833 17 77

Taxis

- Cattaneo Taxi: 0041 (0)81 833 69 69, www.ag-cattaneo-taxi-stmoritz.ch
- Erich's Taxi: 0041 (0)81 833 35 55
- Taxi Alessandro: 0041 (0)81 833 70 49
- Taxi Angelo: 0041 (0)79 312 88 09, www.limousineangelo.ch
- Taxi Bären: 0041 (0)81 833 72 72, www.stmoritz-taxi.ch

Verbier

Extreme in every sense, Verbier is one not to miss.

On the slopes	Rating
Snow reliability	❄❄❄❄½
Parks	❄❄❄
Off-piste	❄❄❄❄❄
Off the slopes	
Après ski	❄❄❄❄
Nightlife	❄❄❄❄
Eating out	❄❄❄❄
Resort charm	❄❄❄

The resort

Verbier is a fantastically fashionable resort and has an equally fierce mountain. If you're a keen freeriding skier or boarder you won't get bored with the mountain or the nightlife, even if you're there for the season.

Verbier's slopes are linked with Thyon, Veysonnaz and Nendaz, which together form the Quatre Vallées (Four Valleys). Although the other valleys have some great terrain, exploring Verbier is enough of a challenge for most and getting over to the other valleys isn't as easy as, for example, France's Trois Vallées. Within Verbier, there are slopes for all levels of rider but it is the freeriders who will really make the most of what Verbier has to offer – steep and deep are what Verbier does best.

After a hard day conquering the Bec des Rosses or back of Mont Fort don't expect a couple of beers then bed. Verbier's après ski is as demanding as its mountain and it's impossible to escape before the early hours. The resort is a popular destination for the rich and famous, many a celebrity owns a chalet here, and some of the bars and clubs reflect this clientele. But Verbier has something for everyone – whatever vibe you're looking for you'll be able to find it somewhere in Verbier.

The mountains

Height: 1500–3330m

Ability	Rating
Expert	❄❄❄❄❄
Intermediate	❄❄❄❄
Beginner	❄❄

Getting about

Verbier is at the far side of the Quatre Vallées, connecting 412km of pistes. The skiing area of the Quatre Vallées links the ski runs of Verbier, La Tzoumaz, Nendaz, Veysonnaz, and Val de Bagnes/Entremont. Most will spend the majority of their time exploring the Verbier slopes but it is worth getting a Quatre Vallées pass to be able to go to the peak of Mont Fort, even if it is just for the view. The Mont Fort Glacier keeps the area pretty snowsure.

> 'The Mont Fort glacier keeps the area pretty snowsure'

Beginners should head to The Moulins or Les Esserts pistes and intermediates to Savoleyres, where you will find excellent snow on the Tzoumaz side and maximum sun on the Verbier side. Les Attelas and Les Ruinettes are also good for cruisy carvers. Experts will find Mont Fort the steepest and most challenging. The piste from the summit of Mont Fort is one of the most beautiful black runs in Europe. This slope hosts speed skiing competitions at the end of the season with a record speed of 201.83kph.

The park

The park, at La Chaux (www.neipark.ch), has been around for a while now, and has a good team of shapers working on it. The terrain is a little strange and the run-ins to some of the kickers are somewhat flat, which makes it hard to get the speed to clear the gaps. However, it does have a few good kickers at the top of the park and a good selection of rails including a C-rail, wall ride and up-flat-up. There is also a great big hip jump located at the bottom of the park. It's not the best place for learning freestyle, but advanced riders will enjoy it. The Verbier Ride Slopestyle event is held here and attracts Europe's best New School skiers. To see this park being ridden at its best, check this event out on www.verbierride.com. Snow cannons mean that two thirds of the park has guaranteed snow cover.

The Nendaz park (www.telenendaz.ch) is huge, with numerous rails, including rainbows, a C-box and a wall ride, as well as hips and a number of kickers. This park is great for all levels of freestyler and you can get to Nendaz from Verbier with a Quatre Vallées pass.

'Numerous rails, including a C-box and a wall ride'

Off-piste and backcountry

Verbier is the freeriding capital of Europe. It is a test for even the world's best big-mountain riders; Seth Morrison has said that this is his favourite area as there is so much challenging terrain. The Bec des Rosses face (home of the O'Neill Xtreme event, see Events) is one of the hardest faces in the world and should only be attempted by seriously good riders, with a guide. Mont Gele is the home of the Verbier Ride event, and once again has extreme terrain and some massive cliffs. There is a cable car up there but it's rarely open, so you usually have a 40-minute hike.

The back of the Mont Fort is another favourite. On a powder day this is the perfect spot to find amazing steeps, gullies and cliff drops. Getting out is quite hairy though, as there is a long traverse along the side of the dam on the way. Its difficulty varies depending on whereabouts you go, though we would not recommend it to anyone who wasn't a competent rider. For those who don't mind a steep climb, check out the Stairway to Heaven. It starts near the Col de Gentianes and takes you right over into the next valley. This place is known for its incredible snow conditions and you won't see many other riders around. If you need shelter from the weather, head across the valley to Bruson, the perfect place to ride through the trees.

Verbier also provides marked ski routes that are not groomed or patrolled. They are great for riders wanting to improve their off-piste riding. Good routes are the Vallon d'Arby and Col des Mines. You can get to these areas from the Lac des Vaux.

We highly recommend that you always carry the right equipment: avalanche transceiver, shovel, probe, helmet, back protector, etc. Also, if you are venturing into the unknown, take a qualified mountain guide to ensure that you get the best out of Verbier's incredible terrain. Three peaks are accessible from Verbier by helicopter: le Petit Combin (3672m), la Rosablanche (3336m) and L'Aiguille du Tour (3540m).

Lift passes

Check the latest prices at www.televerbier.ch

Instruction

Adrenaline Ski and Snowboard School

0041 (0)27 771 74 59
www.adrenaline-verbier.ch

European SnowSport

This is a British-run school with good half-day clinics in moguls, carving and telemarking.
0041 (0)27 771 62 22
www.europeansnowsport.com

La Fantastique

0041 (0)27 771 41 41
www.lafantastique.com

Powder Extreme

0041 (0)76 479 87 71/0208 675 5407 (UK)
www.powder-extreme.com

Verbier Sport Plus

The official ski school can be found here, as well as mountain guides and the parapenting centre.
0041 (0)27 775 33 63
www.verbiersportplus.ch

Warren Smith Ski Academy

Warren Smith is a leading UK freeskier and top performance coach. His Ski Academy has had huge media coverage in recent years with the unanimous agreement that Warren, and his team of talented and personable coaches, will hugely improve your ski technique and your confidence. The percentage of repeat clients speaks for itself.
0044 (0)1525 374757 (UK office)
0041 (0)79 359 65 66 (Swiss office)
www.warrensmith-skiacademy.com

Other activities

Adventure trail: There is an adventure trail open in both winter and summer, with a climbing wall in the summer and ice climbing in winter. Call Verbier Sport Plus (0041 (0)27 775 33 63).

Heliskiing/boarding and off-piste: For off-piste guiding or heliskiing/boarding call Verbier Sport Plus (see above) or Warren Smith (see Instruction).

Paragliding: Call the paragliding centre (0041 (0)27 771 68 18) for an introduction to paragliding, lessons, licence courses and tandem flights. Other paragliding schools are: Fly Time (0041 (0)79 606 12 64/027 776 12 22, www.fly-time.ch), Verbier Summits (079 313 56 77, www.verbier-summits.com), Max Biplace (0041 (0)27 771 55 55).

Sports centre: The Sports Centre (0041 (0)27 771 66 01) has a pool with whirlpools, a sauna and steam bath. As well as ice hockey events you can go ice skating yourself, or play squash or tennis. There are also 6 artificial curling rinks at the multi-sports centre.

Tobogganning: Take a sled down the 10km toboggan run from Savoleyres-Tzoumaz (call Téléverbier on 0041 (0)27 775 25 11).

Events

24 Heures Freeride, in mid-December, is a 24-hour charity event to launch the winter season. Participants ski in teams of 4, accumulate as many kilometres as they can and convert them into Swiss francs. It's also a chance to party for 24 hours with live concerts and DJs set up at Médran.

The **Verbier Ride** in February (www.verbierride.com) is one of Europe's leading New School skiing events. Watch international freeski athletes throw down amazing tricks in this pro/am Big Air and Rail Jam event. Ride Freesport also organises the **Saas-Fee Ride** (see Saas-Fee chapter, page 199 and www.saasfeeride.com) and the **London Ride** (www.thelondonride.com), held at the Metro Ski Show in October.

The **Nissan Xtreme** usually takes place mid–late March (www.xtremeverbier.com). Launched in 1996, this competition brings together the finest freeriders (two-thirds snowboarders, one-third skiers) to compete at Bec des Rosses, opposite Col des Gentianes, on gradients between 45 and 55 degrees, with couloirs and cliff drops. The **Ultime Session**, at the end of April, is a great finish to the winter season. There is a speed skiing race at Le Mont Fort, big air, waterslide concert, equipment testing and loads more going on in bars and clubs later on.

Accommodation

The only 5-star hotel is **Le Chalet d'Adrien** (0041 (0)27 771 62 00, www.chalet-adrien.com), right next door to the Savoleyres lift, but a little walk from the centre of town. For a smart hotel it's very homely, cosy and welcoming, but it does come at a seriously hefty price. The balconies overlooking the valley are well worth requesting and the view from the outside terrace is absolutely stunning. You should also take advantage of the gym, sauna and hot tub, as well as the new indoor swimming pool, which has views over the mountains. **The Lodge** (www.thelodge.virgin.com) is part of Virgin's Limited Edition portfolio, and as such is exquisitely finished and features 9 rooms and suites and a special kids' bunk room. The private pool and indoor/outdoor spa areas make this chalet ideal for the ultimate luxury ski holiday. The Lodge can only be rented by groups for their exclusive use.

If we could stay in any hotel in town, we would choose to stay in the 3-star **Farinet Hotel** (0041 (0)27 771 66 26, www.hotelfarinet.com). It has one of the best locations, bang in the centre of town, only a few minutes' walk from the main cable car. The interior is amazing. All rooms have plasma screen TVs, iPods, free wireless internet, a DVD player, and there is a DVD library downstairs from which you can help yourself. There's even a menu of pillows for you to choose from! There are 16 rooms (all with underfloor heating and south-facing balconies) and 4 big apartments. Not only is it the best place to stay, it's also the best place to enjoy après ski and late-night dancing (see Bars and clubs) and to eat (see Eating out).

Eating out

On the mountain

One of the best mountain restaurants is the **Cabane du Mont Fort** (0041 (0)27 778 13 84, www.cabanemontfort.ch), which serves local Swiss specialities (as well as the odd hot dog) on a beautiful sun terrace with great views of the valley. **Chez Dany** (0041 (0)27 771 25 24), slightly off the beaten track, is a cosy, friendly chalet, again with a great terrace for bathing in the rays. It has a great team of chefs and is open for lunch and dinner. For a quicker, and less expensive, burger and chips, head to **L'Olympique** (0041 (0)27 771 26 15, www.restaurantolympique.ch) at the top of Les Attelas or **Les Ruinettes** (0041 (0)27 771 19 79).

In town

Verbier has loads of restaurants offering a wide variety of food, for a wide variety of budgets. Enjoy local specialities (great fondues and raclettes) in the smart but comfortable surroundings of the cosy and **Swiss Le Caveau** (0041 (0)27 771 22 26, www.caveauverbier.ch). **Au Vieux Verbier** (0041 (0)27 771 16 68) serves more innovative and unusual food, but prepare yourself for the bill.

King's restaurant at the King's Hotel (www.kingsverbier.ch, 0041 (0)27 775 20 35) provides a French/Asian fusion with a wide variety of food on the menu from sashimi to surf and turf, and restaurant **Alpage** (www.kingsverbier.ch/Alpage, 0041 (0)27 771 61 21) is a Swiss/Italian brasserie serving pastas and steak and chips. **Le Millénium** (0041 (0)27 771 99 00, www.lemillenium.ch) is a fantastic restaurant right in the centre of town.

In the **Farinet's** relaxing, cosy and romantic lounge bar (0041 (0)27 771 66 26, www.hotelfarinet.com) you can choose from one of the mouth-watering platters or a simple snack of bread and hummus. For an inexpensive, but superb meal, head to the **Fer à Cheval** (0041 (0)27 771 26 69, www.feracheval.ch) in the centre of town. Enjoy a pizza or local dish, and the very friendly service. The Fer à Cheval has a great little terrace for eating in the sun at lunchtime, if you're not on the mountain. You can also enjoy a great meal downstairs at the **Pub Mont Fort** (0041 (0)27 771 48 98, www.pubmontfort.com), whose food is much smarter than the usual pub grub, or failing that, head to the beautifully cosy **Al Capone** (0041 (0)27 771 67 74, www.alcapone-verbier.com), towards the Savoleyres lift. It has fantastic pizzas, made in the open, wood-fired oven, and you will be welcomed with a smile every time. **Offshore** (0041 (0)27 771 54 44, www.offshorecafe.com), by the Medran lift, has a great surfy atmosphere inside, and it serves the best breakfasts in town. It's great for an informal lunch or dinner, and is a local hangout spot. For something a bit different call **Chez Dany** mountain restaurant (see Eating out On the mountain); you get a skidoo up there and can toboggan back down.

Bars and clubs

Après ski in Verbier is difficult to beat. To start the fun, stop off at the **1936 bar** on the mountain, basically a big tent on the piste and a great place for a beer in the sun and a little something from the barbeque. When down the mountain, head straight to the **Farinet** (see Eating out In town) for the rousing live music. Feel free to stomp on the bar in ski/board boots if the mood takes you. If the music gets a bit much and you actually want to talk to the people you're with, either head inside to the Farinet's lounge bar or sit outside in the sunshine next door at the 'London-esque'

> 'Feel free to stomp on the bar in ski/board boots if the mood takes you'

Central T Bar (0041 (0)27 771 50 07, www.verbiercentralhotel.com). The massive **Pub Mont Fort** (see Eating out In town), open until 1.30am, is popular at all times of the evening; it plays great music, has a great atmosphere and is a staple part of the Verbier scene – no night is complete without a beer here.

There are a few clubs to choose from that are open until 4am. The rich and famous should head to the **King's Bar** and the **Farm Club** both at the King's hotel (www.kingsverbier.ch, 0041 (0)27 775 2010), ridiculously exclusive and expensive, but fun nevertheless.

Getting there

By car

The tourist office website has links to a route planner and information about the current road conditions.

By plane

Geneva (170km) Transfer takes around 3 hours.
Zürich (300km) Transfer takes around 4.5 hours. For a timetable and more information contact CFF (0900 300 300, www.cff.ch).

By train

Take the Eurostar from London St Pancras to Paris, then by train, changing at Geneva and Martigny to Le Chable, and then a local bus (25 minutes) to get to the resort. Contact European Rail (020 7387 0444, www.europeanrail.com). Bus tickets are purchased at Le Chable station. (For people booking through European Rail to Swiss resorts, the rail fare includes the bus connection to resort at no extra cost, so there is no need to pay for a bus ticket.)

Useful facts and phone numbers

Tourist office

T: 0041 (0)27 775 38 88
F: 0041 (0)27 775 38 89
W: www.verbier.ch

Emergency services

- Police: 117 in an emergency or 0041 (0)27 780 64 00 (Police cantonale)/ 0041 (0)27 775 35 45 (Police municipale)
- In a medical emergency call 144 for an ambulance
- Pharmacy: 0041 (0)27 771 66 22/ 0041 (0)27 771 23 30

Doctors

- Dr H Contat: 0041 (0)27 771 70 20
- Dr F Gay-Crosier: 0041 (0)27 771 70 01
- Dr G Bruchez, Le Châble: 0041 (0)27 776 22 23
- Dr M Delgrange, Le Châble: 0041 (0)27 776 22 24

Taxis

- Carron Vincent: 0041 (0)776 28 29
- May Taxis Excursions (24h): 0041 (0)771 77 71, www.maytaxi.ch
- Taxi Edelweiss: 0041 (0)79 460 67 60

Zermatt

A cosmopolitan town with amazing skiing, boarding and nightlife – love it!

On the slopes	Rating
Snow reliability	❄❄❄❄❄
Parks	❄❄❄
Off-piste	❄❄❄❄
Off the slopes	
Après ski	❄❄❄❄
Nightlife	❄❄❄❄
Eating out	❄❄❄
Resort charm	❄❄❄❄

The resort

One of Switzerland's finest resorts, Zermatt provides everything that you might want on a ski holiday. The chalets are all built in typical Swiss 'chocolate box' style and the town is car free, with only electric cars and buses whizzing around. There are hotels, bars and restaurants to suit all tastes and visitors come from all over Europe and beyond, creating a fabulously cosmopolitan atmosphere. Ski bums and billionaires – everyone feels comfortable in Zermatt.

On the mountain there are some great challenges with moguls, off-piste and heli-skiing on offer. There are also plenty of flattering blues and lengthy reds to suit the travelling intermediates. The lift system has been massively improved recently, linking the Klein Matterhorn and Gornergrat areas and making travel between the 2 areas far easier than it has been for those staying in Zermatt and also for visitors coming over from Cervinia.

Zermatt's trademark, the 4478m high Matterhorn, and the other 37 4000m high peaks make for an impressive backdrop. Zermatt also offers the highest glacier palace in the world – take the lift to the glacier palace, walking in through an ice tunnel that is almost 15m below the surface of the glacier.

The mountains

Height: 1620–3899m

Ability	Rating
Expert	❄❄❄½
Intermediate	❄❄❄❄
Beginner	❄❄

Getting about

There are 394km of marked runs and acres of backcountry terrain.There is something for everyone, except perhaps for the complete beginner. In Zermatt alone there are 18 black and yellow pistes (70.5km), 33 red pistes (106km) and 19 blue pistes (17.5km); if you include the runs from Zermatt to Cervinia in Italy (mostly red pistes), you get a total of 394km of marked runs.

The slopes are well-groomed and there are many long, scenic runs, perfect for cruising. It used to be a big grumble that you could not always ride back to the resort, but snow cannons have now been installed all the way to the bottom so it doesn't matter if it has been a little short on snow.

The lift systems in general are not great; on sunny days and weekends there are usually pretty nasty queues to get on to crammed gondolas that will leave you hot, flustered and unable to move. This would be a big setback but, luckily for Zermatt, the memories of the horrendous lift journeys are soon forgotten.

Zermatt consists of 3 separate areas:

The Sunnegga area (including Blauherd and Rothorn) is reached by the underground funicular, located about 5 minutes' walk from the station.

The Gornergrat area (including Hohtälli and Stockhorn) is linked to the Sunnegga area by a 125-person cable car linking Gant to Hohtälli. Gornergrat can be reached directly from Zermatt by trains (Gornergrat–Monte Rosa railway, GGB) that leave every 24 minutes and take 30–40 minutes. The views from this train are definitely worth a look if you're not in a hurry. The red runs from Gornergrat and Hohtälli to Gant are beautiful and Stockhorn is home to 15km of mogul runs.

'The red runs are beautiful and Stockhorn is home to 15km of mogul runs'

The Klein Matterhorn area (including Trockener Steg and Schwarzsee) is the highest region and includes the glacial area used for summer skiing. A huge bonus to the ski area is the cable car link between Furi and Riffelberg connecting the Klein Matterhorn and Gornergrat areas. This cost CHF19 million and can carry 2400 passengers per hour. The Klein Matterhorn also gives you access to Cervinia in Italy (see Cervinia chapter, page 140) – for which you need to buy an international pass or pay a daily supplement on your lift pass. The Klein Matterhorn glacier (now called the Matterhorn Glacier Paradise) is the highest summer ski area in the Alps. It consists of 36km^2 of pistes, 6 in total, and is at a height of 2900–3900m. There are also 6 drag lifts and a cable car. The glacier is open until 2pm, depending on snow conditions.

Park

There are 2 parks in Zermatt, as well as a separate pipe at the Gornergrat that benefits from a bar in the shape of an igloo. The Gravity Park is above the Trockener Steg in the Klein Matterhorn area and the other slightly lower down, used more in the winter as it can get very cold at the top. The parks contain some great rails from easy wide 5m rails to some 8m kinks. Unfortunately there aren't many jumps, but the couple of table tops that there are are always in good condition.

Off-piste and backcountry

The glacier does limit the extent to which you can freely explore the backcountry terrain on the mountain tops but there are plenty of areas to check out.

At the top of the Höhtalli lift is an amazing area for freeride. This always has great snow, and you can get fresh tracks 3 or 4 days after a snowfall. The best moguls around can be found on the slopes between Höhtalli and Gant, at Triftji, where the Triftji bump bash is held each year, organised by the local pros. Above the Höhtalli and Triftji areas is the Stockhorn region, which has been designated as a freeride area. The runs are marked, but not prepared, and not checked at the end of the day. However, the Stockhorn area often doesn't open until around February.

The Rothorn area has diverse terrain and there are loads of amazing and challenging faces to ride. There is a hidden valley in the Rothorn area, but you should hire a guide or local who knows it well if you are going to check it out.

A guide is definitely recommended if you want a full day of adventure on the Schwarzsee tour. It is a good 1.5-hour hike round the back of the glacier and 3–4 hours of non-stop riding back down.

'Zermatt is also famous for its extensive heliskiing opportunities'

Zermatt is also famous for its extensive heliskiing opportunities with trips up to the Monte Rosa at 4250m (a fantastic run down through stunning glacial scenery to Furi), the Alphubeljoch at 3728m and up to the Plateau Rosa at 3479m.

Lift passes

Check the latest prices at www.bergbahnen.zermatt.ch

Instruction

Independent Swiss Snowboard Instructors

0041 (0)27 967 70 67
www.issi.ch

Stoked AG Ski and Snowboard School

This school offers ski, snowboard, freestyle, telemark, guiding and progressive instruction.
0041 (0)27 967 70 20
www.stoked.ch

Summit Ski School

0041 (0)27 967 00 01
www.summitskischool.com

The Swiss Ski and Snowboard School

0041 (0)27 966 24 66
www.skischulezermatt.ch

Other activities

Bowling: There are 4 bowling alleys, darts and table football. Call 0041 (0)27 966 33 80.

Cinema: This is located at Vernissage (see Bars and clubs).

Climbing: Ice climbing is available on a wall that is suitable for all levels or on a tour on steep ice for good climbers only. Alternatively, the Gorge Adventure is a dynamic secured climbing route in the Gorner Gorge. Contact the Alpin Centre (0041 (0)27 966 24 60, www.alpincenter-zermatt.ch).

Fitness centre: Contact the tourist office for more information.

Heliskiing: Extensive heliskiing is available in the area (see Backcountry and off-piste).

Ice grotto: The grotto at the Klein Matterhorn Glacier is the highest glacier palace in the Alps at 3810m. It contains various sculptures and information about glaciers, geology and climbing. Special events can be held in the ice grotto. It is open in both summer and winter.

Ice skating and curling: There are both natural and artificial skating rinks and a curling rink. Contact Obere Matten sports arena (0041 (0)27 967 36 73).

Moonlit skiing/boarding: This can be arranged from the Rothorn area.

Night in an igloo: The igloos on Gornergrat are decorated with artistic sculptures by a local Inuit, and can be rented for the night (see Accommodation).

Night skiing/boarding: This requires headlamps and takes place from Schwarzsee.

Paragliding: Contact Paragliding Zermatt (0041 (0)27 967 67 44, www.paragliding-zermatt.ch). Flights take off from Rothorn and land at Sunnegga, Zermatt or a mountain restaurant of your choice!

Saunas, solariums and massages: These are on offer at a number of hotels at various prices. Hotel Arca (0041 (0)27 967 15 44, www.arca-zermatt.ch), Hotel Christiania (0041 (0)27 966 80 00, www.christiania-zermatt.com) and Mont Cervin Palace (0041 (0)27 966 88 88) are good places to start looking. Zermatterhof's wellness centre, Vita borni (0041 (0)27 966 66 00) includes a pool, whirlpool bath, sauna, steam bath, fitness room and private spa for couples. It is open to the public if treatments are booked.

Sledding: There are 2.5km of sledding runs. Sledding can also be done at night, with a number of additional options such as a party at a mountain hut or a fondue party.

Squash: Call the Hotel Alex (0041 (0)27 966 70 70).

Swimming: There are indoor swimming pools at various hotels including Hotel Christiania (Roger Moore's hotel of choice! – see above) and Hotel Eden (0041 (0)27 967 26 55, www.hotel-eden.ch).

Tennis: Both indoor and outdoor courts are available.

Torchlit skiing: Ski at night by the light of flaming torches, then move on to a fondue party.

Winter hiking: There are 30km of prepared paths.

Summer only

Climbing: Contact the tourist office for more information.

Hiking: There are 400km of marked hiking paths.

Mountain biking: There are 80km of mountain bike trails.

Sports field: Football, volleyball, basketball, tennis and unihockey can all be played here. Contact Obere Matten sports arena (0041 (0)27 967 36 73).

Events

The **Triftji Bump Bash** mogul competition (www.bumpbash.com) is held every year on the infamous mogul runs.

Accommodation

In 1838 the local surgeon opened the first guest house that could accommodate 3 people, called the Hotel Mont Cervie (which was later changed to Monte Rosa). Zermatt can now accommodate 14000 guests in 112 hotels (6800 beds) and around 2000 holiday apartments. There are 3 5-star hotels, 36 4-star, and 45 3-star. The other 28 hotels are 2-star or less.

You should take care when choosing the location of your hotel/apartment as the resort does sprawl a long way. The best location is probably near the Gornergrat and Sunnegga railways, as here you are close to 2 of the lifts and the main street. You will need to take a bus to the Klein Matterhorn lift from here unless your hotel offers a free shuttle.

On a budget there are few decent places to stay. There is a **youth hostel** in Zermatt (0041 (0)27 967 23 20), located about 400m from the main lifts in the centre of town. This is fairly cheap and offers half-board accommodation.

The **Admiral Hotel** (0041 (0)27 966 90 00, www.hotel-admiral.ch) is a very friendly 3-star hotel, with lots of character and charm. The rooms are cosy and have fantastic views of the Matterhorn from their balconies. The hotel is located right next to the Sunnegga-Rothorn lifts, and 5 minutes' walk from the centre of town. The bus stop for the Klein Matterhorn is a few seconds' walk away.

The **Omnia** (0041 (0)27 966 71 71, www.the-omnia.com) is gorgeously modern, elegant and a member of www.designhotels.com Weirdly, rooms are not numbered, but listed A–Z. For sheer luxury, book yourself into the stunning, 5-star **Mont Cervin Palace** (0041 (0)27 966 88 88, www.montcervinpalace.ch) in the centre of town.

For a bizarre experience, stay in an **igloo village** (0041 (0)41 612 27 28/0800 11 33 55 (in Switzerland), www.iglu-dorf.com) below the Gornergrat, at 2700m! There are romantic suites for 2 people, or group igloos sleeping 6. There is also a whirlpool to relax in whilst enjoying the awe-inspiring views above Zermatt.

Eating out

On the mountain

There are 38 restaurants on the mountain, with nearly every one having a reputation for serving excellent food. It is also difficult not to have beautiful scenery on the mountains of Zermatt – even the couple of ugly concrete restaurants have stunning views. At Findeln, below Sunnegga, are several busy, rustic and atmospheric restaurants. Of these, **Chez Vrony** (0041 (0)27 967 25 52, www.chezvrony.ch) is the most widely esteemed. Between Furi and Zermatt is another hamlet of restaurants including **Simi** (0041 (0)27 967 26 95) and **Zum See** (0041 (0)27 967 20 45, www.zumsee.ch), which are both fantastic. Also at Furi, the **Farmerhaus** (0041 (0)27 967 39 96) is a beautiful, traditional rustic chalet with a big log fire inside. Outside you will find a large terrace with a bar and pizza hut. This place really comes into its own after 4pm for après ski when the live music starts. The food ranges from pizzas and crepes to pastas and steak. To get to this cluster of restaurants you need to take the red run from Schwarzsee to Furi. This is a very scenic route through the trees and there are cannons to make sure that there is always decent snow cover.

Further down the mountain is **Hennu Stall** (0041 (0)79 213 36 69, www.hennustall.ch), another great place for loud live music during après ski. The hotel restaurant at **Schwarzsee** (0041 (0)27 967 22 63, www.zermatt.net/schwarzsee), right at the foot of the Matterhorn, has a massive terrace with incredible views of the Matterhorn and glacier. Booking is recommended.

In town

There is no doubt that Zermatt is an expensive place to eat. If you are on a strict budget then you should hit the supermarkets (or even McDonald's – not that this is particularly cheap). However, as there are around 100 restaurants in Zermatt with a huge range of cuisines, it would be rude not to indulge a little.

Grampis (0041 (0)27 967 77 55, www.grampis.ch) is right in the centre of town; you can't miss it for the sparkling fairy lights. It has a funky bar/club downstairs and serves good pizzas and pastas upstairs at decent prices. The **Brown Cow Snack Bar** (0041 (0)27 967 91 31, www.hotelpost.ch) in the Hotel Post serves good burgers and sandwiches and always has a busy, fun atmosphere.

Hotel Albana Real (www.hotelalbanareal.com) contains 2 restaurants: **Rua Thai** (0041 (0)27 966 61 81) and **Fuji** (0041 (0)27 966 61 71), a Japanese restaurant where teppanyaki dishes are prepared in front of you. For something very different, **Restaurant Al Bosco** (0041 (0)27 966 05 07, www.riffelalp.com) at the 5-star Riffelalp hotel produces pizzas in the shape of the Matterhorn – 10 points for originality go to them.

The 5-star restaurants have posh nosh if you fancy it. Try **Prato Borni** in the Zermatterhof (0041 (0)27 966 66 00, www.zermatterhof.ch) and the restaurants at the **Mont Cervin Palace** (0041 (0)27 966 88 88, www.montcervinpalace.ch). These restaurants are no doubt a gourmet treat but are the same as other 5-star restaurants that you would find anywhere around the world. For superb food in very smart but cosy surroundings, **Le Mazot** (0041 (0)27 966 06 06, www.lemazotzermatt.ch) is the place. The owner's pride in the restaurant and dedication to service make it really stand out above the rest. The cuisine is dominated by lamb, the restaurant's speciality. To complement the dishes is a menu of 150 different European wines. You should book a few days in advance.

Bars and clubs

Zermatt has 44 bars and a buzzing, year-round nightlife.

For a good après ski scene, try **Papperla** (0041 (0)27 967 40 40, www.papperlapub.ch) where the club downstairs is popular with the workers. The **Country Bar** (0041 (0)27 967 31 74, www.elite-zermatt.ch) offers the internet, karaoke and a game of pool. If you fancy drinking and eating with the seasonaires, The **North Wall** bar (0041 (0)27 966 34 10, www.northwallbar.com) hosts numerous fancy dress nights (Faschnacht). Sunday and Tuesday are the nights to be with the locals, while Saturdays are more touristy.

> 'The bar hosts numerous fancy dress nights'

For getting drunk quickly, **Z'Alt Hischi** (0041 (0)27 967 42 62, www.hischibar.ch) pours the biggest measures ever. For drunken partying later in the evening, Hotel Post (0041 (0)27 967 19 31, www.hotelpost.ch) has loads of bars and restaurants to check out, but the main partying tends to occur in the cave-type club at the bottom of the building, the **Broken Bar**. Everyone should go to the über-cool **Vernissage** (0041 (0)27 967 66 36, www.vernissage-zermatt.com). Its bizarre décor really works, with chandeliers made out of chains, loads of candles, and comfy sofas. It serves food at night and downstairs you will come across an art gallery and cinema! You can take your drinks downstairs for the film and later on the chairs move away, a DJ gets on stage and it turns into a club.

For the more discerning drinker, **Pink** at Hotel Post (0041 (0)27 967 19 31, www.hotelpost.ch) has live jazz music every night and a great atmosphere. It's also in the same building as the cheesy parties, so when you're done being civilised you can join in the carnage. **Elsie's Bar** (0041 (0)27 967 24 31, www.elsiebar.ch), opposite the church on the main street, is tiny but atmospheric. It tends to attract the 25+ age group, who have enough cash to splash out on a decent bottle of plonk. Elsie's also serves as a restaurant with fresh oysters every day.

Getting there

By car

The drive time from Calais is 10 hours (1070km). From Geneva, take the N1/N9 via Sion to Sierre. Then take the E62 to Visp, where you will turn and head towards Zermatt via Stalden.

Cars have to be left in a car park in Täsch in open-air or covered car parks. A shuttle train runs from the car park to Zermatt every 20 minutes (www.mgbahn.ch). If you would prefer a taxi to pick you up from the car park there are a number of options – try Taxi Eden (0041 (0)27 967 64 44) or Taxi Schaller (0041 (0)27 967 12 12).

By plane

Geneva (244km) Transfer by bus (around 4–5 hours) or train (4 hours, see www.rail.ch), or car (3.5 hours).

Zürich (248km) Transfer is 5 hours by train, 3.5 hours by car.

Milan (234km) Transfer is nearly 4 hours by train, 3 by car.

You can take trolleys on to the train up to Zermatt and wheel them off the other end, which can save a lot of hassle. Your hotel should arrange an electric car to pick you up from the station; just give them a call on the free phones at Zermatt station. If not, taxis are available (see opposite).

By train

Take the Eurostar from London St Pancras to Paris, then an overnight train, changing at Zürich and Brig to arrive at Zermatt station in the resort. Contact Rail Europe (0870 830 4862, www.raileurope.co.uk) or European Rail (020 7387 0444, www.europeanrail.com).

Useful facts and phone numbers

Tourist office

T: 0041 (0)27 966 81 00
F: 0041 (0)27 966 81 01
W: www.zermatt.ch

Emergency services

- Fire brigade: 118
- Police: 117
- Ambulance/rescue service: 144 or Air Zermatt ambulance service: 0041 (0)27 966 86 86
- Police station: 0041 (0)27 966 22 22 (community police), 0041 (0)27 966 69 20 (cantonal police)
- Mountain Guide's Office: 0041 (0)27 966 24 60
- Avalanche situation: 187 (excluding foreign mobile phones)

Doctors

- Dr Ch Bannwart: 0041 (0)27 967 11 88
- Dr P Brönnimann: 0041 (0)27 967 19 16
- Dr E Julen: 0041 (0)27 967 67 17
- Dr D Stoessel: 0041 (0)27 967 79 79
- Hospital in Visp: 0041 (0)27 948 21 11
- Hospital in Brig: 0041 (0)27 922 33 33

Electric taxis

- Taxi Zermatt: 0041 (0)848 11 12 12
- Taxi Schaller: 0041 (0)27 967 12 12, www.taxischaller.ch

Index

Page references for rated facilities in **bold** for 5-star rating and *italic* for 4-star rating.
Resorts:
(And) = Andorra
(Aus) = Austria
(Fr) = France
(It) = Italy
(Nor) = Norway
(Swe) = Sweden
(Sz) = Switzerland